ELEGANCE

ELEGANCE

THE SÉEBERGER BROTHERS AND THE BIRTH OF FASHION PHOTOGRAPHY
1909-1939

Sylvie Aubenas
Xavier Demange
with Virginic Chardin

CHRONICLE BOOKS
SAN FRANCISCO

First published in the United States in 2007 by Chronicle Books LLC.
First published in France in 2006 by Seuil/Bibliothèque nationale de France.

Photo Credits:
Apart from the photographs that belong specifically to the Séeberger family collection, all the photographs reproduced in this work are preserved at the Department of Prints and Photography of the Bibliothèque nationale de France. The prints were made by the Reproduction Department of the Bibliothèque nationale de France.
Copies made by Seuil Publications (Jacques Vasseur) from the photographs in the Séeberger collection appear on the following pages: 15, 16, 17, 21, 23, 24, 27, 198, and 203.

Library of Congress Cataloging-in-Publication Data available.

ISBN-10: 0-8118-5942-8
ISBN-13: 978-0-8118-5942-4

Manufactured in Italy.

This English edition produced by APE Int'l, Richmond VA
Translation from French: Dr. Pippin Michelli

Distributed in Canada by Raincoast Books
9050 Shaughnessy Street
Vancouver, British Columbia V6P 6E5

10 9 8 7 6 5 4 3 2 1

Chronicle Books LLC
680 Second Street
San Francisco, California 94107

www.chroniclebooks.com

ACKNOWLEDGMENTS

Our deepest gratitude goes first and foremost to the Séeberger family, who accommodated us with generosity and opened the family archives to us: Cécile Séeberger, Michèle Séeberger, M. and Mme Daniel Séeberger, Geneviève Séeberger, and Frédéric Séeberger.

We would also like to thank the following for their assistance: Prince Charles d'Arenberg, Philippe Bérard, Anne Biroleau-Lemagny, Michel Cabaud, Roxane Debuisson, Hervé Degand, Robert Delpire, Françoise Denoyelle, Marie-Caroline Duburch, Guy Feinstein, Agnès Gagnès, Stephan Garrion, Cécile Kambouchner, Patrick Lamotte, Sylvie Lécallier, Countess Edouard de Leusse, Claude Malécot, Bruno Martin, Catherine Mathon, Bernard Minoret, Jean-Daniel Pariset, Hélène Pinet, Florence Quignard-Debuisson, Patrick Ragot, Françoise Reynaud, Hélène Rochas, Catherine Tambrun, Dominique Versavel, Mme Vittu-Tétard, and Jean-Baptiste Woloch.

CONTENTS

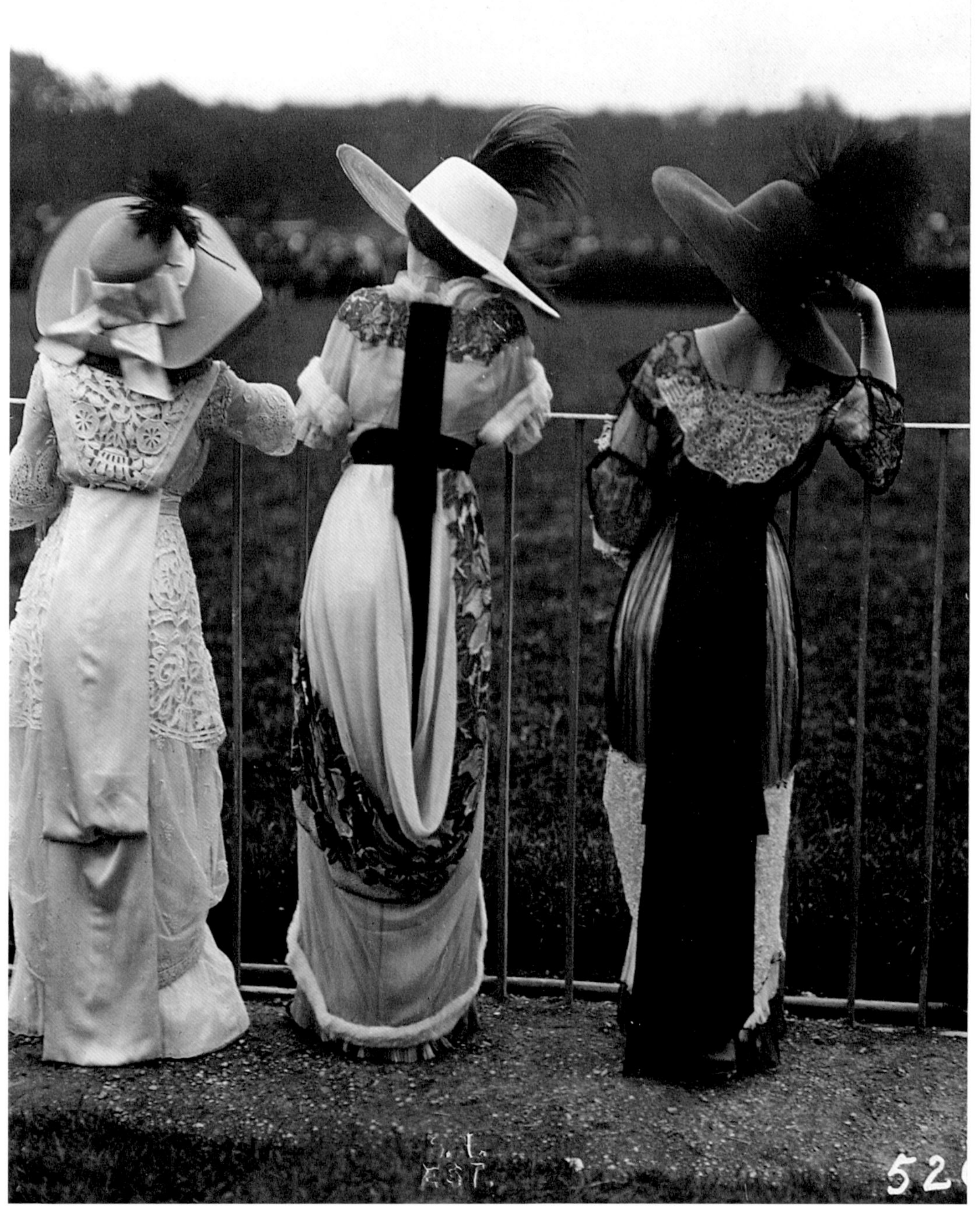

Grande Course des Haies, Auteuil, June 1912.

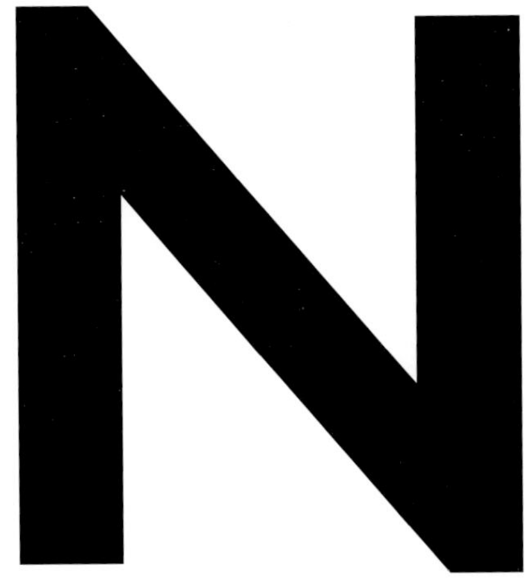

othing is more difficult than to preserve the memory of ephemera. Yet, what could be more important? So often—paradoxically—the volatile, the frothy, and the superficial mold the core of an evolving society with particular precision. Moreover, the Bibliothèque nationale de France is particularly concerned with offering its visitors just such evanescent and incalculably valuable items—from digitizing the content of old periodicals to registering image copyrights. Clothing fashion, which by nature is fleeting and "dies young," as Jean Cocteau once remarked, is a strong presence in our collections and our concerns. This was recently and effectively underscored by the *Revue de la Bibliothèque nationale de France*: issue 21 (winter 2005) was devoted to the history of clothing from the 1700s to the end of the twentieth century.

The couturier Christian Lacroix, the inspired originator of the exhibition *Rouge. Des costumes de scène, XVIIIe XXIe siècle* (Red: Theatrical Costume, eighteenth to twenty-first centuries), which was presented in Fall 2005 at the Library-Museum of the Opéra, recently emphasized, "In fashion, it is hard to ignore a desperate plea to the past." He recalled that in the twentieth century only the "optimistic decades"—the 1920s and 1960s—were creative enough to remain a rich resource for contemporary couturiers even today. In that same spirit I wish to publicize the invaluable Séeberger photographs held in the Prints and Photography Department. This family, who worked for the media and the fashion industry for many years, from 1909 to 1977, entrusted some 60,000 negatives and prints to the Library when they ceased to be active.

Up until the Second World War, the core of their work consisted of society journalism from Longchamp to Biarritz. Fashion historians will find a rich treasure trove of documents here that were either unpublished or scattered among numerous newspapers. Photography specialists will truly appreciate these excellent artists. Finally, it is my hope that the general public will take rare pleasure in immersing themselves for a while in this refined, frivolous, and fragile world.

Jean-Noël Jeanneney,
President of the Bibliothèque nationale de France

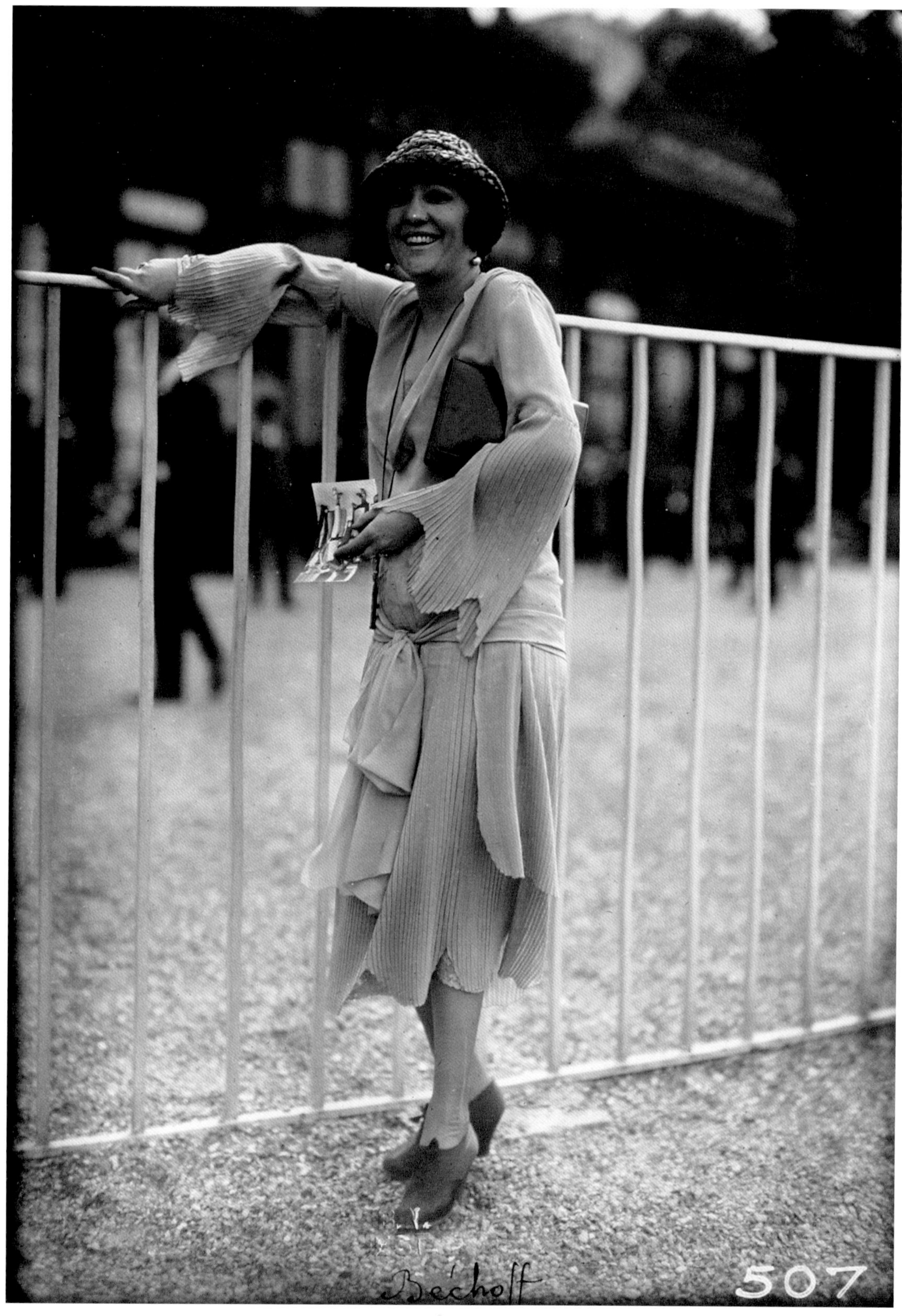

Young woman in a Béchoff dress, holding a Séeberger photograph in her hand, summer 1924.

THE SÉEBERGERS, FASHION PHOTOGRAPHERS: REDISCOVERING THEIR PLACE

Sylvie Aubenas

FASHION PHOTOGRAPHY BETWEEN 1909 AND 1939

In the last thirty years, there has been an explosion of research, study, exhibitions and all kinds of institutional initiatives regarding the history of photography and fashion. Unfortunately, however, fashion photography, which combines these two fields, has not attracted many researchers' attention; it has only been the subject of a few general studies (though there are numerous monographs).[1] Fashion photography in the first half of the twentieth century is closely linked to the development of the illustrated press, and more precisely, of course, to periodicals illustrated by photography. Indeed, until the very recent time when fashion photographers achieved a place of honor on gallery and museum walls, there was no other outlet for their work. The use of photography in periodicals only became technically possible in the early twentieth century, and truly widespread from the period between the World Wars.

Strictly speaking, fashion photography as we understand it didn't exist in the nineteenth century, but from the 1890s we do begin to find engravings made from photographs by Leopold-Emile Reutlinger, William Henry Fox Talbot, Boyer, Taponnier, Paul Nadar, and others. The vast majority of illustrations in women's fashion and style magazines relied on drawings, or drawings of photographs, until World War I. Indeed, it wasn't until the 1920s that increasing numbers of fashion photographs appeared in specialized and general publications. Drawings persisted even after World War II, in spite of technical constraints, because they offer specific advantages: silhouettes are conveyed in broad outlines, essential details are clarified, and colors are emphasized. Drawings can focus on the construction of clothing or accessories to a far greater degree than photography. At that time it was important for readers to have a precise representation of the models for reference, as these designs were destined to become the latest fashion and—especially—to be copied. At a time when ready-to-wear clothing didn't exist, magazines and newspapers provided inspiration for homemakers and seamstresses, who would copy the haute couture fashions that were otherwise inaccessible.

To a large extent, the great fashion photographers—their talent, personalities, and careers—are those associated with the development of *Vogue* and *Harper's Bazaar*, two now-legendary periodicals. Their ranks include Baron Adolphe de Meyer, Edward Steichen, George Hoyningen-Huene, Martin Munkacsi, Horst P. Horst, and Erwin Blumenfeld. Working for these two elegant magazines, which did not focus on providing patterns for less affluent readers to re-create, they were able to develop unusually personal work. Plentiful drawings printed alongside the photos alleviated the need for precise representation of fashions, freeing them to give their talent and imagination free rein to evoke the world of haute couture, rather than simply document seasonal innovations. They worked according to the spirit rather than the letter, catering to the dreams and fantasies of the viewers, contemporaries of their models, women who not only personified an ideal of beauty, but were modern and desirable, as well. This freedom allowed them to create images, of an evening gown by Gabrielle Chanel or Madeleine Vionnet, for example, that conjured the realm of luxury, wealth, and happiness implied by simply having such clothing, rather than featuring the construction of the gown itself.

Clearly, these renowned fashion photographers were first and foremost great artists, and their work kept pace with the development of the medium as a whole. It evolved from the pictorialism of Baron de

Meyer and Edward Steichen between 1910 and 1920, through the modernism of George Hoyningen-Huene and the surrealism of Horst and Man Ray to the realism of the subverted journalistic style or amateur photography of Martin Munkacsi or Toni Frissell. In fact, the history of fashion photography, even more than that of photography in general, focuses on the analysis of these significant artists.

Prior to Munkacsi, the presentations—or more precisely, the stagings—of the clothing were highly refined and intellectual: artificial universes with heavily coded references to painting, classical sculpture, and the cinema. Generating images in the studio, almost systematically, allowed complete control of composition, light, and poses. The liberation of manners and (inseparably) the body, enhanced by participation in sports and the outdoor life, are subtly present in these photographs. They reflect the evolution of society in its more narcissistic and apparently more superficial and frivolous modes. Today, there is no need to quote Jean Cocteau or Oscar Wilde to be convinced that, in fact, it is precisely these nonessentials that are essential. This truth established itself in the first half of the twentieth century, and the progressive democratization of beautiful clothing led to the development of a trade—or, rather, an industry—that had nothing frivolous about it. The preeminence of French haute couture in the world has been irrevocably established, and the illustrated newspapers, directly and indirectly, play a paramount role in its promotion. Indeed, these images are in every respect closely related to general advertising photography between the World Wars, which promoted idealization of the collective aspiration to wealth and modernity. Staging the presentation of objects such as clothing is the work of photographers—often the same avant-garde artists (such as Tabard, Laure Albin-Guillot, or Man Ray) whose aesthetic inventions, such as solarization, recourse to the pure and dry lines of modern architecture, were recycled in advertising. Events like the Great 1925 Exhibition of Decorative Arts or the World Fair of 1937 in Paris perfectly illustrate this alliance between the most innovative art and the interests of the biggest industries.

Their professional work did not exclude the parallel development of a more personal and less forced oeuvre; indeed the connection between it and the latest artistic innovations always shone through—even if this was at the cost of conceding to majority taste.

Similarly, many of the great couturiers—Paul Poiret, Gabrielle Chanel, Elsa Schiaparelli, Jeanne Lanvin, or the milliner Agnès—developed close ties, both business collaborations and friendships, within the artistic world and artists. The artists' influence is clearly evident in their fashion creations, as well as in the decor of their salons and private residences.

THE SÉEBERGER FASHION PHOTOGRAPHERS

Jean and Albert Séeberger contacted the Bibliothèque nationale de France in 1975,[2] when the brothers were about to close a business that had been established in 1909. The original Séebergers were the three brothers Jules, Louis, and Henri; two nephews, Jean and Albert (sons of Louis) joined the firm in 1927 and 1930. Some 60,000 negatives and prints represent the family's work in this specialty within photography. Concerned that this wealth of material should be neither lost nor dispersed, Jean and Albert Séeberger contacted our institution, which thus acquired a collection that is priceless in every respect.[3] Referring to the correspondence exchanged at the time, and the arguments advanced for this enrichment of our collections,[4] the initial interest seems to have been documentary, a matter of gathering a complete iconography of the history of fashion in the twentieth century. In fact, what they offered was an unparalleled collection of exclusively outdoor shots until 1939, and studio production and photos taken in natural contexts after World War II.[5]

The difference between the pre- and post-war material is fundamental. Prior to the war, the Séebergers were essentially journalists. They recorded society events where the latest haute couture creations were worn (and if the couturiers sent models to mingle with this fashionable crowd, it isn't always easy to distinguish them from the elegant customers). Indeed, the Séebergers' first business stationery with a motto announced, "High-Fashion Snapshots. Photographic Accounts of Parisian Style."[6] After 1945, on the other hand, the Séebergers' photo shoots took place in the studio or outdoors, and the models were chosen and the clothing borrowed as needed for each assignment.

Thus, to our eyes, the photographs taken before 1939 are richer and more varied in content. Often taken spontaneously, as snapshot photography dictates, these pictures were taken with a portable camera,

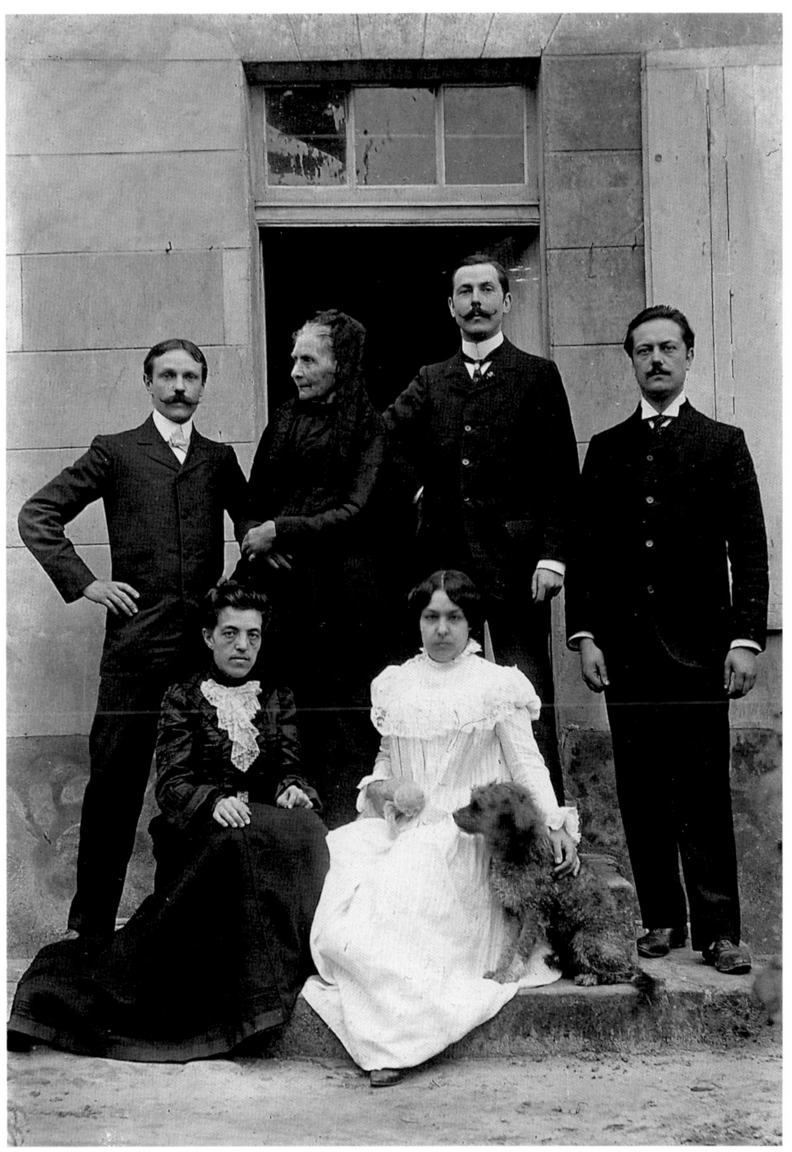

Portrait of the three brothers.
From left to right: Jules (1872–1956), Louis (1874–1946), and Henri Séeberger (1876–1956); sitting on the left in the foreground is their half-sister, Félicie, ca. 1900.
Séeberger family collection.

a "Klapp Nettel 13 x 18 or a Thornton Picard equipped with a Tessar Krauss lens"[7] working with negatives on 13 x 18 cm glass plates (illus. p. 24 and p. 27). This equipment guaranteed fabulous clarity of the prints, which were "contact prints," i.e. in the same format as the negative plates. Although Kodak invented the flexible negative in the late 1880s, most professional photographers, including press photographers, who generally worked without a tripod,[8] were still using glass plate negatives after the turn of the century. The Séebergers, for example, didn't acquire Rolleiflex cameras (this time equipped with flexible negatives), which were much lighter and more manageable (illus. p. 23), until 1935. The rising generation, Jean and Albert (both sons of Louis), undoubtedly spearheaded this change: photographs from 1935 are the product of a Rolleiflex test session conducted by Jean and his uncle, Henri.

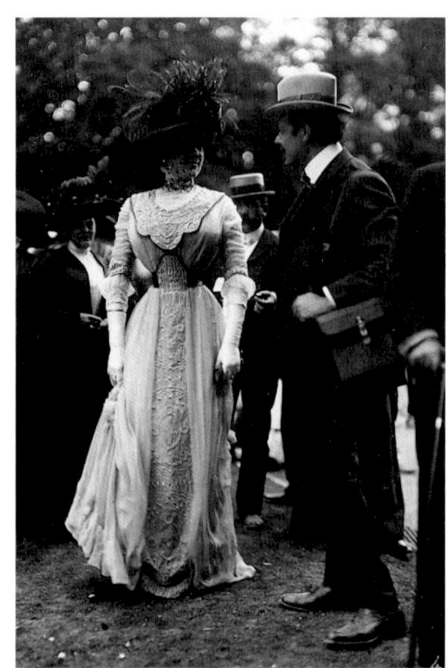

It was also around this time that the Séebergers annual output increased notably, as well as the quantity of orders placed by their customers. Prior to ceasing entirely in 1940, their activity in the pre-war years was as frenetic as the high society life they covered.

The modus operandi for these snapshots was photo journalism, and they are hardly comparable with the studio work that characterized the Séebergers in later years, as mentioned above. Nonetheless, these Séeberger pictures were published in the same magazines[9]–*Vogue, Harper's Bazaar, Le Jardin des Modes, Femina*, etc.–albeit alongside a different kind of article, under headings similar to those found in more general publications, such as *L'Illustration, Vu*, and *Excelsior*. These were two-page spreads that chronicled in images the main venues and highlights of the social season: the racetracks, first and foremost, but also seaside resorts, winter sports, and more; of course with detailed commentaries on the personalities and their appearance and attire. Many pictures appeared the very same day they were taken, cropped or cut out, with or without their backgrounds.

Henri Séeberger (1876–1956) at work at the races, 1909 or 1910.
Séeberger family collection.

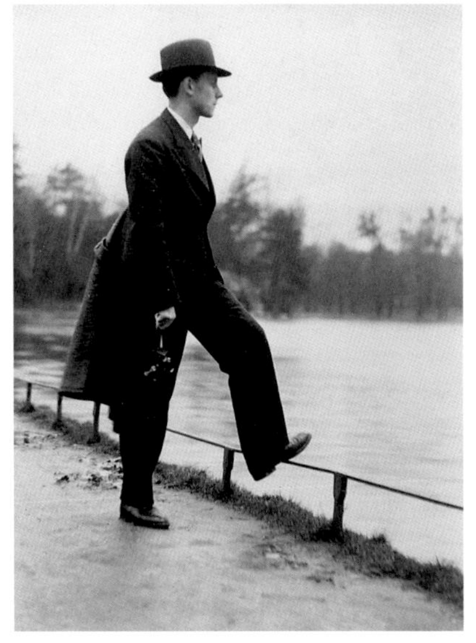

The ritzy locations and the names of the celebrities and couturiers made enthralling "photo-novels" for the readers. This concept, which stimulates great curiosity and imagination, is inexhaustible: it is still found in many news and fashion magazines, even those that are generally more concerned with social and cultural news than haute couture.

The Séeberger brothers did not have a monopoly on this kind of production. In the 1910s, just after they launched this specialty, magazines such as *La Mode Pratique*, *Les Modes,* and even *L'Illustration* generated a demand for photos of the raceways, and there were many news photographers and services to respond to the need. Apart from the Séebergers, who started out in 1909, Paul Géniaux, Royer, the Rol and Meurisse studios (among others) deserve mention. Throughout the period between the wars, packs of photographers gathered trackside at the great racing events and prowled the fashionable holiday resorts, lying in wait for the stars (this can be seen in some of the pictures).

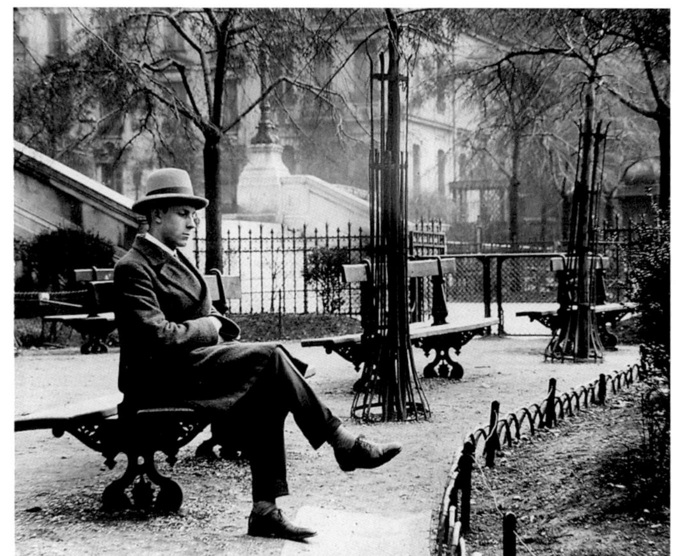

The Séebergers were thus neither the first nor the only of their kind, but they were completely unique in being able to develop and refine their family's expertise over two-thirds of the twentieth century. It was this strong sense of purpose—of contributing to the family oeuvre—that led them to keep and preserve the records of their activity. This unified collection is all the more interesting in

Henri Séeberger
Portraits of his nephew, Jean Séeberger.
Test shots with a Rolleiflex that
Henri Séeberger was considering purchasing, 1935.
Séeberger family collection.

that the Séebergers demonstrate a remarkable stability in their professional and private lives, at a time when everything around them teetered and changed as never before. The same Henri Séeberger who photographed corseted women in gowns with trains and weighed down by oversized hats in 1909 also took snapshots of their daughters less than thirty years later, quite at ease in their summer attire of loose hair and two-piece swimsuits. Through the Séeberger collection we can track the total and unprecedented upheaval of dress codes they witnessed through images of similar kinds of people, taken in the same places, by the same photographers.

A story that might have been a tiresome and incomplete reconstruction of images from agency archives and published documents is presented in this book in its entirety, bringing every chapter to completion, whether or not the images have been previously published.

A PARTIAL RECOGNITION

Such a profusion of images could not have gone unnoticed and, in fact, the Séeberger oeuvre is not unknown in publications about fashion. As a rule, however, the Séebergers are mentioned briefly and only in reference to the hesitant beginnings of the genre of fashion photography prior to World War I, as if their principal merit belonged to that first generation and their documentation of the pre-1914 styles that now seem so extravagant. This is how Nancy Hall-Duncan treats them in *The History of Fashion Photography*, a standard reference work. In the first chapter, which is devoted to the beginnings of the genre, she disposes of them as follows: "If the work of the Séebergers is entrancing, this, with a few rare exceptions, is due more to the charm of the attire than to the beauty of the photographs."[10] Similarly, the catalogue for the 1993 exhibition *Vanités. Photographies de mode des IXe et XXe siècles* ("Vanities: Fashion Photographs of the Nineteenth and Twentieth Centuries") also reproduces only Séeberger pictures from the races between 1909 and 1919, and comments, "The work of the Séeberger brothers smacks more of journalism about a few dress codes of the Parisian aristocracy than of true fashion photography."[11] As for the *The New History of Photography*, edited by Michel Frizot and published the following year, it fails to cite the Séebergers either in the chapter on fashion or anywhere else. In the minds of historians—and picture researchers, as well, judging by their many publications on this period—there is a strong correlation between the Séebergers and the Belle Époque—that is, France before 1914. Yet they continued to be professionally active into the mid-1970s.[12]

Although many publications have been devoted to this family of photographers, they pass quickly over the longevity of their careers and still confine themselves to the pre-1914 work. They focus on the Séebergers' images of Paris around the turn of the twentieth century: the Seine flooding, children in parks, or diverse news items[13]—always exploiting the nostalgic seduction of a Paris yet untouched by the great changes the twentieth century would bring.

In 1979, however, in London, Célestine Dars published *A Fashion Parade: the Séeberger Collection*, a work that finally considered the family's entire fashion production. She presented a wide range of their images, and her exposition of the Séebergers was rendered particularly sympathetic by her meeting with the brothers Jean and Albert. Dars' text is a rather free evocation of fashion and the personalities wearing them. It seems to have resonated more with the history of fashion than that of photography, which is primarily used to provide contemporary illustrations of various models. This is laudable in itself, though, since it takes into account the entire period during which the studio was active, right to the end. The work of author Jean-Claude Gautrand, *Séeberger. L'aventure de trois frères photographes au début du siècle* ("The Séebergers: The Adventure of Three Photographer Brothers at the Beginning of the Century"), again devoted to the pre-1914 period, describes their initial forays into fashion photography in much greater detail.

But the only publication that goes beyond the seduction of pre-war images to consider the Séebergers' work for women's magazines in a broader historical context is *La Lumière de Paris. Les usages de la photographie: 1919-1939* ("The Light of Paris: The Uses of Photography, 1919-1939"). In it, author Françoise Denoyelle devotes a chapter to fashion photography, recognizing the Séebergers' place in the particular context of this period. She notes, as do we, that studies on fashion photography are generally condensed to a succession of great names, and that photographers like Diaz, Saad, Dorvyne, Scaïoni—

and, we would add, Séeberger—seem negligible because they did not initiate the formal revolutions we owe to Steichen or Horst. While that is accurate, it is no less true that it was these photographers and agencies, now forgotten, who provided the vast majority of the magazines' images. It was the Séebergers, Rol, Meurisse, Wide World Photo,[14] and others who nourished these essential chronicles of fashionable life. To cite just one example from the late 1930s, the magazine *Chapeaux Mode* presented the latest hat styles in two-page spreads. Every issue required dozens of signature images by Dorvyne, Lipnitski, Scaïoni, Diaz, Dax, and others: pure illustrations exploiting the precision of photography.

THE SÉEBERGER BUSINESS

This exceptional collection of Séeberger images allows us—through original prints, neither cropped nor spoiled by second impressions—to measure the interest and quality of this kind of body of work. Let it be noted that the history of these newspaper spreads in which fashion mingles with the social column and seasonal news remains to be written.

Nevertheless, thanks to the family archives kindly placed at our disposal by Cecile Séeberger (the widow of Albert Séeberger), we can outline the professional activity of this studio until 1939. Although the documents from this period were not preserved in their entirety, the registers and books that survive are precise enough to provide much new and significant material.

The first indications lie in the very nature of these documents. Their simplicity—basic notebooks, alphabetically recorded journals, and then from the 1930s onward, commercial registers with pre-printed headings—testifies to the extremely limited, even rudimentary, organization of the company. These material proofs corroborate the evidence gathered by the first people to research this family:[15] the Séebergers were an extremely close-knit family, living and working together first at 13 rue Fénelon, then at 33 rue de Chabrol in the popular 10e arrondissement of Paris. Fittingly, this district was the heart of the clothes industry: wholesalers, various middlemen, and clothing exporters all ran their businesses side by side. Many customers noted in the registers were close neighbors.

A photograph taken prior to 1914 (below) shows the Séeberger family gathered around the dining table, with children on their parents' knees; on the wall to the right a heavily retouched photograph of a woman testifies to Jules' pictorialist period. All the family portraits testify to a certain simplicity, to a patriarchal life still reinforced by strong religious principles. This orderly state was maintained by the widowed Mme Séeberger, mother of the three brothers, as well as by her daughter from a first marriage, their half-sister Félicie, a benevolent and gruff old maid, and guardian of the virtues of the hearth. These two raised the children, prepared the meals, and kept the household and business accounts. But they did not hesitate to lend a hand, whether for photo shoots at the races or studio portraits. The memory of this family saga, in which Jules seems to have been the artist of the group and Félicie the eccentric, is kept alive in anecdotal stories about each of them.

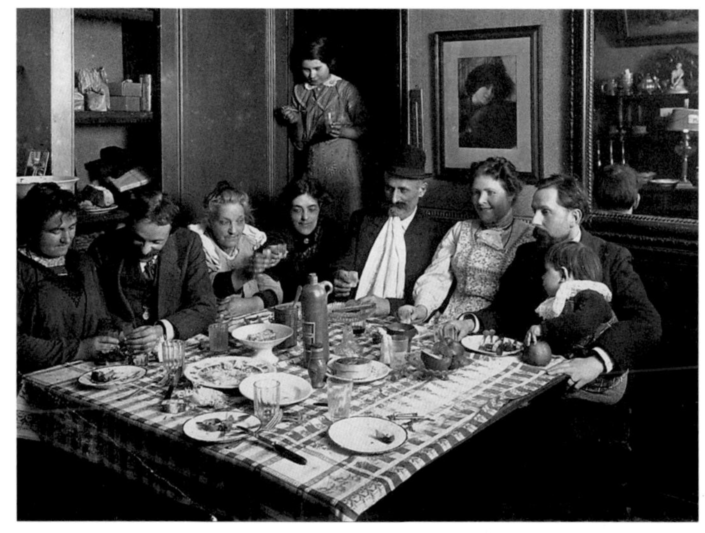

A touching example is a book kept by the matriarch Mme Séeberger during the war of 1914. Her sons Henri and Louis had both been mobilized, and Jules, whose health was more fragile, was working alone. She kept records of all visitors received during his absence. Thus, in the middle of the list of calls made by the tradesmen of the district, one finds records of images sold to *La Maison Vogue* or *La Mode Pratique*. This impression is further reinforced by perusal of the expenses listed in the books until 1939: every taxi ride, every entrance ticket to the racetrack, every trip to Deauville or Saint-Moritz, and every purchase of photographic material is carefully entered and specified to the exact centime. This helps us appreciate what an investment every photo shoot represented, especially knowing the pictures were not always sold in advance.

Evening meal in the apartment at 13 rue Fénelon in Paris.
Henri Séeberger is on the left, and Louis is on the right with his son Jean in his lap, ca. 1913.
Séeberger family collection.

"We always lived modestly, working twelve to fourteen hours a day, more interested in the quality of our work than our fame,"[16] Albert Séeberger told Françoise Denoyelle. There is similar testimony from Daniel Séeberger,[17] who proudly mentions the complexity of the photo shoots and the sophistication of the lighting equipment they used. It is clear, at least, that the brilliant universe in which they carried out their daily work did not turn the family's heads. Where one might expect anecdotes of famous beauties or crowned heads, the family lore instead focuses on technical prowess.

This modesty puts into context the small-scale character of France's luxury industry in the first half of the twentieth century. At that time, France's supremacy in the fields of style, elegance, and fashion was universally recognized. Yet the creations featured on the glossy pages of magazines and in the most renowned boutiques in major cities around the world were developed with an expertise that, while it was certainly fostered by talent and technical innovation, was above all passed from one generation to the next through the daily routine of the family-based business. The journalism of humanistic photographers between 1930 and 1960, with a certain affection, emphasizes the labor-intensive and modest side of these small-scale enterprises. The workshops of the great couture houses were thus home to a whole population of dedicated and conscientious employees,[18] just as families often worked together in the directors' offices of these same houses.

This is the light in which we should understand the modus operandi of the Séeberger family: an enterprise in which quality and independence were the supreme characteristics. This is also what differentiates them fundamentally from Man Ray and Beaton, who frequented their circle as equals or, almost, as clients.

A VARIED CLIENTELE

Another point the registers highlight is the diversity of the Séebergers' customers. In addition to photo shoots on location, which constitute the most remarkable aspect of their production, they also worked directly with the couturiers, manufacturers of fabrics and accessories, the press, exporters—and especially American exporters.[19] Thus two record books that itemize the work the Séebergers completed for Louchel publications between 1919 and 1938–*La Femme Chic* ("The Stylish Woman") and its spin-offs, such as *La Femme Chic à Paris* ("The Stylish Woman in Paris")–list the sales of photos taken at racing events as well as photo shoots of specific models, from in front and behind, of hats, etc. The seasonal round of high-society events alone certainly wouldn't have been sufficient to generate images every day, as the Séebergers did, and the off-season would have been too long. Indeed, the races occupied them mainly on Sundays during the year, and summer or winter holiday reports at fashionable places like Cannes or Deauville were limited to quite short periods.

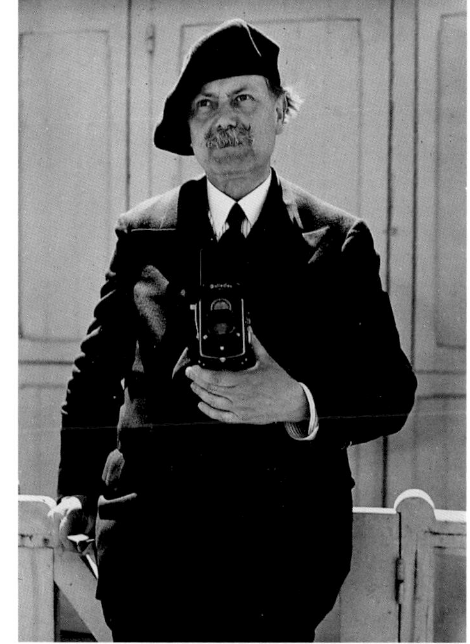

The variety of these other customers is impressive, and the quantity of picture sales recorded day by day is a very precise indication. There are alphabetical binders in which occasional customers have an entire page dedicated to them, and there are separate binders for the biggest ones. The price of prints varied considerably and depended on several criteria: the number of photographs sold, the volume of transactions with the individual or company, the material provided (a photo shoot especially for the occasion versus the sale of prints from preexisting plates), the purpose, whether partial or complete rights were transferred, and so on.

In January 1918, for example, eight photos of gowns for Louchel came to 48 francs, three pictures of hats for *Les Élégances Parisiennes* cost 21 francs, and four for *La Mode Pratique* totaled 20 francs. However, seven pictures for the *Dry Goods Economist* came to only 21 francs, while an unspecified agency on rue Trévise was invoiced 15 francs for a single image, and *Vogue* paid 30 francs for two prints. In 1935, the Eaton Company, which purchased dozens of photographs every month, paid approximately 6 francs each,

Photograph taken by Jean or Albert Séeberger, Henri Séeberger, Cannes, spring 1937. Séeberger family collection.

whereas in same period the Gimbel Brothers paid closer to 8 or 10 francs, and Louchel, which had many publications, paid 20 francs for every racetrack or news photo and 35 francs for every commissioned shot.

The Séebergers were also accustomed to offering prints to the models themselves (illus. p. 10) and to the celebrities and society figures they had captured particularly well in their press coverage.[20] They did this

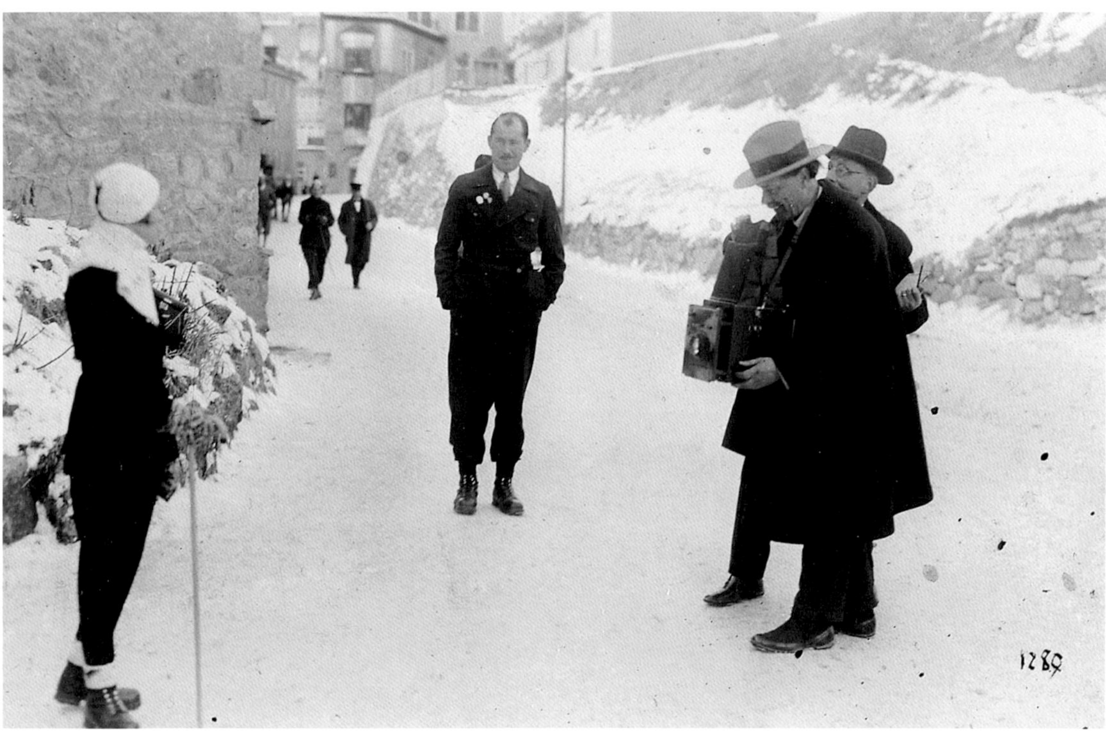

both in order to maintain good relations and to stimulate sales: they would select the best shots and send them to the subject by mail to generate an order. Also worthy of mention is the Séeberger's collaboration with the Palace Hôtel in Saint-Moritz–where they often stayed and enjoyed steeply discounted rates–

Anonymous, Henri Séeberger (1876-1956) with Mr. and Mrs. R. Parke, Saint-Moritz, ca. 1935. Séeberger family collection.

and especially with the Saint-Moritz Office of Tourism, with which they exchanged quite a delightful correspondence. H. Schiller, the press officer for Saint-Moritz, wrote to them in 1938, "the following subjects interest me particularly: style and female beauty, hotel balls, children merry and funny, good-looking sportsmen, etc."[21]

Taking all of this information as a whole, it becomes clear that while the collection now at the Bibliothèque nationale corresponds to a production culled by the Séeberger family from their entire output,[22] other work done in response to specific requests from their clients were sold, often with their negatives, and are therefore now dispersed.

The fact that the Séebergers' frequented the widest variety of locations on a daily basis, from the simplest to the most luxurious, were familiar with the whole chain of fashion production–including the production and distribution of fabrics, lace, clothing, and accessories–does them no disservice in our eyes, nor does it diminish their standing among photographers. On the contrary, it provides the key to their extraordinary effectiveness in the field of social journalism. The essential difference between them and the agency photographers who covered the race meets as if they were football matches or school openings, is that they successfully developed a sound knowledge of every component of fashion, and could identify the best angles of good styles and designs with a single glance. This advantage allowed the Séebergers to meet the magazine publishers' needs in the best way possible.

AN INDIVIDUAL STYLE?

Can an individual style be attributed to an oeuvre created by five people over two generations, with no way of distinguishing between the photographers? Can a long-term collective oeuvre show distinctive talent? At any rate, a clear evolution over time can be noted: a better way of selecting a particular model, of working the scene or exploiting the available decor. The fairly static images of the 1910s lead to a much more lively series in the 1930s and, ever more frequently, to genuine masterpieces. Their gradual mastery of the construction and technical features of the Rolleiflex alone do not explain the progression: as photography experts know, while fate plays an important part in photo shoots, she seldom smiles on artists who lack talent.

The early days of the Séebergers, with due caution, have often been compared to the work of the very young Jacques-Henri Lartigue, the superlative photographer who began chronicling his life and times at the tender age of six. The subjects they focused on are sometimes similar—high society at the race and on the hunt—even if their intentions and results are ultimately quite different. Indeed, up until the 1930s, there is a parallel between Lartigue's world and models and those of the Séebergers. They tread the ground of the same elegant venues but, if their paths cross there, they don't really meet; each remains true to their particular form. When Lartigue took photos of people in Cannes (illus. p. 177), he was not so much a photographer as a society man among his peers.

If one looks closely at the Séebergers' pictures, one can infer their trick—necessitated by shooting on the fly—of exploiting everyday settings to best advantage in order to accentuate the style of a garment. It may come as no surprise that from the 1950s onward, this artifice in fashion photography, which was once a journalist's coping mechanism, became an aesthetic choice. A real pleasure of the Séeberger oeuvre is to discover among its 35,000 prints hints or foreshadowing of the entire modern vocabulary of fashion photography (or street journalism), which was developed in such a masterly fashion by Lartigue, Blumenfeld, Frissell, Bourdin, or Erwitt. These provide clues that help us better understand the development of a complex and ambiguous genre. For this reason, and for certain images that should be included in every anthology of fashion photography—the Hitchcockian profile of Dulce Liberal Martinez de Hoz (illus. p. 102), or the same woman in a white fox fur coat surrounded by men in black (illus. p. 89), for example—the Séebergers richly deserve to be given the recognition that their modesty always prevented during their lifetimes.

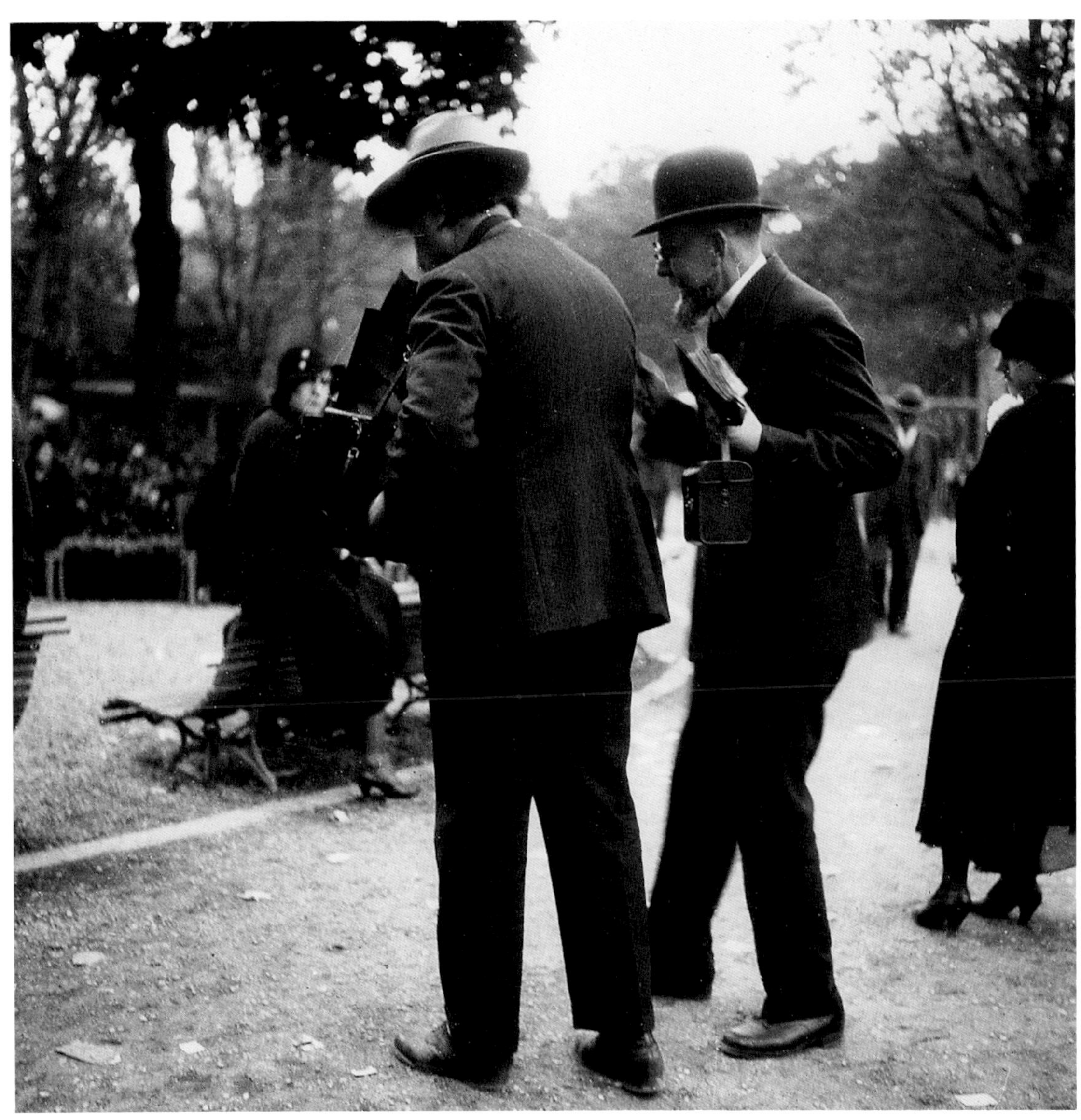

Henri (1876-1956) and Louis (1874-1946) Séeberger
at work in the Bois de Boulogne, 1927.
Séeberger family collection.

TREND SETTERS AT THE RACETRACK

Xavier Demange

Vividly I remember the wonder I experienced as a young child peering into the eyepiece of an antique stereoscope and saw a procession of painted photographs of fairy queens and other creatures of Second Empire theater. Many years later, I felt a similar giddiness when I discovered the collection of photographs the Séeberger brothers donated to the Bibliothèque nationale de France. Ladies who had slumbered for years awaiting the slightest signal to rouse from their long sleep leapt from the surface of the plates, little windows behind which they had been unjustly imprisoned. Swathed in silks and furs or swishing with fringes and feathers, bristling with plumes or helmeted with felt, coiffed, outfitted, and bejeweled according to latest dictates of fashion, they processed through racetracks, beach piers, beauty contests, and hotel lobbies, superb and nonchalant, looking for admiring glances, and amused or occasionally annoyed by potential onlookers. These forsaken beauties are guardians of a vanished way of life in which society demanded that one take their time, and intense enjoyment of life was a reason for living. Both witnesses and arbiters of the mode of their times–which they created season by season–they released women from the social straitjacket imposed over centuries into playful fashion. Softening the silhouette in subtle ways while opening up an overly restrictive outfit here, splitting an over-tight skirt there, adopting a more comfortable or more becoming form of hat, loading their gowns with feathers and drapes or (by contrast) revealing their triumphant bodies, season after season they created new definitions of feminine style.

It was a formal laboratory, a permanent tightrope walk between what was permissible and what was desired. Through their lenses we see the fashion designers' proposals taking form before our very

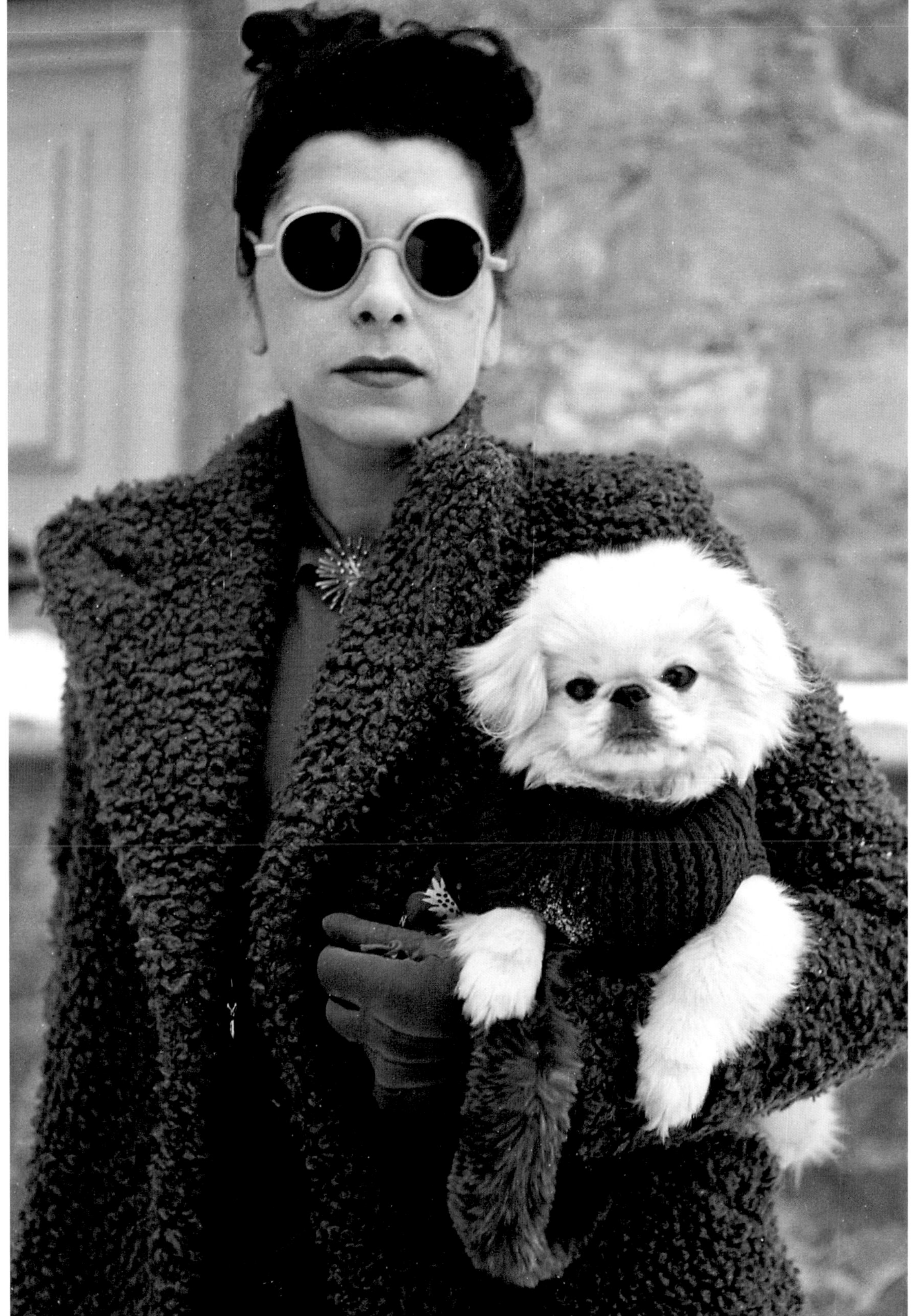

Mme Ulam-Krauss, Saint-Moritz, New Year's Eve, 1939.

eyes, day by day. In thousands of plates, the Séeberger brothers indefatigably recorded the fugitive metamorphoses of fashion, and it is this coherence over a period spanning almost seventy years that provides a unique working tool for historians of fashion and fashion photography in the first half of the twentieth century.

MAGAZINES

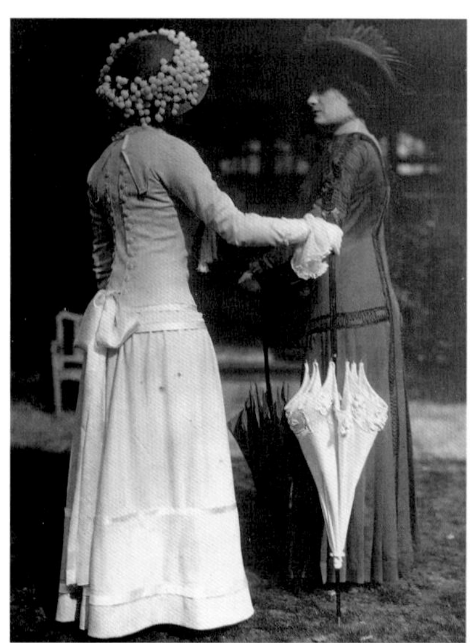

At the beginning of the century, two approaches to representing fashion in photography existed side by side. The luxury magazine *Les Modes* published very careful portraits, mostly in color, of high society women or actresses posing in the studio wearing outfits that were designed by renowned couturiers. These portraits bear the signatures of well-established studios such as Reutlinger or Manuel. In the period between the wars, amateur models tended to disappear, gradually yielding way to professional models in the fashion magazines. *Vogue* and *Harper's Bazaar*, however, maintained the great tradition of the fashion portrait by publishing photos of society personalities wearing the great couturiers' latest modes.

During this period, the magazine *Fémina* pioneered the publication of photos of women at the racetracks. Remaining closer to journalism than to fashion features, they sought to be a sort of illustration for the late editions that the big national daily newspapers such as *Le Figaro* and *Le Gaulois* had been publishing since the Second Empire. Citing the Parisian personalities at the races by name, these dailies often added a short description of their attire. The idea caught on and, as of 1902-1903, high-circulation magaziness began regularly publishing photos of notable personalities—first at the races, then later at seaside resorts, both abroad and in the places frequented by high-society cosmopolitans. In this way, they responded to an

The first fashion photograph by the Séebergers to be published in La Mode Pratique, *1909.*

increasingly evident curiosity on the part of their readers, who wanted to figure out for themselves not only what the fashion designers hoped to impose on their wealthy clientele, but also what was actually being worn in the fashionable world.

This appetite for "real clothing" was initially exploited by photo journalists, obscure amateurs like Carle de Mazibourg or Edmond Cordonnier, who in 1901 - 1902 took the first trackside snapshots at the race courses—the primary location for making and unmaking fashion. Their photos were published in popular magazines like *Paris Illustré* or *La Nouvelle Mode*. Little by little, the illustrated newspapers adopted the practice of including a few photos of fashionables at the track under the rubric "Society News." Thus, when Jules and Henri Séeberger submitted their first race meet photos to Mme de Broutelles, who published them in her magazine *La Mode Pratique* from May 22, 1909 onward (illus. facing page), they were actually latching onto a process that already dated back several years. Some of their images were even granted a place of honor later, featured on the cover, whose glazed paper permitted better reproductions of photoengraving. Generally taken during the major racing events held in the spring and fall, these photos—which represent a veritable goldmine of information on the evolution of fashion—were published according to a set calendar.

THE CALENDER

The racecourses around the capital opened their season in mid-February and closed in mid-July, with an additional, abbreviated session from mid-October to December 15. The culmination of the Parisian racing season took place at Longchamp, at the end of June, with Grand Prix Sunday. This was *the* day when new fashion trends were established, when couturiers and fashionables observed a pause and agreed on what would be worn in the coming year. Thereafter, the entire *beau monde* would scatter to seaside resorts or spas, to deluxe hotels and country seats, in order to preach Parisian good taste to populations thirsting for innovation. Hence the importance of publishing those trackside photographs: they played an essential role in the diffusion of fashion and the development of the clothing industry, not only throughout France, including the most obscure backwaters, but also abroad, where thanks to this periodical documentation,[23] Paris held an unquestioned prestige in the field until World War II.

If fashion, which is essentially transitory, fluctuated week by week, the racing calendar was immutable: Monday at Saint-Cloud, Tuesday at Enghien, Wednesday at Tremblay, Thursday at Auteuil, Friday at Maisons-Laffitte, Saturday at Vincennes, and Sunday at Longchamp.[24] The important prizes were the Grand Prix de Paris (Longchamp, in June), The Drags (Auteuil, in June), the Prix du Jockey-Club (Chantilly, in June), the Grand Steeplechase (Auteuil, in May), the Prix de Diane (Chantilly, in June), and the Prix de l'Arc de Triomphe (Longchamp, in October).

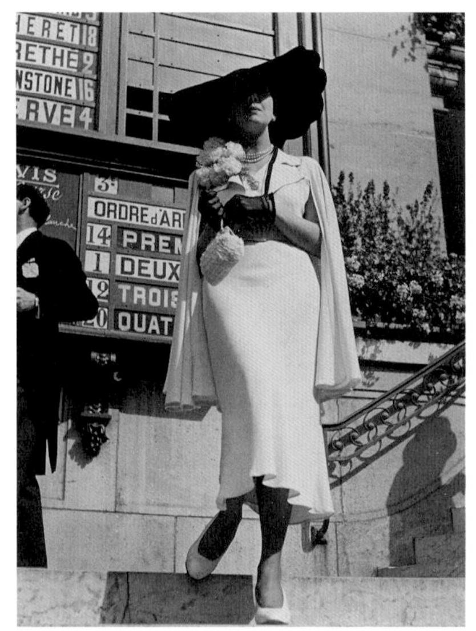

The meeting place of anyone who was anything in Parisian society until 1891 (the year when parimutuel betting was established), until World War II the race course remained the arena where two distinct populations rubbed elbows: those who came to see the races, and those who came to be seen. Among the first group numbered stable owners, trainers, racing fans, bookmakers, and track staff. The second group comprised members of high society, professional models, fashion designers, journalists, stage and screen personalities, and stargazers. The latter milled around the track, the stands—reserved for horse owners and their spouses—the paddock, and the betting office. The same onlookers could be found between the two World Wars on the beaches at Deauville, on the Promenade des Anglais at Nice, at Chambre d'Amour (a beach in Biarritz), or on the snowfields of Saint-Moritz, at dates arbitrarily fixed by fashion: January in the Bavarian Alps and then the Tyrol, March on the Riviera, June in Paris, August in Deauville and Touquet, September in Biarritz or Venice. After the war, the airplane upset these immutable rites and the café society disappeared, to reemerge in the 1960s jet set.

Ellen von Lee wearing a Toutmain gown and Marlène hat, Grand Prix de Longchamp, June 26, 1938.

PROFESSIONAL MODELS

There were two kinds of models, the professionals and the fashionables. The models of the great houses (Poiret, Lanvin, Worth, Patou) were recognizable by their youth, their slim figures, and their characteristic poses.[25] They tended to stick together and form groups. Then came the occasional models, who generally presented styles by small couturiers or houses just launching themselves; these often eccentric garbs served as publicity stunts for their creators. These models strolled about alone or in pairs, but seldom in groups. Wearing the insignia of a workroom on their backs, employees from the lowliest to the most prominent–such as the designers and even directors–of smaller couture houses (Mme Georgette, Mme Melnotte-Simonin; illus. p. 80, bottom left) paraded at the great June gatherings at Longchamp or Auteuil. With the exception of Charlotte Révyl (Prémet) and Schiaparelli (on rare occasions), when the great couturiers themselves were present, they generally did not advertise their designs at the racetrack. Sometimes a couturier's wife (Melnotte-Simonin) or mistress (Paul Poiret) would wear his creations.

As for the milliners, creators and purveyors of stylish headwear, they often presented their hats on the couturiers' models and never hesitated to wear their latest creations themselves (Agnès, Mado, Corinne, Gaby Mono, Suzy, and Maria Guy). Lucienne Rebaté–who ran the house of Mme Reboux (the greatest milliner between the wars) in the 1920s–was an exception to this rule; she never made appearances at the racecourses.

Alongside professional models who were paid by the day were the fashionables: well-known personalities who wore the great designers' latest creations. Within the world of couture they were informally called "amphibians" or "jockeys," or officially "society consultants."[26] These women were given significant discounts on their purchases (up to seventy-five percent) on the condition that they wear these clothes to the most important society gatherings; and if a particular model had already been worn in a private showing, they paid nothing. Any spots were removed, hems were resewn, and seams repaired; the once-worn gown would then be returned to the designer. All the great houses had their "stables" of fashionables (a dozen on average). Patou claimed to have outfitted a hundred of them in 1934 alone.

To uphold her part of the bargain, the "jockey" had to be recognizable by photographers and, preferably, by the readers of fashionable magazines, wear the outfit well, and be clearly visible. Their popularity generally lasted about five years, although a professional model such as Mlle Darteix "survived" nearly twenty years at the races and the tall Laure Jarny's career extended over fifteen years. This draconian rule did not apply to the exquisite, universally recognized elegance of Mme Martinez de Hoz or Mme Revel (illus. p. 104), whom the Séebergers continued to photograph well after World War II.

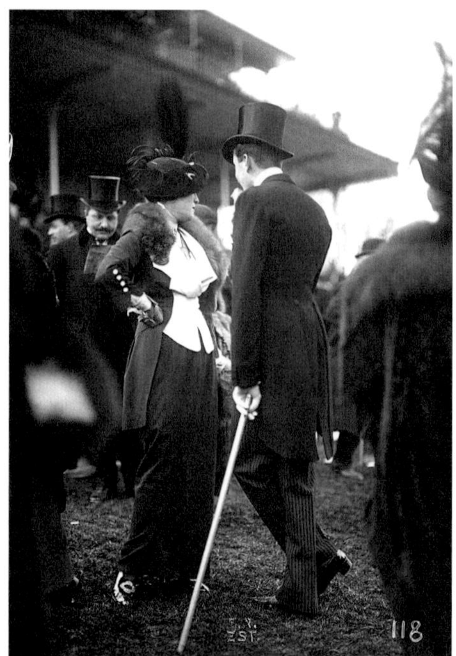

The social origin of those whom the society chronicles indicated with the general term "fashionables" was of minor importance, as media celebrity took precedence over status. Thus great courtesans (Jacqueline Forzane, Laure Jarny, Yvette Laurent), music-hall artists (Mistinguett, Régine Flory, the Dolly Sisters), boulevard actresses (Alice Cocéa, Maud Loty, Spinelly), and movie stars (Francesca Bertini, Josette Day, Arletty) often launched the styles that ladies with greater titles both in France and abroad adapted to their taste and subsequently established.

POSING

The fashion pose, which was originally static to let the eye take in every detail of the toilette, evolved just as clothing fashions did. Poiret's models[27] launched the *à la russe*, or "Russian style" in the period immediately prior to World War I (1910–1914). Facing forward, with the feet forming a right angle, hands on the hips (illus. above), this posture lent itself to the Directoire fashions, with their high waists, split skirts, plumed hats, and fur wraps. After the war (1919–1929), fashion touted the silhouette known as the "slouch": round back, sunken shoulders, outstretched neck,

An elegant couple at the races, March 1913.

and bent knees (illus. facing page). At that time it was all about privileging the straight line of the dress tube, with no chest or hips, and the top of the face was hidden under a cloche. Finally, the 1930s saw the gradual return of the natural forms, updated through narrow gowns with increasingly voluminous sleeves that rendered women caryatid-like: breast shown through a broad vent, arms playfully spread, chin raised (illus. p. 50, bottom left).

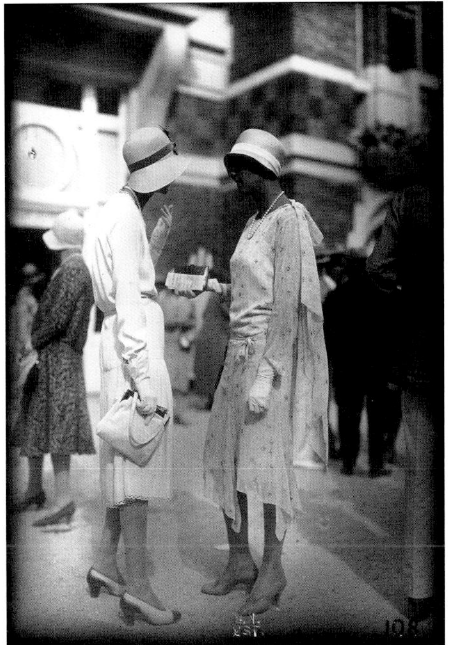

On the periphery of the racecourse, the professional model would interpret these edicts entirely to her own advantage and—with the photographer's complicity—set up spontaneous scenarios to enact. She could be seen stepping onto a chair to board a train, crossing her perfect legs under a short skirt (illus. p. 109, bottom), resting against a barrier to emphasize a beautiful arm (illus. p. 103, top right), or generating an original silhouette with a suggestive swing of the hip (illus. p. 32). Some would shimmy for the camera to make fringes and feathers dance (illus. p. 36), twirl, laugh, comment, grimace, look askance, shake a finger, or frown. There was often a tacit complicity between photographer and model, especially if she was a professional or a stage personality accustomed to the tricks and demands of the trade. The most photographed society women were also in perfect control of their image, even in less photogenic situations—sitting on their stadium seats or in animated conversation with friends—but one rarely senses any collusion between them and the camera. Rather, they behaved like queens of the track, accustomed to the homage and dumb worship of the crowd. In any case, press photographers like the Séebergers had no prestige in their eyes, unlike the great studio photographers, who would become fixtures in the "Parisian" scene in a class of their own from the end of the 1920s; every "fashionable" came to count on photographers such as Hoyningen-Huene, Horst, de Meyer, Cecil Beaton, and others.

Mme Martinez de Hoz (right) wearing a Madeleine Vionnet gown, Deauville, August 19, 1928.

If the Séeberger brothers did not yet have expert control of their subjects when they began in 1909 (taking shots of women in groups, for example, which tends to blur the details of each costume, or choosing overly crowded backgrounds, thus losing the model against the mass of spectators),[28] they soon mastered the challenging art of the snapshot, capturing a distinct silhouette by isolating it against a neutral ground, or cropping drastically to bring out details of a garment. In this, they were inspired by the layouts of contemporary fashion illustrators such as Drian, Barber, or Van Brooke, who could evoke the atmosphere of the racetrack through a series of evocative details: a track barrier, a distant horse and jockey, empty seats, or even tickets scattered on the turf.[29]

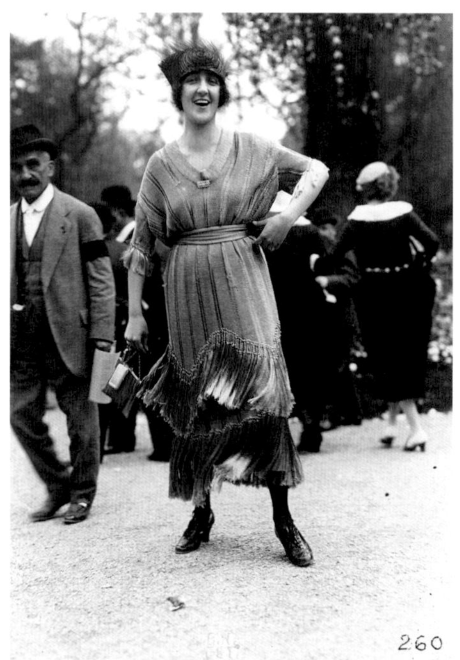

While it would be misleading to classify the Séebergers with the forerunners of fashion photography—this belongs to Nadar, Reutlinger, or Baron de Meyer—they should indeed be counted among the virtuosi of the fashion snapshot. Some of their compositions verge on great art, especially considering how little time they had between finding a suitable model to be photographed and choosing the best camera angle.

It should also be noted that the Séeberger photos published in contemporary magazines seldom did justice to their virtuosity: they were chosen only for their documentary value. This explains the lack of interest that historians of fashion photography have accorded to this aspect of their work until now. Their artistic sense and their undeniable contributions to the representation of fashion could be appreciated only with the passage of time and a thorough study of the collection they left to the Prints and Photography Department of the Bibliothèque nationale de France. Today we can, without hesitation, classify the Séebergers among the great twentieth-century masters of the snapshot.

Longchamp, May 15, 1919.

At the races, May 1914.

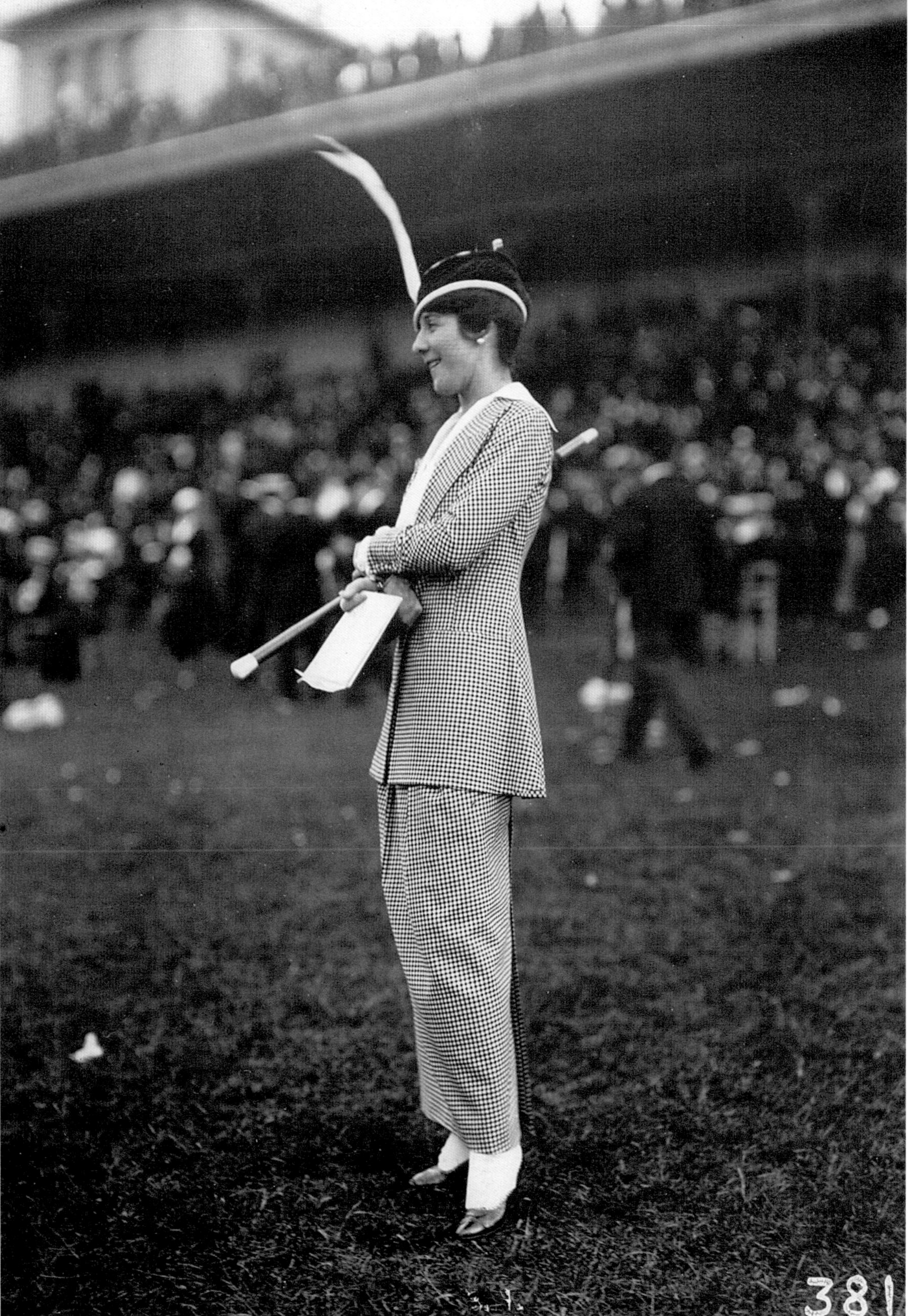

THE EVOLUTION OF FASHION AS SEEN BY THE SÉEBERGERS

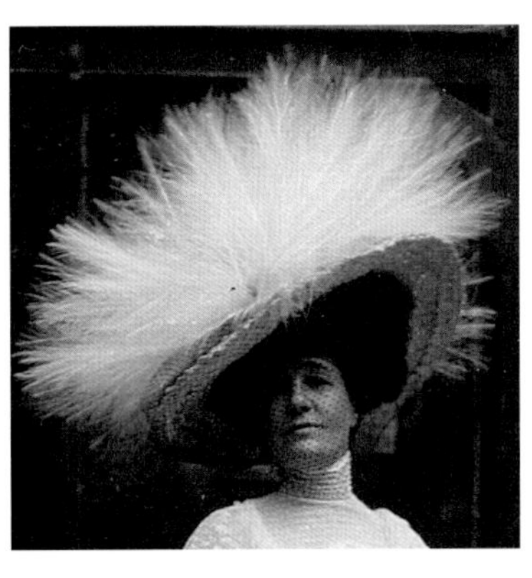

THE EVOLUTION OF FASHION AS SEEN BY THE SÉEBERGERS

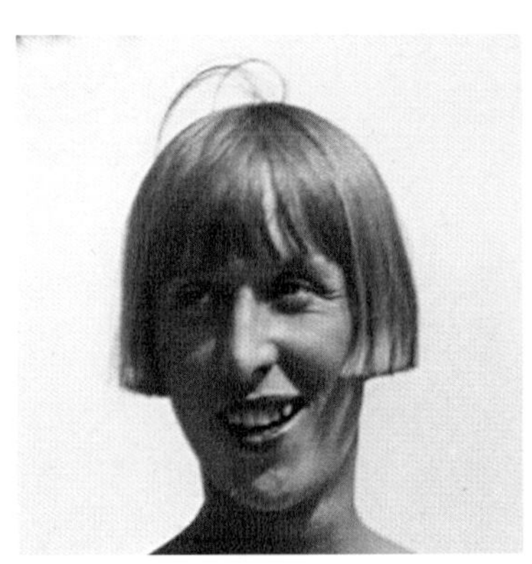

THE EVOLUTION OF FASHION AS SEEN BY THE SÉEBERGERS

Xavier Demange

The decision to focus on the Séeberger oeuvre in the time span from 1909 to 1939 was not an arbitrary one. These photographs happen to cover the period in which two of the greatest twentieth-century upheavals in the history of female fashion occurred: dresses were shortened to the knees, and women began to wear pants. A brief backward glance helps clarify the age in which the Séebergers began their careers on the Paris racetracks. In 1909, the fashionable woman's silhouette was still that of an hourglass, with the waist nipped in by a corset and hips and chest jutting out in contrast, as fashion had decreed for over thirty years. The head was laden with hair pieces topped by immense head coverings overloaded with feathers, flowers, or lace trims; the nape of the neck was stiffened in a whalebone collar, the arms swathed in shawls and feather or fur boas, the hands occupied with a parasol, fan, hand bag, or muff—all of which contributed to create a fragile, ethereal creature who was completely anachronistic in a world that was increasingly mechanized and ever less inclined to be nostalgic.

1909–1918: THE CORSET – THE EMPIRE WAIST – THE BALLETS RUSSES – THE CRINOLINETTE

And then along came Paul Poiret. Taking the artist David as his starting point, who had released women in the early 1800s from the complicated fashions of the *ancien régime* by invoking a reformed and restated Greco-Roman antiquity, Poiret raised the waistline to just under the breast after 1910, freeing women from the corset[30] and draping their forms in vague folds and shortened sheaths that allowed a view of feet clad in cothurnes (Greek sandals; illus. p. 127). At the same time, grafted onto this tasteful "antico-mania" was the Orientalism of Diaghilev's Ballet Russes, assailing heretofore tasteful but bland toilettes with the most vivid colors, and framing faces with the folds of turbans adorned with show-stopping plumage (illus. p. 47), advocating harem pants, the bayadere belt, and cascades of pearls at the collar and wrists.[31]

Between 1912 and 1914, an expansion of styles complicated the clarity of the debut: the rococo style (faux panniers, tricorn hat), the *japonaiserie* style (kimono coat, obi sash), and the androgynous style (culottes, flat chest; illus. p. 52) all blended and gave rise to new creations, half-Odalisque, half-Mme de Pompadour.[32] Particular references were lost in the avalanche of overloads that quickly tired the eye of the beholder. On the eve of World War I, a new silhouette emerged. A short waist from which a loose skirt with generous folds (*crinolinette*) hung to mid-calf, worn with high laced boots and a boater tilted over the eyes became the uniform the fashionables adopted during the war (illus. p. 48, top left).

1919–1929: THE LOW WAIST – THE SHIFT DRESS – THE FLAPPERS AND GARÇONNES – THE SWEATER – THE CLOCHE

In 1918, the skirt became outright short, as did the bob haircut, known as a "Joan of Arc" in France. Attire remained pared down, without the frills that could destroy the simple and surprisingly modern line. It was the great lesson of the war years: elegance in sobriety (Chanel would take this up again later, in her own way). Illustrating the deep upheavals in French society caused by the war, and especially the new role played by women in the realm of work, the general look prefigured the garçonne, or flapper, of the 1925–1928 period. But when the Séeberger brothers returned to the racecourses in 1919 to document the changes that had taken place in fashion, the silhouette was sobering up again. Skirts lengthened season after season, and the waist sat at the kidneys and then disappeared, ceding place to the shift dress, which had a straight line from shoulder to ankle, virtually erasing both hips and bust (illus. p. 167). All of this gave free rein to the fabric designers (Bianchini-Ferrier, Dufy), who wove fabrics with bold cubistic patterns (illus. p. 128–129). In 1924, when the hat was reduced to a little cloche pulled down low over the nose (illus. p. 133), the silhouette of the decade had reached its full development and would be pass down to posterity under the vague term "flapper style" without further precision. The complex (and until recently) poorly understood genesis of this style is well documented by the Séeberger brothers.

Once the vocabulary was established, this fashion carried on without great innovation until 1929. The female ideal tended to favor the gawky shape of a young girl who has grown too quickly. The skirt, which had been lowered almost to the ankle, gradually rose to the knees, and then lengthened markedly again, to allow couturiers to exercise their full imagination between belt and hemline. Into that restricted space went a riot of flounces, stitches, pleats, and fur or feather appliqués, rendering the top of the dress so unpleasantly plain by contrast that it, in turn, had to be brightened up with snazzy sweaters, dramatically colored scarves, and masses of long necklaces (illus. p. 62, top right).

But an important variant also had its day in the sun. Rejecting frills and jewels, this style sought simplicity of line by borrowing its look and clothing from men.[33] *La Garçonne* (translatable as "The Boyish Girl"), the literary scandal of 1922, lent its name to an androgynous style launched the same year by the House of Prémet, consisting of close-cropped hair, a man's shirt and tie, smoking suit, soft felt hat, and low-heeled shoes (illus. p. 49, bottom left). Once the shock had passed, the extremes of the garçon style became obsolete quite quickly and were adopted only by a few eccentrics. Nonetheless, this abortive attempt at masculinizing fashion led to a greater simplification of daily wear and the introduction of pajamas. Hiding under these modest garments is one of the most dramatic clothing revolutions of the twentieth century: the introduction of pants into the female wardrobe.

1930–1937: PAJAMAS – LONG DRESSES – PICTURE HATS – LEGS

Worn since the war by both sexes as casual, indoor clothing, pajamas appeared at the beaches and casinos in 1929 and received their popular name in the summer of 1931. Ridiculed, sung about, and prohibited by the Church, pajamas were finally accepted when the couturiers thought to feminize them and erase any hint of ambiguity. The Séebergers photographed the best of these styles, worn in Biarritz from autumn 1929 until 1939, a period during which pajamas were transformed into slacks– something else altogether. Pants were worn, as were shorts, by all the fashionables, any time sportswear was expected (illus. p. 56).

Paradoxically, the adoption of male pants went hand in hand with the post-1929 abandonment of the 1920s' geometric lines and silhouette, and a return to the narrow, fluid princess line. The skirt lengthened, erratically at first, and then fell right to the ankle, the waist returned to its natural location, and the use of light fabrics such as crepe georgette, muslin, and silk jersey, as well as bias cuts, furthered the return of natural forms. Between 1930 and 1935, there was an odd revisiting of an ultra-feminine style reminiscent of 1900, in some cases carried to the point of caricature.[34] Women in frilly, frothy dresses and great broad-brimmed hats seemed to inhabit a permanent garden party in search of a bygone era (illus. p. 157).

From all these excesses, street fashion settled on a new calf-length skirt, the layering of garments of different lengths, and a boldly tilted felt hat. A sleek silhouette was born that was all about legs, whose length was emphasized by the small waist. In some of their photos, the Séebergers also managed to capture the subtle eroticism of this active and independent woman who could play off her newly rediscovered femininity (illus. p. 51, top right).

1937–1946: PADDED SHOULDERS – GRAND HATS – PLATFORM SHOES – LONG HAIR

On the eve of World War II, women seemed to hesitate between two ages: heads had femme fatale proportions, while feet were boy-like. At that time, Max Factor and Hollywood–whose influence was omnipresent–decreed a new face for women with composite features: plucked eyebrows like Jean Harlow, square-shaped lips like Joan Crawford, false eyelashes like Marlene Dietrich, not to mention the strawberry-blonde permanent of Ann Sheridan. As from the 1930s, the face became a fashion object in photography thanks to the close-up, borrowed from the language of the cinema. The

Séebergers used this technique to document variations of the hat, in particular, itself a pretext to compose genuine portraits of women in traditional silhouette form.

To crown this artificial mask, women began to wear increasingly voluminous hats, perched on top of the head or forming a halo around the face (illus. p. 141). The breasts were restored to a place of honor, and the elastic girdle molded the hips and emphasized the chest, slightly at first and then increasingly aggressively. Rehabilitating the waist at the same time it was trimmed down, a widened torso that exaggerated the puff sleeve (launched by Suzanne Talbot and Marcel Rochas) was adopted on the street at the end of the decade. The general outline of the fashion of the war years–platform shoes (illus. p. 144),[35] square shoulders, short dresses, and long hair–was initiated around 1937.

A new factor–young people's influence on fashion–began to make its mark. Until this point, teenagers' clothing was hardly different from that of adults, but from 1936-1937, the differences became radical. American music invaded Europe, establishing the youth as a new market, and launched the "swing" style: ankle socks, flat shoes, short skirt, fitted sweater, sunglasses, and a head scarf.

It is worth considering the major factors that caused the female silhouette to change in one direction or another. Of course, the motivations that led skirt hems to be lengthened or shortened, the adoption of a particular form of dress or hat, and the acceptance of pants or shorts into the fashionable wardrobe are largely lost to us. Yet the evidence lies before our eyes like a strictly factual police report, written without emotion. We can piece together the colossal, 35,000-plate puzzle left to us by the Séebergers to give it meaning and tease out the general logic.

What is behind each of these moments in fashion crystallized on paper? The identity of the model, the creative imagination that clothed her, the artistic influences at work in her choice of accessories, fabrics, and colors, the social context that accepted this fashionable emulation–all of these can be sought mainly in printed media of the period: memoirs, newspaper articles, best-selling novels, various happenings, artistic events, and so forth abound with contemporary testimonies. All these will help us figure out who these women and men were, who appear so familiar and yet so distant.

Let us investigate one of the Séebergers' photos more thoroughly: the bare-headed singer Suzy Solidor in a white dress at Deauville in August 1923 (illus. p. 46). Her bobbed haircut, called the "Joan of Arc," is radically short. The first women to cut their hair in this style, as early as 1910–1911, were painters' models at Montparnasse. Famous actresses (Sorel, Mona Delza, Vera Sergine) appeared on stage with a bob during the war of 1914–1918, and fashionable personalities (Misia Sert, Mme Letellier, Chanel) followed around 1917. The trend had been launched, but it was initially followed only in the narrow circle of the world of show business and haute couture. Women who had acquired some independence during the war and were dissatisfied by the roles to which they were consigned after the armistice used this symbolic style as a sign of protest. In 1923, Suzy Solidor's haircut still incurred the disapproval of the moral majority, and men in general. The previous year, author Victor Margueritte had published a vaguely pornographic bestseller entitled *La Garçonne*, creating a kind of sexually emancipated young woman of intense modernity. Any asexual fashions began to be called *à la garçonne*,[36] and public opinion considered the women who adopted them to be both loose-living hussies and (with respect to Solidor, who also vaunted her preference for women) a threat to the social order.

In the Séeberger photo, Solidor scrambles the aggressive message projected by her ultramodern hairstyle by wearing "chaste" clothing: a white dress with a romantic look that would normally be worn on very formal occasions. It is one of those full skirts known as "robes de style" that were made fashionable by Jeanne Lanvin in reaction against the blandly geometrical shift dress. The boat neck and long, puffed skirt are reminiscent of the Louis-Philippe period. Only the low waist is a concession to the contemporary line. Under the translucent muslin of this "robe de style" a shorter, more "modern" skirt can be seen. This photograph is an instructive illustration of a hinge moment between two periods—the nineteenth and the twentieth centuries—and two visions of woman: at once modern and traditional.

For the fashion historian, the documentation provided by the Séeberger brothers is crucially important. Not only does it cover an essential period in the evolution of feminine clothing in the twentieth century, in addition, each photograph is a nuanced narrative that can be read on various levels. Long and meticulous interpretation remains to be done, and this publication hopefully will provide a useful impetus in that direction.

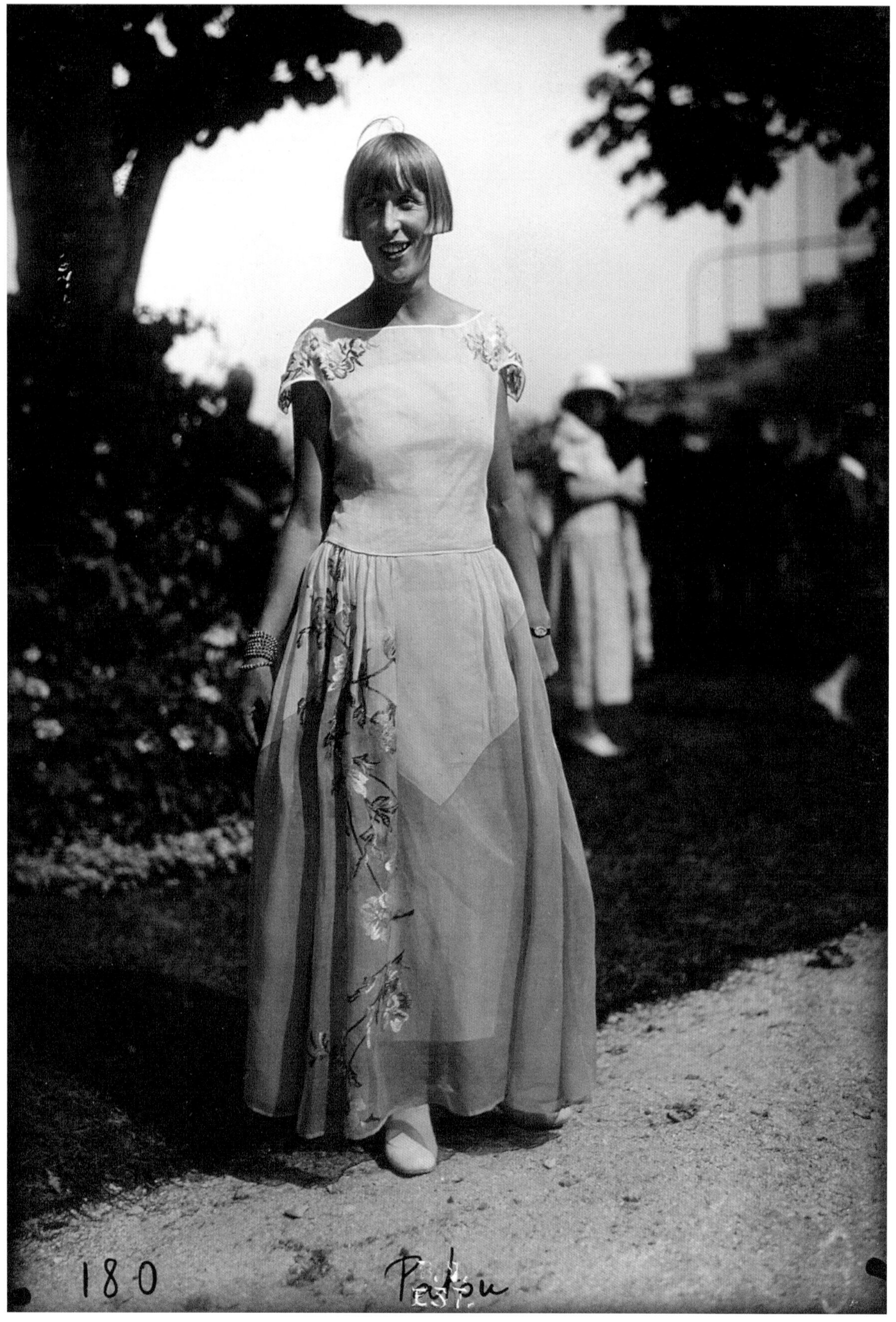

Suzy Solidor (1900–1983), with a garçonne *haircut and wearing an embroidered gown by Patou, Deauville, August 12, 1923.*

Summer, ca. 1907.

Summer 1909.

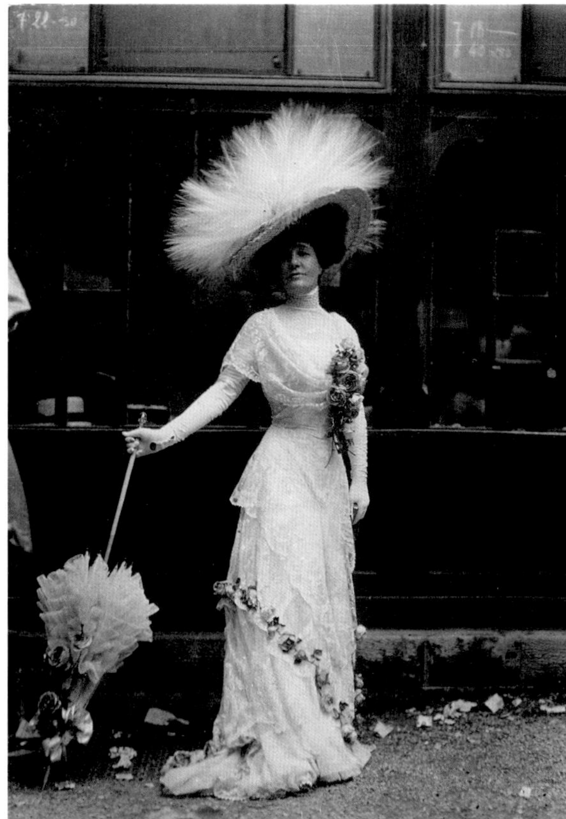

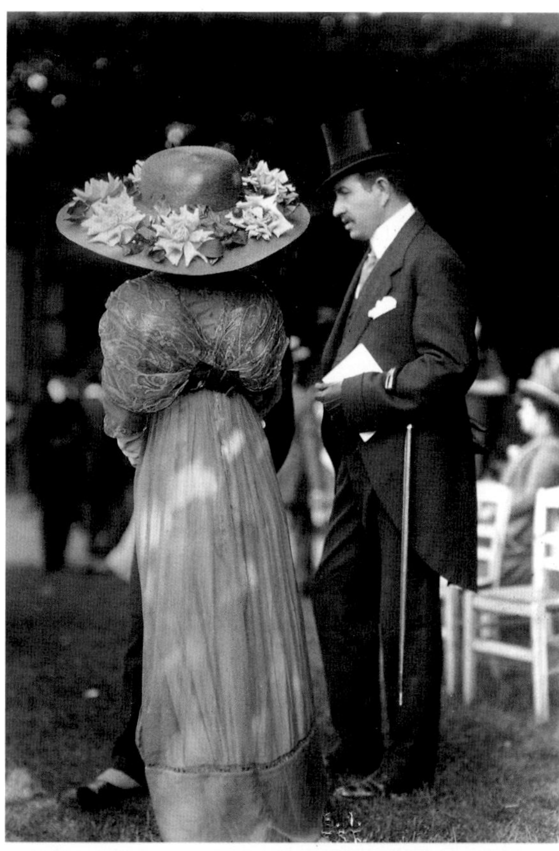

Beginning of 1912.

Autumn 1913.

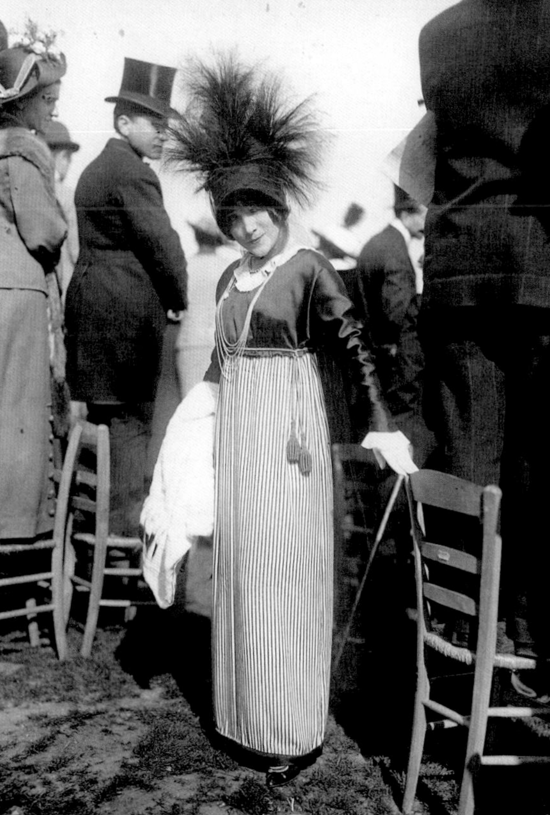

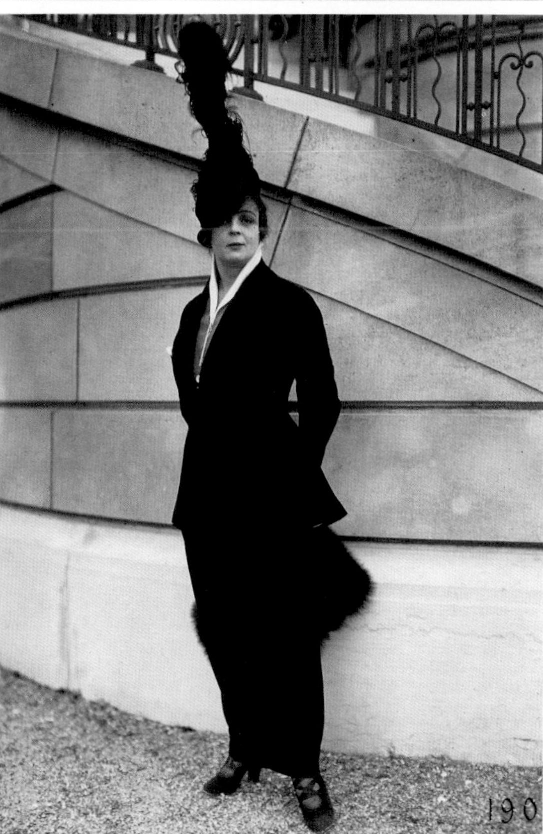

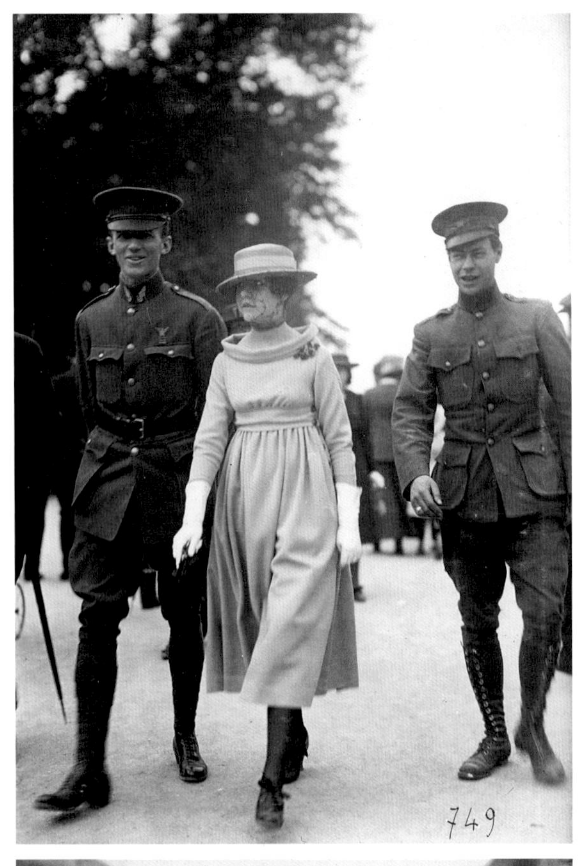

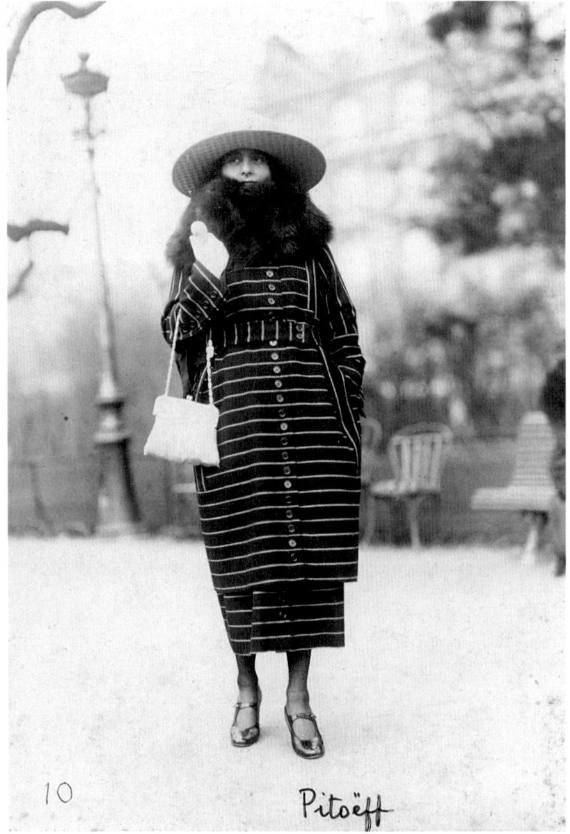

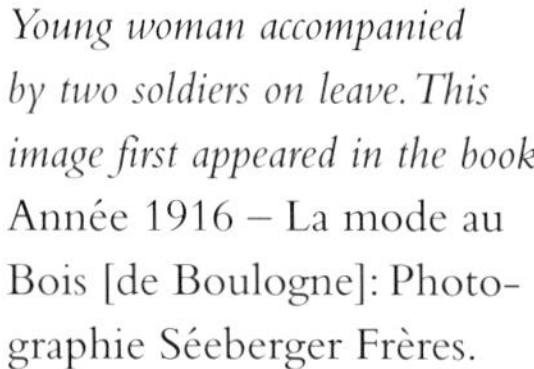
Young woman accompanied by two soldiers on leave. This image first appeared in the book Année 1916 – La mode au Bois [de Boulogne]: Photographie Séeberger Frères.

Striped dress and coat, by Pitoëff, January 1919.

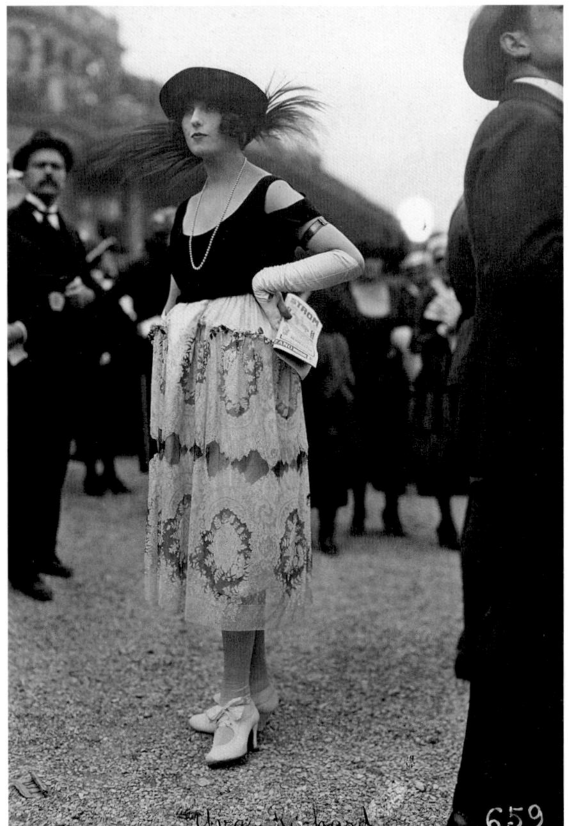

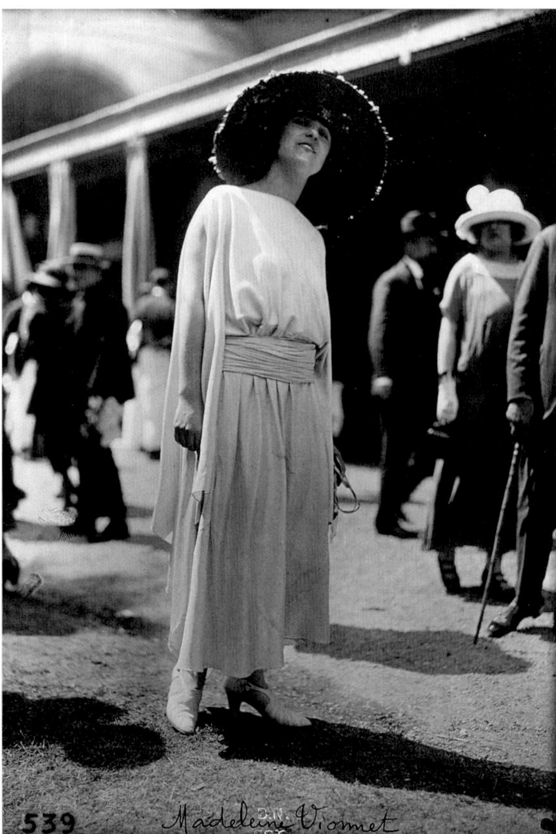

Yva Richard dress at the Grand Prix de Paris, 1920. Nativa and Richard L. had a fine lingerie business, under the pseudonym of Yva Richard, whose styles were disseminated through highly suggestive photographs.

Gown by Madeleine Vionnet, Chantilly, Prix du Jockey Club, June 11, 1922.

Lanvin suit, Auteuil, March 25, 1923.

Joseph Paquin outfit, Bois de Boulogne, 1925.

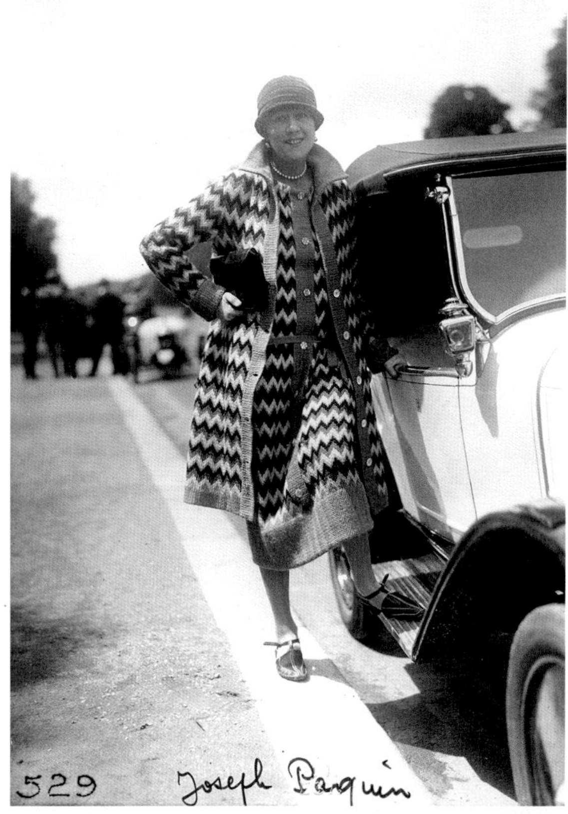

Laure Jarny at the races, winter 1927.

Deauville, La Grande Semaine, summer 1925.

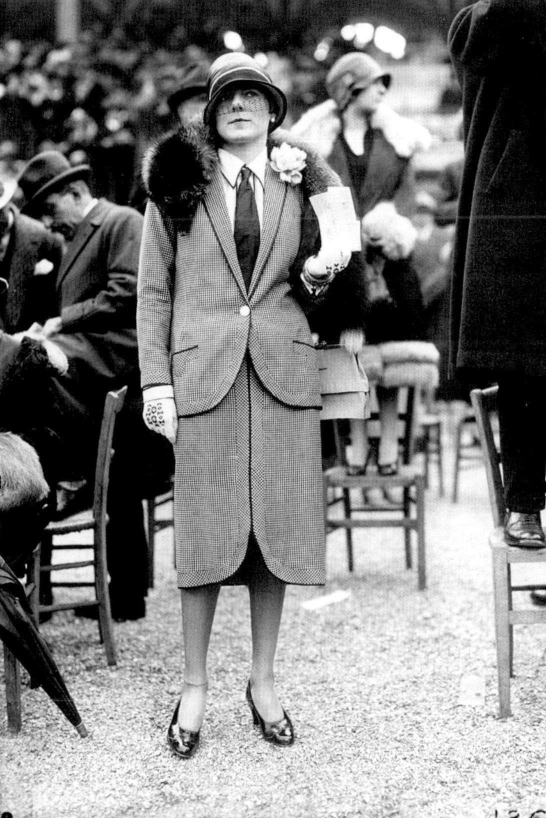

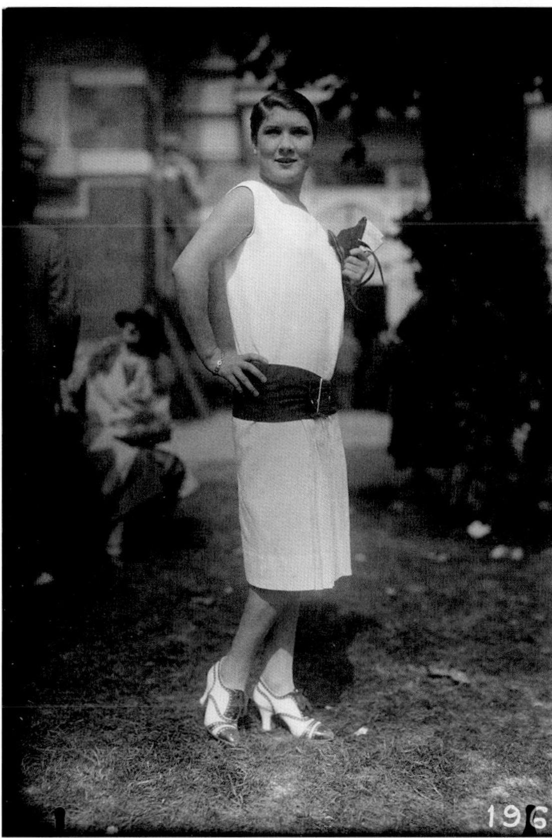

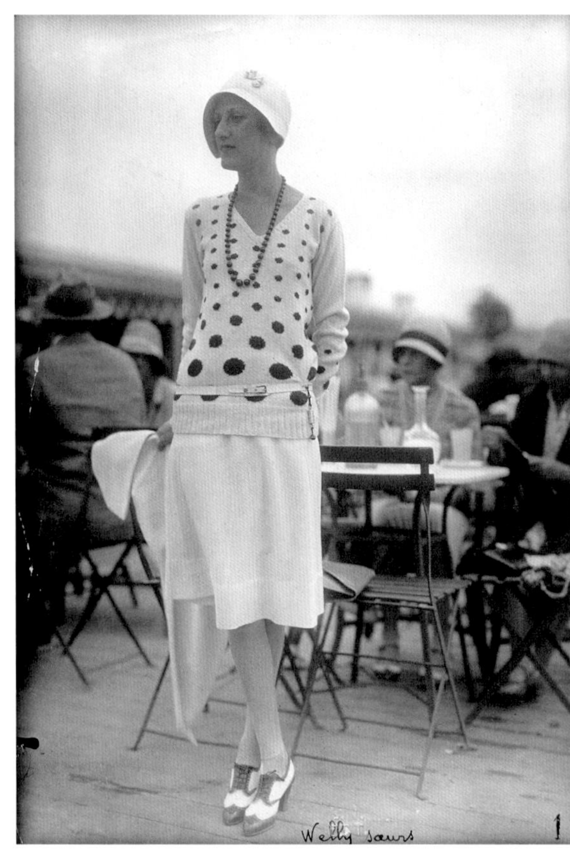

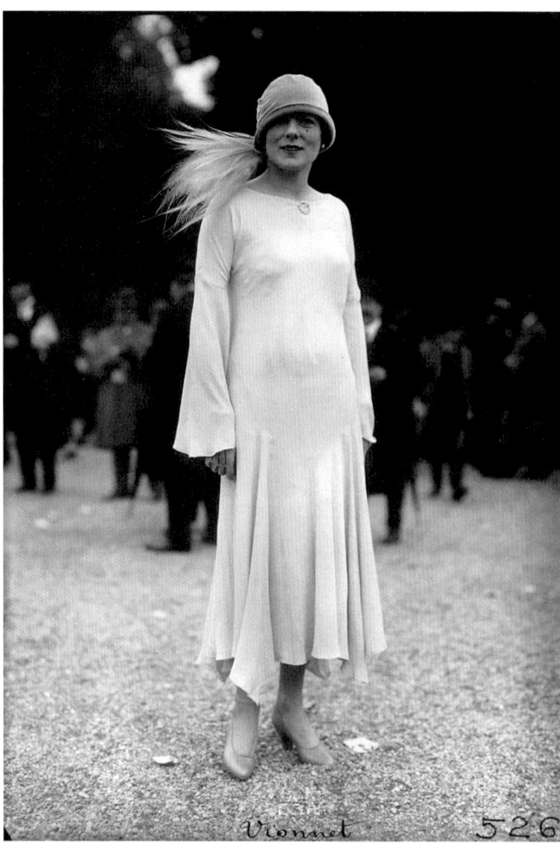

Welly Sisters outfit, Deauville, August 9, 1928.

Madeleine Vionnet dress, worn by Laure Jarny, summer 1924.

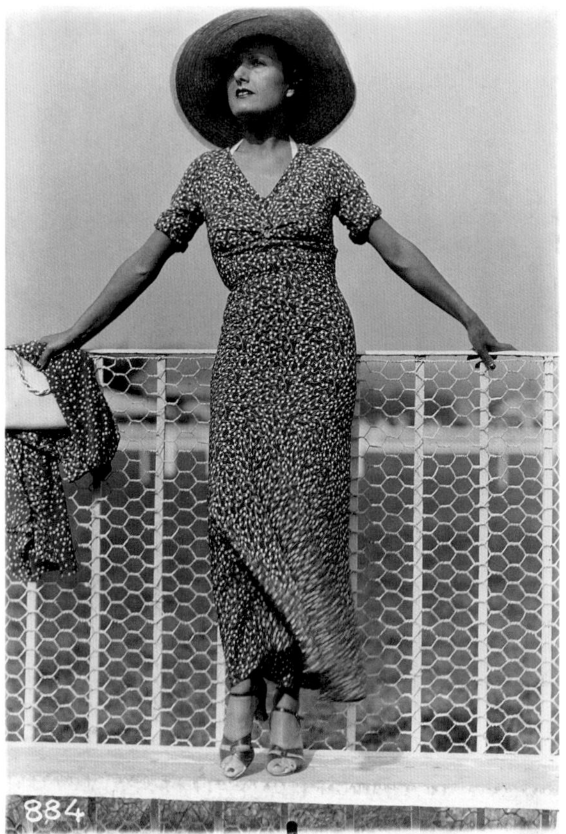

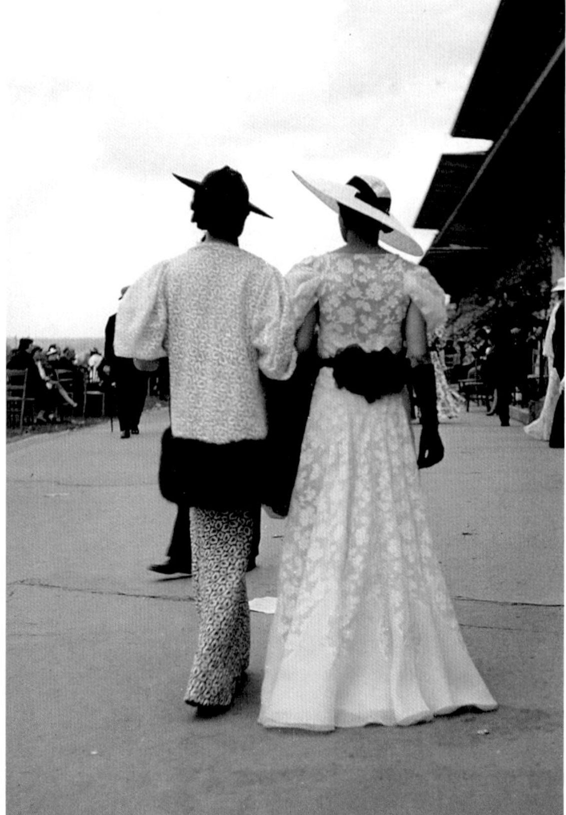

Francesca Bertini, Italian silent film star, later Countess Cartier, outfitted by Lucien Lelong, Deauville, August 1932.

Back view of women in designs by Jane, Auteuil, Grande Course des Haies, June 26, 1935.

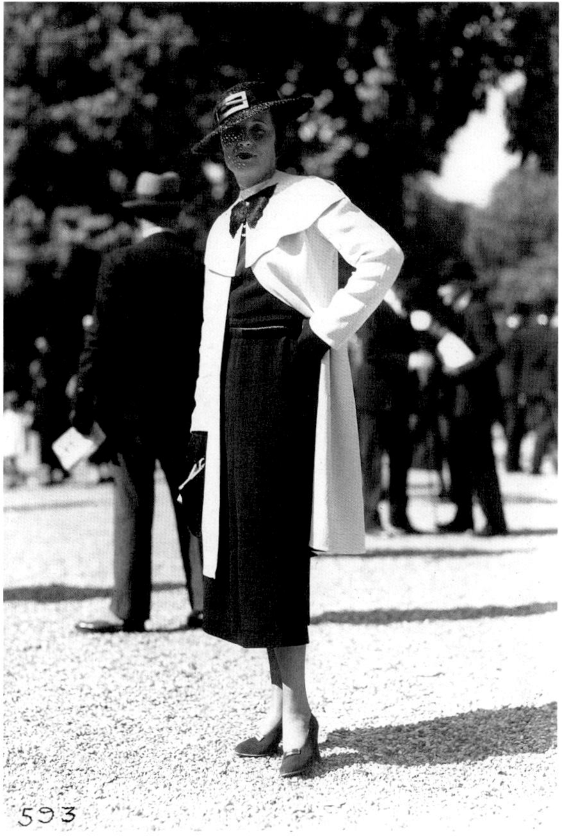

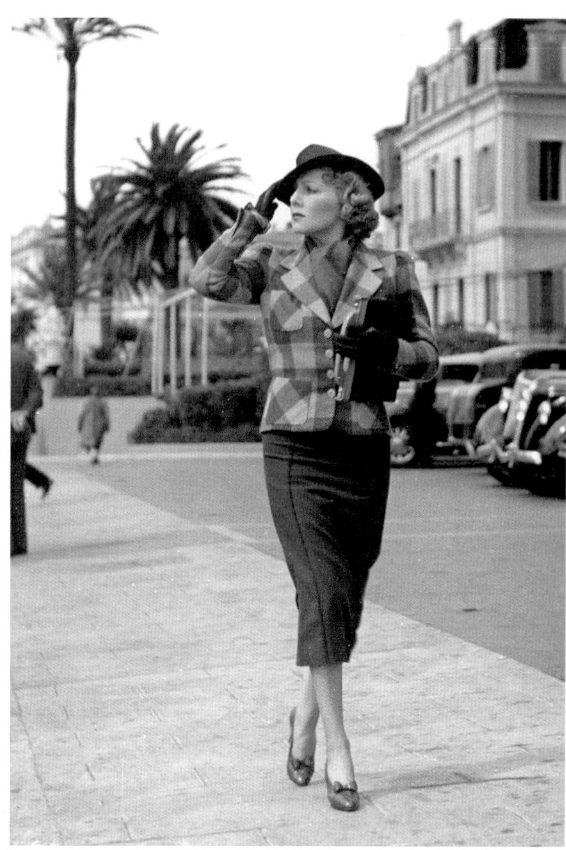

Begum Aga Khan (1898–1976), née Andrée Carron, third wife of Aga Khan III, outfitted by Worth, Longchamp, Prix du Cadran, May 6, 1934.

Young woman walking along the Croisette, Cannes, Easter 1937.

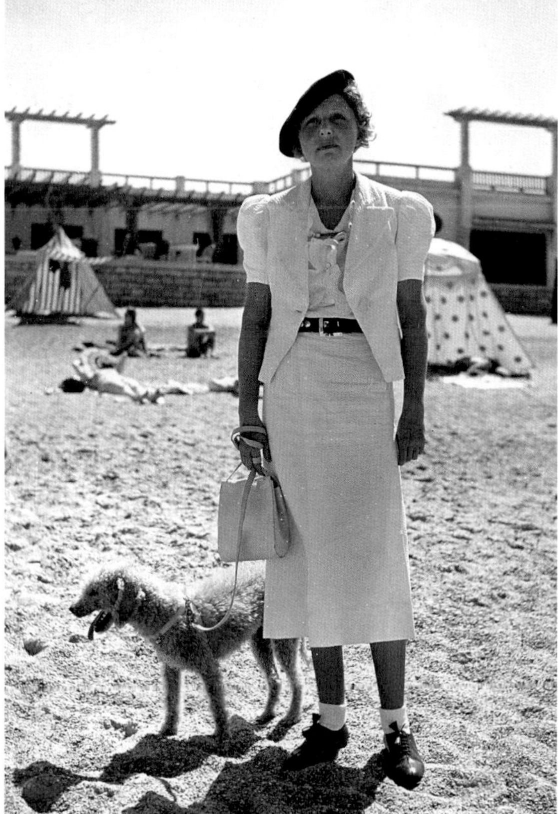

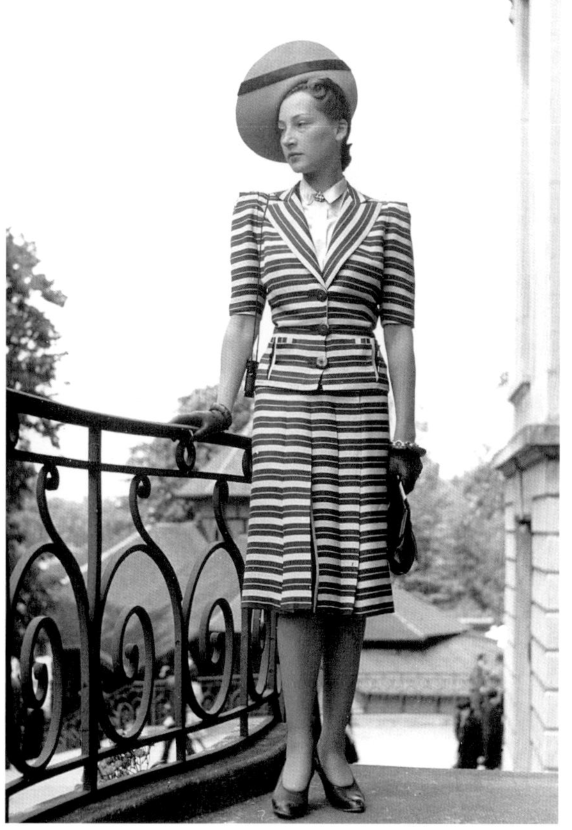

Countess Marie-Thérèse Du Bourg de Bozas, née Fuller-Feder, wife of Guy de Bozas, wearing an outfit by Marcelle Dormoy, Biarritz, September 1936.

Mlle Kramer, in a Mendel suit and Erik hat, Grand Steeplechase d'Auteuil, June 18, 1939.

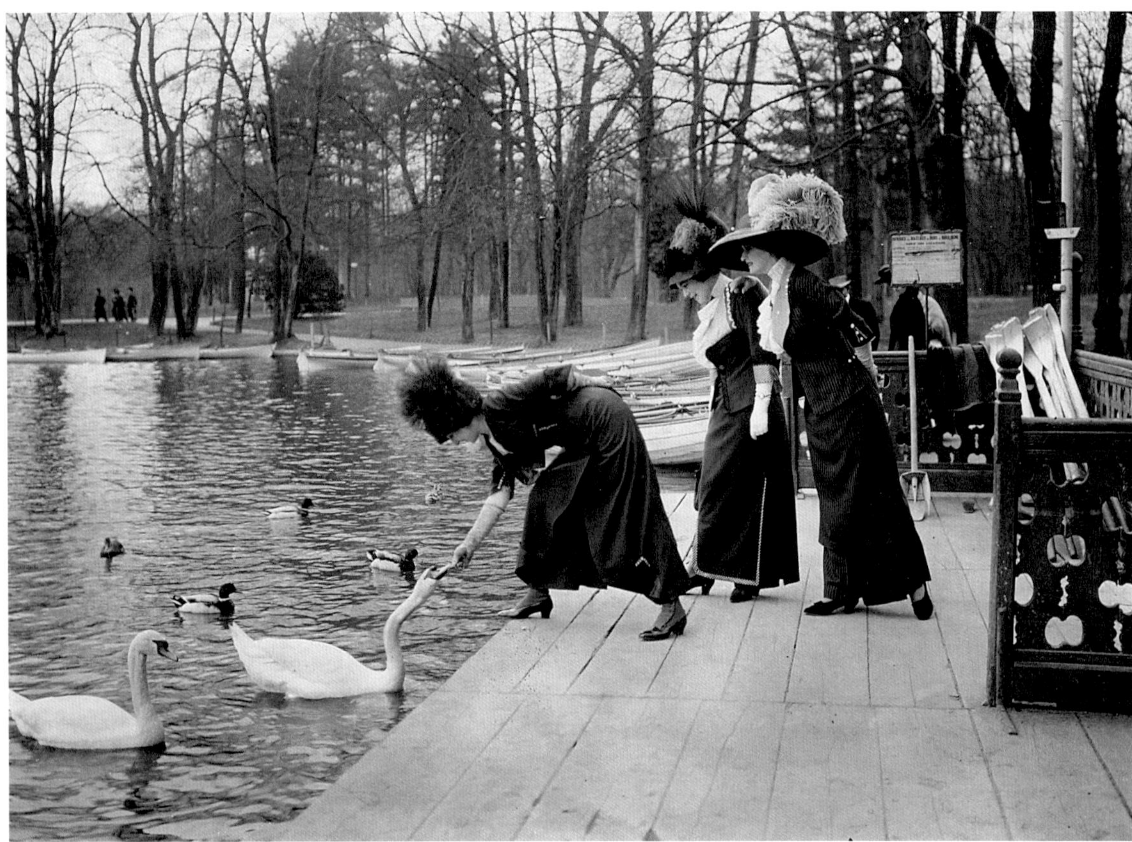

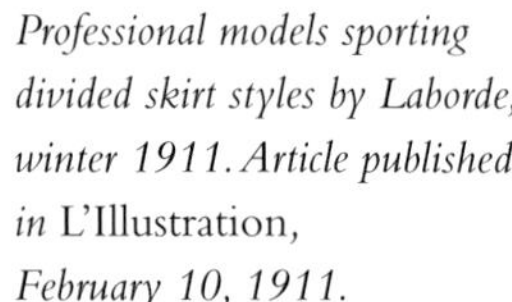

Professional models sporting divided skirt styles by Laborde, winter 1911. Article published in L'Illustration, *February 10, 1911.*

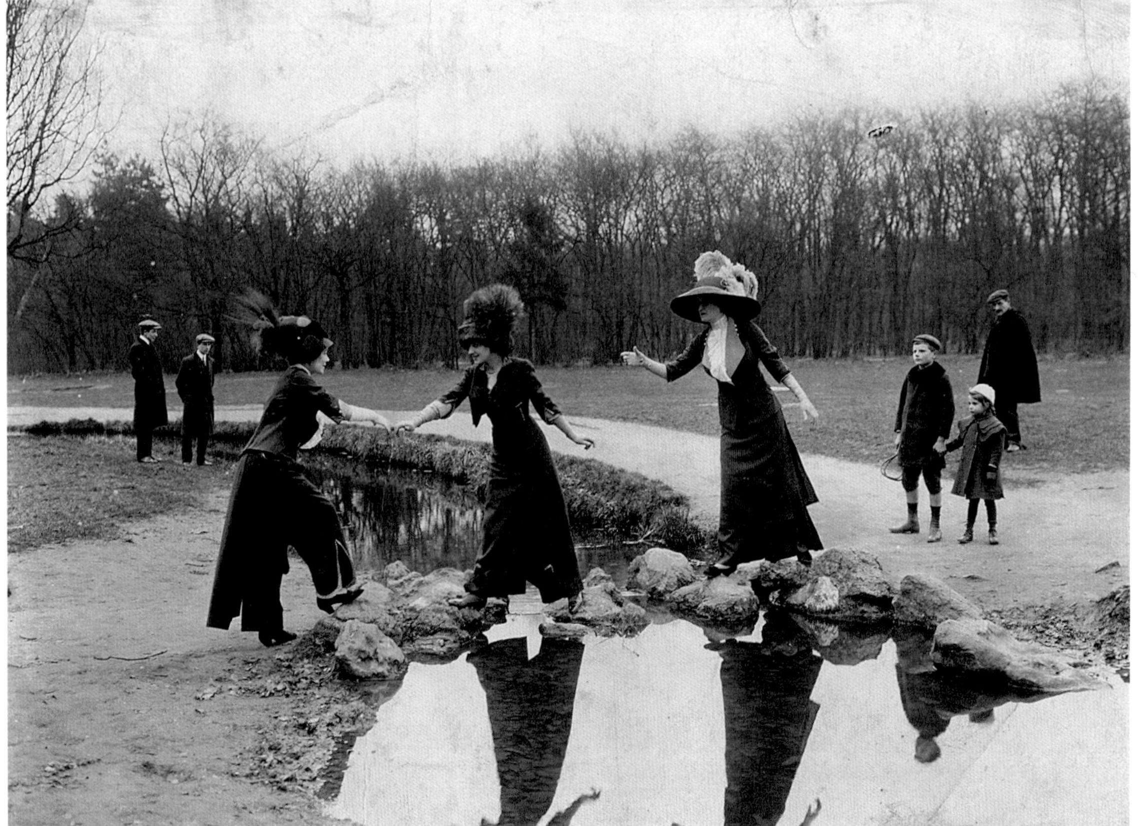

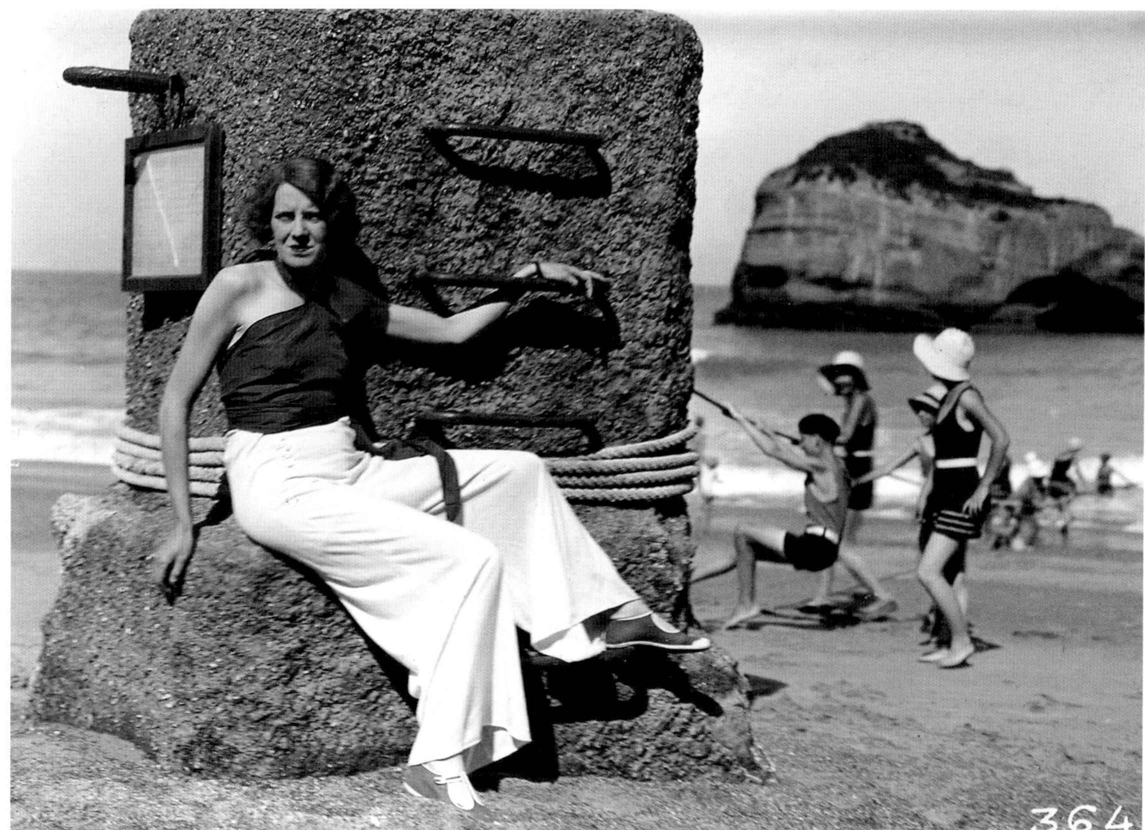

Young woman in a Heim pantsuit on the beach of Biarritz, September 1931.

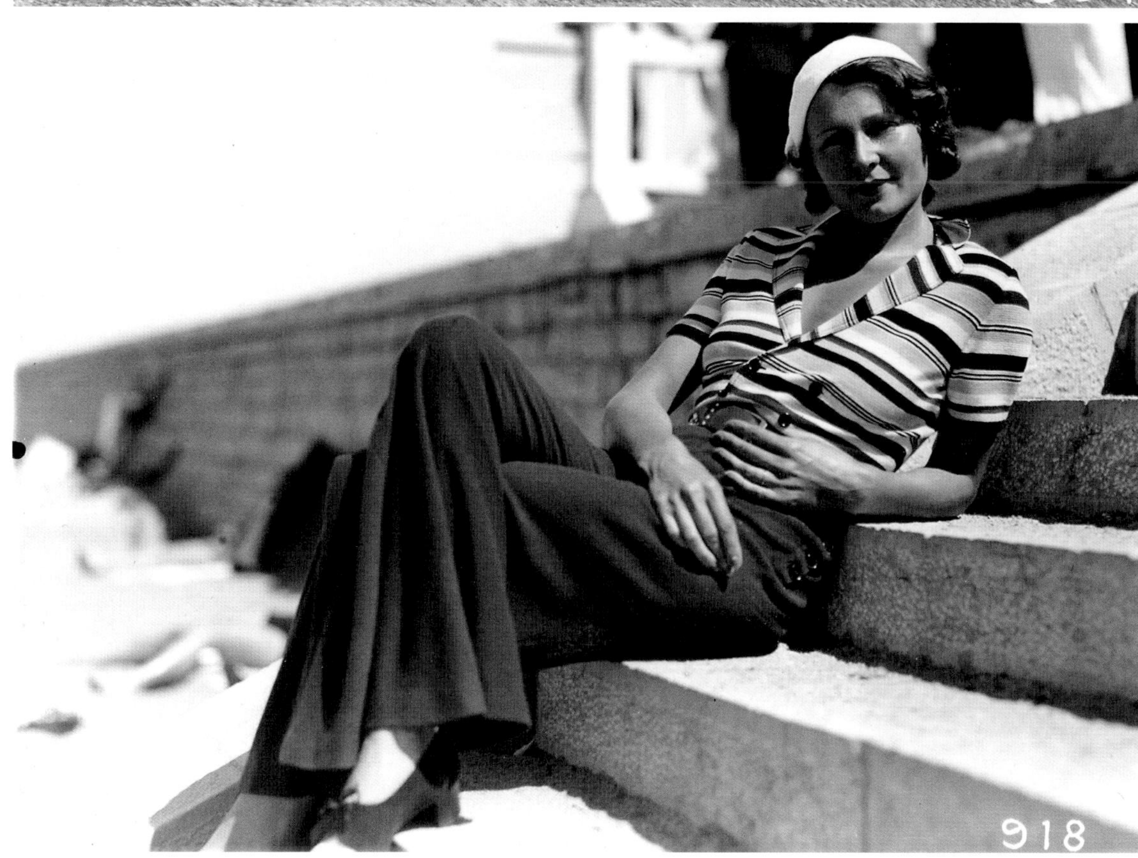

Mme Barret-Décap in a Chanel pantsuit, Biarritz, September 1932. The Barret-Décap family, established in Biarritz, had inherited a series of Impressionist paintings from the Parisian collector Edmond Décap, including several by Renoir, Monet, and Sisley that are now in major American museums.

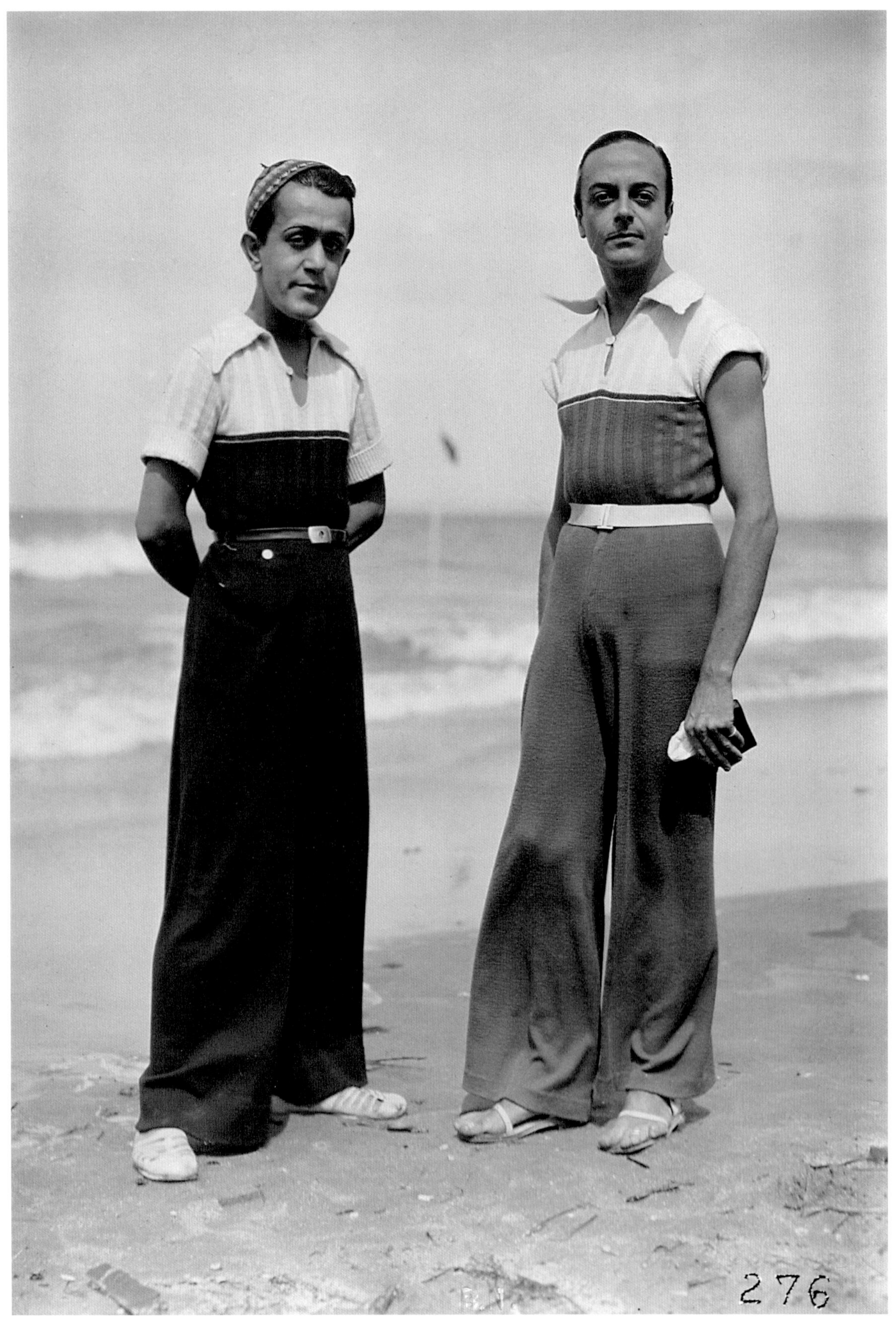

Two young men in beach pajamas by Lucien Robert, Deauville, August 15, 1931.

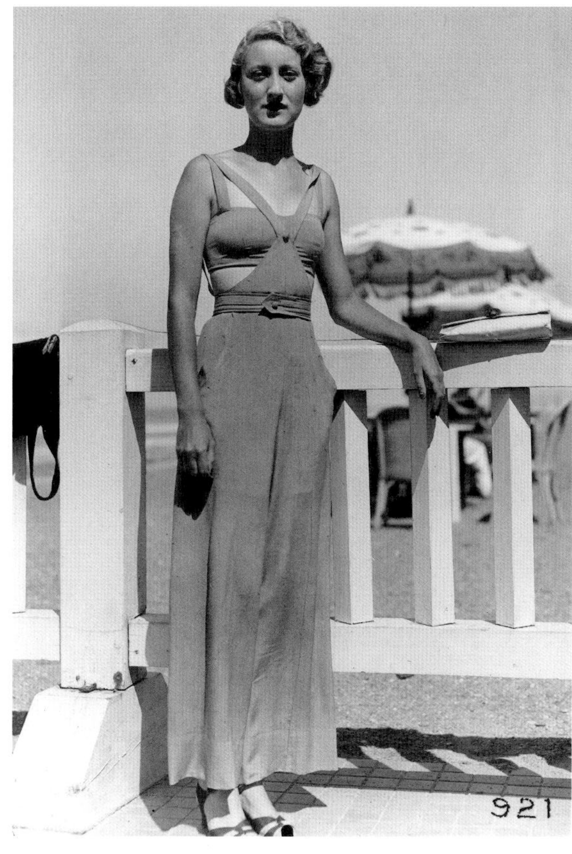

Mme Mansfield wearing Chanel, Biarritz, September 1932.

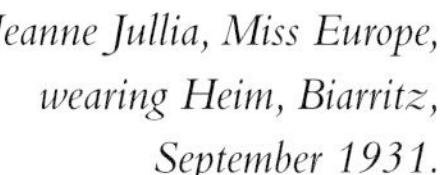

Jeanne Jullia, Miss Europe, wearing Heim, Biarritz, September 1931.

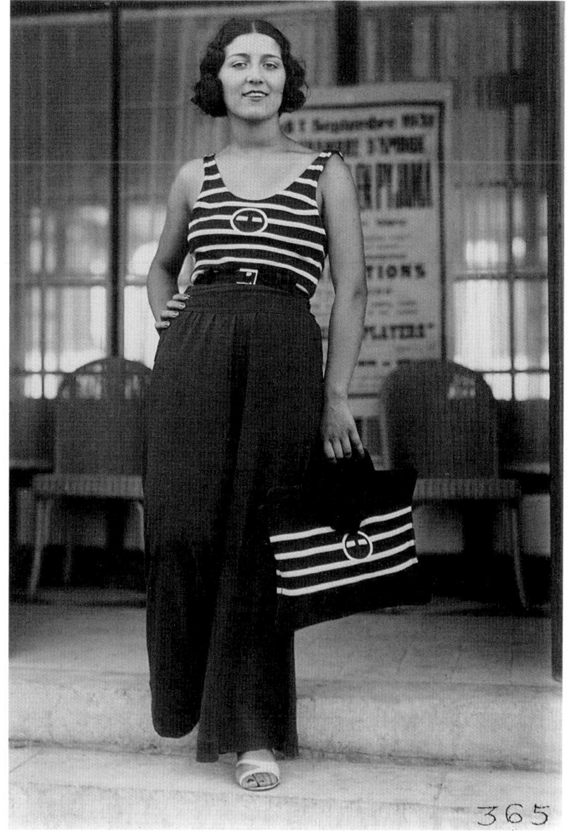

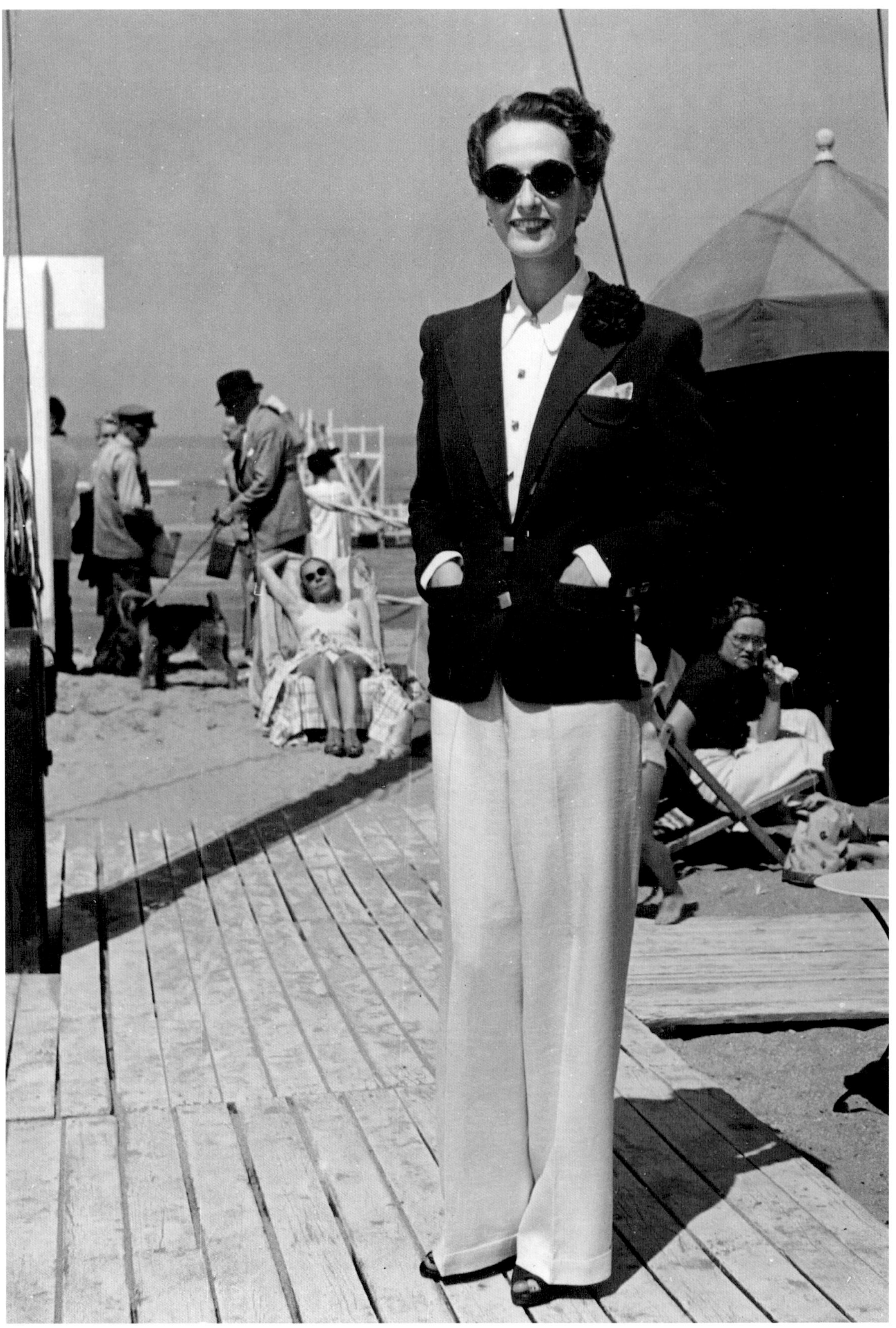

Hélène Arpels (née Ostrowska), wife of the jeweler Louis Arpels, wearing Maggy Rouff, Deauville, August 13, 1939.

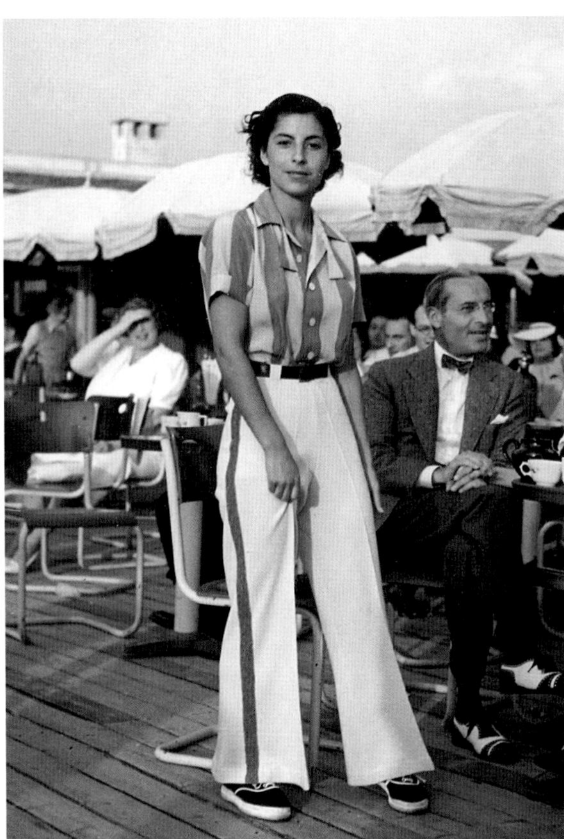

Mlle Dorys wearing Ahetze on the beach at Deauville, summer 1937.

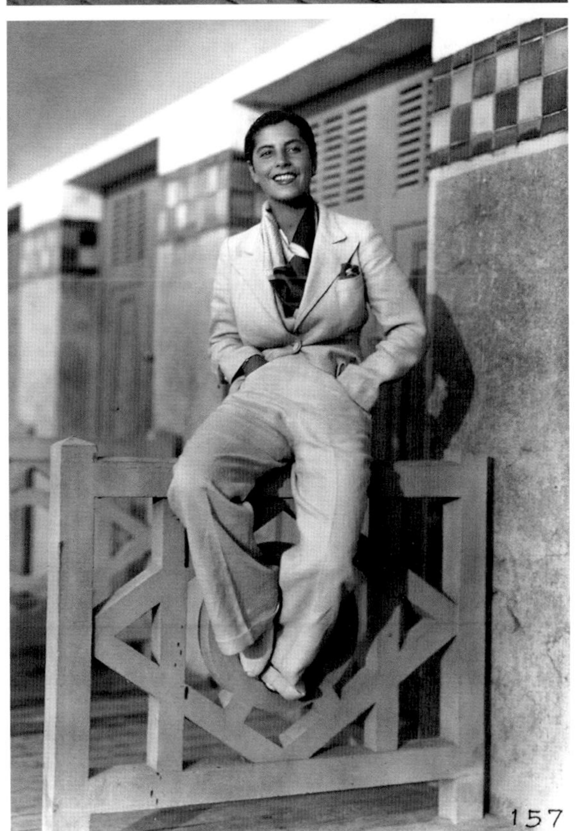

Mlle Dorys in a pantsuit sitting in front of the changing rooms, Deauville, summer 1934.

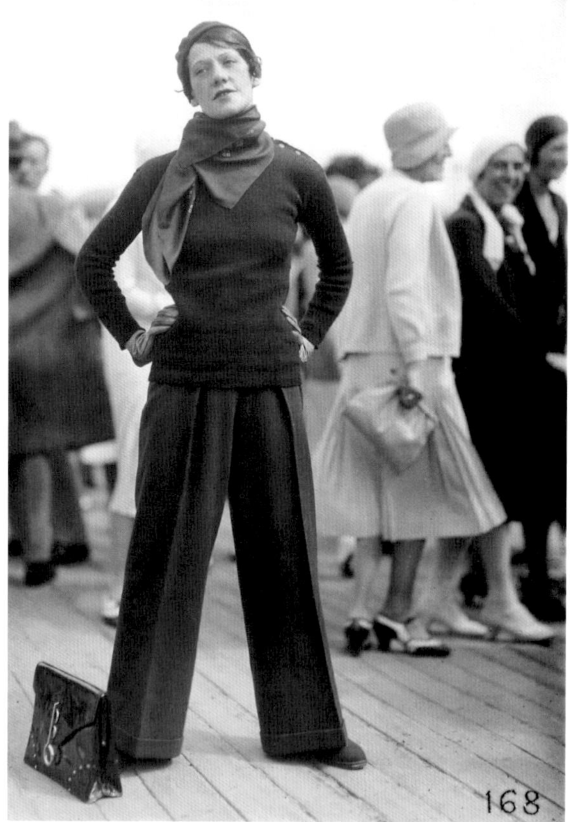

Young woman in a Worth pantsuit, Deauville, Grand Prix, August 1930.

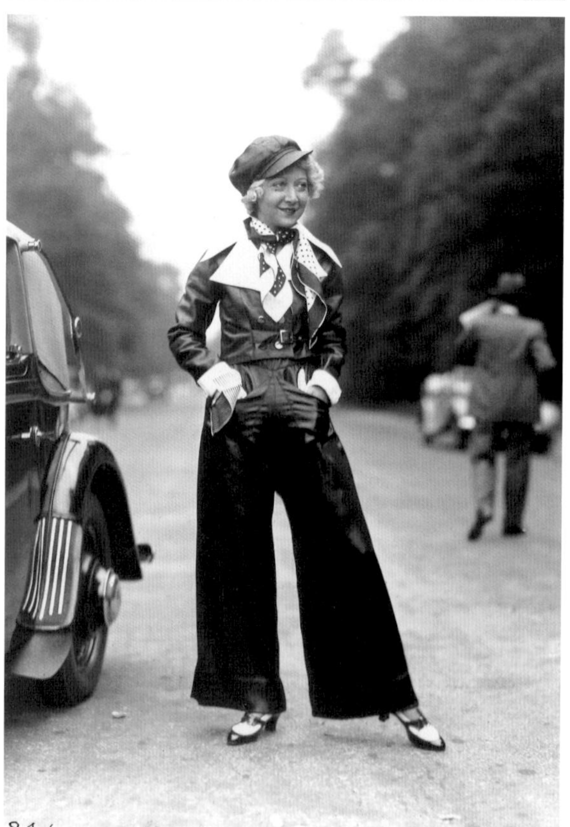

Moussia de Breteuil (née Volguine) wearing a Bussoz leather jacket and Fairyland pajama pants to the concours d'elegance custom automobile show at Bagatelle, June 1933.
A cabaret artist, she also appeared on screen in the 1930s.

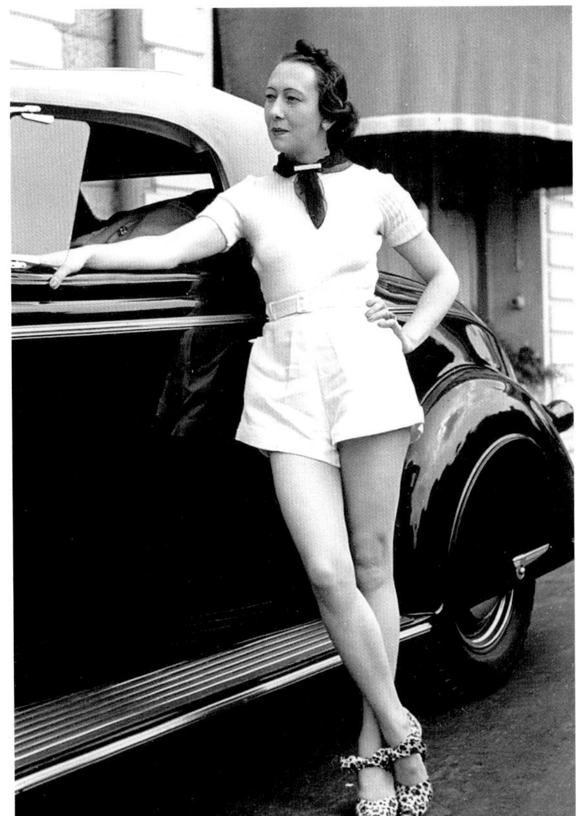

Ellen von Lee, Cannes, end of April 1938.

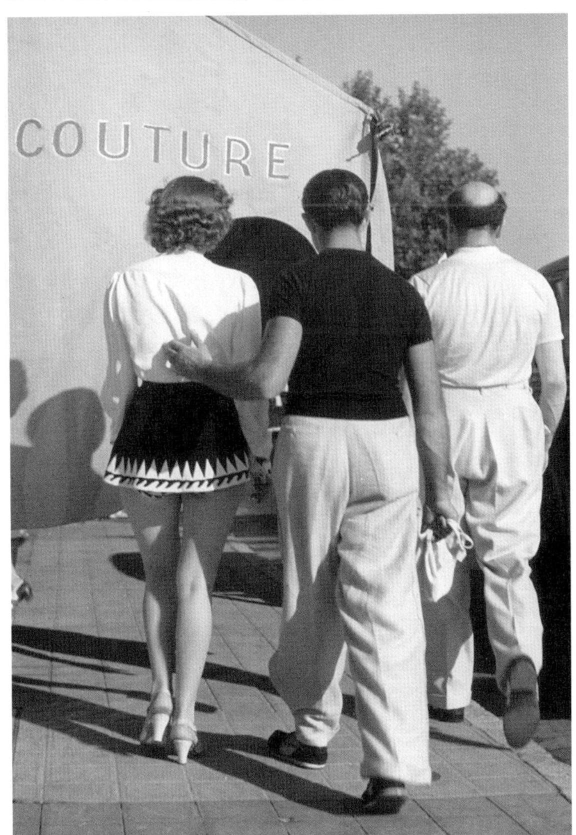

Cannes, late August 1937.

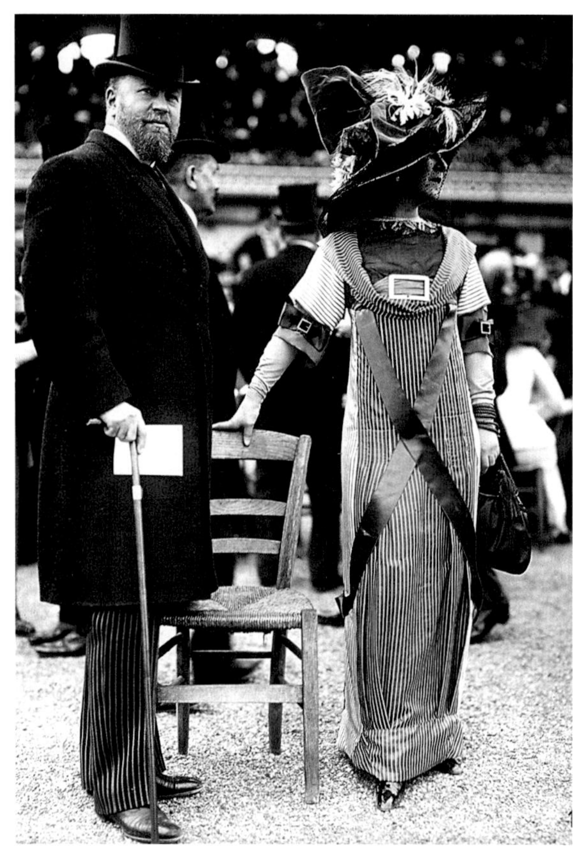

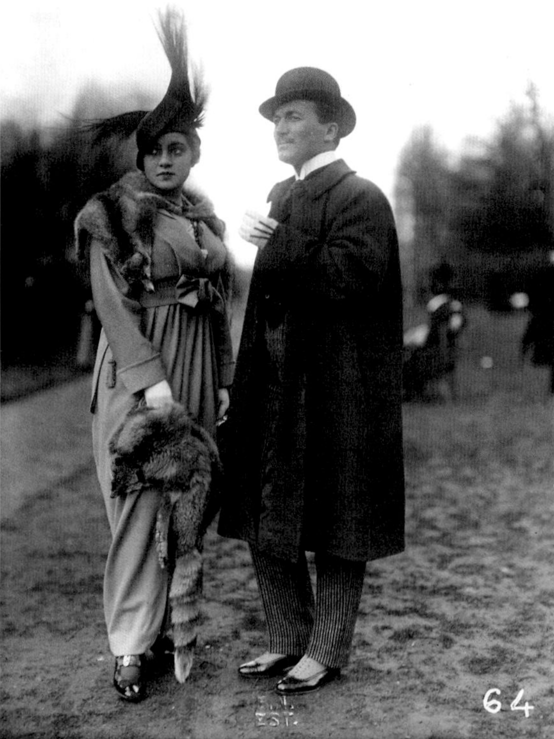

Summer 1911.

February 1914.

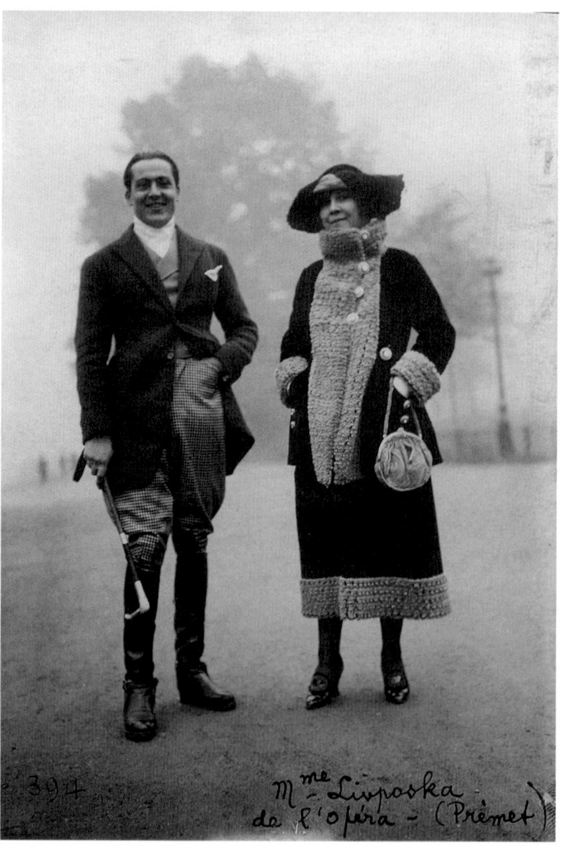

Lydia Lipkowska (1882–1958), née Marschner, a Russian soprano, wearing a Prémet outfit, with her husband Richard-Pierre Bodin (1892–1932), October 26, 1919, in the Bois de Boulogne. Richard-Pierre Bodin was one of the models for Chéri, *by the author Colette.*

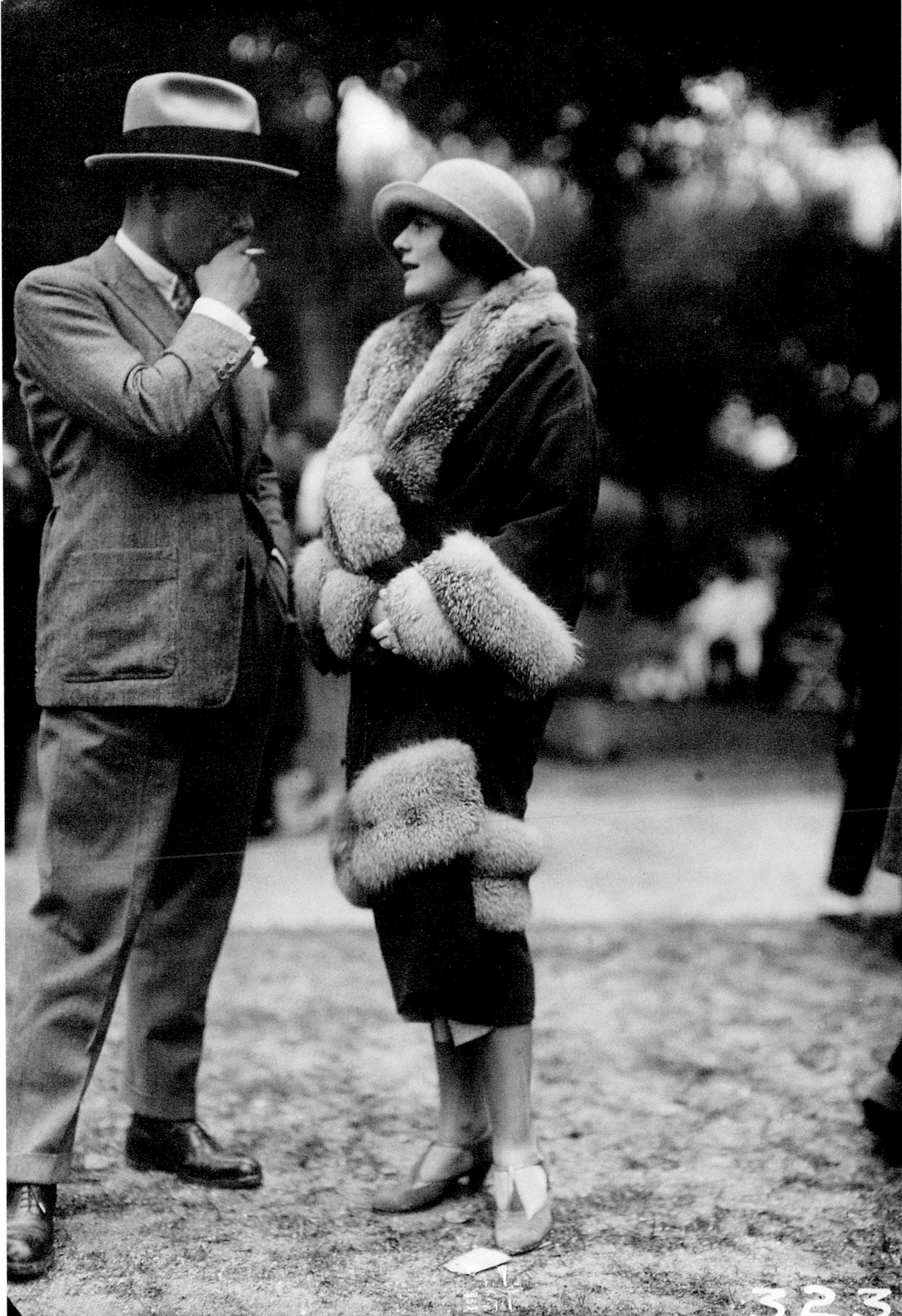

Grand Prix de Deauville,
August 24, 1924.

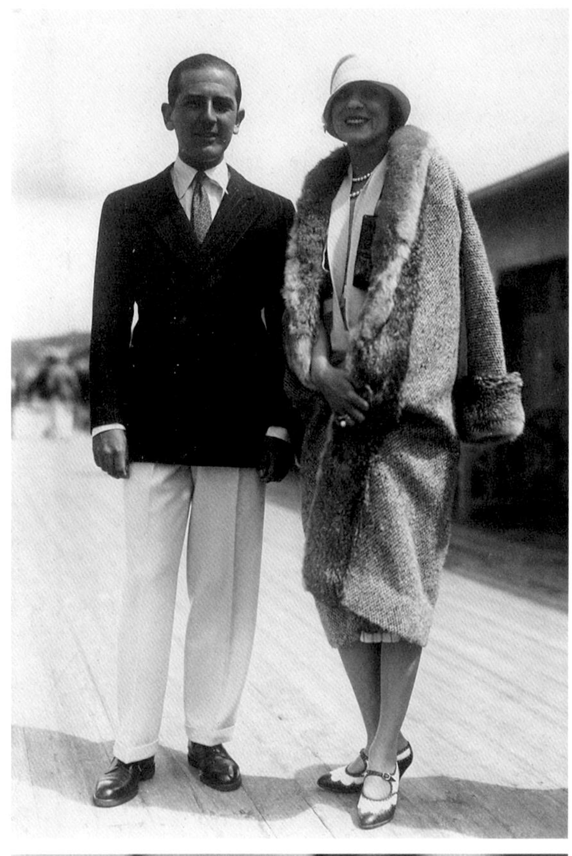

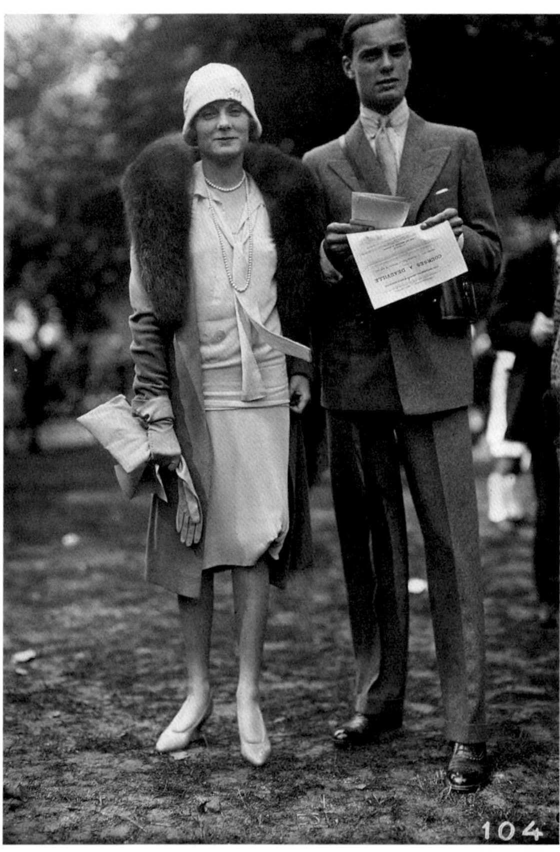

Lady Mortimer Davis, Grand Prix de Deauville, August 1927.

Deauville, August 14, 1927.

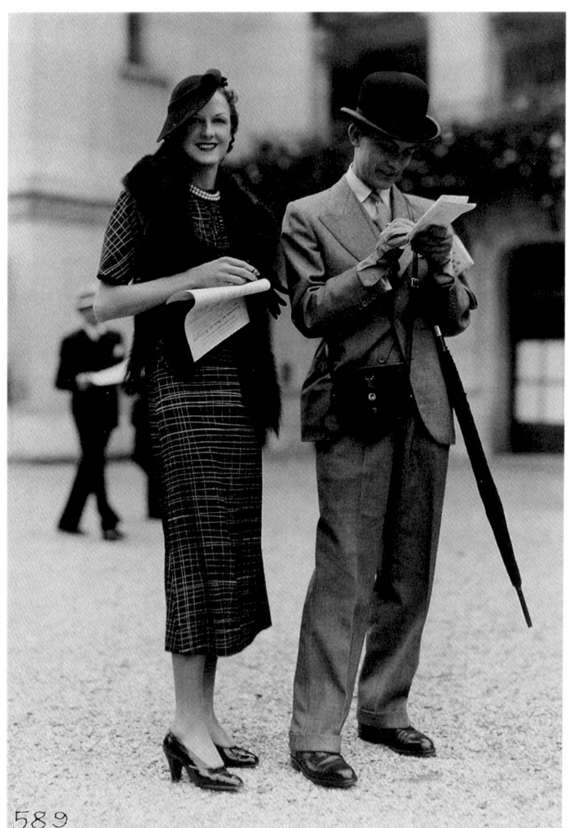

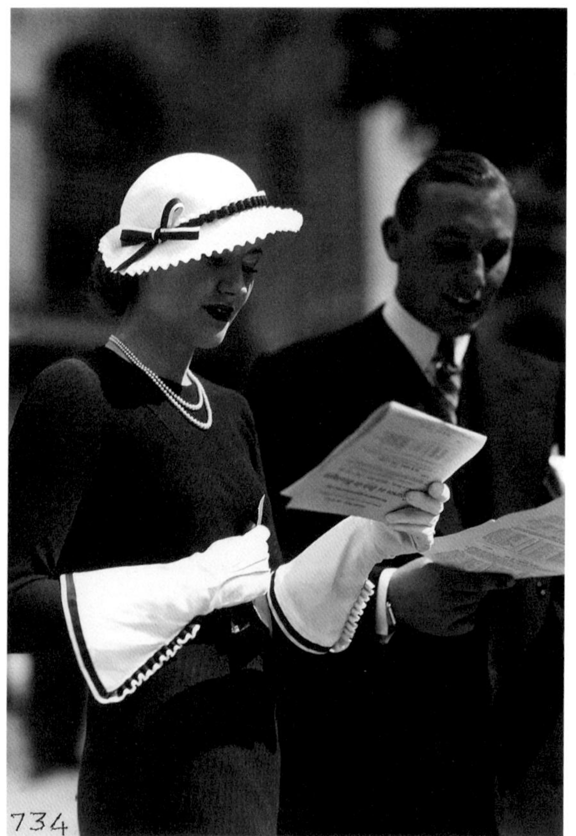

Countess Alain de La Falaise wearing Schiaparelli, Longchamp, Prix Henri-Delamarre, September 30, 1934.

An elegant couple; the young woman is wearing a hat by Suzanne Talbot, Chantilly, Prix de Diane, June 4, 1933.

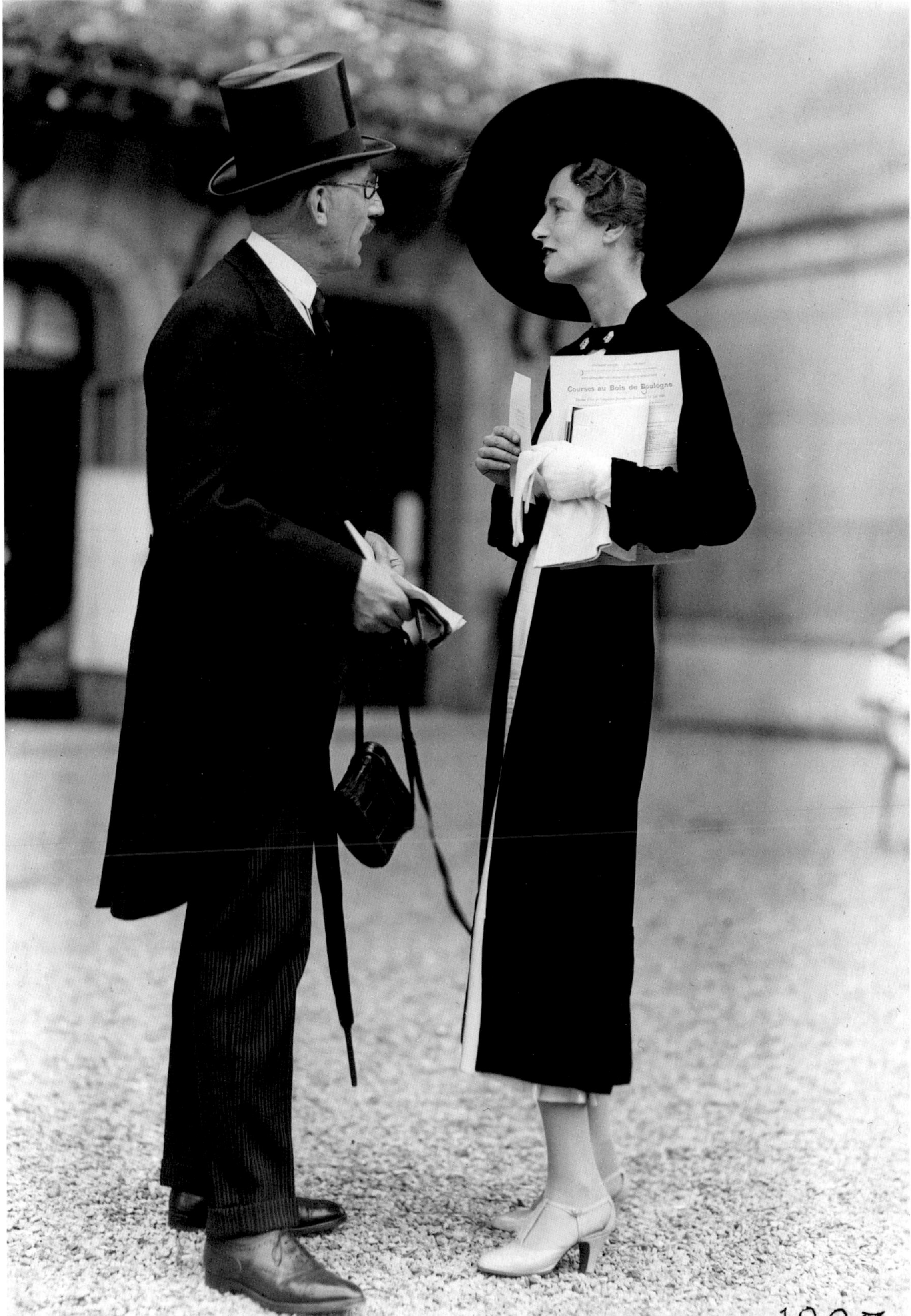

Countess Élie de Ganay, née Nadège de Fontenay, wearing Worth, Grand Prix de Longchamp, June 24, 1934.

THE GREAT COUTURIERS: STYLE PERSONIFIED

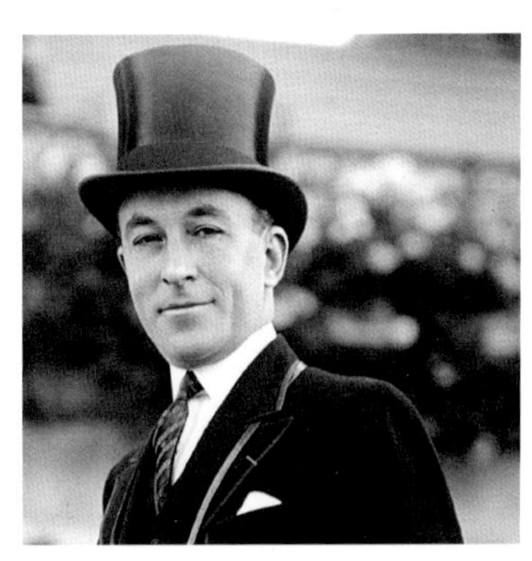

THE GREAT COUTURIERS: STYLE PERSONIFIED

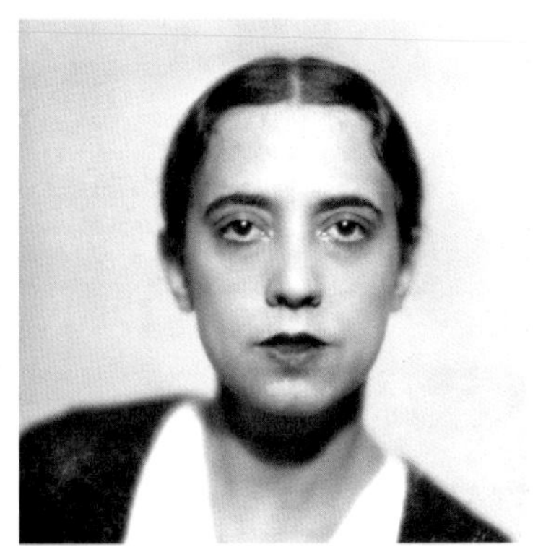

THE GREAT COUTURIERS : STYLE PERSONIFIED

Sylvie Aubenas

The Second Empire witnessed the birth of a personage who would come into full force in the first third of the twentieth century: the great couturier as a fixture of social and fashionable life. Even under the reign of Napoleon III, great couture houses (such as Camille Roger or Palmyre et Vignon) had sustained their reputation by means of prominent women wearing their creations. The first to avail himself of this system for a self-launch was the young Charles Frederick Worth (1826–1895): in 1858, he offered Princess de Metternich, wife of the Austrian ambassador, two dresses at prices far below their standard price. One of the most elegant and spirited women in the capital, whose unconventional charm earned her the nickname of "the best-dressed monkey in Paris," she wore one of Worth's first gowns to a ball at the Tuileries, a design in white tulle embroidered with spring flowers, whose freshness and simplicity suited her so well that Empress Eugenie immediately demanded the designer's address. The Worth house was made for a century.

Worth's other trick, which also augured a great future, was to dress general society as well as high society, both respectable women and kept women, without offending the former. And, finally, he managed to be a charming man so pleasing to converse with that the same Princess de Metternich remembered him in her memoirs with as much fondness as the dinners to which she was invited at his house in Suresnes.

In the succeeding generation, Jacques Doucet (1853–1929) established himself as a great collector of objets d'art, paintings, prints, and books. A well-read, generous patron, he was advised by the young André Breton, who introduced him to Man Ray and Picasso. Then came Paul Poiret (1879-1944), whose flamboyant personality and costly extravagance will not be forgotten. This megalomaniac and inspired demiurge was the true archetype for those who followed close behind, resembling him in many points. His complicities with the world of art and the theater, his talent for organizing festivals—or "events"—made him one of *the* personalities of Paris between 1910 and 1925. But the financial troubles born of this frenzy delivered his house and his property to implacable administrators, broke his spirit, and prevented him from finding a second wind. The romantic insanity of his excesses marginalized him from his contemporaries, who did not consider it necessary to drown the commercial aspects of their activities in Eastern ostentation. Although they belonged to the same generation, they had understood that it was now possible, and even obligatory, to earn a great deal of money with a more pragmatic elegance.

After Worth, Doucet, and Poiret—figures of truly outstanding individuality—many talented individuals emerged, bringing an extraordinary brilliance to the already preeminent French haute couture, along with stunning commercial success.

Among these new luminaries, many benefited from established knowledge, starting out in less glorious houses before finding their wings. Others were unexpected shooting stars. Jeanne Lanvin (1867-1946) began as an apprentice milliner at Mme Félix in 1883 before founding her own house in 1889; Madeleine Vionnet (1876-1975) began at the workshop of Mme Gerber, one of the Callot sisters, where she remained until 1907; Jean Patou (1880-1936) took his first steps with a furrier uncle before launching a first collection that was abruptly halted in August 1914; Lucien Lelong (1889-1958) inherited the family couture house (which he had personally directed since 1910) in 1925, just as Jacques Heim (1899-1967) took over the house of fur founded by his parents in 1898.

Although we know that Gabrielle Chanel (1883-1971) worked in a house of "trousseaus and layettes" at Moulins when she was twenty, her debut as a milliner in autumn 1910 at 21 rue Cambon, with the financial assistance of her friend Arthur Capel, remains very private. Similarly, Elsa Schiaparelli (1890–1973), a Roman aristocrat, owed her 1927 plunge into the world of fashion to an unhappy marriage and financial losses. Finally, the meteoric career of Jacques Fath (1912–1954) was born of a major vocation, although going back to his great-grandparents there were a few Second Empire fashion magazine illustrators in his family.

These strong characters gave their houses flair. Their charm, their beauty—or, better still, their style—were the best publicity they could generate for their clothing. As Edmonde Charles-Roux confirmed in a celebrated biography of her in 1974,[37] Chanel has emerged as the figurehead of the haute couture of the flapper years: the incarnation of the liberated woman, wearing her hair short and stringing together stories of love, high society, and performing artists, without forgetting to make a fortune along the way. But she must not be allowed to eclipse all the others. There was Jean Patou, a great seducer but eternal bachelor, creating gowns "for the woman of his dreams: the one he would like at his side, at home, at the theater, or at a restaurant." Inspired by sportsmen, film actors, and other new kinds of heroes, he lived like a Paul Morand character, playing hard and dying of exhaustion while still young. Schiaparelli, like Poiret, drew her inspiration from ancient art or from her artist friends, translating her admiration of Dalí's work into hats and accessories. Jeanne Lanvin, a great collector of Impressionist paintings, linked to the aristocracy through her daughter, Marie-Blanche de Polignac. Madeleine Vionnet, in love with a young Russian, Dimitri Netcholodoff, offered him a career as a chic shoemaker. Finally, in 1928 Lucien Lelong married the very beautiful Princess Nathalie Paley, daughter of Grand Duke Paul (uncle of Czar Nicholas II), and a refugee from the Bolshevik massacres. Just before the war, the exceptionally handsome, fun loving and scintillating Jacques Fath exploited his image as a young star, and that of the dream couple he evoked with his young wife Geneviève, for the benefit of his label.

For their couture salons and their apartments or private residences, they called on the most renowned decorators of the time: Jean-Michel Frank for Schiaparelli; Süe and Mare and Boutet de

Monvel for Patou; Armand-Albert Rateau for Jeanne Lanvin; and Lalique, George de Feure, and Boris Lacroix for Madeleine Vionnet, offering their customers a luxurious yet especially refined and modern environment. Photographs of these interior décors were published as benchmarks by illustrated magazines such as *Vogue* or *La Demeure française*.

Their connections, and their collaborations with stage and film directors—who systematically commissioned them to create costumes—lent the couturiers' designs additional allure. The fashion world was no longer an expression of the expensive whims of wealthy women: its interaction with the greatest artists had given it a status of its own.

Fashion also became a very profitable business, to the point of representing up to fifteen percent of French foreign trade in the 1930s. The couturiers quickly built enormous fortunes, thanks especially to perfume and licenses granted to foreign manufacturers, which allowed them to live the same life of ease as their customers—or even, quite often, an easier one still.

The progressive declassification of society caused their clientele to diversify: the royalty and aristocracy, wealthy foreigners, and wives of industrial tycoons were now joined by actresses, champion athletes, and, above all, completely unknown women. Celebrated, sought-after, and hosting the most exclusive soirées in their own homes, the fashion moguls were no longer discrete clothing suppliers, but friends around whom the greatest snobs gathered.

And finally, in a reversal of previously established mores, it was the couturiers—the Chanels, Schiaparellis, and Patous—who were in a position to pick and choose from among the international nobility their models, their sales force, and their boutique managers. In this way, too, they gave women confidence that they were on familiar territory, and had not moved into a different world when they crossed the threshold of their salons.

Today we have completed the evolution that spanned the twentieth century: the notoriety of the fashion designers now completely eclipses that of their customers.

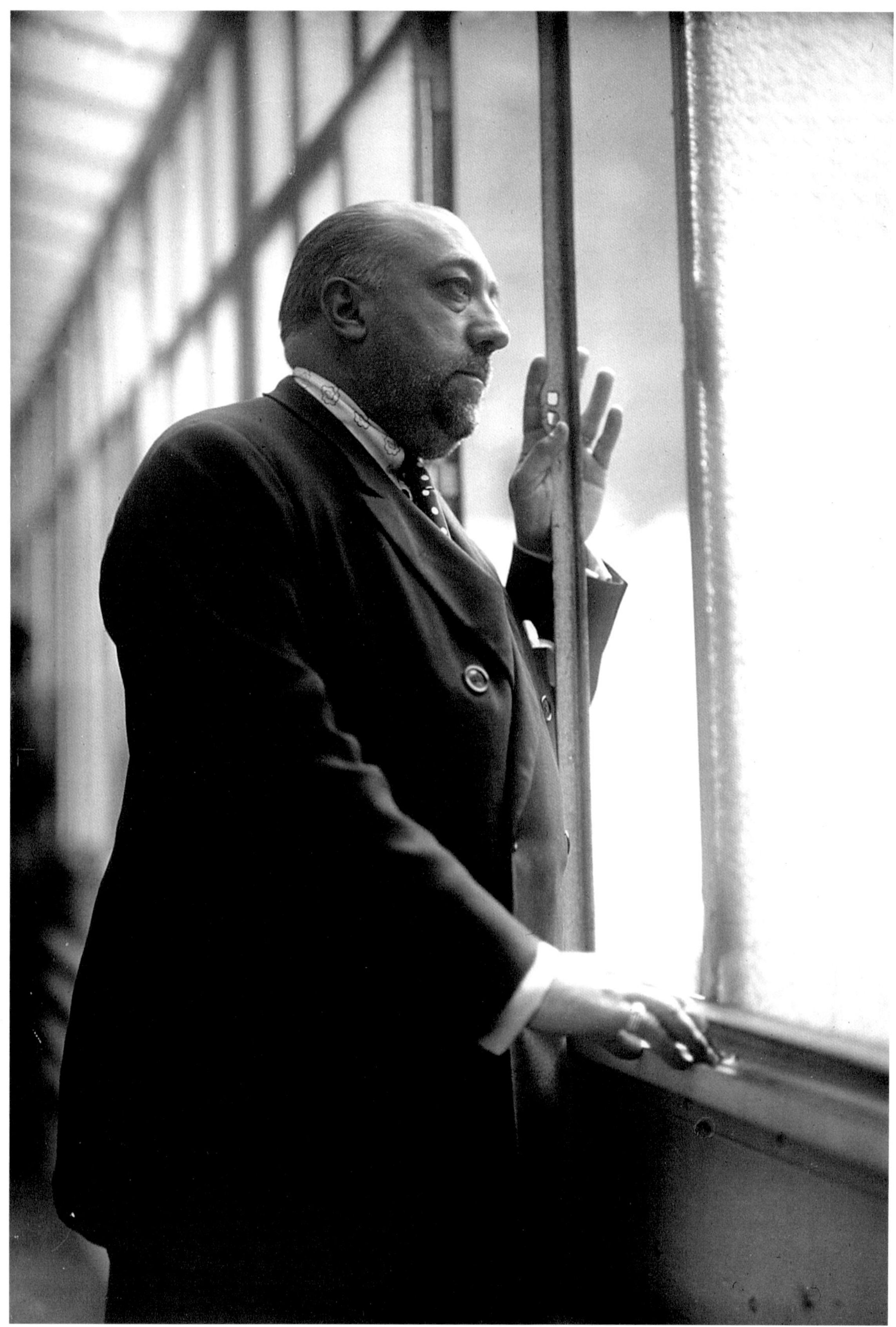

Paul Poiret (1879–1944) in his studio on avenue Victor-Emmanuel, 1927.

A model wearing Joseph Paquin (left) with Jeanne Paquin (right) at the races, Deauville, August 15, 1919. The house of Joseph Paquin had nothing to do with the infinitely more famous house of Jeanne Paquin (1869–1936). Joseph Paquin was sued for taking the same name.

Jeanne Lanvin (1867–1946) at the reopening of the restaurant des Ambassadeurs, MYCCA (Motor Yacht Club de la Côte d'Azur) party, May 11, 1939.

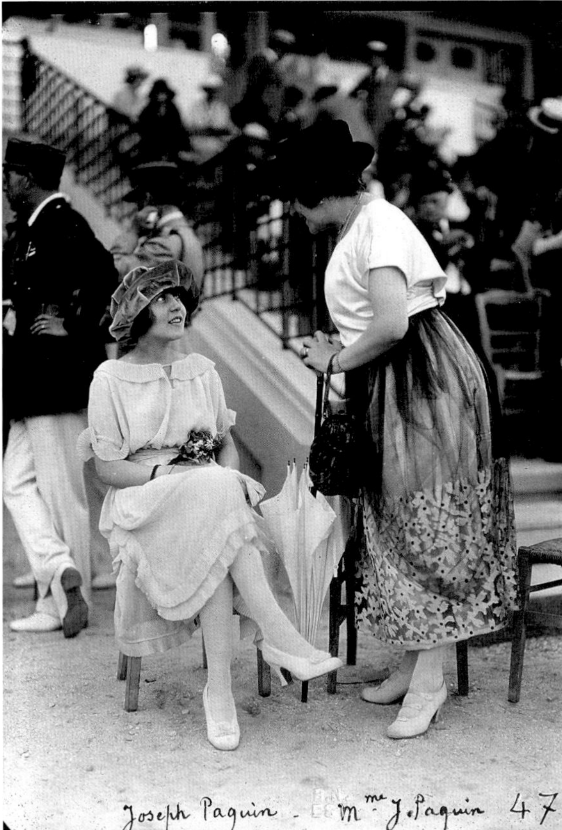

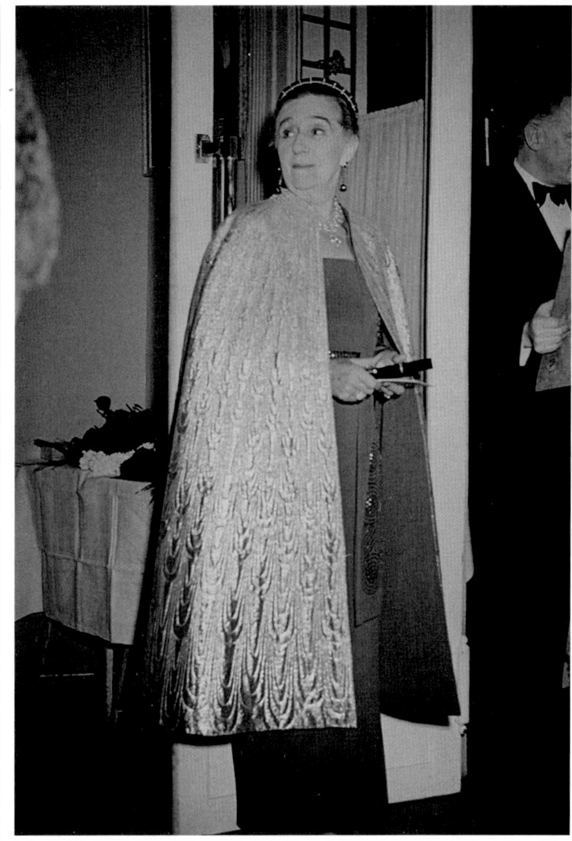

Jeanne Lanvin's salons, rue du Faubourg-Saint-Honoré, in 1936. Jeanne Lanvin entrusted the decoration of her salon (as well as her private mansion in the rue Barbet-de-Jouy) to Armand-Albert Rateau (1882–1938).

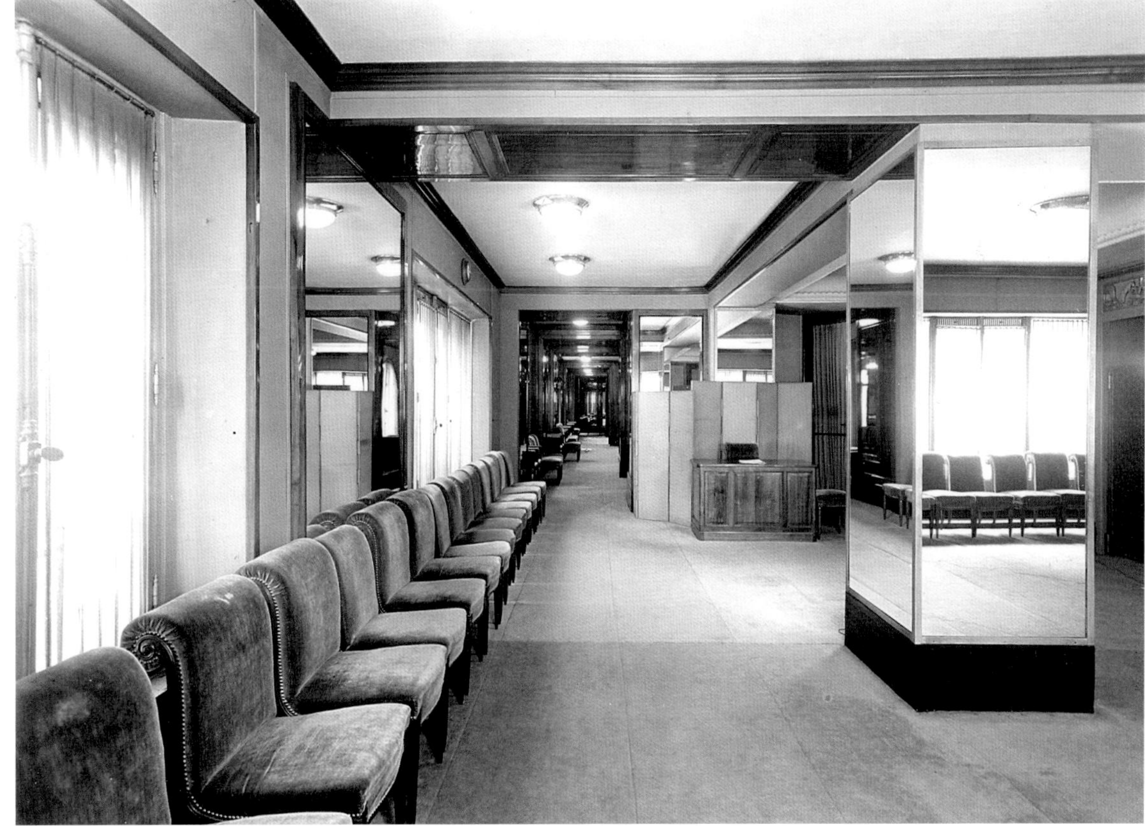

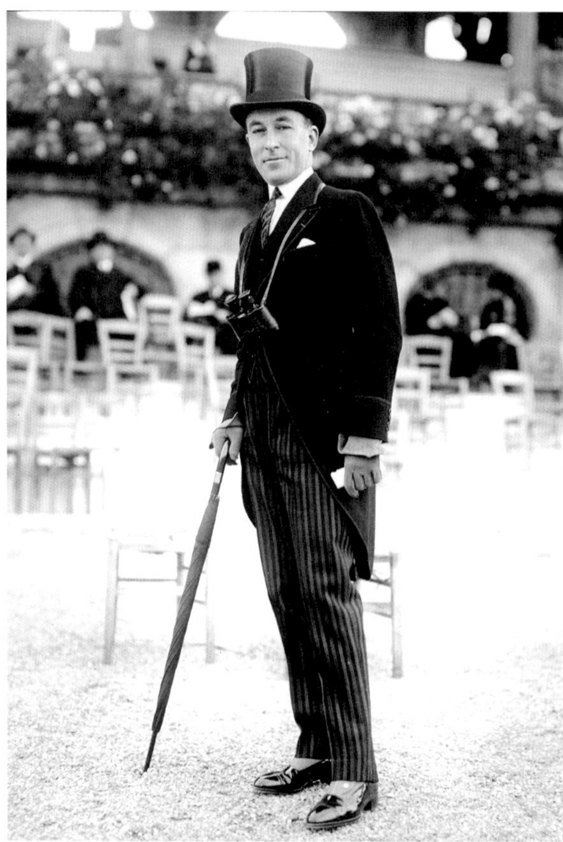

Jean Patou (1880–1936) at the races, 1927.

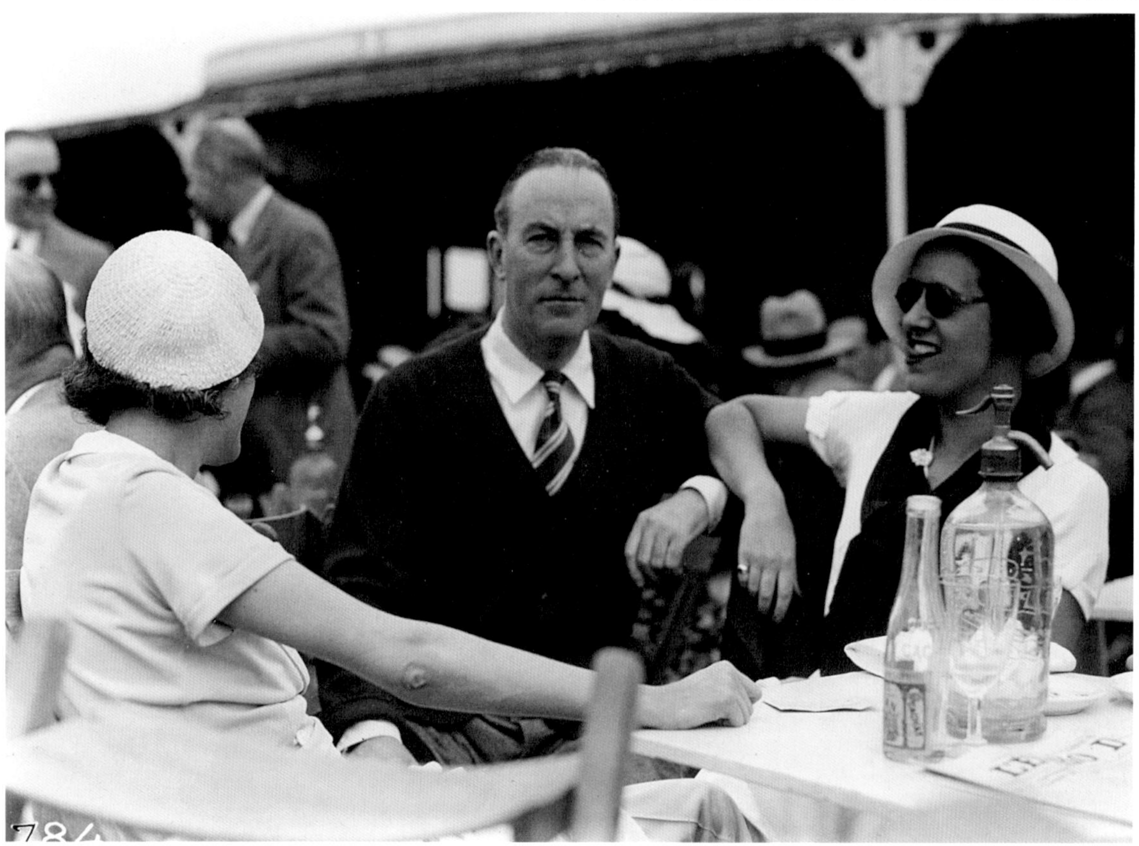

Jean Patou, Deauville, August 1934.

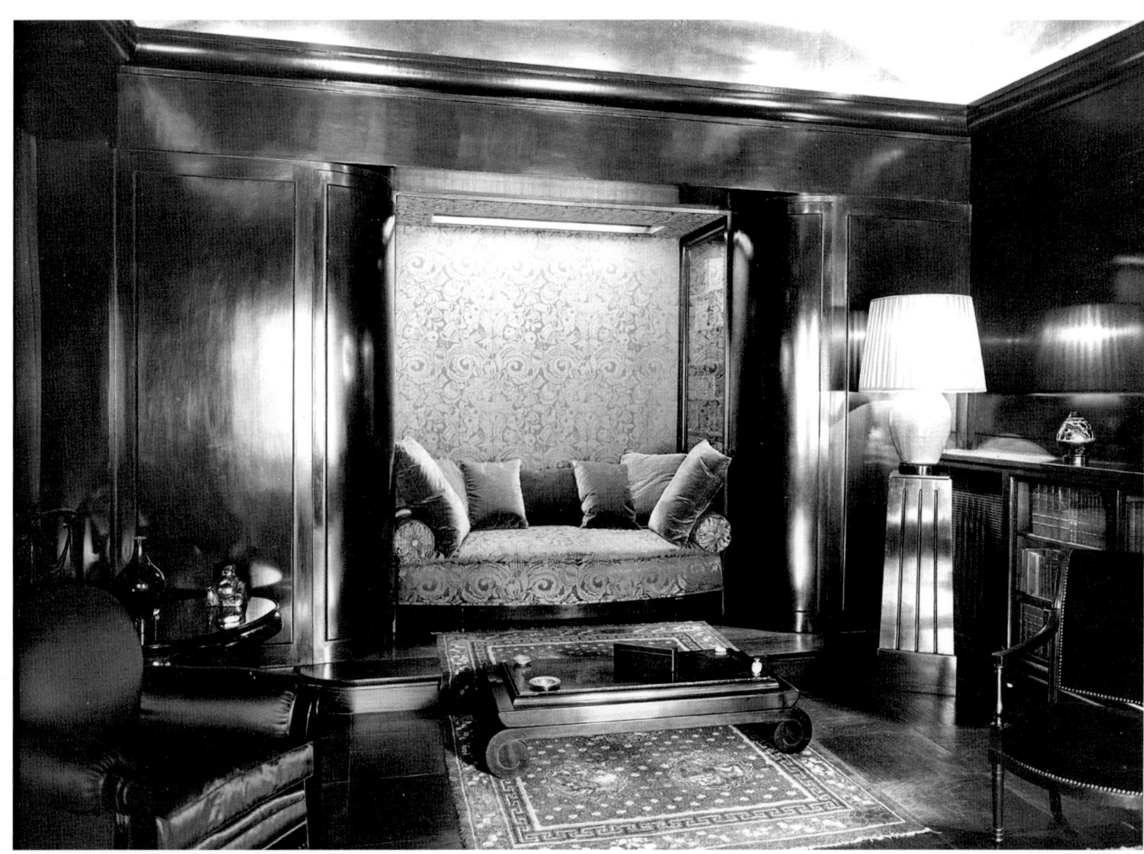

Jean Patou's mansion, 55 rue de la Faisanderie, in 1925. This set of photos was published in 1926 to illustrate an article by René-Jean, "Süe et Mare chez M. Jean Patou" in La Demeure française, *nr. 1, spring 1926, pp. 39–52.*

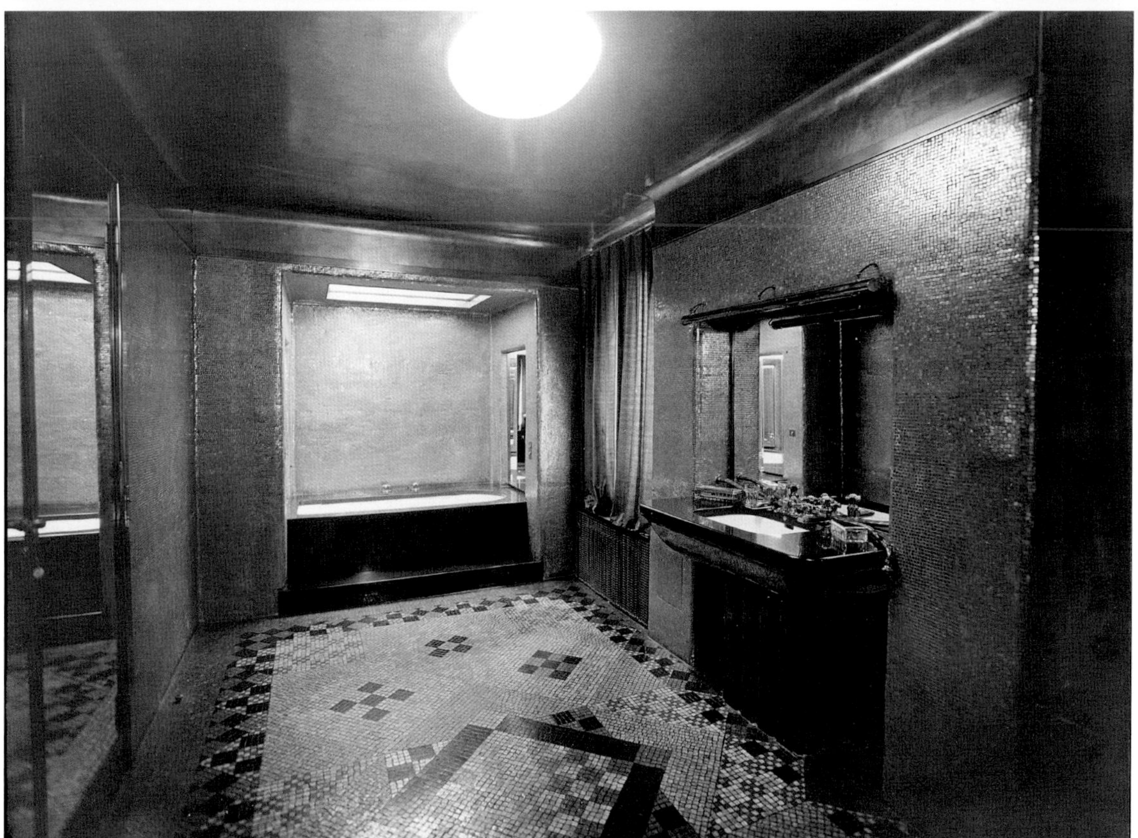

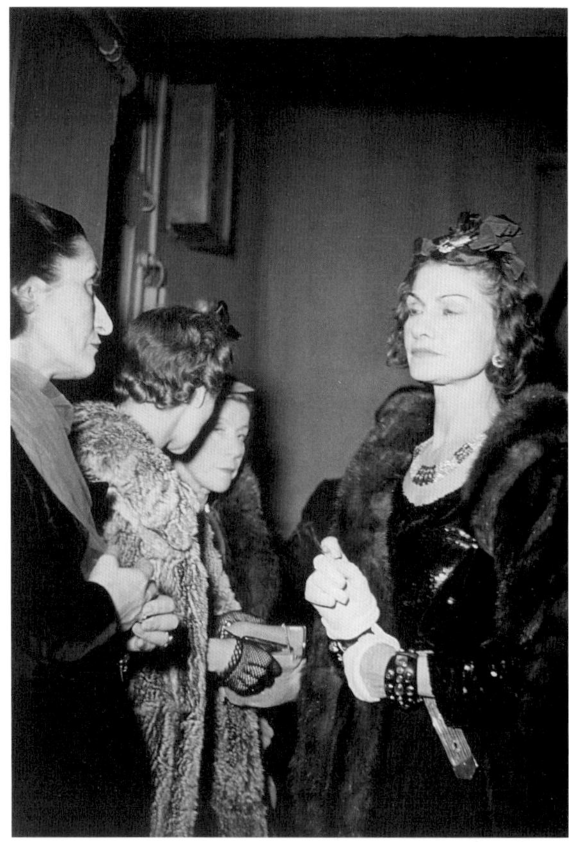

Left and opposite:
Gabrielle Chanel (1883–1971) on the opening night of Marcel Achard's play Adam *at the Théâtre du Gymnase, November 1938.*

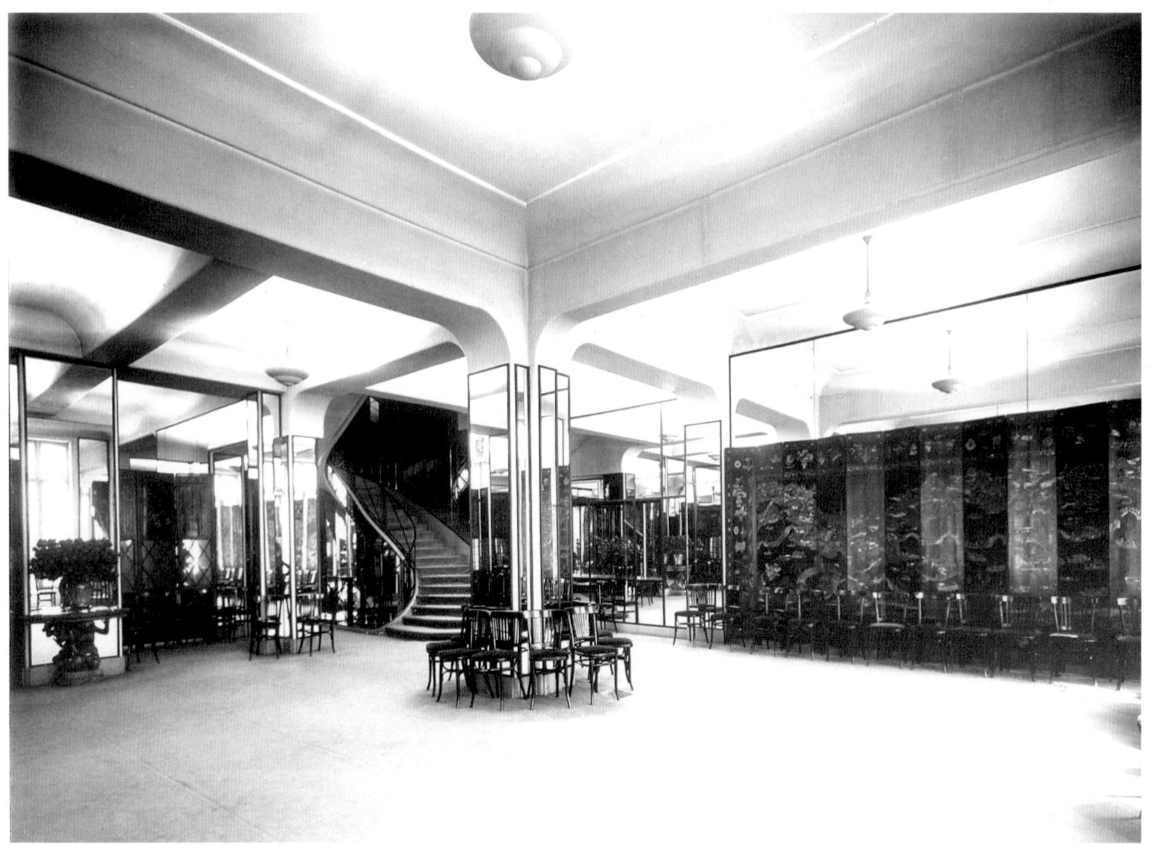

Gabrielle Chanel's salon, 31 rue Cambon, in 1936.

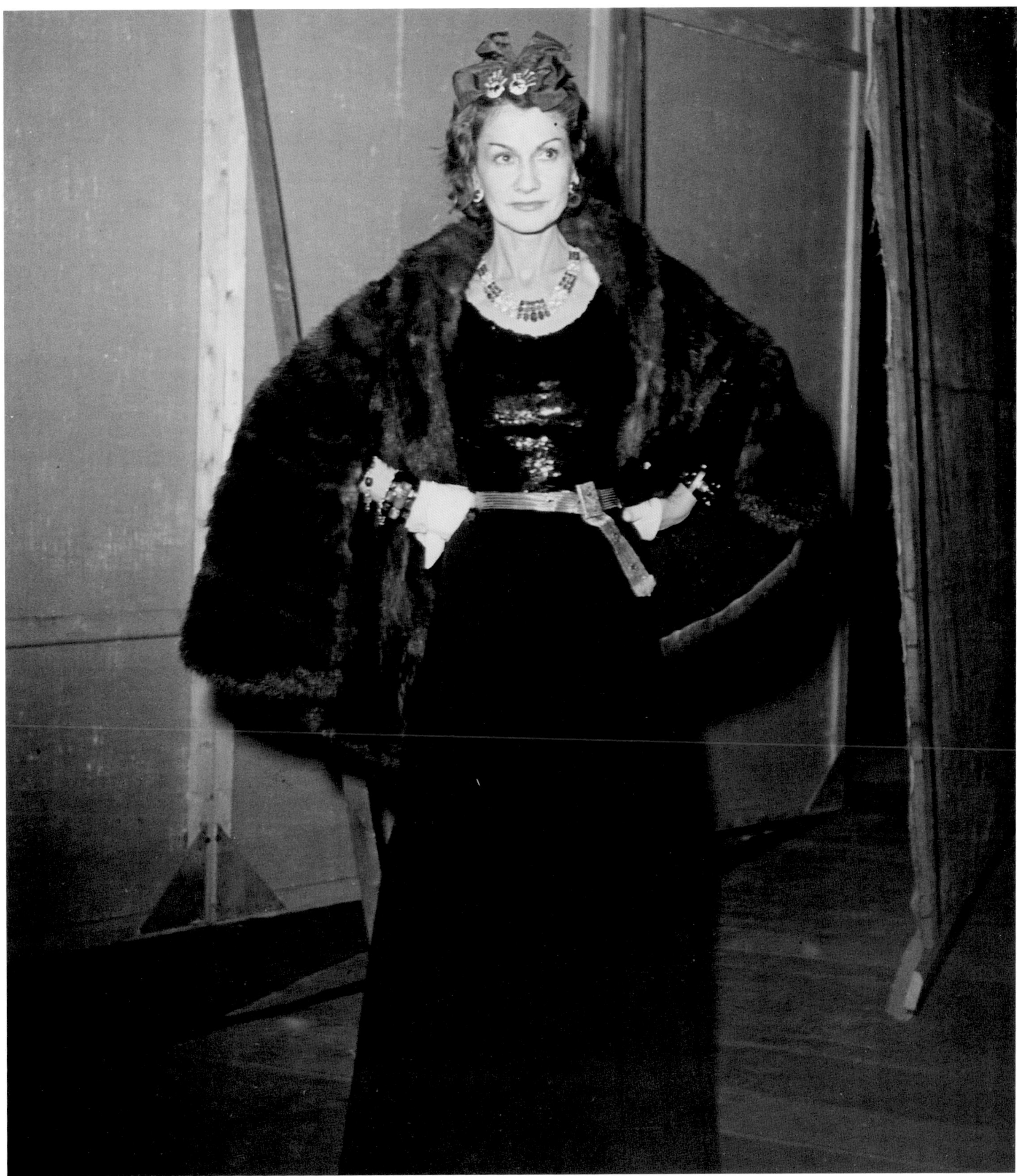

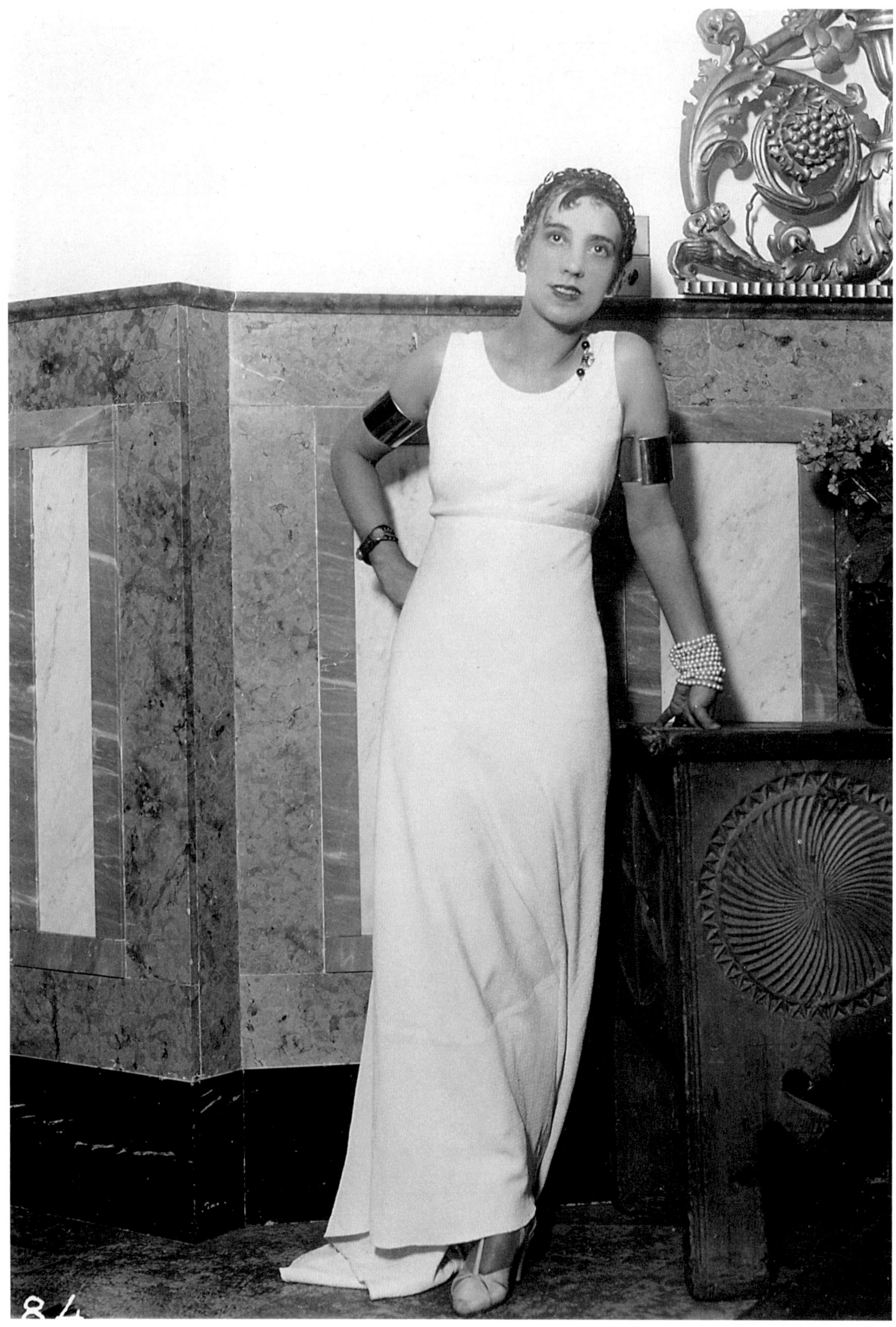

Elsa Schiaparelli (1890–1973)
coifed by Antoine,
New Year's Day, Saint-Moritz,
January 1932.

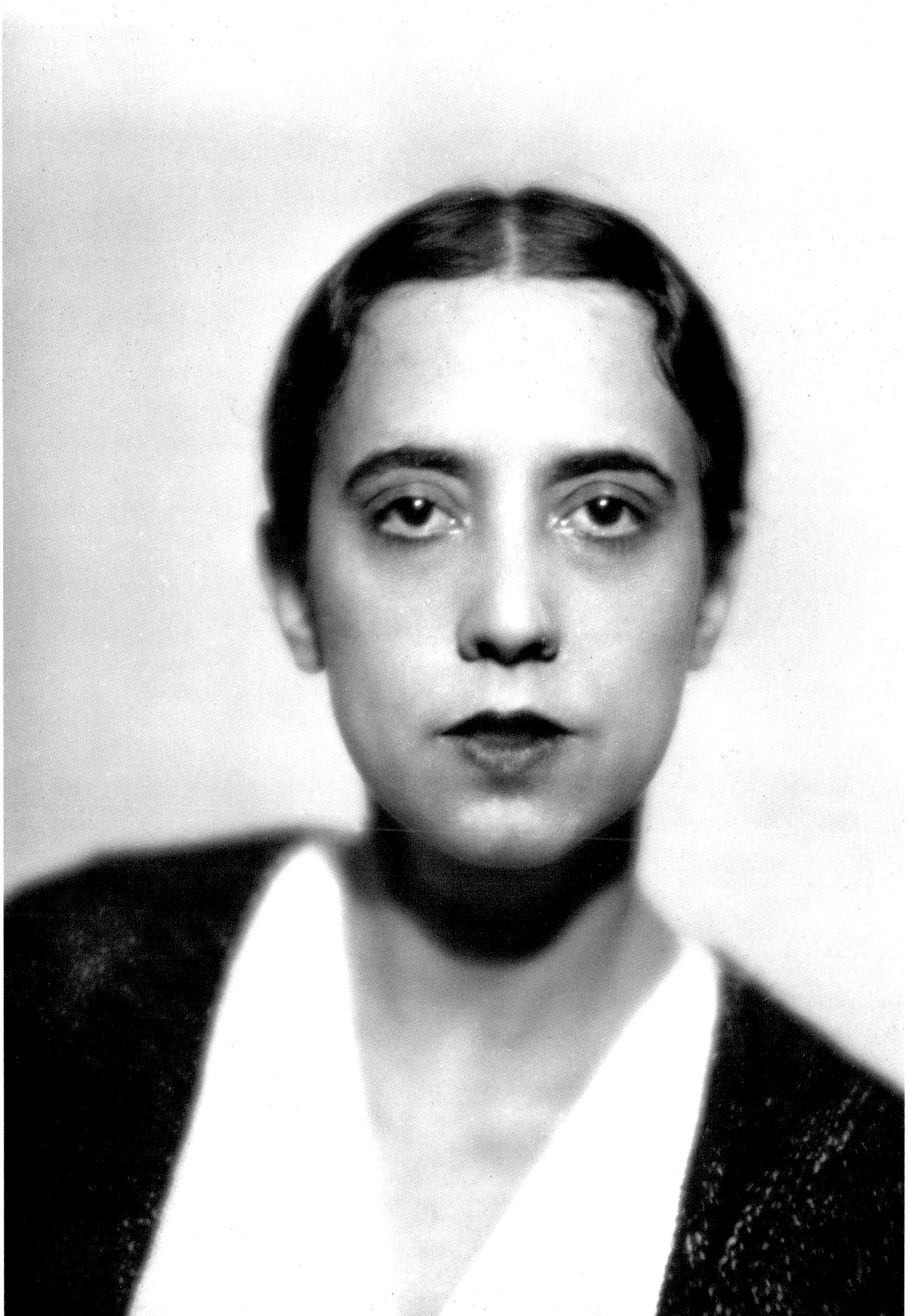

Portrait of Elsa Schiaparelli, 1930.

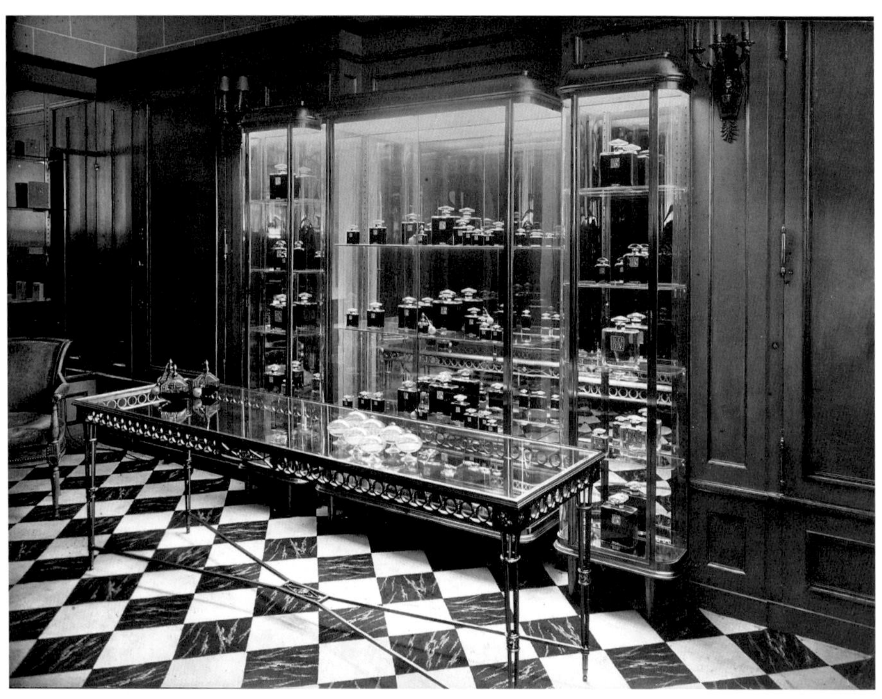

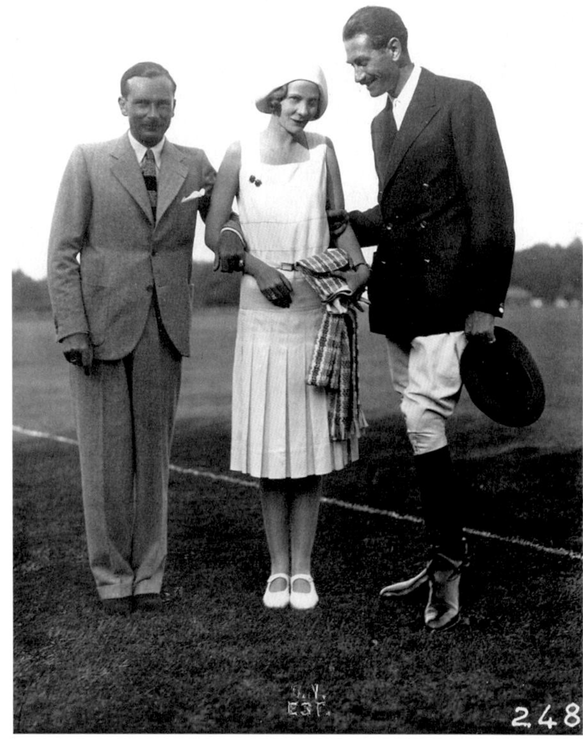

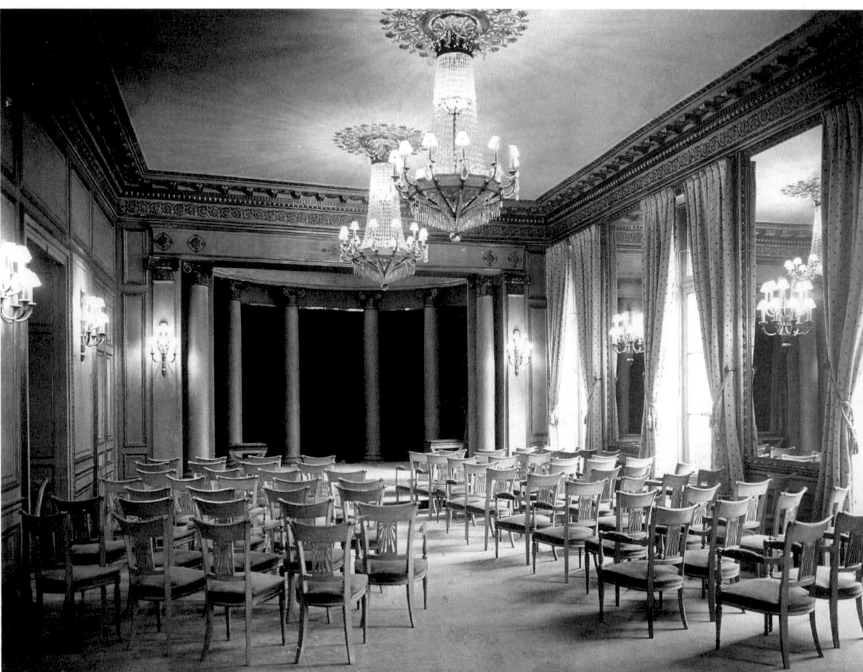

Lucien Lelong (1889–1958) with his second wife, the princess Nathalie Paley (1905–1981), and Count Hubert de Montbrison, Biarritz, September 1929. Nathalie Paley, daughter of Grand Duke Paul (uncle of the czar Nicholas II), married couturier Lucien Lelong in 1927. Her great beauty and elegance contributed much to the luster of her husband's creations; her cinema career was launched in 1933 and she made several films with Marcel L'Herbier and Georges Cukor. In 1950, Count Hubert de Montbrison became the second husband of her sister, Irina.

Salon of Lucien Lelong, installed in a city mansion at 16 avenue Matignon from 1924 (here in 1927).

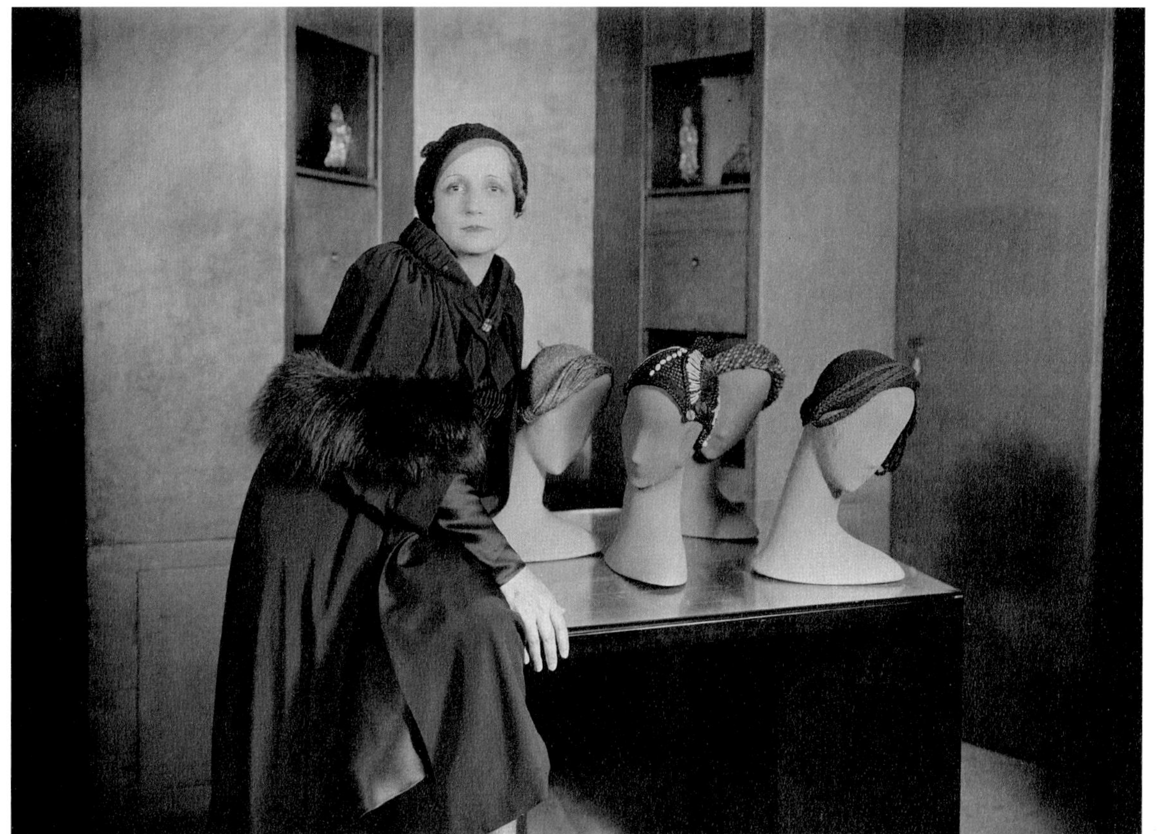

M[me] Agnes, milliner, in her rue Saint-Florentin salon, in 1930. Jean Dunand, with whom she was very close, created pieces of furniture and decorative objects for her.

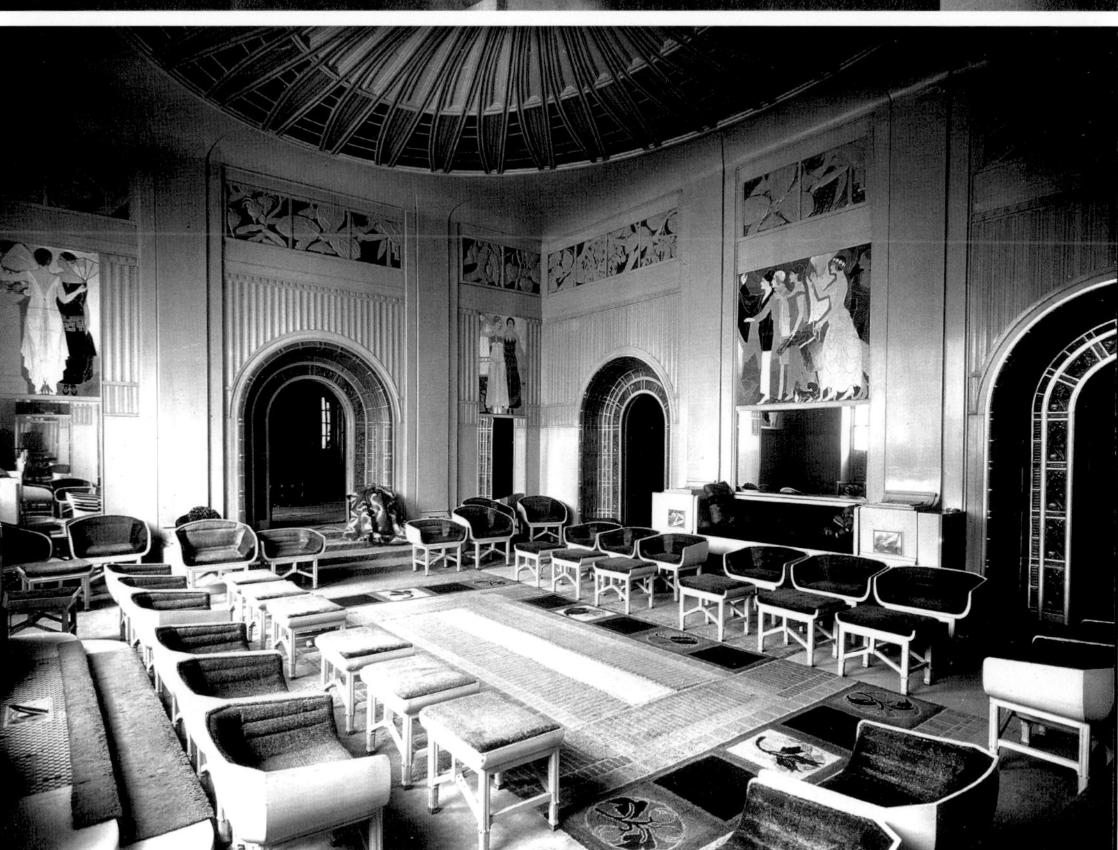

Salons of Madeleine Vionnet (1876–1975), 50 avenue Montaigne. Installed at this address in 1923 with financial assistance from Bader, owner of the Galeries Lafayette, she entrusted the decoration of the former Hôtel Lariboisière to Georges de Feure, Lalique, and Boris Lacroix (seen here in 1936).

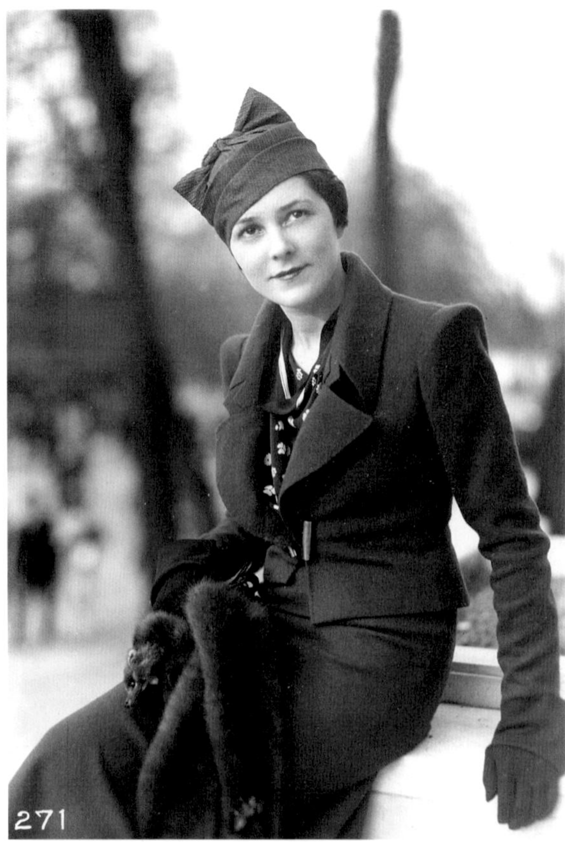

The milliner Mlle Mado at the Prix d'Auteuil, March 12, 1933.

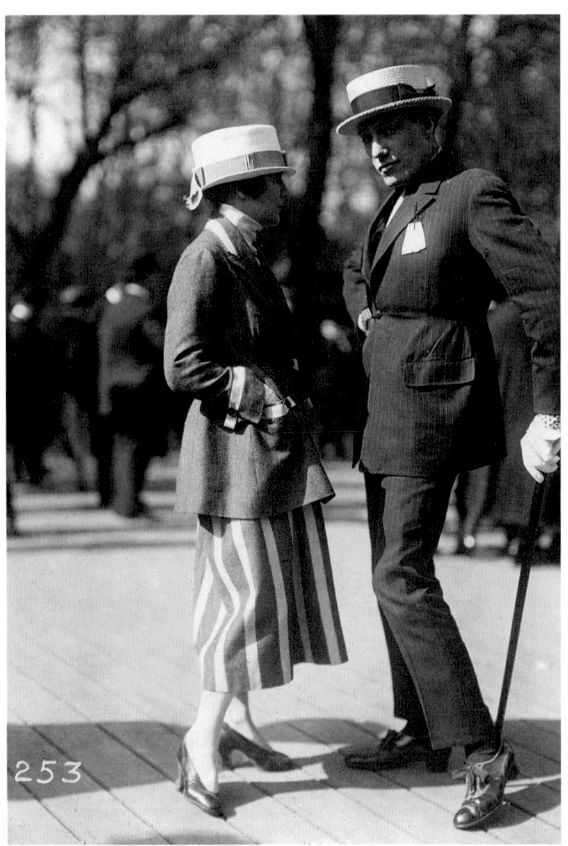

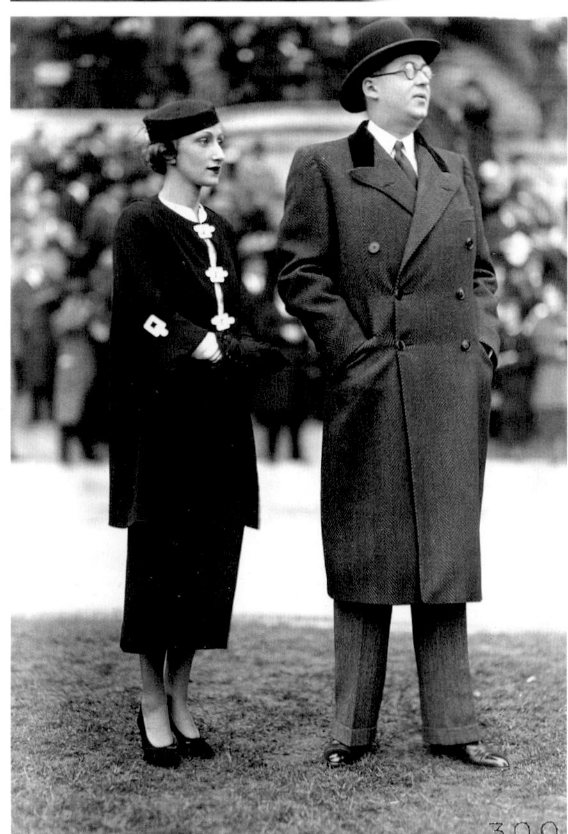

The Melnotte-Simonins at the races, March 28, 1920. This couturier team, now long forgotten, was in vogue during the 1920s; in 1924, they commissioned Robert Mallet-Stevens to design the presentation salon of their Parisian couture house.

Jacques Heim (1899–1967) and his wife, née Simone Lion, Auteuil, Grand Prix du Printemps, March 25, 1934.

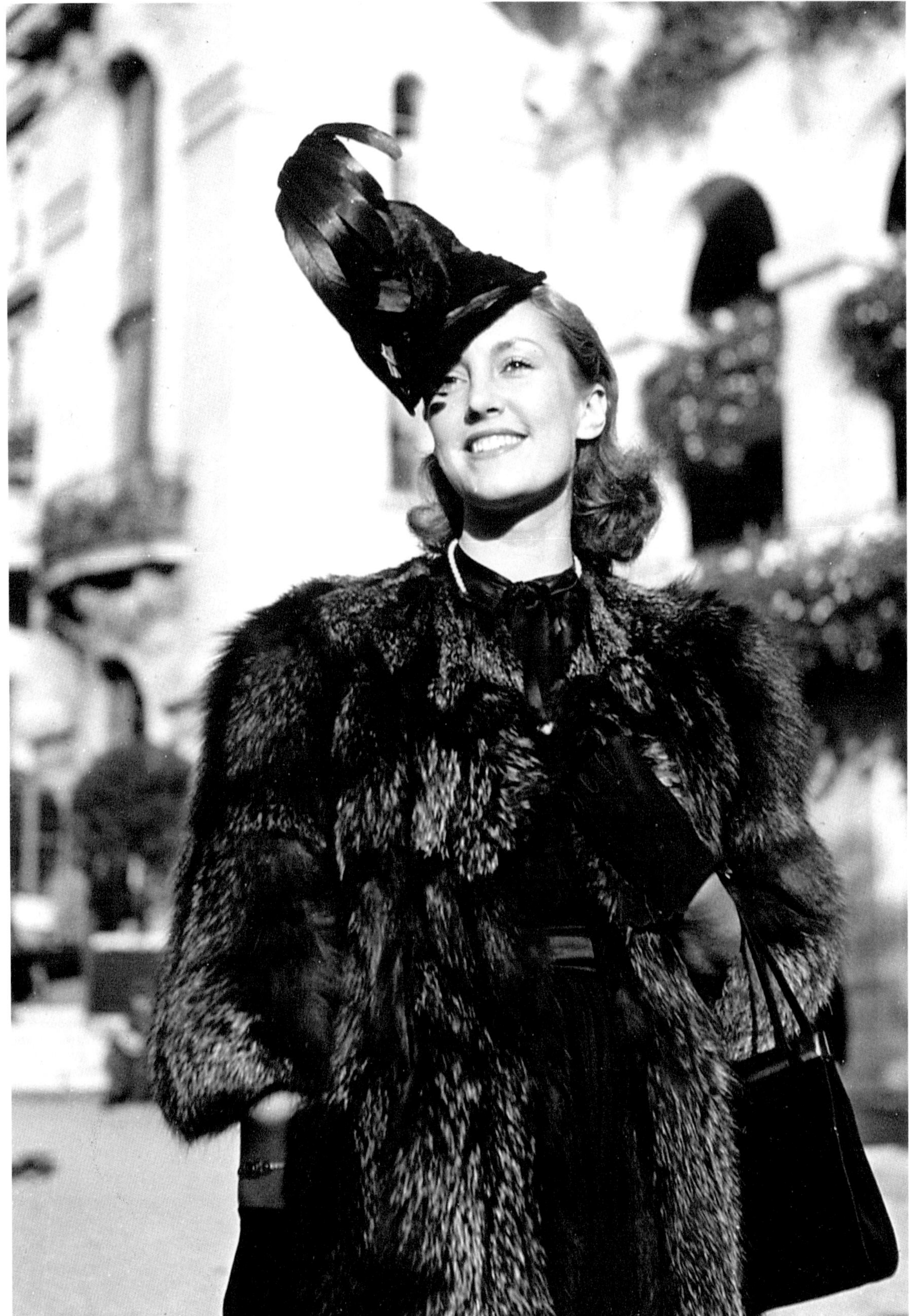

Geneviève Boucher (1914–1993) wearing Jacques Fath, capped with an Erik hat, Longchamp, Prix du Conseil Municipal, October 23, 1938. A professional model, she married Fath in February 1939 and continued to present his designs for the press and on foreign promotional tours.

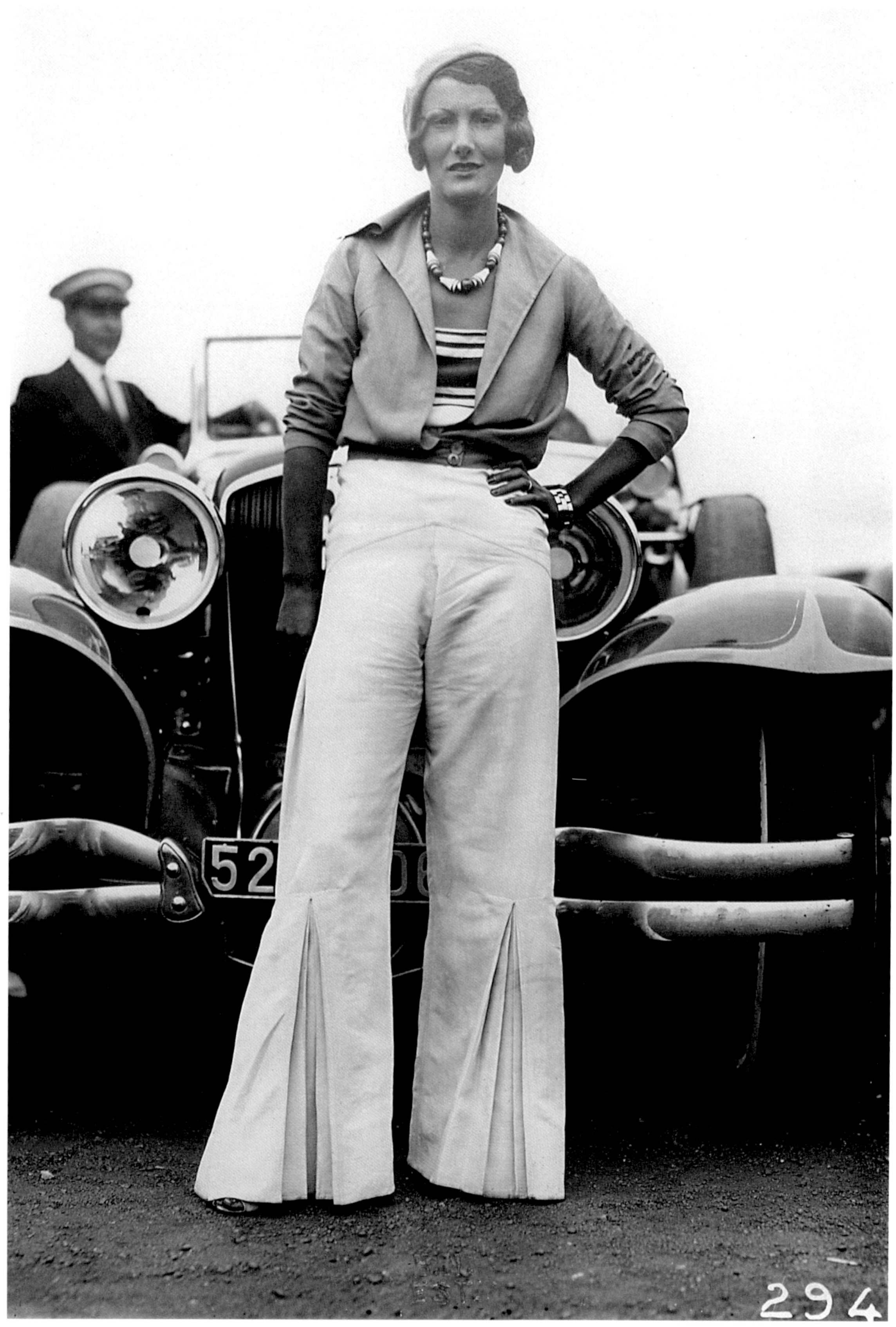

Rina Rochas (née Rosselli) in Biarritz, September 1930. A painter, decorator, and creator of ballet sets and costumes, Rina Rosselli divorced Marcel Rochas in 1941; his second wife, Hélène, became the emblem of his couture house after the war.

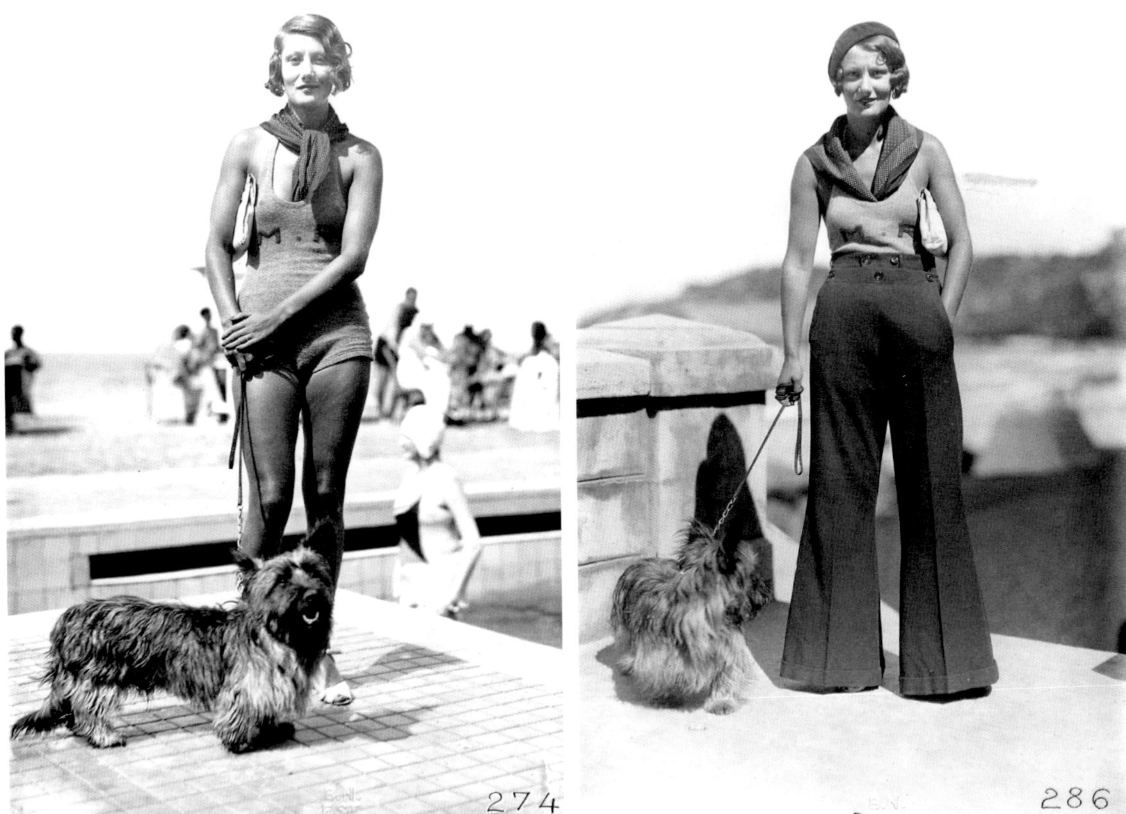

Rina Rochas in a Rochas swimsuit and Rochas pants, Biarritz, September 1930.

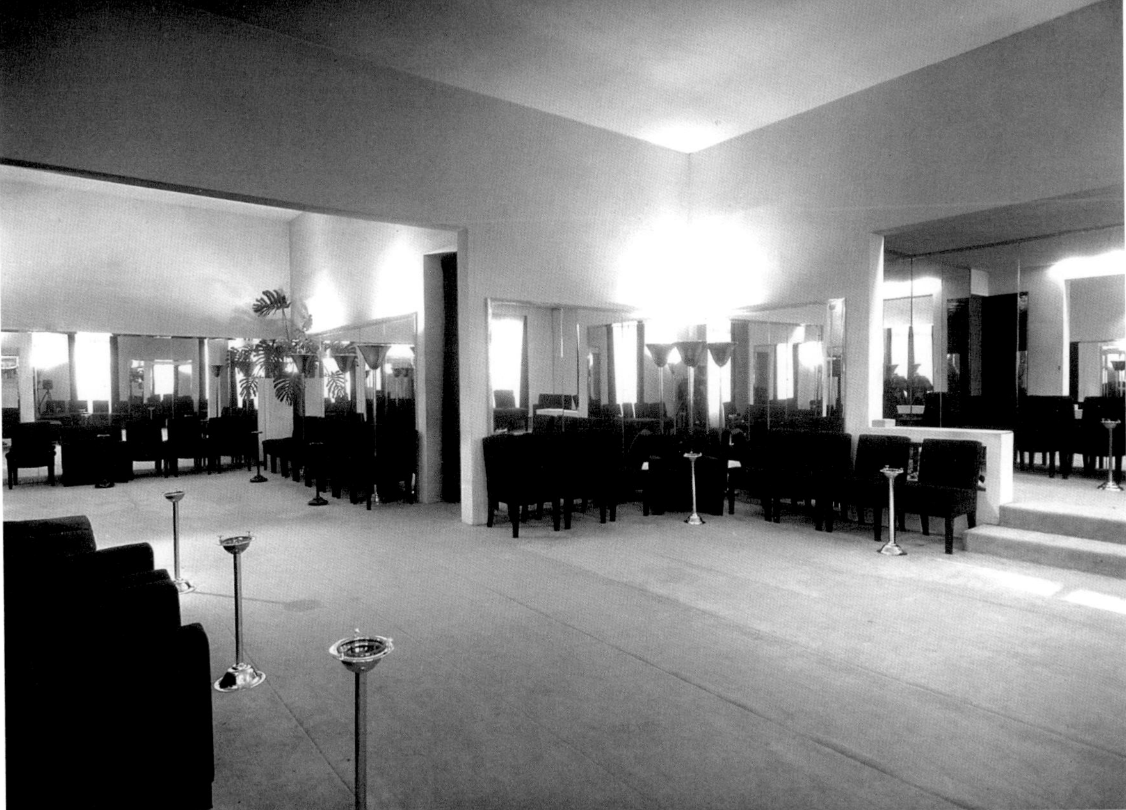

Salon of Marcel Rochas (1902–1955), installed at 12 avenue Matignon in 1931 (seen here in 1936).

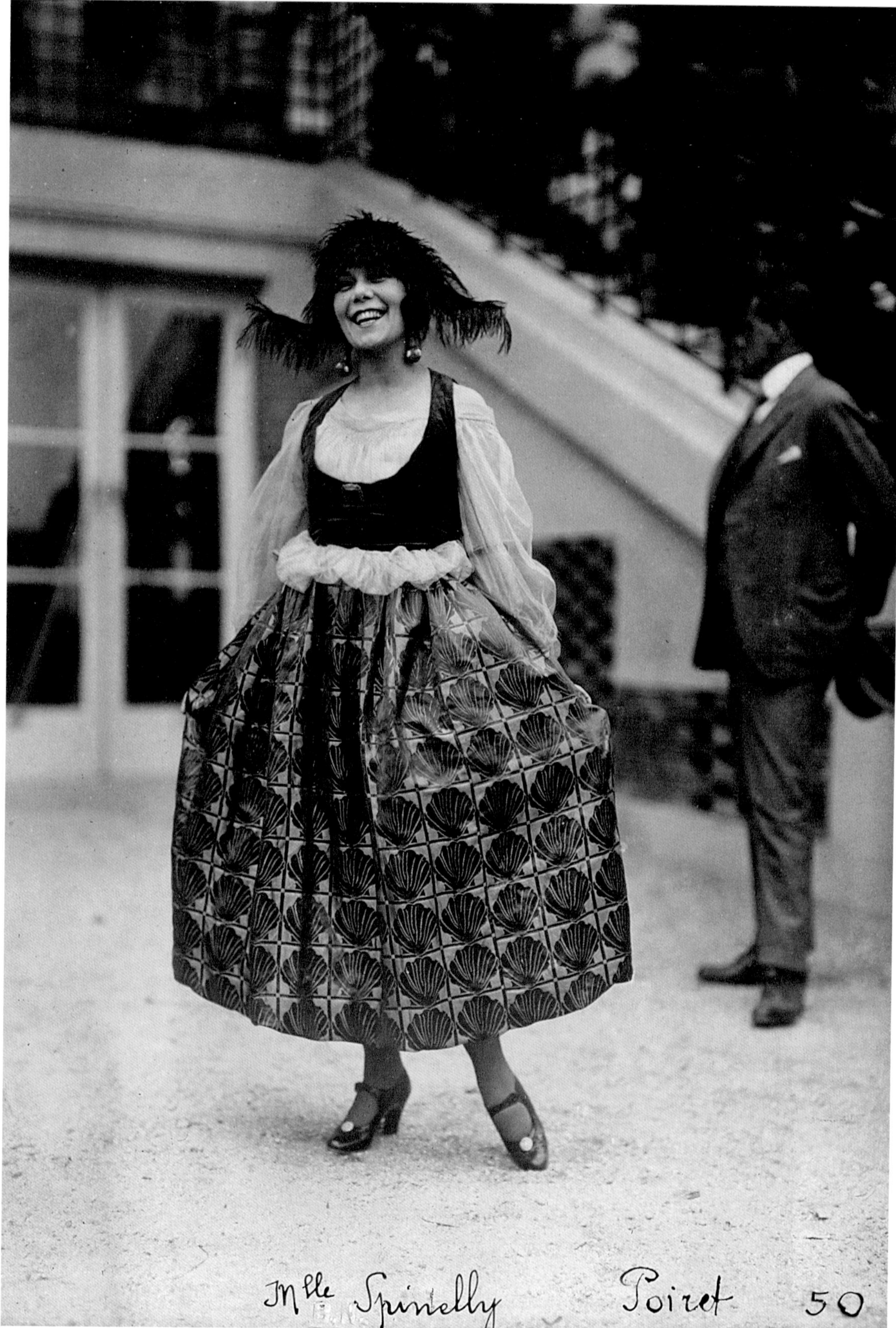

Mlle Spinelly (née Élise Fournier, 1890–1966) in Poiret, Grand-Prix de Deauville, August 15, 1920.
This theater actress was outfitted by Poiret from 1912, both about town and on stage; after 1920, he became her appointed couturier and created entire wardrobes for her, and especially for her foreign tours.

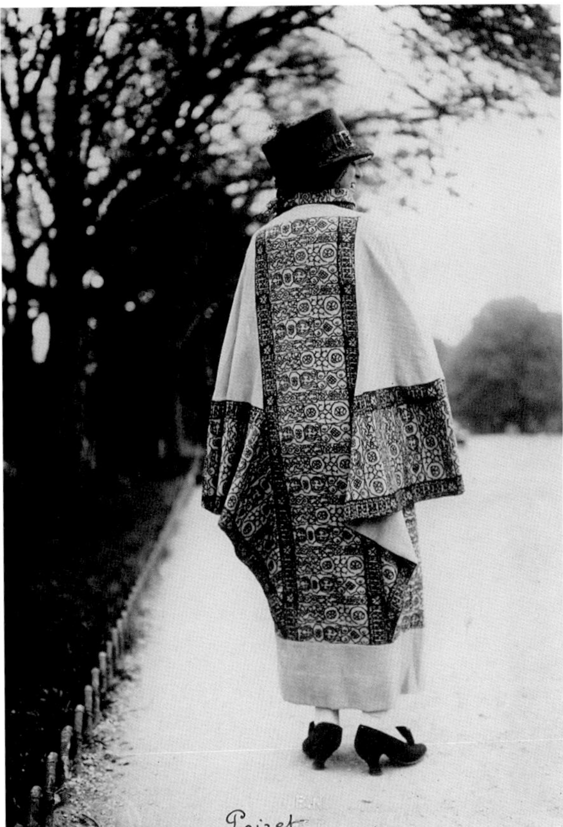

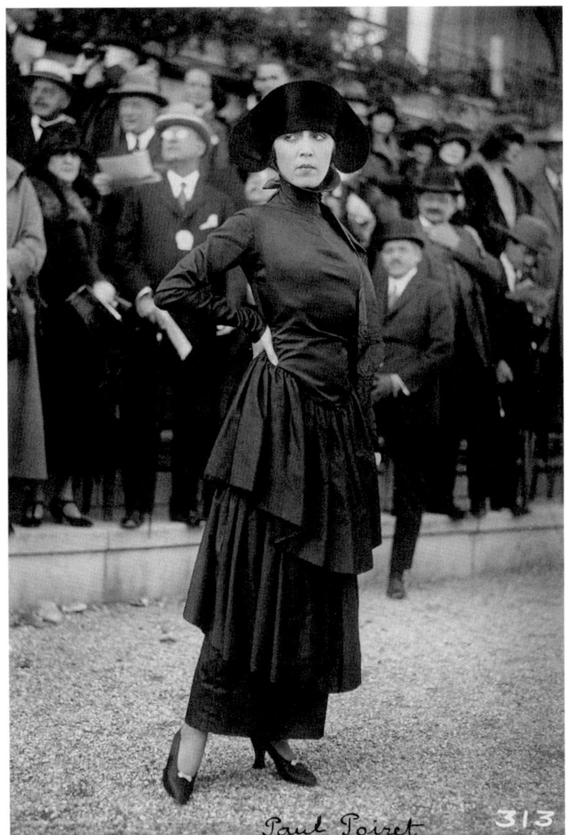

In the Bois de Boulogne, April 1923.

At Longchamp, September 23, 1923.

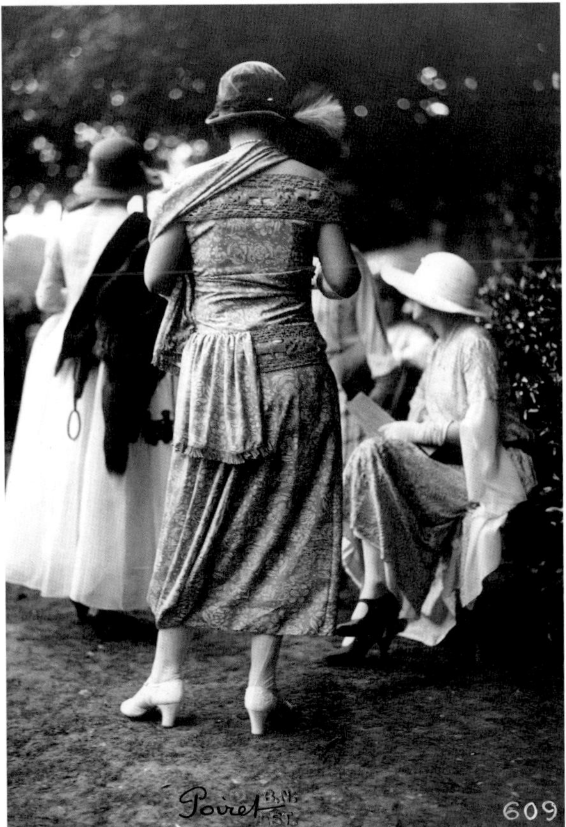

At the races, June 21, 1922.

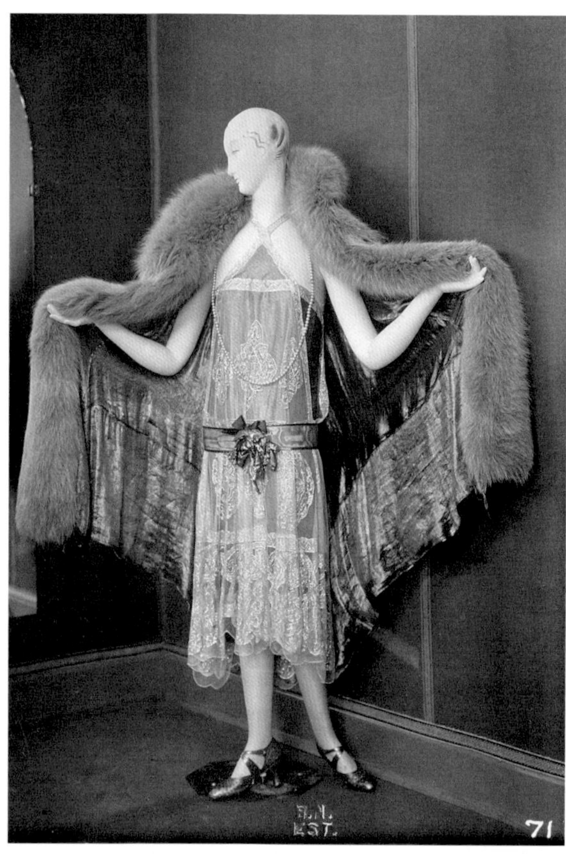

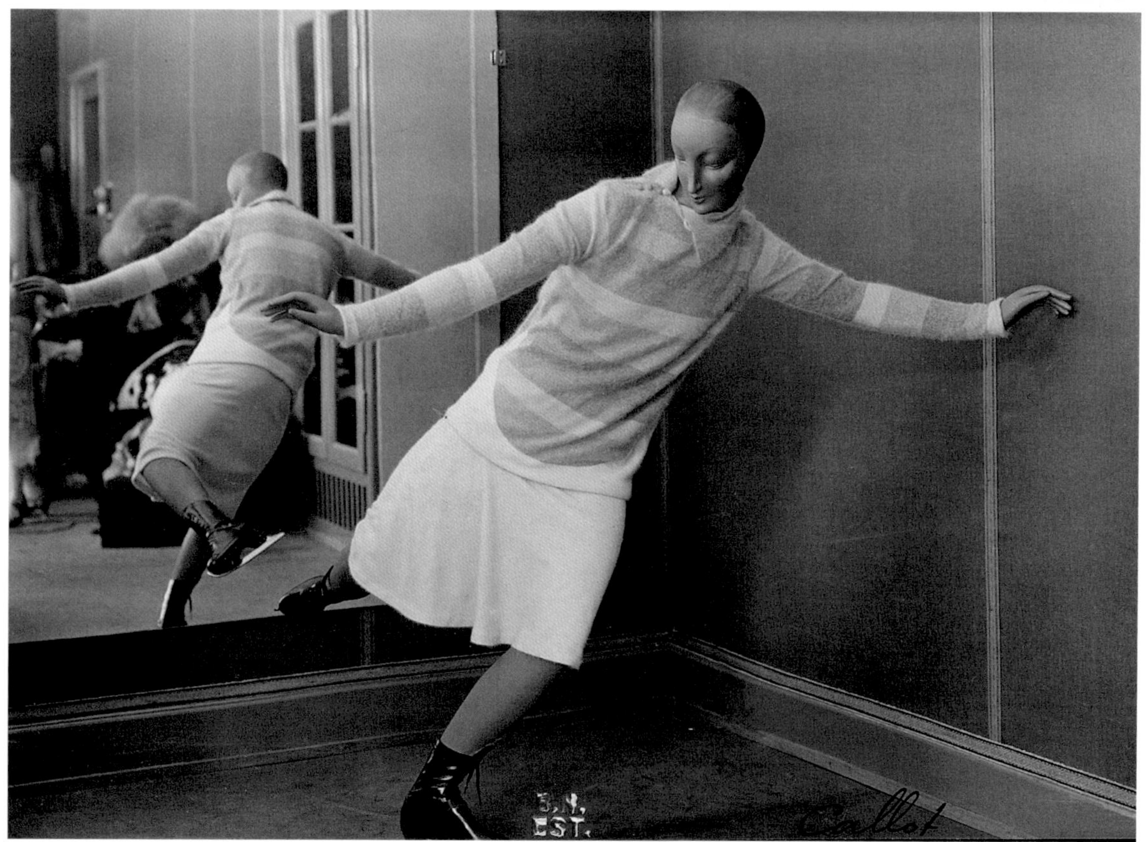

Display of Callot designs on mannequins in a store window, Saint-Moritz, January 1928.

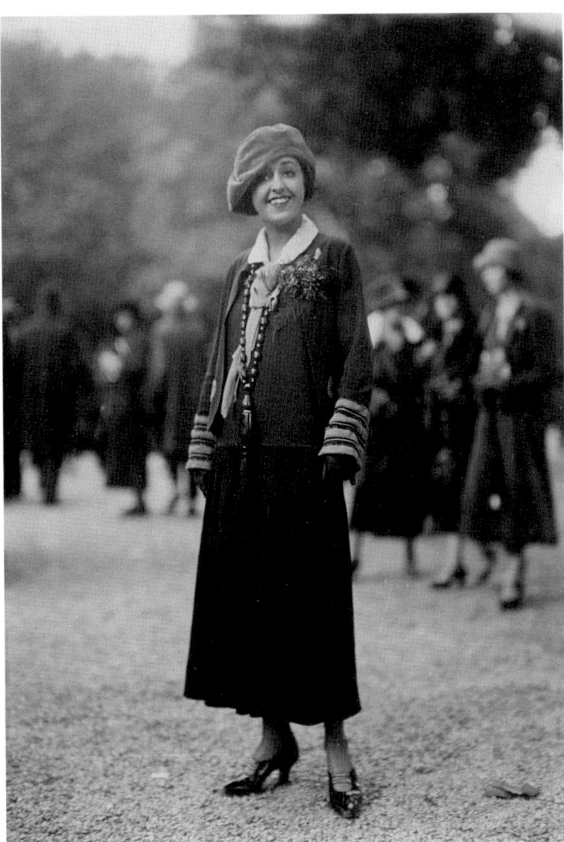

Mlle Rahna, a performer at the Paris Palace, wearing Lanvin, Longchamp, October 5, 1924.

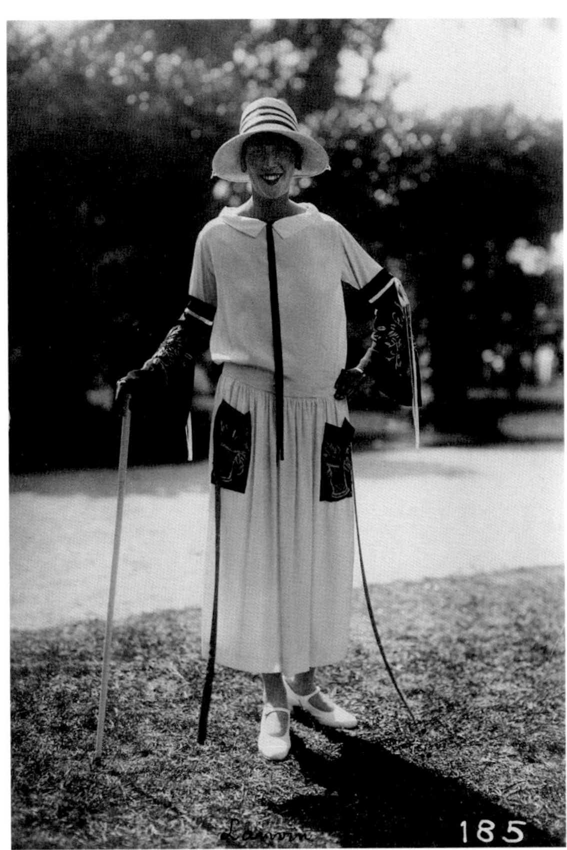

Singer Suzy Solidor (1900–1983) wearing Lanvin, Deauville, August 10, 1924.

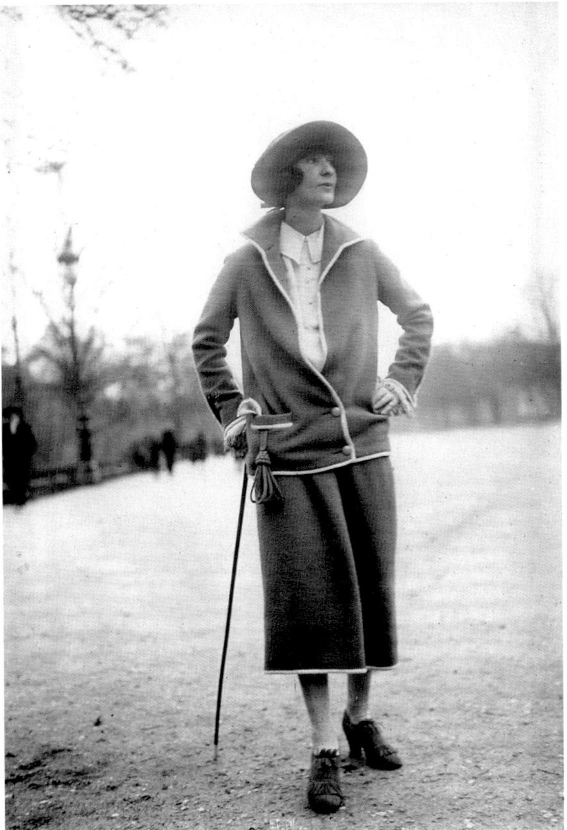

Lanvin sports suit, Bois de Boulogne, winter 1922.

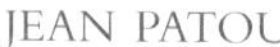

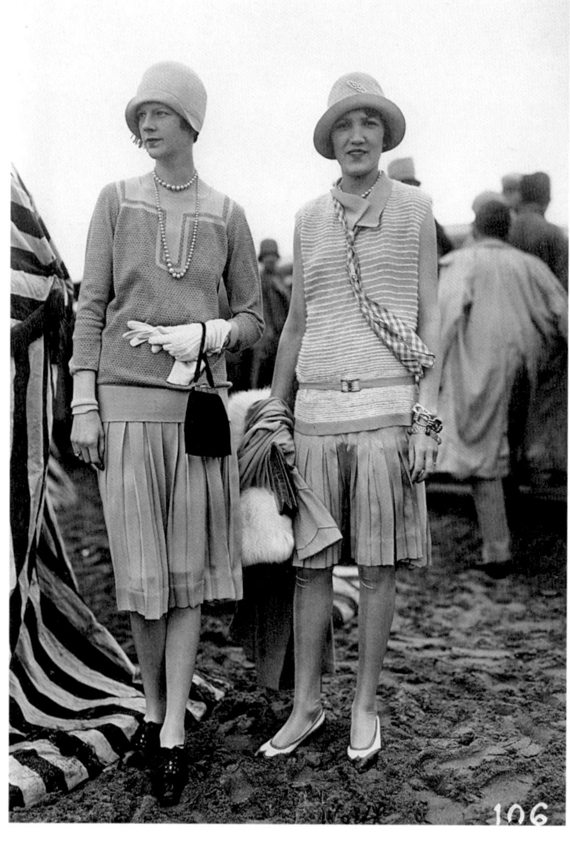

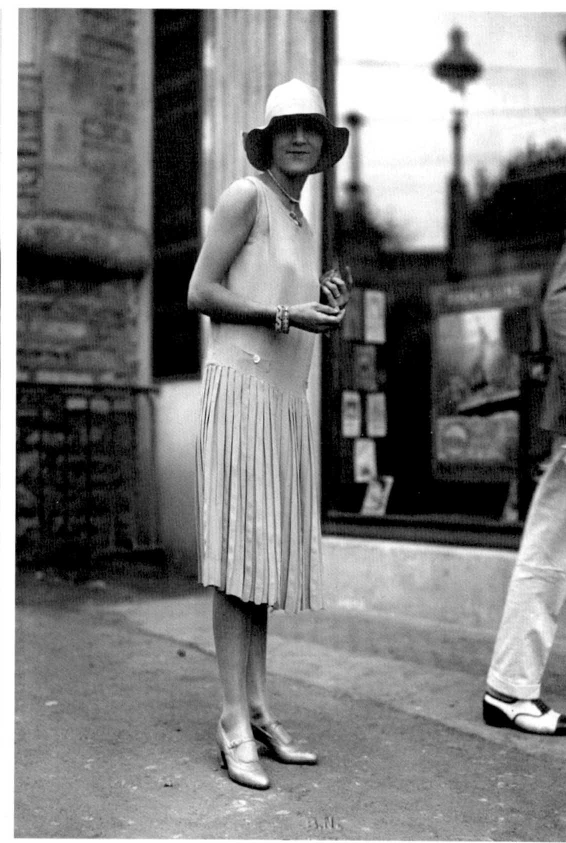

Jean Patou outfits, Deauville, August 14, 1927.

Jean Patou dress, Biarritz, September 10, 1926.

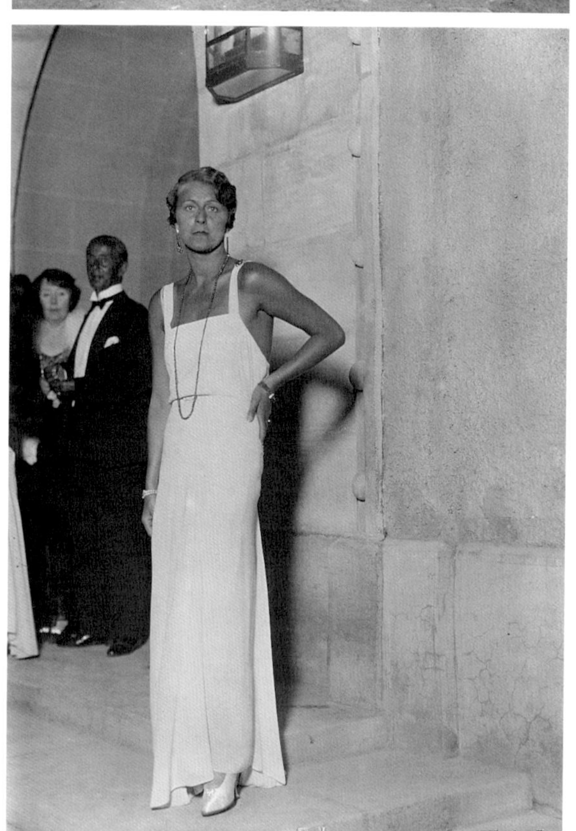

Mme Naes in a Patou evening gown, Biarritz, September 1930.

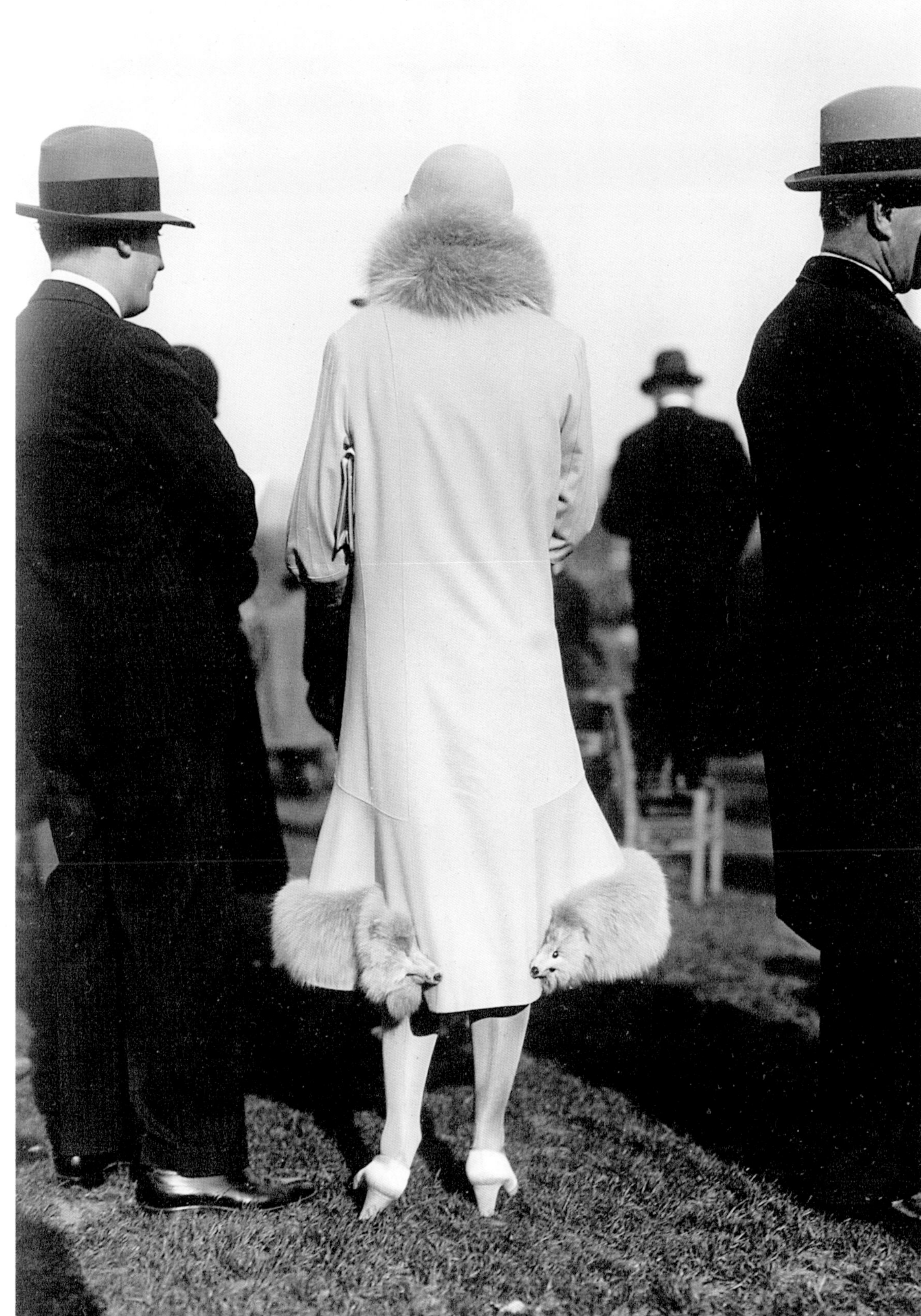

Dulce Liberal Martinez de Hoz (1900–1987), wife of Eduardo Martinez de Hoz, dressed by Patou, at the Auteuil races, March 24, 1929.

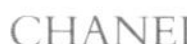

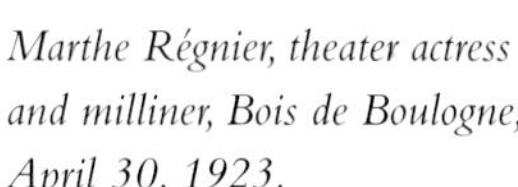

Marthe Régnier, theater actress and milliner, Bois de Boulogne, April 30, 1923.

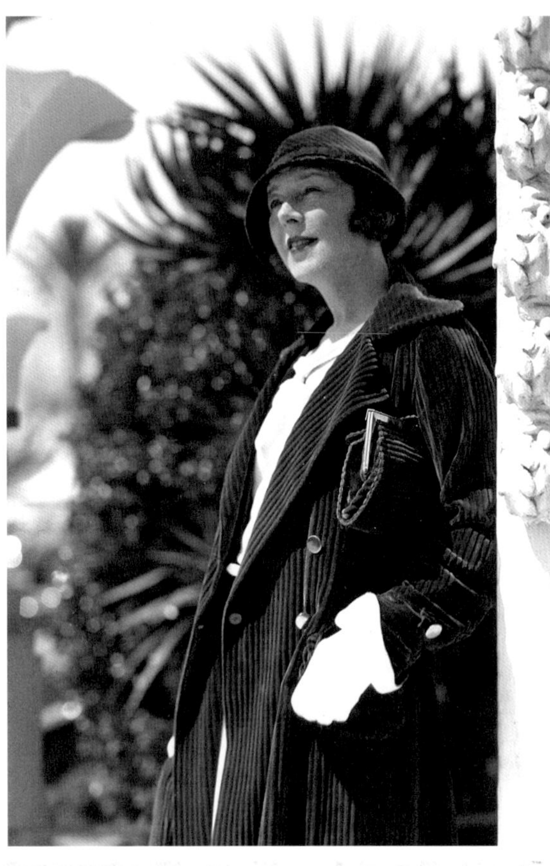

Julia Thompson in a Chanel corduroy trench coat with matching bag, Cannes, April 1933.

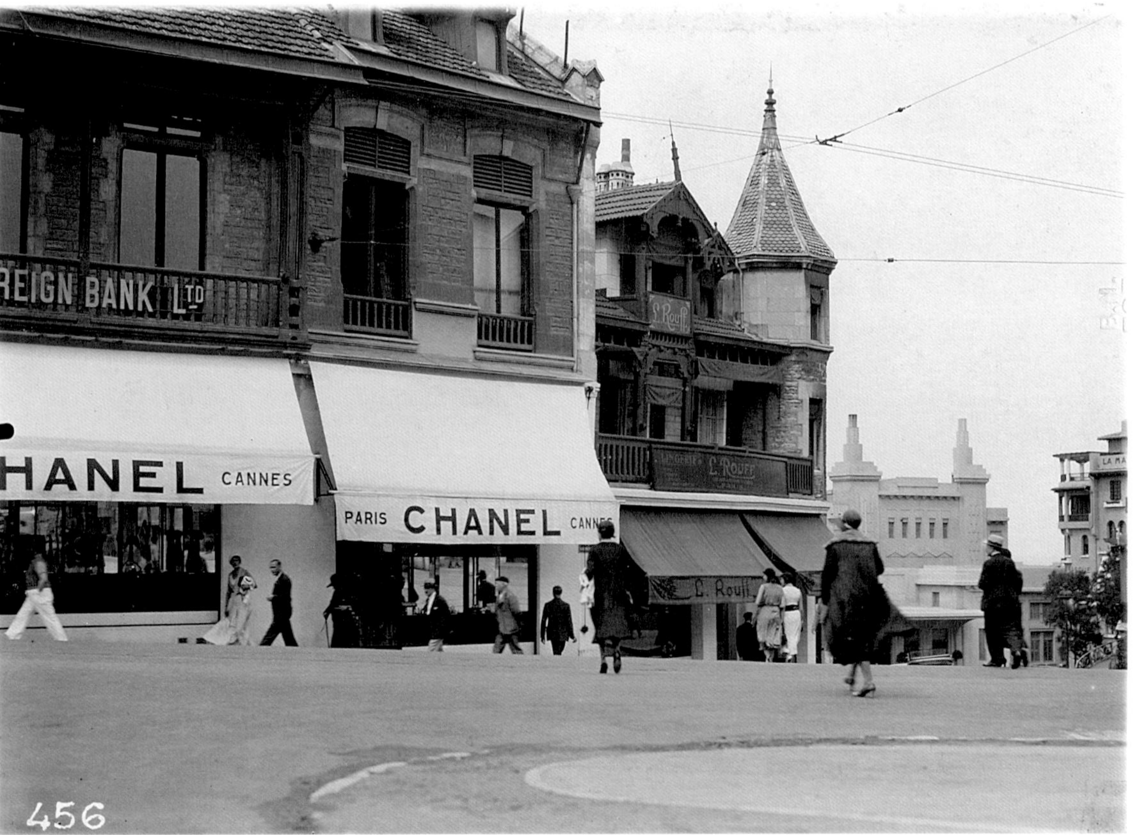

The houses of Chanel and L. Rouff, Biarritz, August 15, 1931.

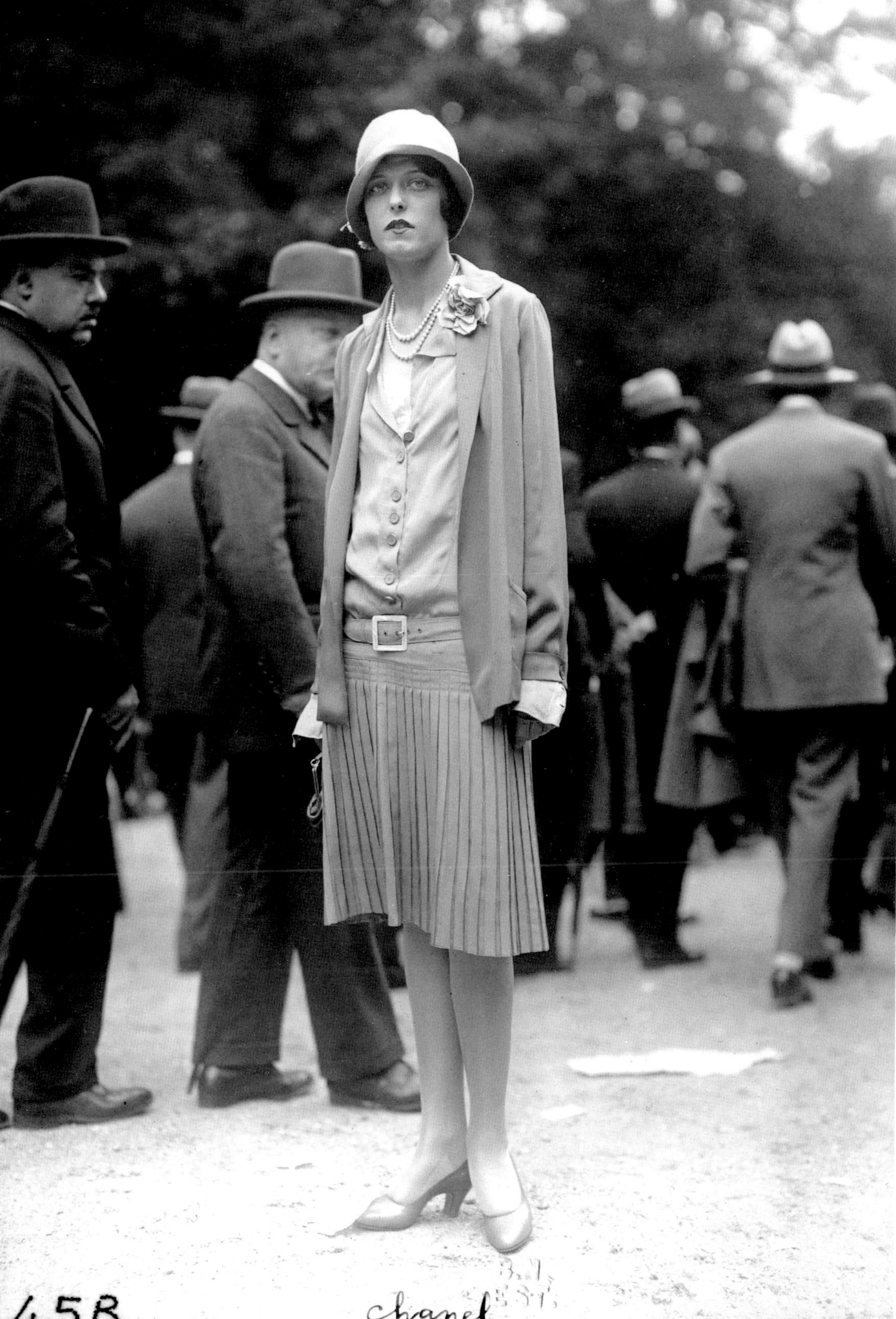

Yola Letellier, née Henriquez, at the Grand Steeple-Chase d'Auteuil, June 19, 1927. A ballerina at the Opéra, at a very young age she married Henri Letellier, publisher of the daily newspaper Le Journal *and mayor of Deauville from 1925 to 1928. She inspired the novelist Colette's character of Gigi.*

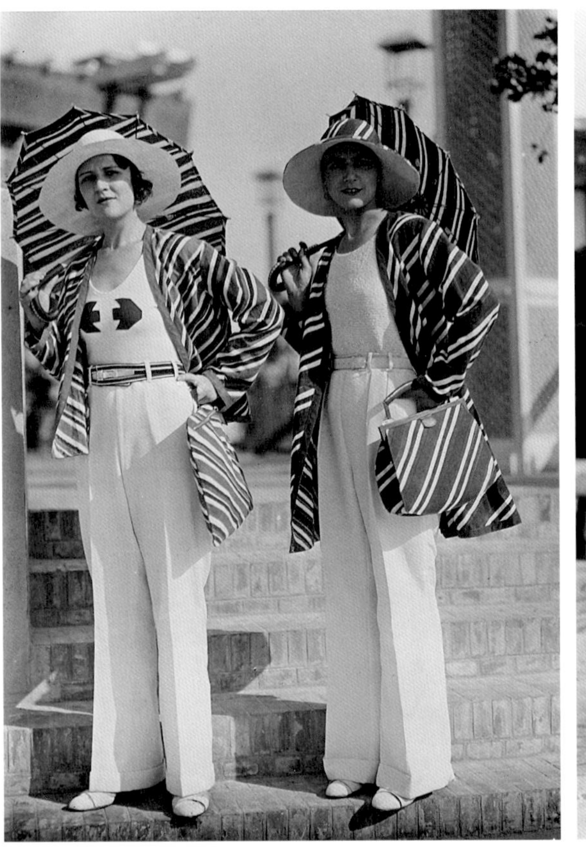

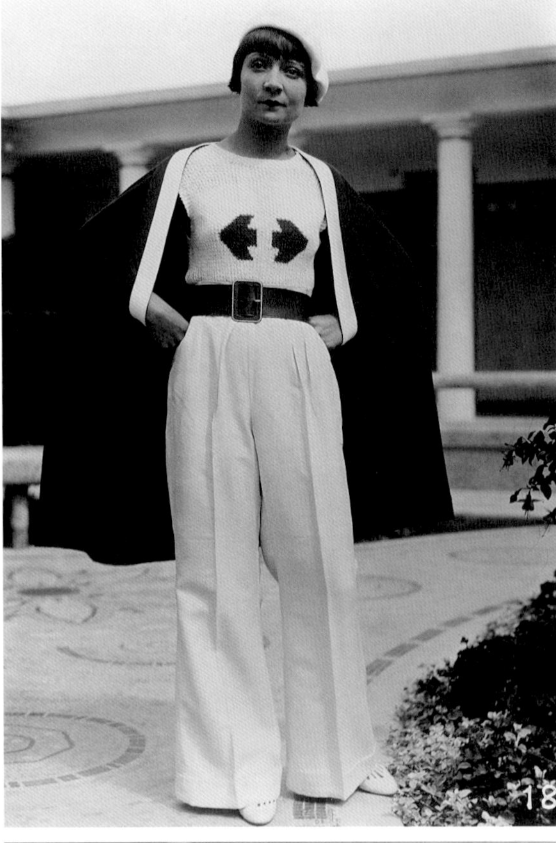

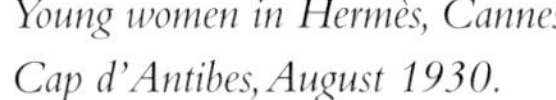
Young women in Hermès, Cannes, Cap d'Antibes, August 1930.

The actress Germaine Auger (1899–2001) in Hermès at the Grand Prix de Deauville, August 24, 1930.

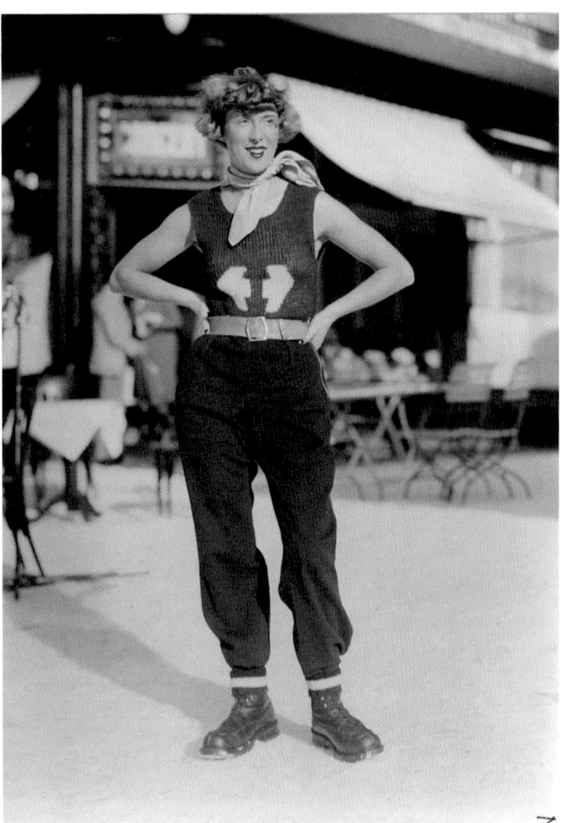

The singer Suzy Solidor in Hermès at Saint-Moritz, January 1931.

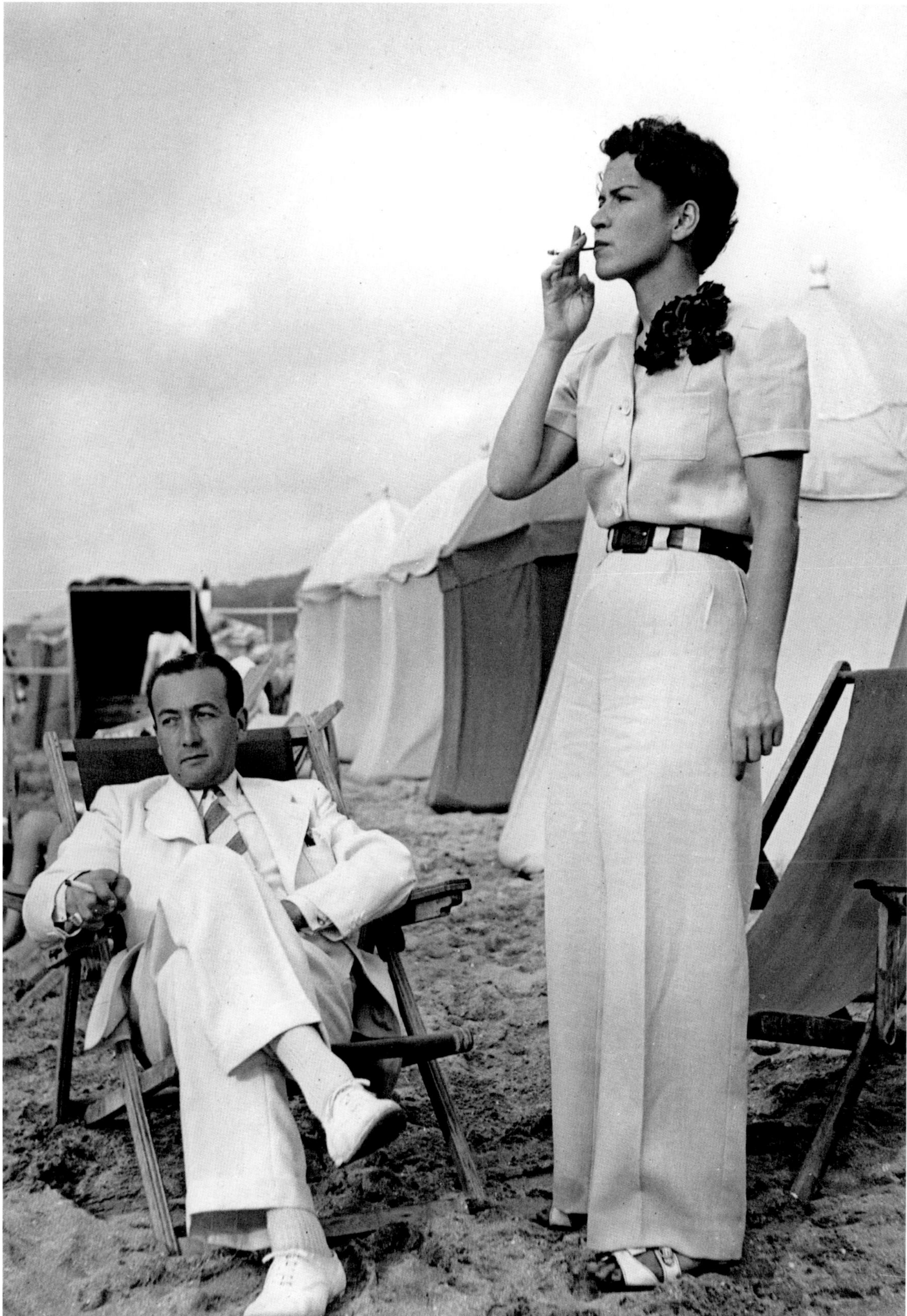

Hermès models, Deauville, August 6, 1939.

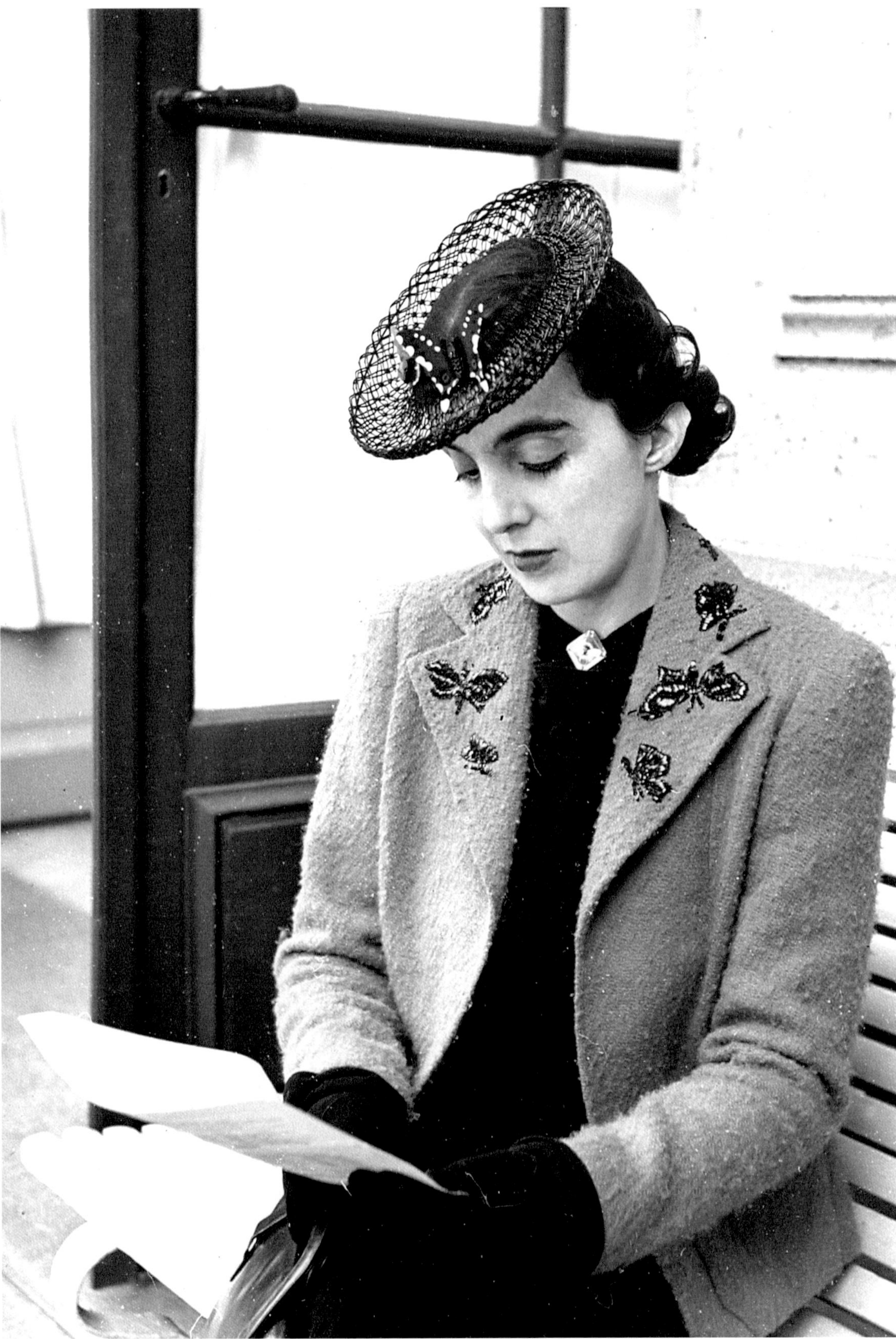

Countess Alice de Montjou, née de La Laurencie, wearing Schiaparelli, Longchamp, April 25, 1937.

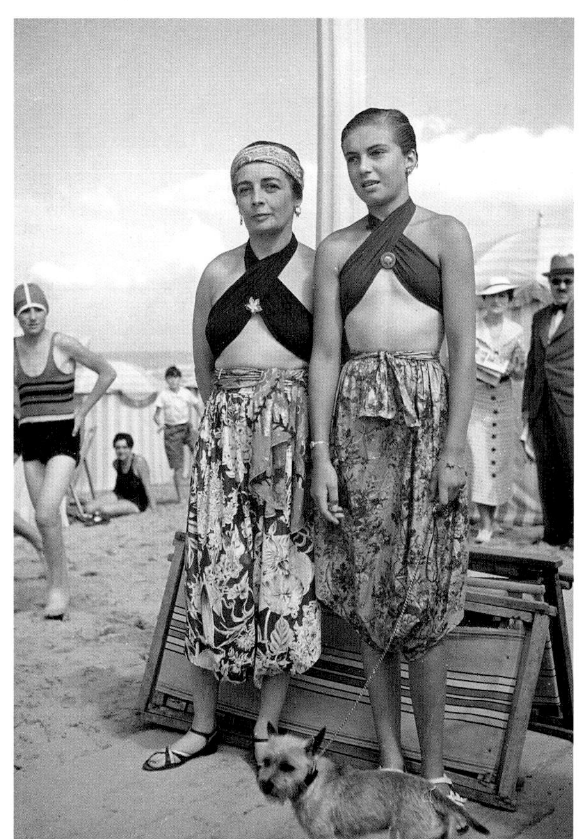

Mme and Mlle Hasselbach in Schiaparelli, Deauville, August 25, 1935.

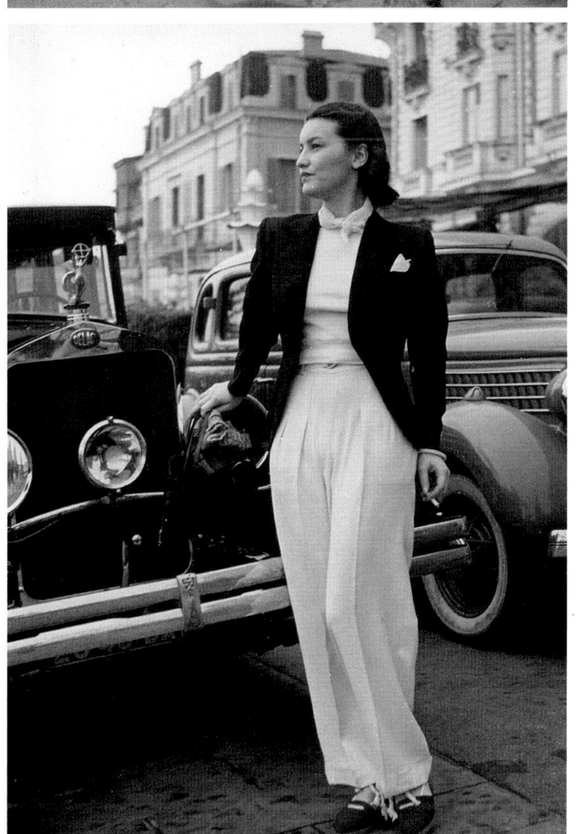

Schiaparelli pants, Cannes, April 1939.

LEADING LADIES OF FASHION

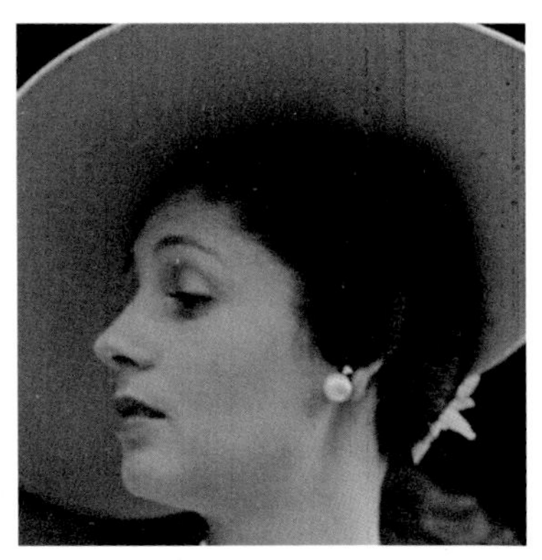

LEADING LADIES OF FASHION

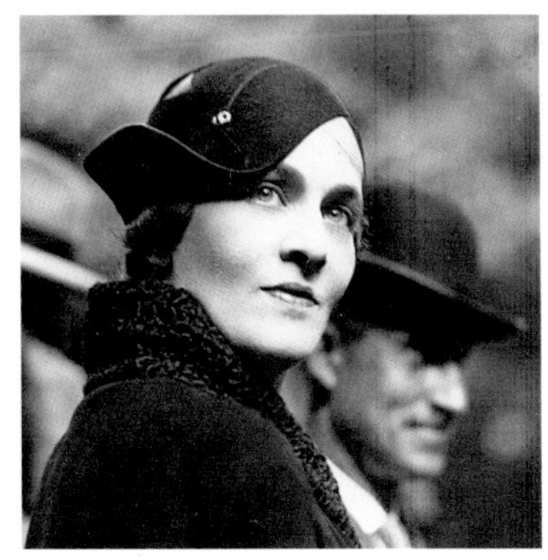

LEADING LADIES OF FASHION

Xavier Demange

In its art and literature, every century celebrates a small, select group of women who crystallize all the physical graces and intellectual refinements of their time: these are *Les Précieuses*, or pretentious young ladies, of the seventeenth century, *petites-maîtresses* of the eighteenth century, the scandalous *merveilleuses* of the Directoire period, and the romantic muses, the "Cocodettes" of the 1860s, and grand courtesans of the fin de siècle. With the development of photoengraving at the beginning of the twentieth century, the runaway success of the commercialized concept of the "fashionable woman" by such high-circulation magazines as *Femina*, *Vogue* and *Harper's Bazaar* did away with the social significance of fashion entirely, giving preference to the form to the detriment of the substance.

In response to the general post-war denial of femininity, the clothing industry advocated a uniformity of silhouette, falling quickly into a caricature of bad taste. This was during the years 1920-1925, when fashion sought every opportunity to plaster down every supposedly superfluous female trait, namely the breasts, hips, legs, and–to a lesser extent–the hair and eyes. "I'll do them in black!" trumpeted Chanel to complete this demolition work. The haute couture reaction was not far behind: Lanvin, Dœuillet, Worth, and Lelong added the bias cut and assymetrical hemline to their collections from 1927, gradually imposing a sleek, new elongated silhouette.

Recognizing their error, women decided to compromise, although without giving up the moral, professional, and aesthetic gains won during this brief period of sexual anarchy. Fashion brought back the legs, the fabric tightened around the hips, and hat brims were raised to reveal the eyes and face. Fashion accepted, in short, that women had assets and would insist on showing them off.

The Séebergers followed this gradual change, season by season, leaving a well-documented iconography of this return of the feminine to fashion. It is interesting to note that while actresses seeking to please the general public often preferred brash styles between 1920 and 1925, after 1927/1928 a small group of society women emerged who were "complete knock-outs." Three of these led the field for years: Mme Martinez de Hoz, Mme Revel, and Mme Arpels. A few lines must suffice for this attempt to convey their well-deserved reputations.

The first was of Brazilian origin and married to an Argentinean. Dulce Liberal (1900–1987) was married to Eduardo Martinez de Hoz, a great horse owner and president of the Jockey Club of Buenos Aires. The couple settled in France in the early 1920s and became firm fixtures at the Parisian tracks where his horses raced. In 1925, Martinez de Hoz was the first owner to win the fabulous sum of 39,800,000 francs with two of his horses, Tricard and Tric-Trac.

Dulce Liberal Martinez de Hoz was tall and slim, with an enchanting Creole face. She was first seen through a Séeberger viewfinder in the spring of 1925, and the photographer's fascination for his model continued undiminished until 1939. The Bibliothèque nationale de France has no fewer than 240 photographic portraits of her by the Séebergers. Some are very successful. Others are less so, but none are dull, as the model had a natural radiance. She wore only the designs of the great couturiers (Vionnet, Paquin, Lelong) and selected her hats entirely among those by Caroline Reboux. She sought not to be original, but only to be perfectly dressed. In 1927, the magazine *Femina* admired a particular coat by Paquin trimmed with two silver foxes, and periodically waxed lyrical about her hats.[38]

Vogue also devoted an article to her beauty secrets. In it, readers learned that she slept eight hours per day, awoke at 9 o'clock in the morning and stayed in bed until 11 o'clock, that she did not smoke, and maintained a strict diet that allowed neither fruits nor sauces, milk nor alcohol, only fresh vegetables and roast meats.[39] This regulated life, dedicated entirely to her own beauty, was crowned by the ultimate reward: Mme Martinez de Hoz was elected the best-dressed woman in the world in 1949.

Another woman followed her closely in the great style marathon of the period between the wars: Mme Robert Revel, wife of a great Parisian notary. Née Alice Rosenau (Paris, 1894–1977, London), she married her second husband, Count René de Chavagnac, in 1947. Her daughter from her first marriage, Christiane, married Count Bernard de Montesquiou-Fezensac in 1938. The two women were regulars at the racetracks; Alice Revel was particularly noted for her impeccable taste in clothing.[40] The Séeberger brothers tracked her, too, as she migrated to Deauville and Saint-Moritz from 1927 right into the 1950s.

The beautiful Alice Revel wore nothing but the great couturiers' most flattering designs (Molyneux, Vionnet, and Madeleine de Rauch, for example) and, like Dulce Liberal Martinez de Hoz, wore only hats created by the house of Reboux. She became known as a leader of fashion. The magazine *Femina* thus declared in the summer of 1933 that "ostrich plumes were challenged by Mme Revel, whose big flat-brimmed boaters by Reboux made a sensation."[41] She wore these innovations with such distinction that she seemed to embody one definition of French elegance: moderation and simplicity.

Finally, one additional leading lady of fashion should be introduced: Mme Louis Arpels, wife of the famous jeweler. Even prior to the vogue for star models of Slavic origin, including such names as Lud or Alla,[42] Mme Arpels (née Hélène Ostrowska) attracted widespread attention with her slender figure and exotic features. The Séeberger brothers noticed her for the first time in Deauville in August 1927. She seems to have been working as a roving model for the house of Worth at that time, and for several years she could be seen lending her sleek silhouette to creations by Schiaparelli and Reboux, among others. Then, in 1933, she married Louis Arpels (1886–1976), one of the brothers who owned the famous jewelry store Van Cleef & Arpels on the Place Vendôme. She continued to appear at all the great society gatherings in Paris and Cannes until World War II, dressed exclusively by Maggy Rouff, whom she must certainly have represented as a "jockey," (see p. 33) unless she had some financial interests in the house.[43]

As a professional model, Hélène Arpels knew how to take full advantage of the camera. At the Prix de Diane in Chantilly, June 1934, the magazine *Femina* noted that, "the standard gesture of the day was the one made by Mme Arpels as she held the edge of her broad-brimmed black Reboux hat."[44] Over time, other fashionables would adopt this gesture—a gracious feint—like queens waving to their crowd of admirers (illus. p. 51, top right).

This discrete little hand gesture is how the dream should come to a close, leaving in memory only the sweetness and enjoyment of a period that would forever be darkened in the storm of the war years. The great merit of the Séebergers is to have fixed thousands of fleeting moments on paper, in respectful homage to a group of leading ladies and the society that gave rise to them.

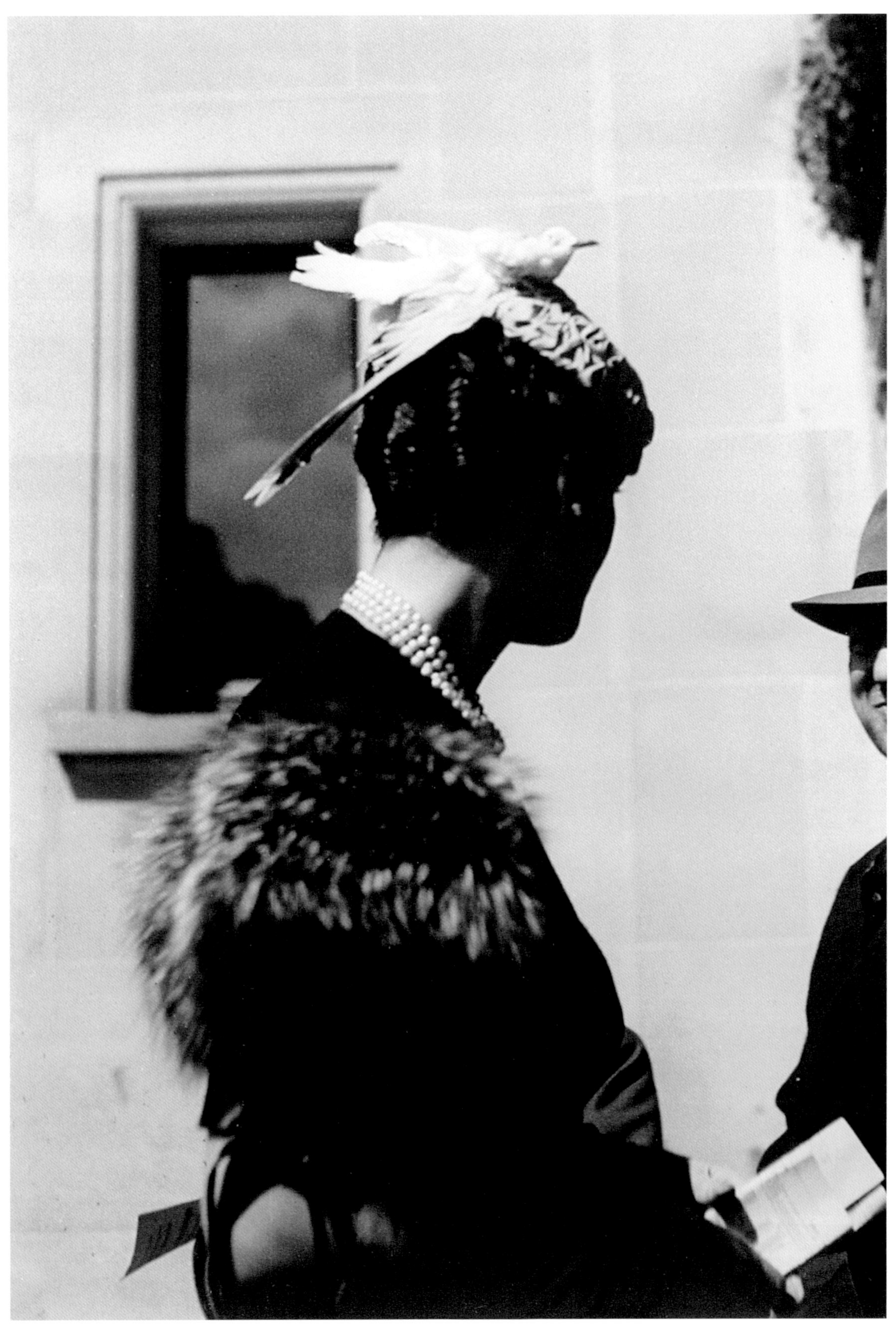

Dulce Liberal Martinez de Hoz (1900–1987), wife of Eduardo Martinez de Hoz, at Longchamp, May 28, 1939.

Dulce Liberal Martinez de Hoz, wearing a hat by Caroline Reboux, Chantilly, Prix du Jockey-Club, June 14, 1931. She is with Ellie G. Blake (1893–1961), née Ellie Malcolm Lawson, wife of the Scottish author George Blake.

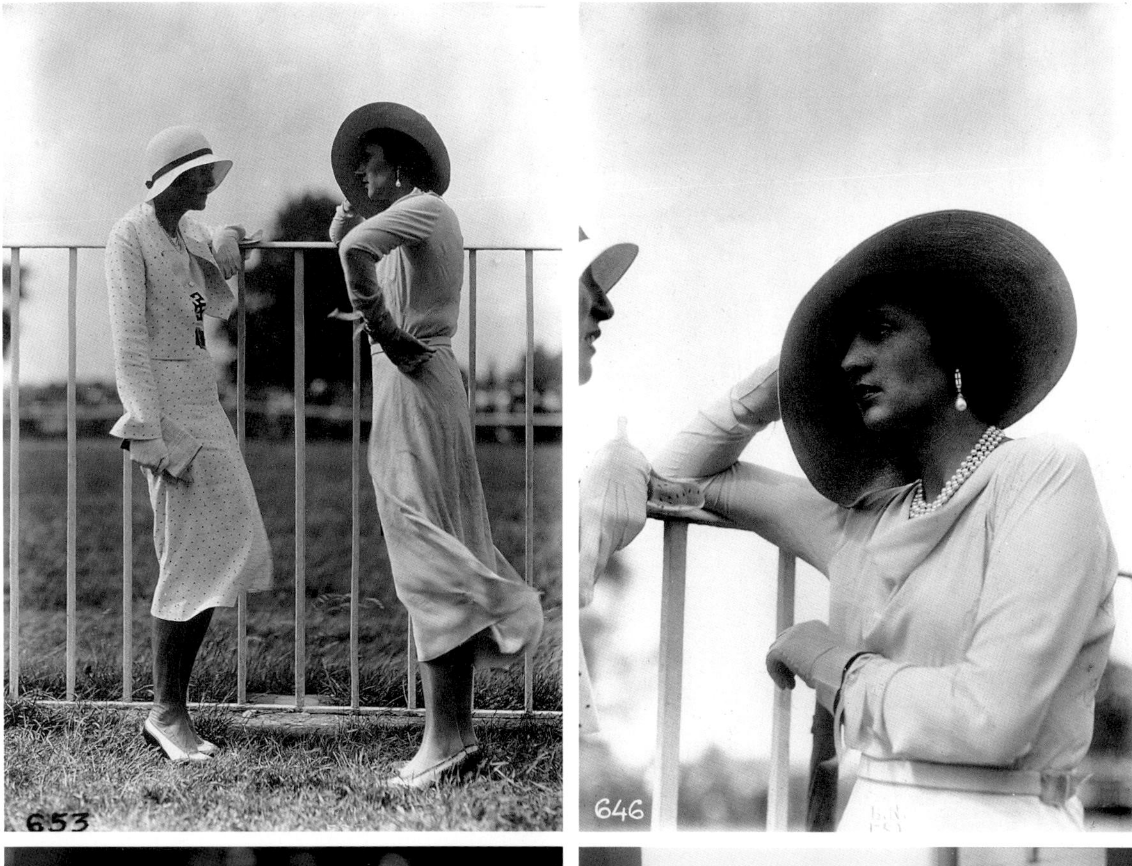

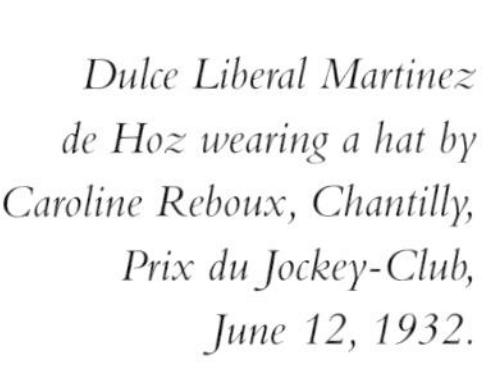

Dulce Liberal Martinez de Hoz wearing a hat by Caroline Reboux, Chantilly, Prix du Jockey-Club, June 12, 1932.

Dulce Liberal Martinez de Hoz with her son at Longchamp, April 15, 1934.

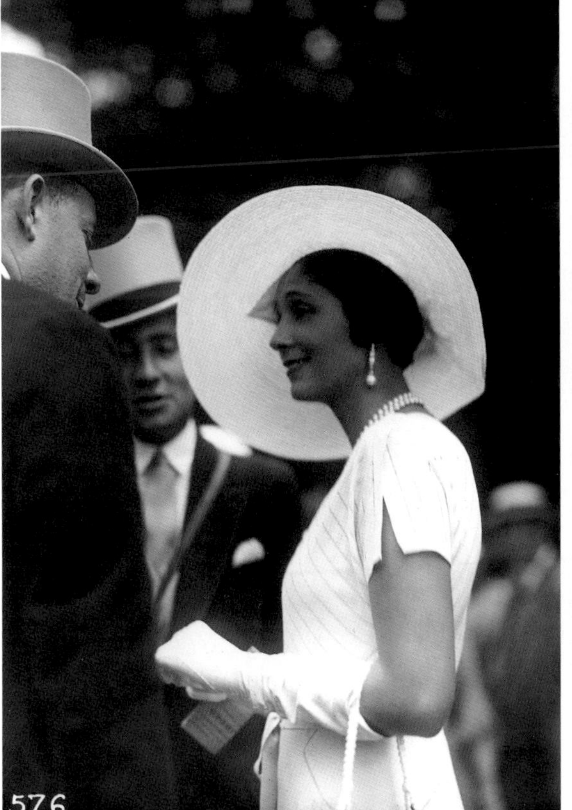

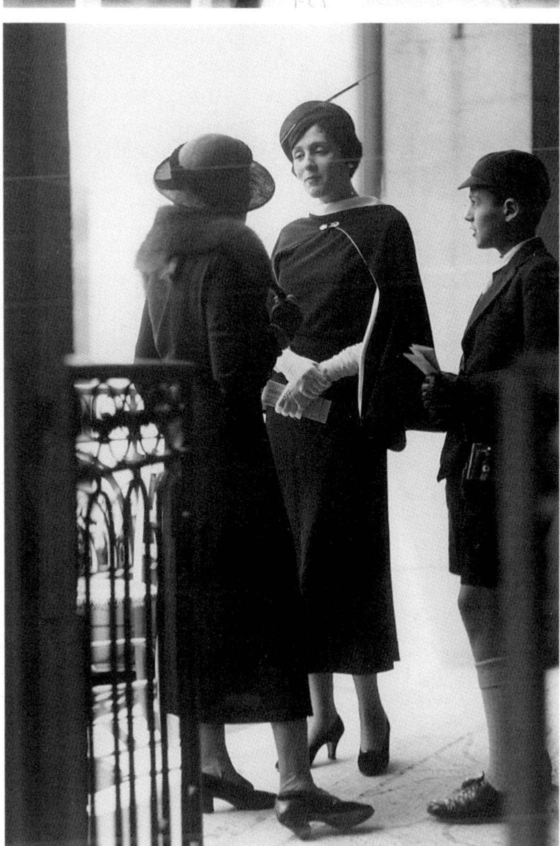

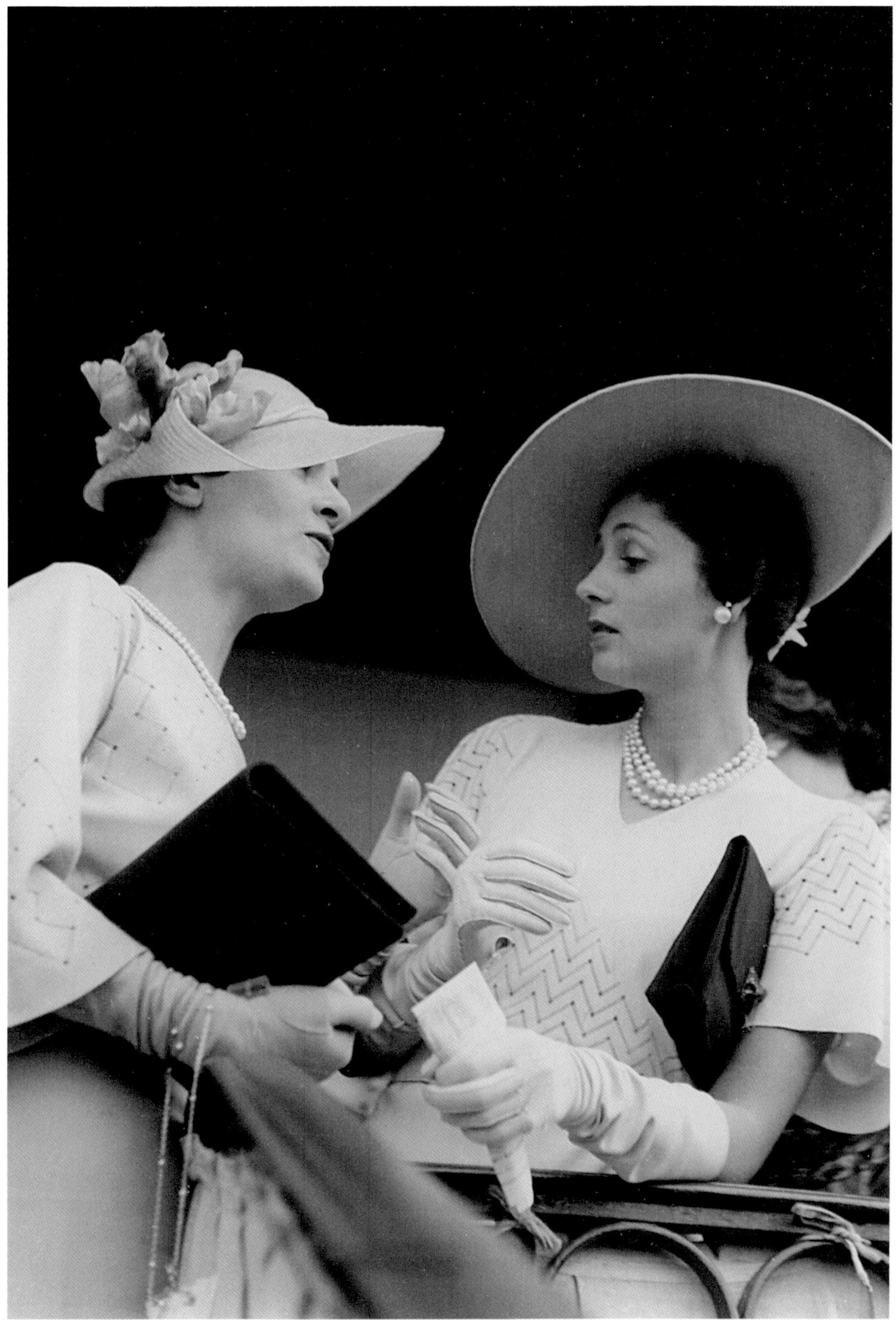

Dulce Liberal Martinez de Hoz with Alice Revel at Chantilly, Prix de Diane, June 9, 1935.

Alice Revel, née Rosenau (1894–1977), wearing a hat by Caroline Reboux at the reopening of Longchamp on September 18, 1932.

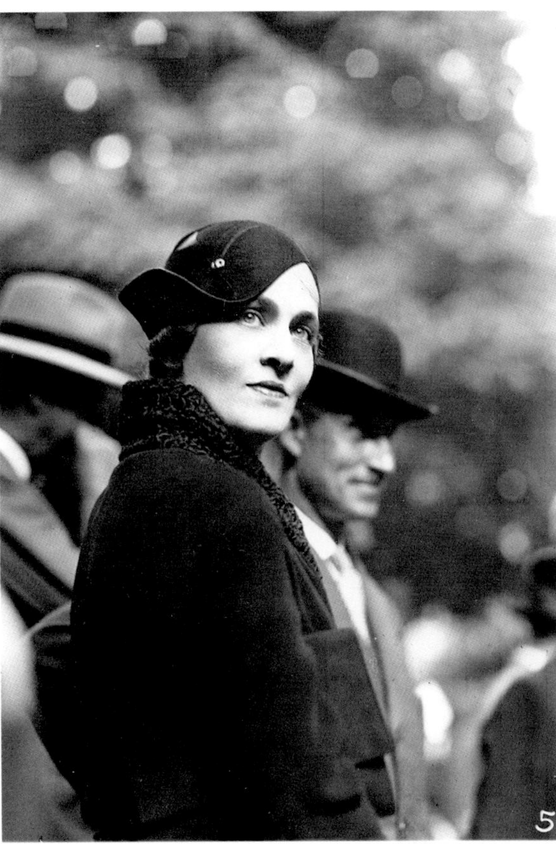

Alice Revel in a skating outfit by Madeleine de Rauch, Saint-Moritz, January 1933.

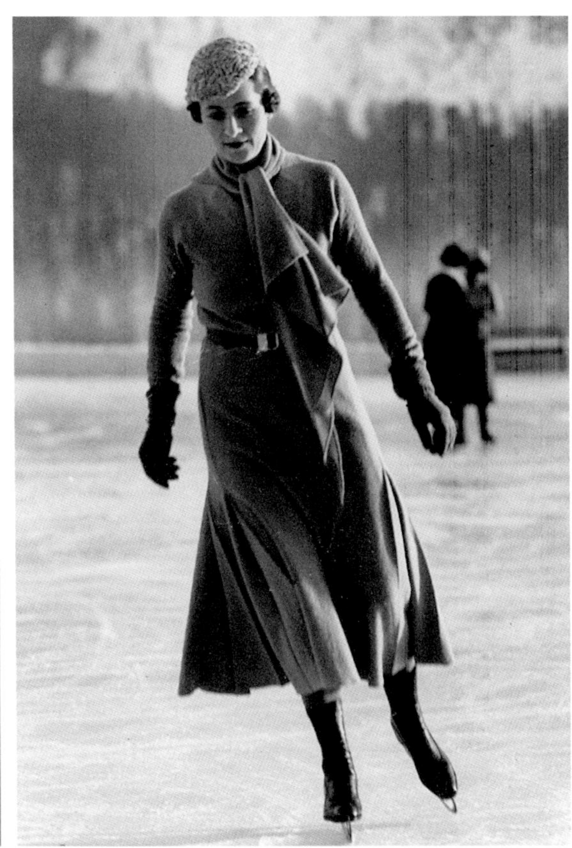

Alice Revel, Deauville, August 12, 1934.

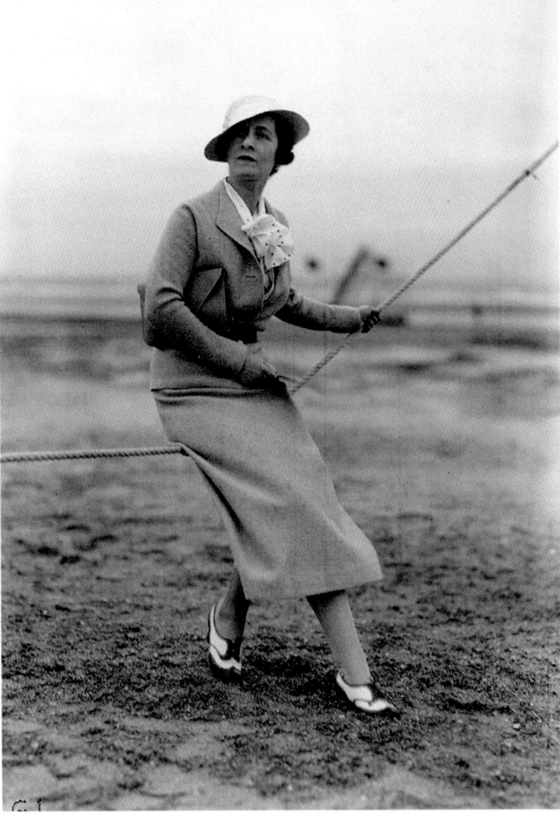

Alice Revel wearing a hat by Caroline Reboux, Longchamp, October 21, 1928.

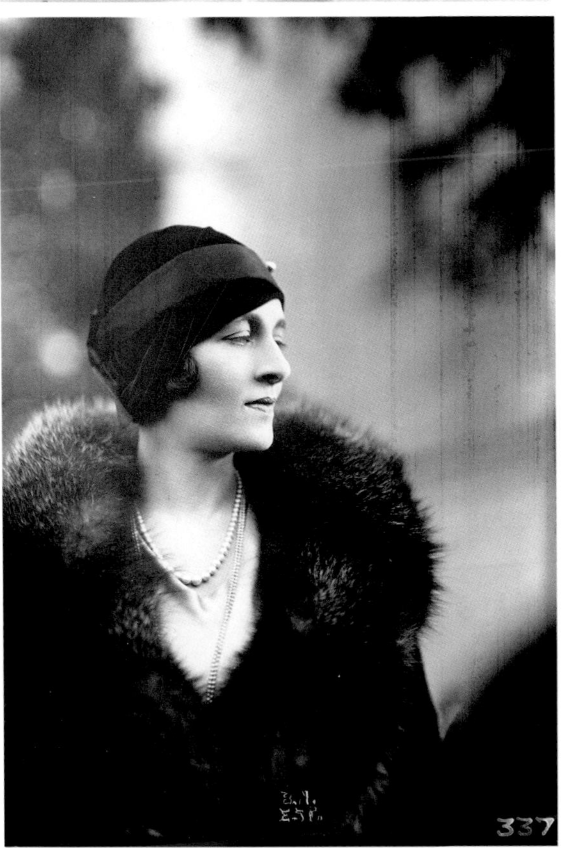

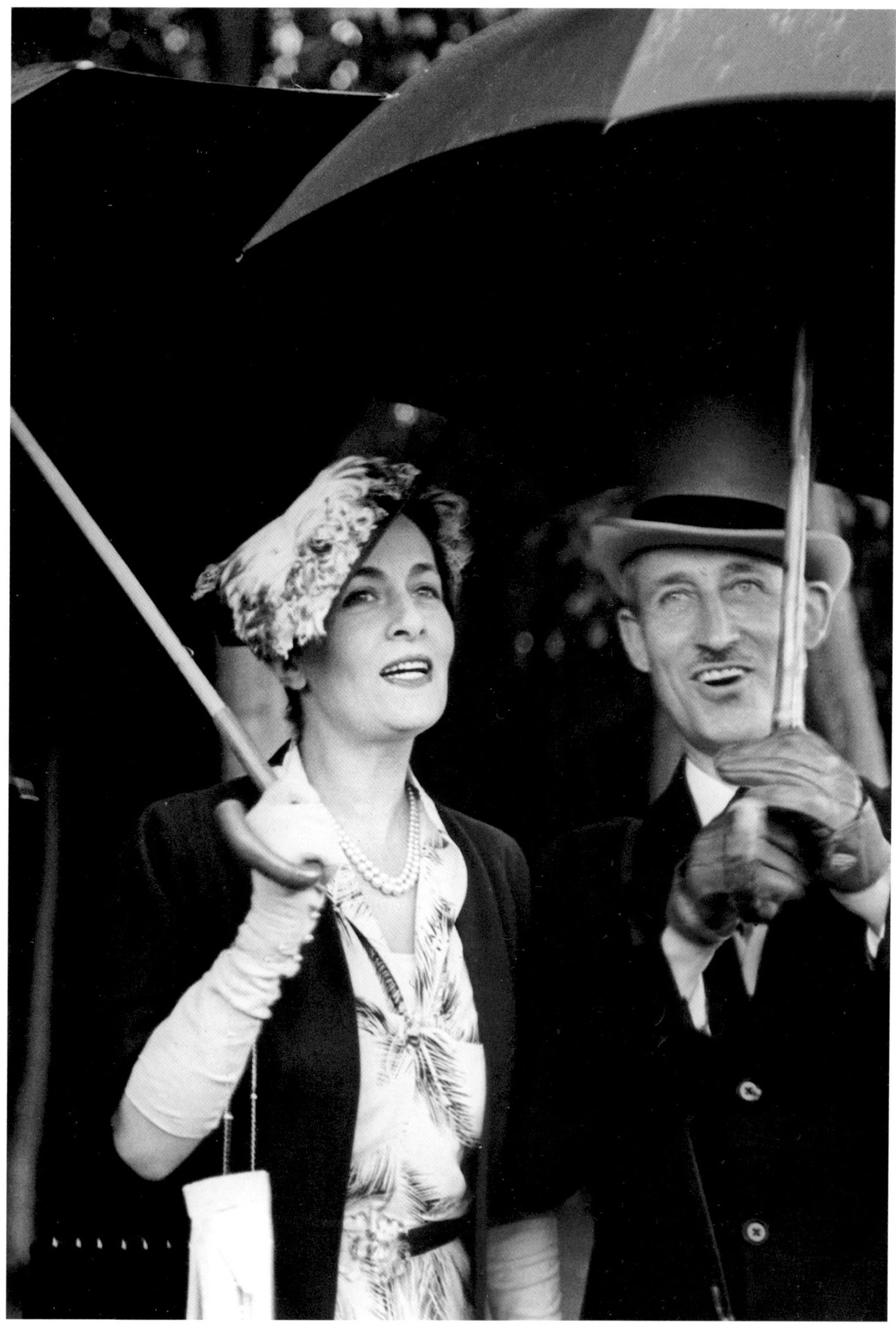

Alice Revel and her future second husband, Count de Chavagnac, wearing a hat by Caroline Reboux, Chantilly, Prix de Diane, June 5, 1938.

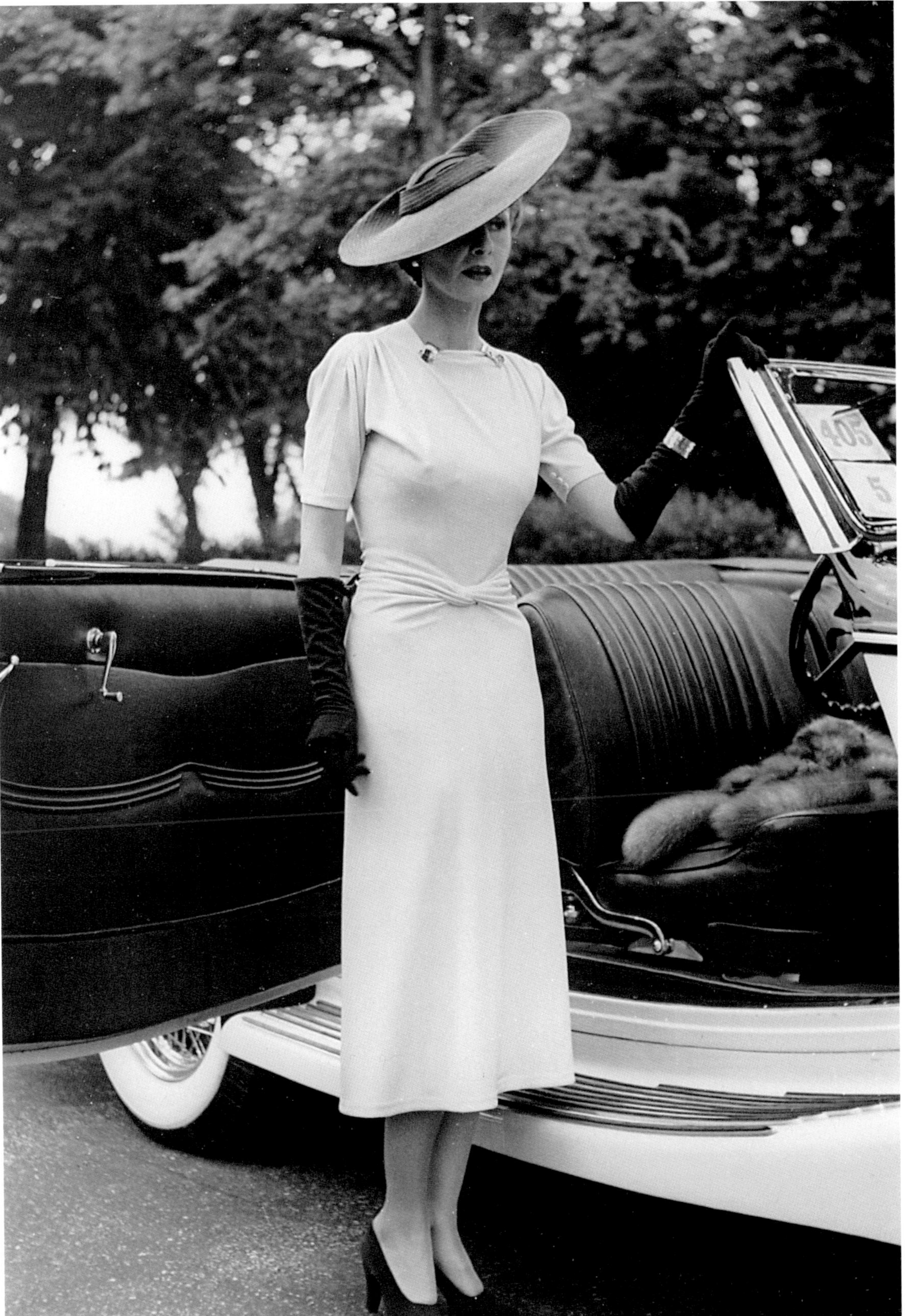

Hélène Arpels (née Ostrowska), wife of jeweler Louis Arpels, in a dress by Maggy Rouff, hat by Caroline Reboux, concours d'elegance custom automobile show, June 20, 1937.

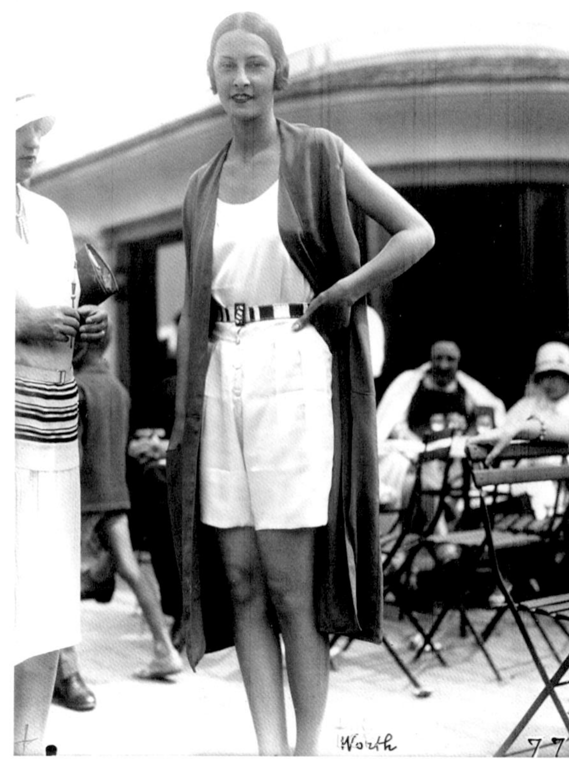

Hélène Ostrowska before her marriage to the jeweler Louis Arpels in 1933, wearing Worth, Deauville, August 15, 1928.

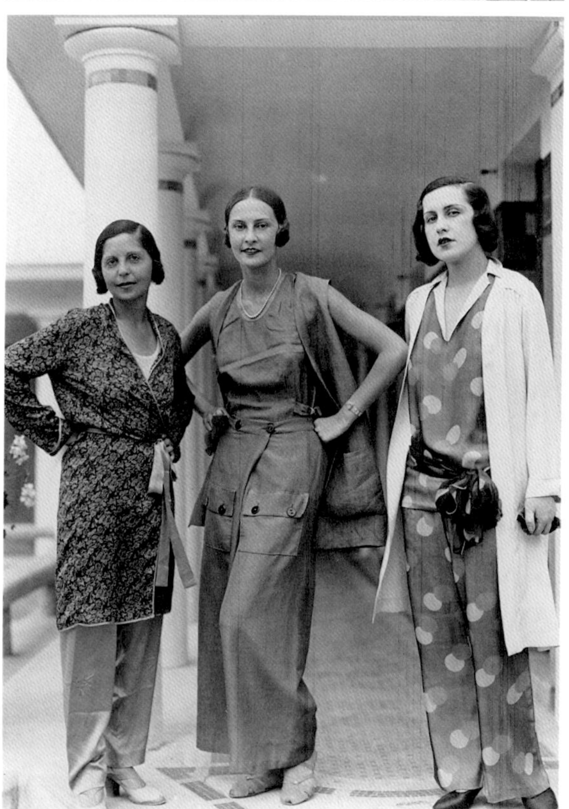

Hélène Ostrowska in Schiaparelli, Deauville, July 1929.

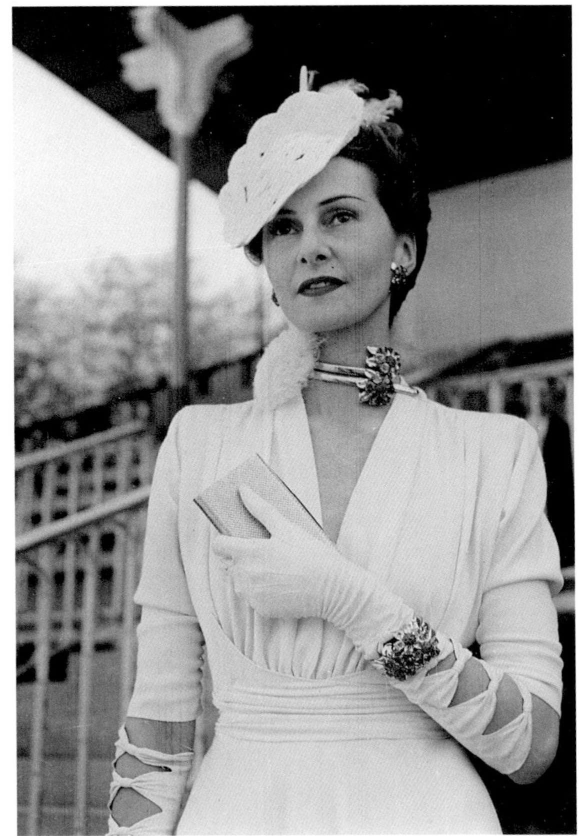

Hélène Arpels outfitted by Maggy Rouff, hat by Caroline Reboux, at the Prix de Diane, Chantilly, June 4, 1939.

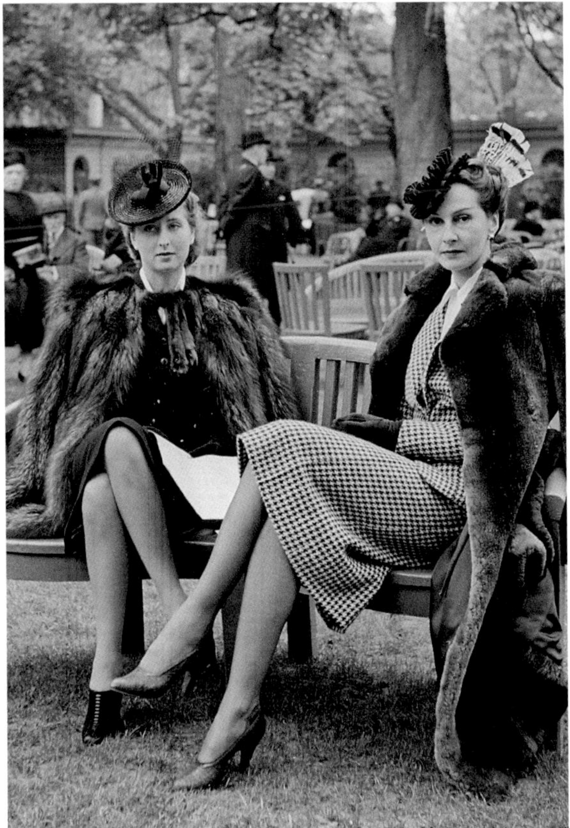

Monique Louis-Dreyfus (née de Nervo) and Hélène Arpels, Longchamp, Prix Daru, April 30, 1939.

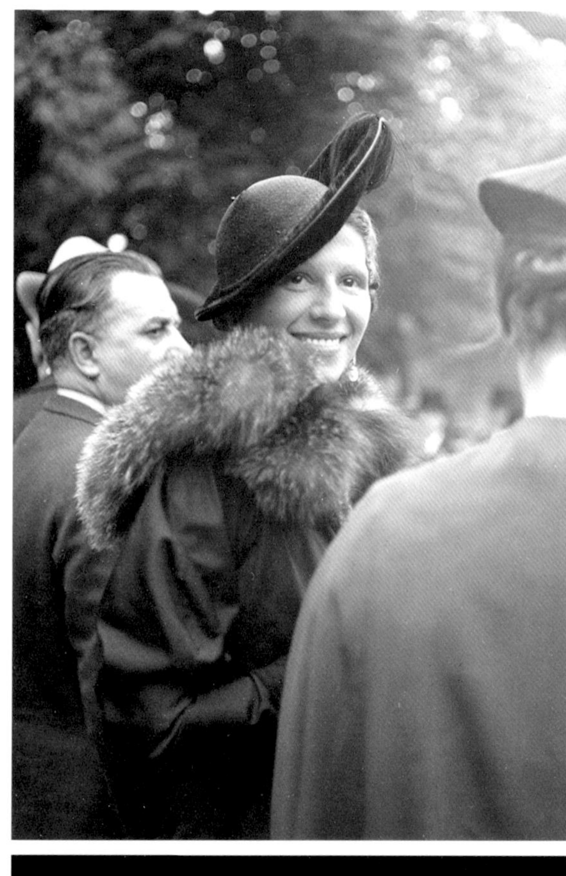

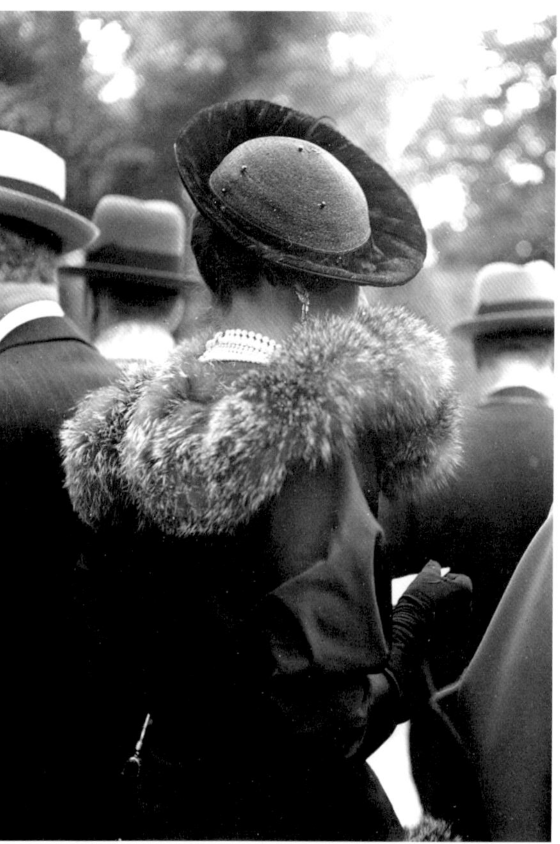

Mme Robert Lazard at Longchamp, May 24, 1936.

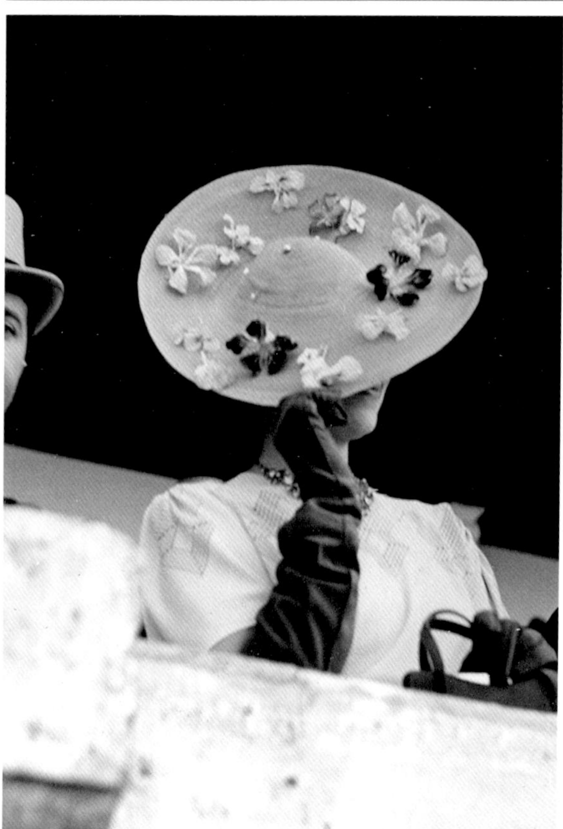

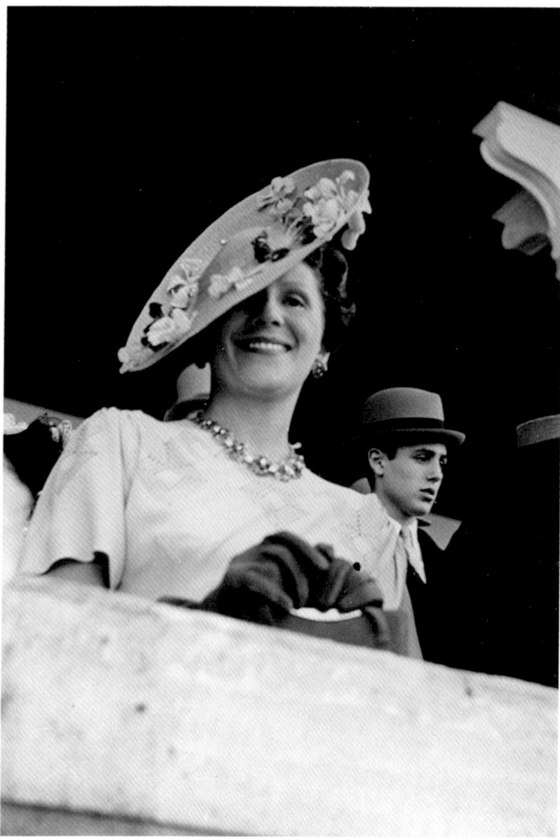

Mme Robert Lazard wearing a hat by Caroline Reboux, Chantilly, Prix de Diane, June 4, 1939.

Yola Letellier, née Henriquez, wife of Henri Letellier, director of the daily newspaper Le Journal *and mayor of Deauville from 1925 to 1928, wearing a hat by Marthe Collot, Auteuil, March 25, 1928.*

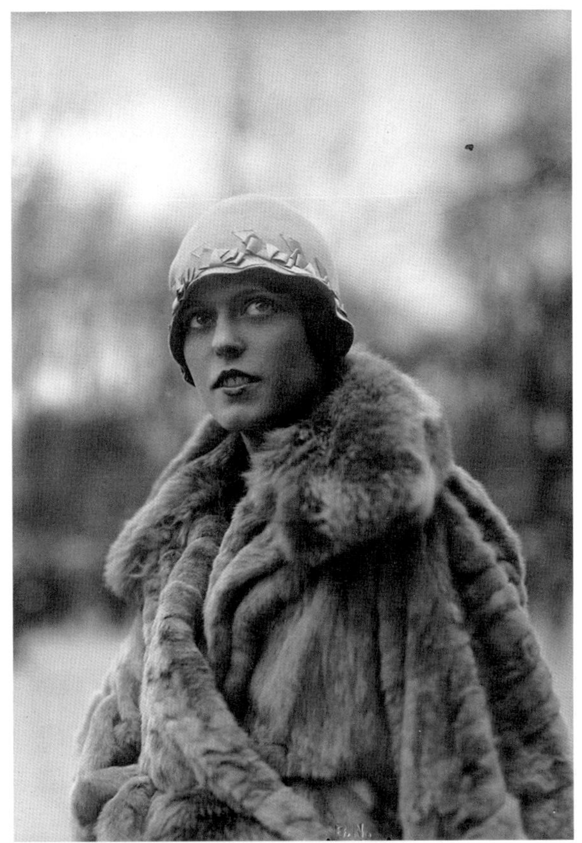

Yola Letellier dressed by Callot, Grand Prix de Longchamp, June 1926.

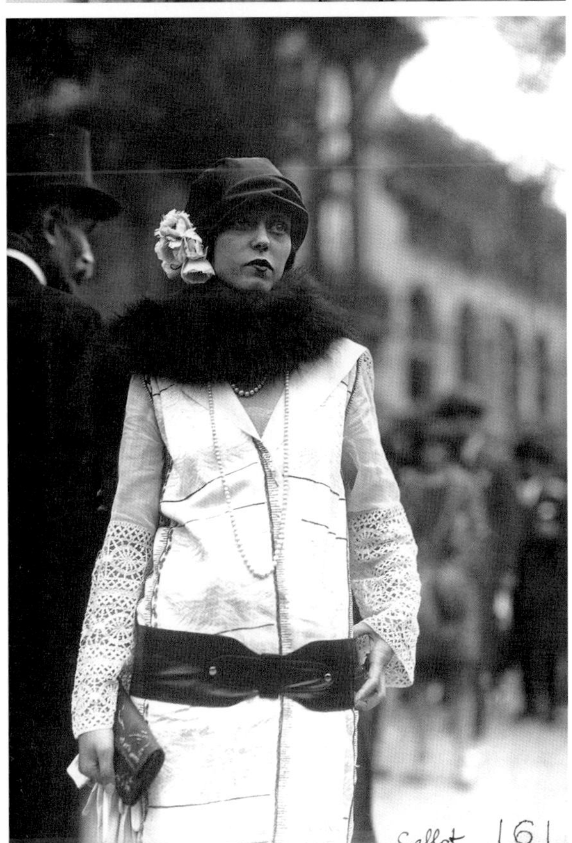

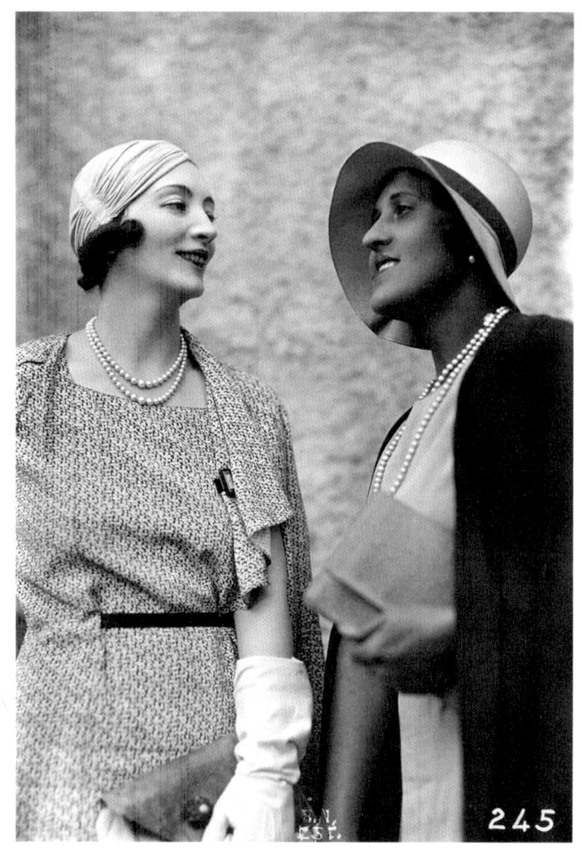

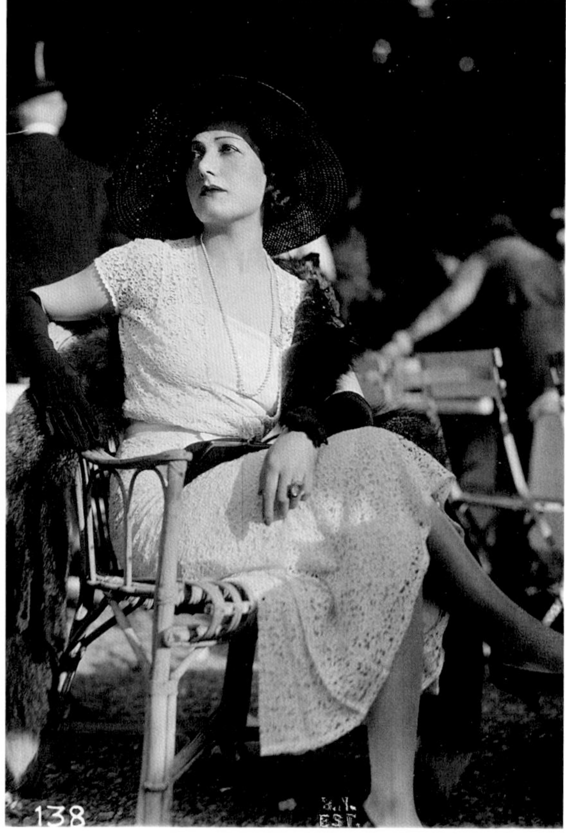

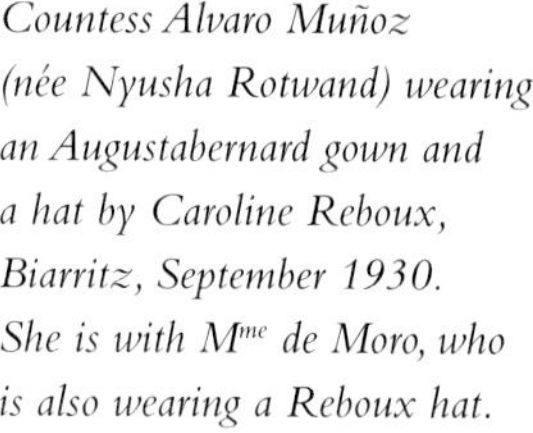

Countess Alvaro Muñoz (née Nyusha Rotwand) wearing an Augustabernard gown and a hat by Caroline Reboux, Biarritz, September 1930. She is with Mme de Moro, who is also wearing a Reboux hat.

Francesca Bertini (1892–1985), née Elena Vittello, Italian silent movie star and later Countess Cartier, in Worth and a hat by Marguerite Paraf, elegant polo fête at Bagatelle, June 27, 1931.

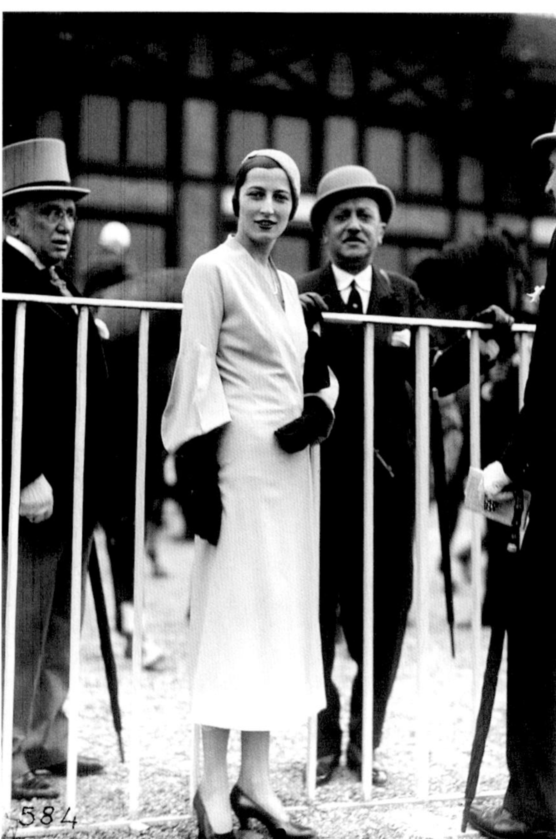

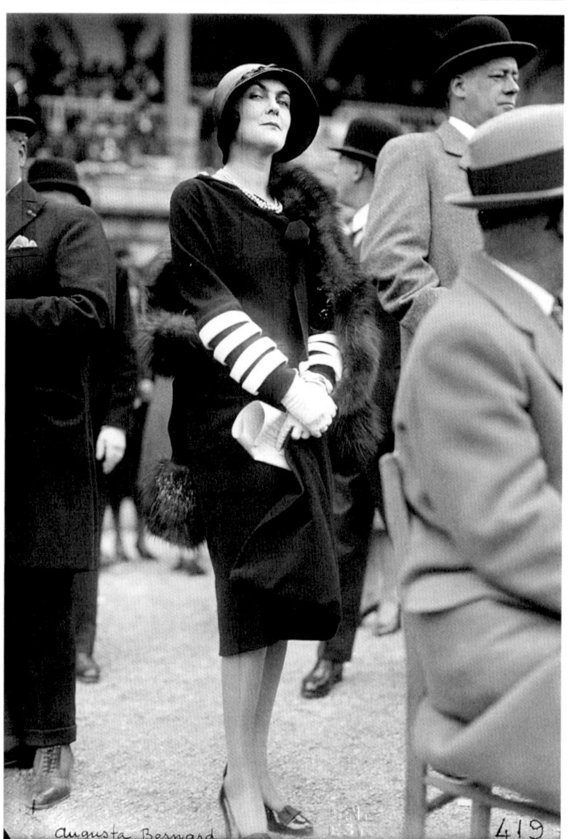

M[lle] Jaguenaud in a Marcelle Dormoy dress, Chantilly, Prix du Jockey-Club, June 12, 1932.

M[me] Yvan Maquinay wearing an Augustabernard outfit, Longchamp, May 12, 1929.

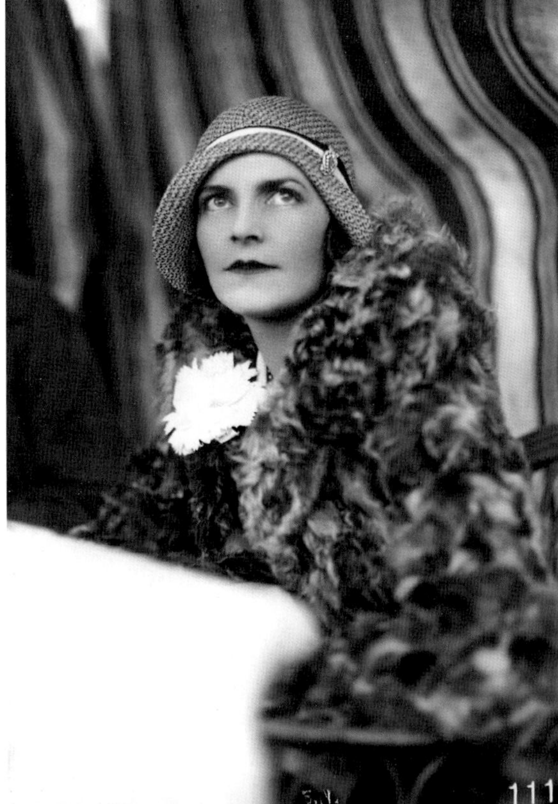

Lady Edwina Mountbatten (1901–1960) wearing a hat by Marie-Christiane, Deauville, August 1930. After an active society life, Lady Edwina, wife of Lord Mountbatten, emerged as a heroine of the Second World War and a remarkable political woman when she served as the last vicereine of India in 1947.

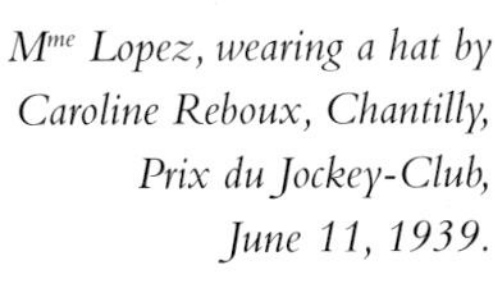

Mme Lopez, wearing a hat by Caroline Reboux, Chantilly, Prix du Jockey-Club, June 11, 1939.

Countess Celani, née Bichette Amor de Yturbe, wearing a hat by Suzanne Talbot, Auteuil, Grand Steeple-Chase, June 22, 1930.

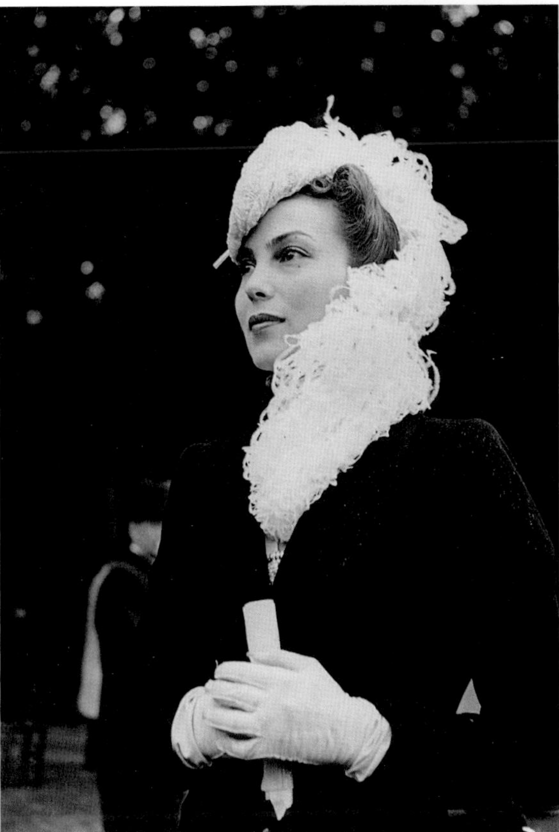

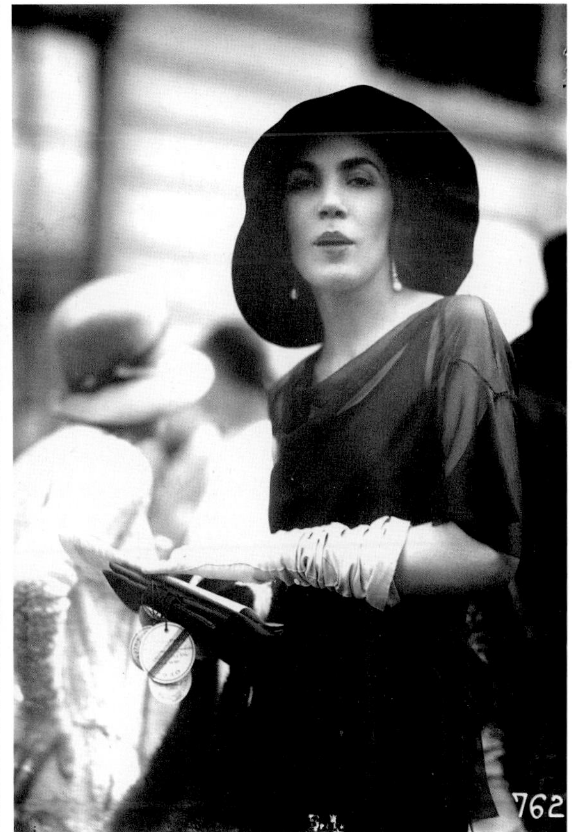

FASHION ACCESSORIES

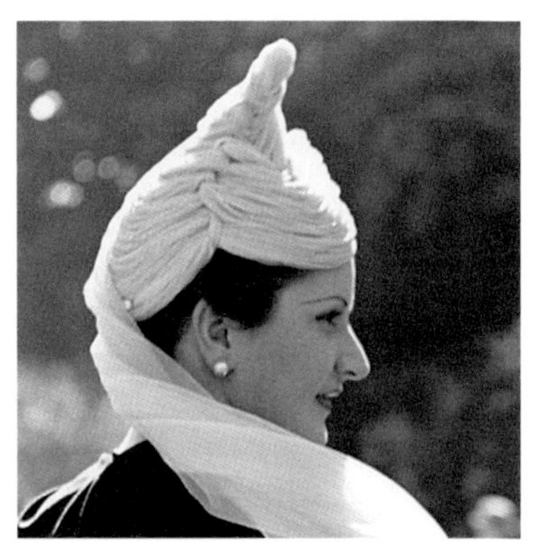

FASHION ACCESSORIES

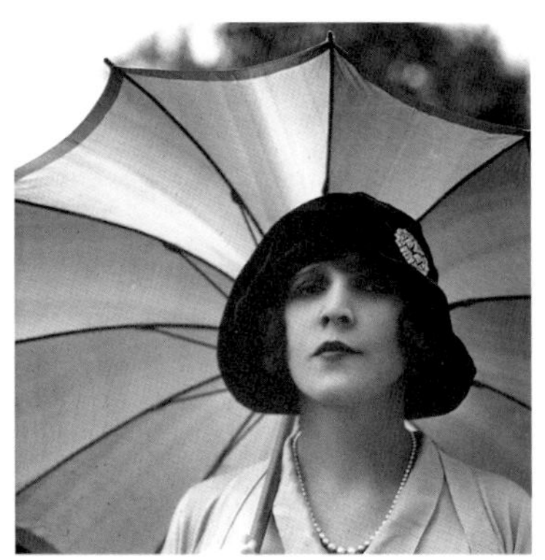

FASHION ACCESSORIES

Sylvie Aubenas

"The choice of accessory (which is important in its own right) must be made with extreme care, an almost mathematical precision. It will not brook the slightest sloppiness."
– Maggy Rouff, *La Philosophie de l'élégance* (*The Philosophy of Elegance*), 1942

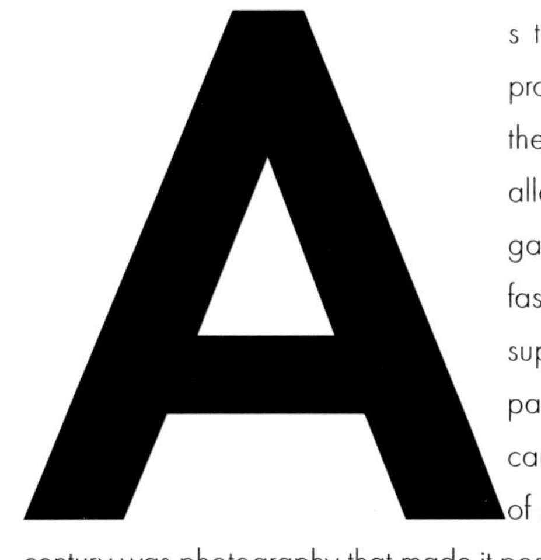

s time passed, the Séeberger photos conferred increasing prominence on fashion accessories, and it seems clear that after they adopted the Rolleiflex in 1935, their new apparatus allowed them greater flexibility in capturing the details of elegant attire. Their pictures reflect a general evolution in the fashion industry. Obviously, accessories had always existed to supplement or enhance an outfit–Balzac ably described the pangs of ambitious young people for whom the choice of tie, cane, or fashionable boots might decide the success or failure of an intrigue. The new feature at the beginning of the twentieth century was photography that made it possible for the press to disseminate general views of these items that were so essential to "lift" an outfit. From that point on, entire magazines–abundantly illustrated–were devoted to them. It frequently took two or three views to make sense of a hat (hardly an accessory, actually, since it is the veritable focal point of any feminine look). This was seldom necessary for a dress.

While the importance of the hat prior to 1939 is undeniable, it is notable that other accent pieces, which had been far less obvious or even non-existent until then, were gradually achieving their present prominence in fashion, business, the media, and roused the interest of many more people: fashion jewelry,[45] handbags, shoes, sunglasses, sunshades, and even pets. Their increasing variety enables us to grasp two realities of the period: the extreme sophistication of the fashion codes and, in an apparent paradox, the slow democratization of haute couture by means of these items that were less expensive but much more profitable than the actual clothing.

FASHION CODES

Accessories must follow the general evolution of fashion. Thus hats and even sunglasses display the furs or feathers of the day, be it black or white monkey, ermine, fox, or cockerel. But an accessory must also have its own personality, and there was a hierarchy of style among milliners just like that governing couture. The importance of houses like Caroline Reboux, Lewis, Mme Agnès, Jeanne Blanchot, and Gaby Mono can hardly be exaggerated, as couturier Maggy Rouff recalled in her memoirs: "Thanks to the natural specialization of the milliners, a single fashion provided an infinite range appropriate for every face and every kind of woman, according to her taste. Thanks to them, every woman could be fashionably coifed without sacrificing any aspect of her character, her taste, her personal inclinations, and–if it is necessary to go so far–without having to disavow anything, or to renounce any part of herself. Glamorous hats from Reboux, hats both classy and unique from Suzy, exotic turbans from Maria Guy, inimitably smart felt sports hats from Rose Descat, delightful whimsicalities by Albouy, inspired brilliance by Agnès ... and finally Mme Legroux, that poet whose hats pass through her hands to take on some subtle enchantment–what a romantic, moving dream! Seeing these, you could believe you were reading verses by the Countess of Noailles."[46]

First Jeanne Lanvin and then Chanel began as milliners. Great couture houses recommended their own hats–Schiaparelli, Lanvin, and Patou, for example–or even forged privileged bonds with milliners, such as Madeleine Vionnet and Caroline Reboux.[47]

The spectacular evolution of women's clothing between 1910 and 1940 was accompanied by that of the hat. After reaching an irrational width prior to 1914, during the 1920s it evolved into the cloche, the cap, and the close-fitting beret, changes related to the trend toward short, straight hairstyles. In the 1930s, the vogue for skillfully waved and crimped hair knocked the hat backwards, or tilted it to the side, which allowed it to take on particularly daring and occasionally even highly eccentric forms in 1938 and 1939.

Every season, different materials for the hat itself would appear, or reappear—felt, velvet, velours, straw, horse hair, tulle, draped fabric, etc.—along with new inventions in the trims—flowers, fruits, feathers, bird wings, complete birds, furs, cockades, buttons, drapes, knots, frills, ribbons, veils, and matching scarves—that were made marvelously clear in large photographic prints.

While granting that milliners were almost the equals of the couturiers, their leather creations, such as bags, gloves, and shoes, seem rather more subordinate to the general line. The names of great houses are far fewer: Henry a La Pensée for handbags, gloves, and sunglasses; Édith for coordinating handbags and shoes; and Alexandrine for gloves. These accessories were highly codified and their choice very much dependent on the outfit as a whole. Even so, novelty handbags begin to appear, for example fish, plush animals, and clock faces in the spirit of the designs developed by Schiaparelli.

The magazines that peremptorily decreed what should be worn outlined precisely which outfits were suitable for each moment of the day and for every social and fashionable function; and for every gown or suit, there was a matching bag, shoes, and gloves. It was only grudgingly allowed, as a concession to the faster pace of modern women's lives, that the same items could be worn with different clothing.

Although the Séebergers present fewer examples of these, the changes in this field are perfectly visible even if they are seldom the intended subject of particular shots: the shorter skirt and finer stockings that emphasized the multi-strapped shoes known as cothurnes in 1920 were followed by bobbin heels, and finally slip-on pumps. Summer shoes were more varied and casual, including the espadrille borrowed from traditional Basque costume[48] and sandals—open-toed shoes (not unconnected to the invention of nail polish in the mid 1930s)—but the true revolution was the platform sole launched in 1936 by Ferragamo and reproduced by all shoemakers the following year.

The photographers caught new feminine gestures in action: the use of powder compacts for touching up in public, the cigarette, and sunglasses worn in summer or in the mountains in winter (these appeared sporadically in the mid 1930s, but became thoroughly fashionable in 1939). Certain status objects also appeared, including a photographic apparatus casually balanced on a manicured hand: little movie cameras that were taken to the beach.

ACCESSORIES BY COUTURIERS

Haute couture, now more familiar thanks to illustrated magazines, cinema, the stage, and advertising, began to create items worn or carried by a larger clientele than could afford their clothing. Many great houses grasped the extraordinary importance of accessories for the financial prosperity of their businesses. In the early 1920s, Jean Patou invented what he called *les riens*, "little nothings," a clever way of suggesting that, on the contrary, they were everything: scarves, gloves, bags, and perfumes all matched the clothing of the brand. In 1922, Patou first had the idea of affixing his own monogram to his line of sport clothes—an idea that was quickly taken up by Chanel and Hermès. While up to that point the customer had marked her linens or luggage with her own name, a discreet and useful sign of ownership, it became more stylish to display that of the supplier—whose label even became a status symbol.

The first couturier perfumes were another Poiret innovation. He launched his own line in 1911 under the name of his daughter, Rosine; Chanel followed in 1921 with N° 5 in a bottle that was as revolutionary as her clothing. Patou unveiled Amour Amour in 1925 and his signature fragrance, Joy, in 1930. Also in 1925, Jeanne Lanvin offered the evocative My Sin, and Arpège in 1927 (its black spherical bottle with a gilt figure of mother and daughter created by Albert Rateau and Paul Iribe remains a masterpiece of the genre). More provocative was the bottle for Shocking, in the form of a bust, released by Schiaparelli in 1938. These creations were closely linked to the style of each house, and helped disseminate their spirit. They remain the best example of couture accessories.

Alongside the designers of fine jewelry, couturier fashion jewelry appeared. Chanel launched costume jewelry, flashy and showy, the epitomy of chic—especially when combined with genuine jewels—and Elsa Schiaparelli, with the aid of artists like Dalí and Giacometti, created jewelry in which her designer Jean Schlumberger used unexpected combinations of materials, such as plastic and metal or porcelain.

For the neophyte who finds the subtlety of drape or the imperceptible shortening of a hem as dry as dust, these refinements of detail—that go so far as to match a dog to a dress—are certainly the most enjoyable way to grasp the vagaries of fashion.

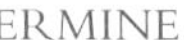

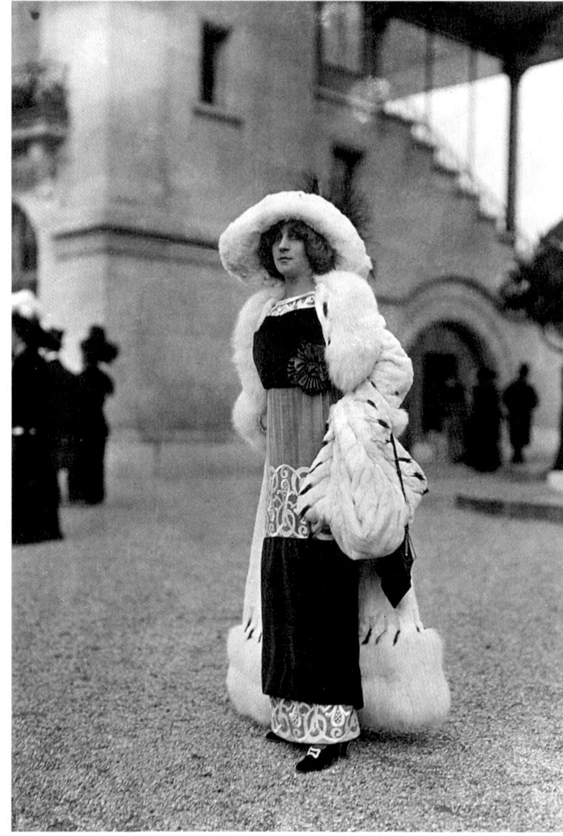

Liane de Lancy, with ermine trimmings, autumn 1909.

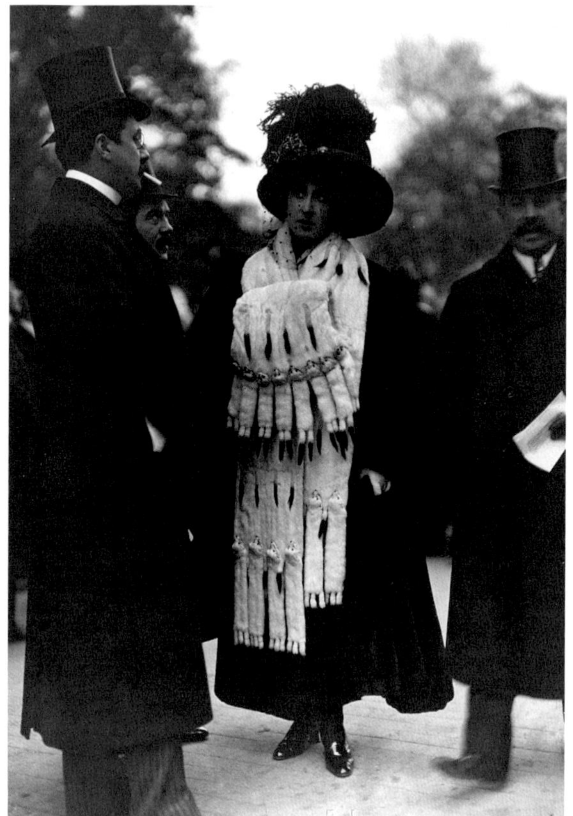

At the races, autumn 1909.

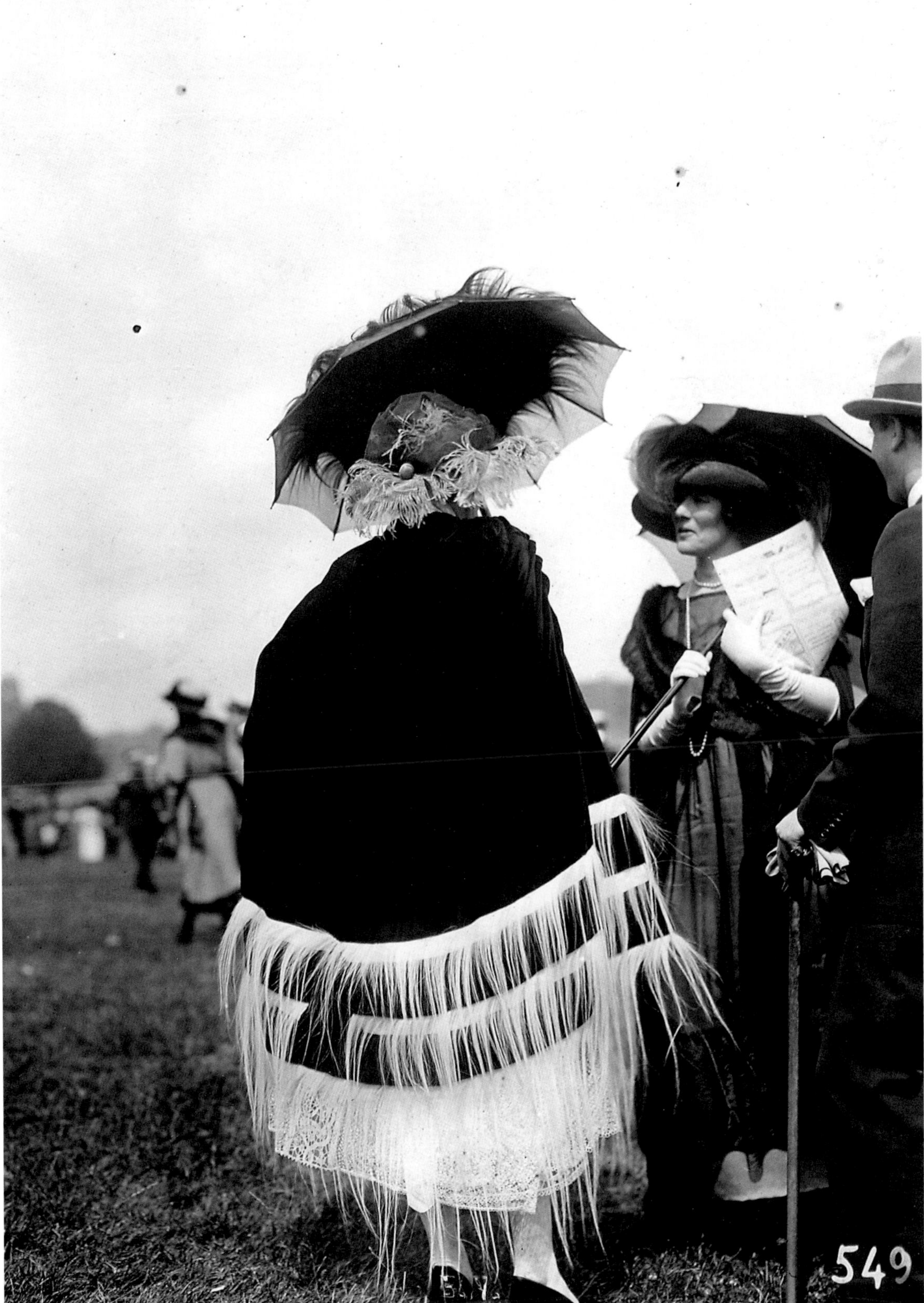

Callot cape, trimmed with white monkey fur, Auteuil, Grande Steeple-Chase, 1919.

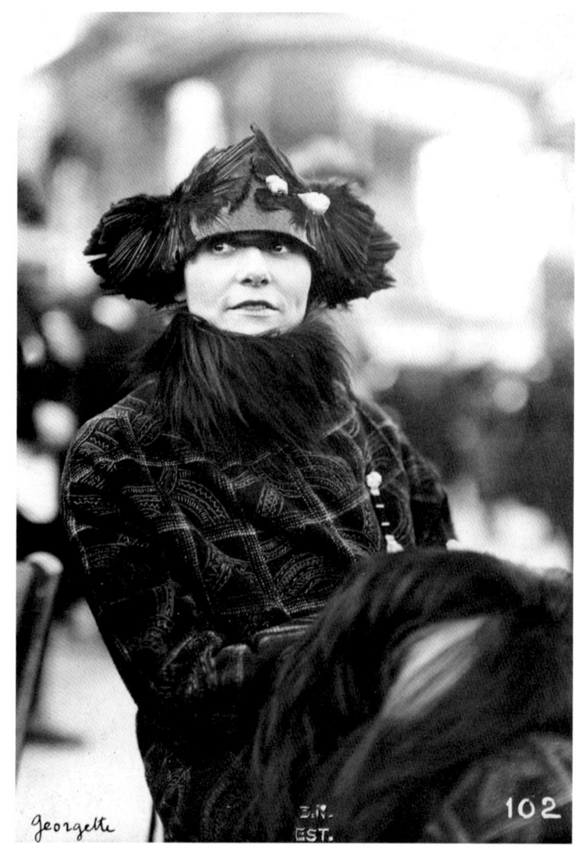

Seated woman outfitted by Georgette, coat trimmed with monkey fur, Bois de Boulogne, 1920.

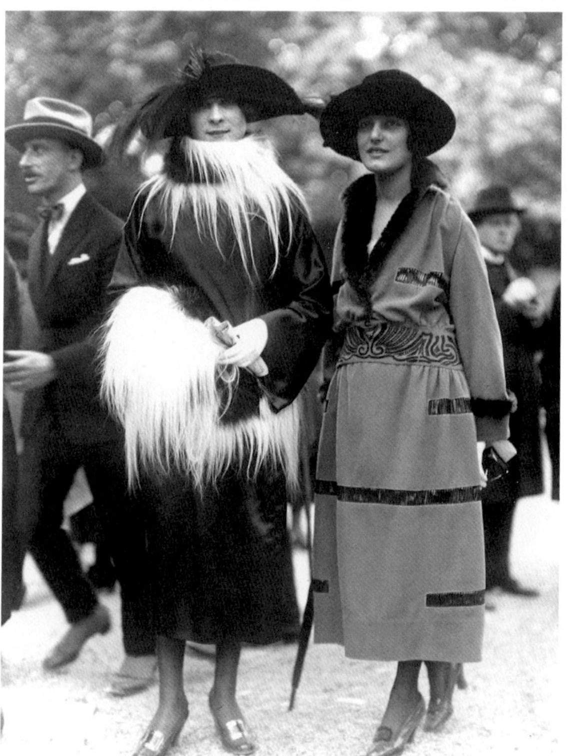

Juliette Courtisien coat, trim and cuffs of white monkey fur, Longchamp, Prix d'Arc de Triomphe, October 3, 1920.

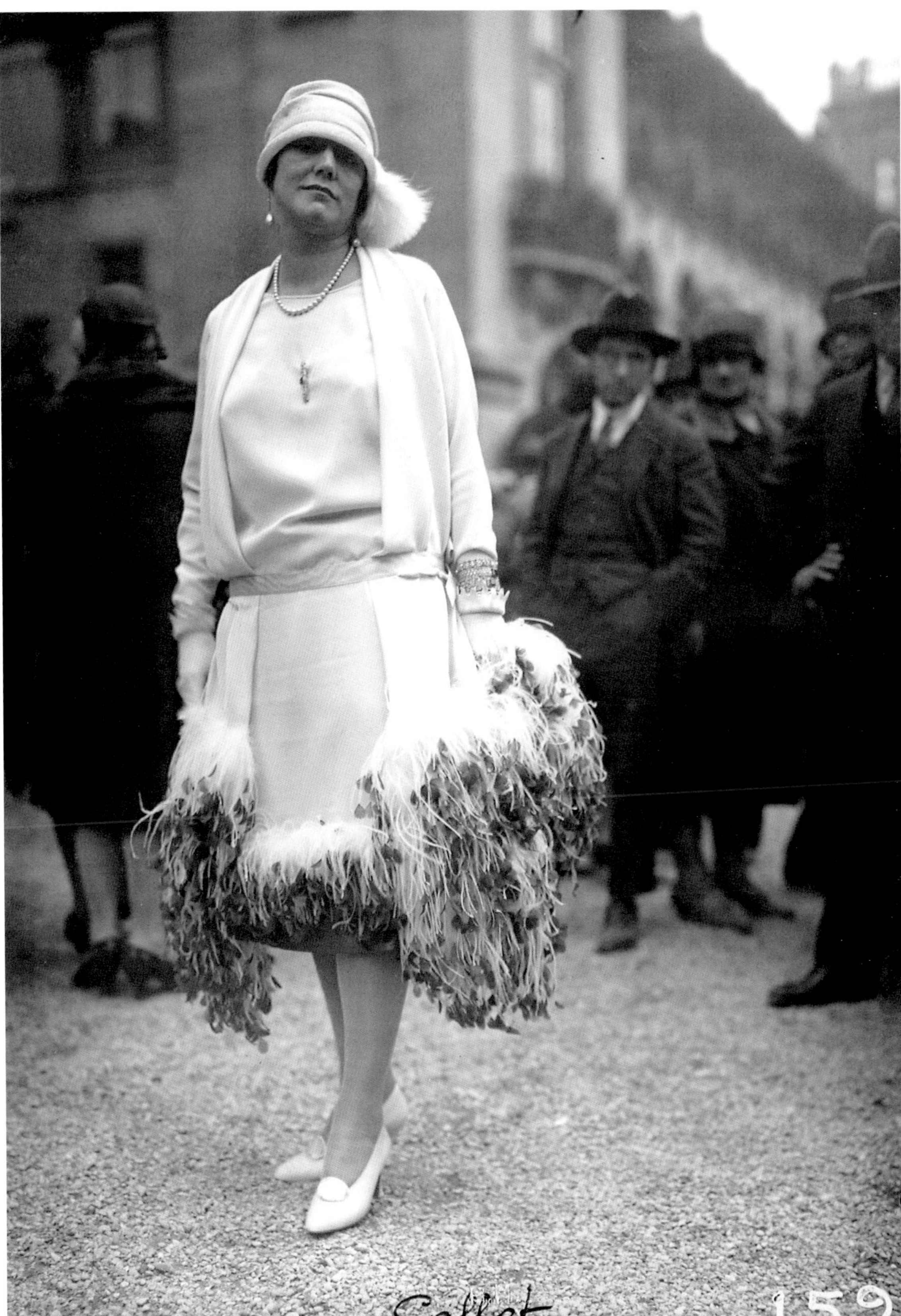

Callot outfit trimmed with feathers, Grand Prix de Longchamp, June 1926.

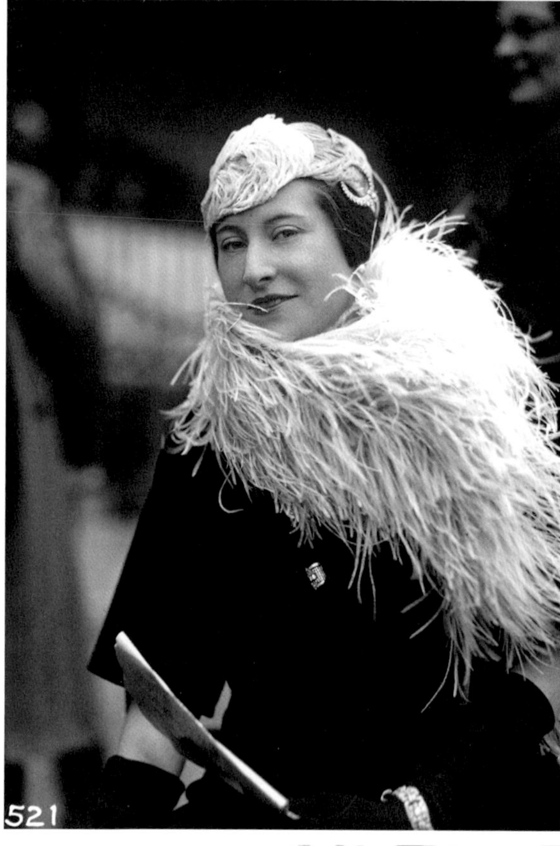

Adry de Carbuccia, née Turpin-Rotival, wearing a hat by Caroline Reboux with a matching feather boa, Chantilly, Couturier, June 5, 1932. Wife of Horace de Carbuccia, director of the daily Gringoire *and Deputy of Corsica, through her mother's second marriage, she was also daughter-in-law to the Chief of Police in Chiappe.*

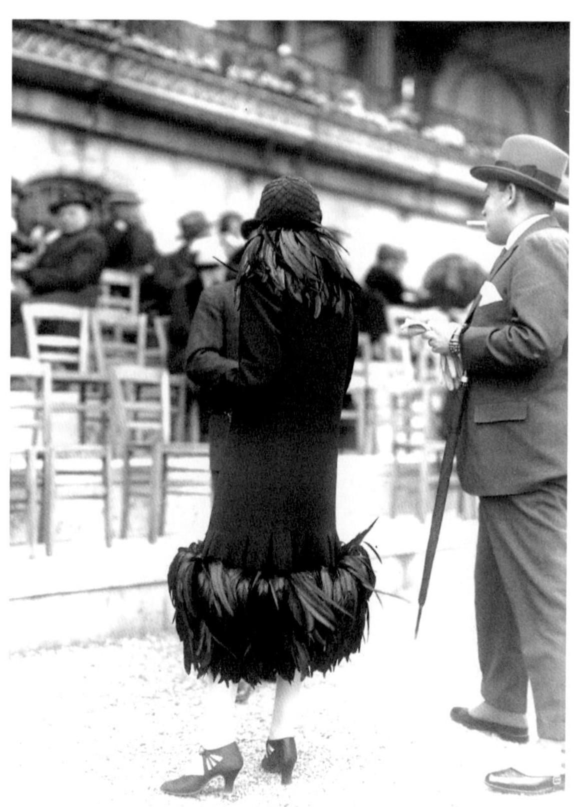

Hat and coat trimmed with cockerel feathers, at the races, 1925.

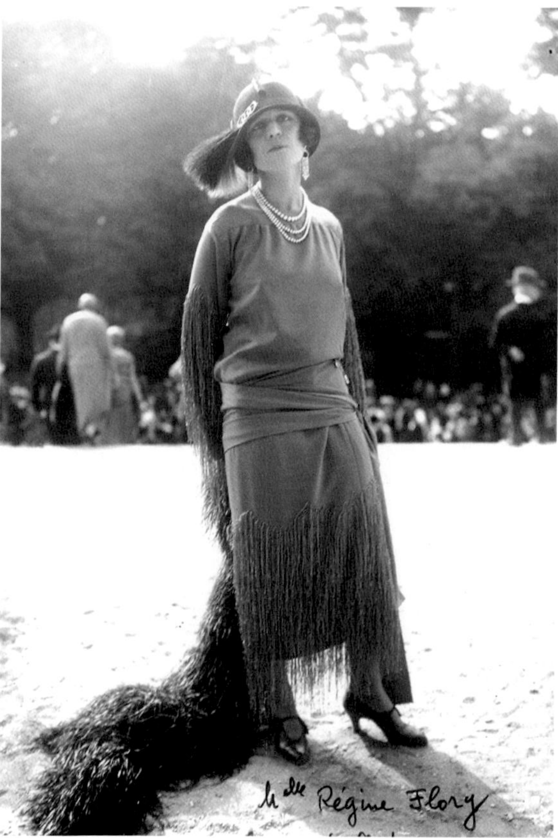

Régine Flory (1892–1926), née Marie-Louise Artaz, a music-hall dancer, wearing a Callot gown and feather boa, Auteuil, the Drags course, June 27, 1924.

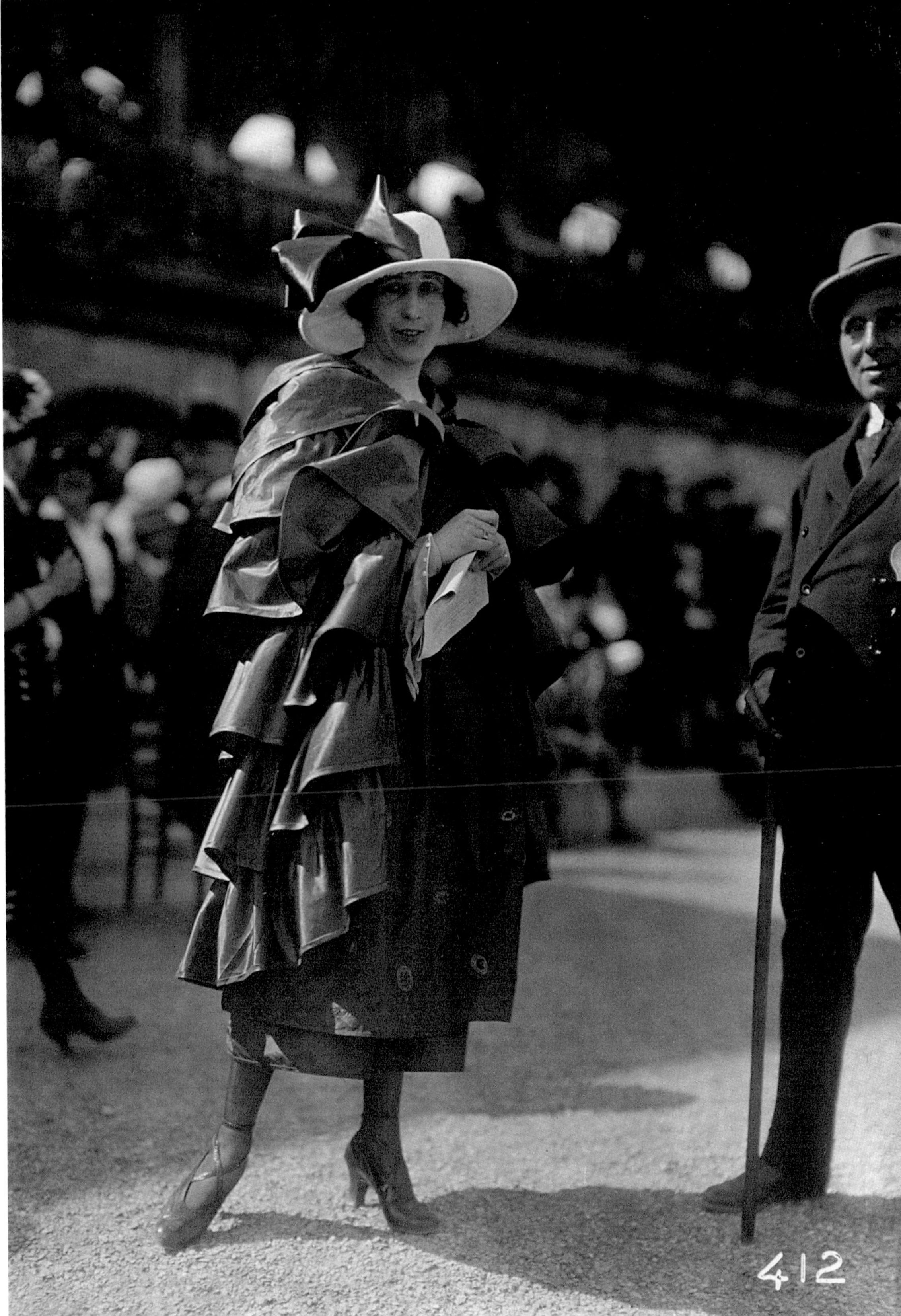

Tiered cape, Longchamp, May 23, 1920.

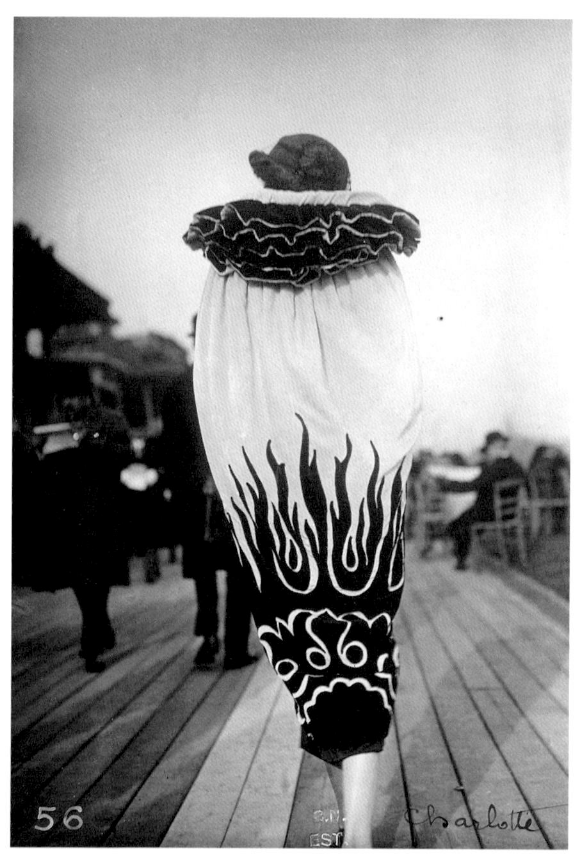

Charlotte cape, worn by Laure Jarny, Auteuil, February 20, 1921.

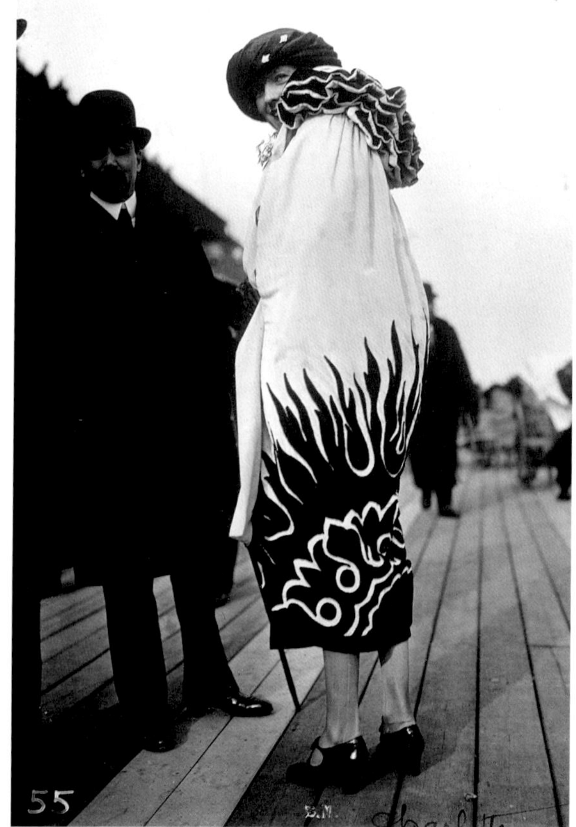

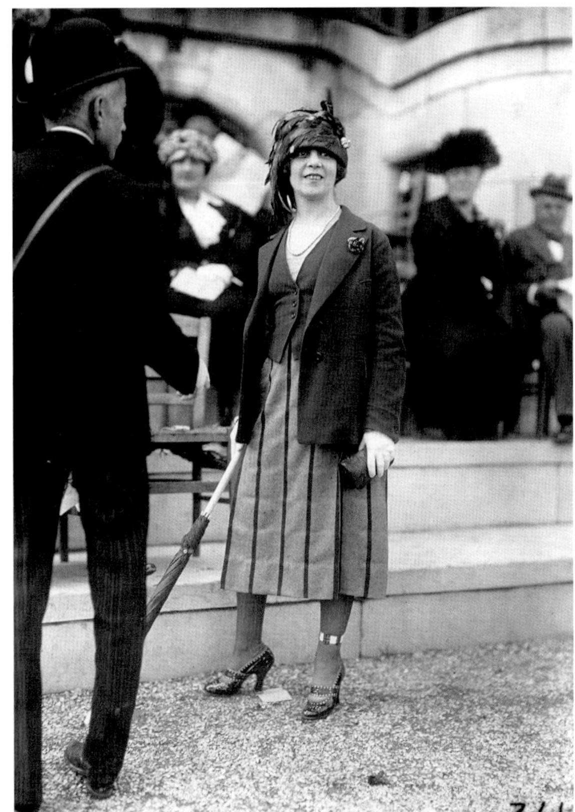

Longchamp, May 2, 1920.

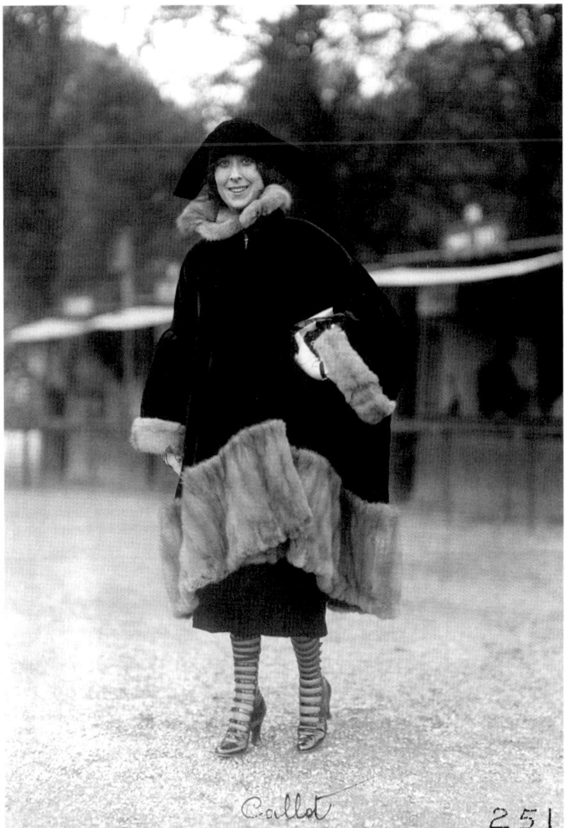

Callot coat, shoes with straps extending halfway up the calf, Longchamp, October 24, 1920.

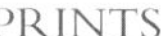

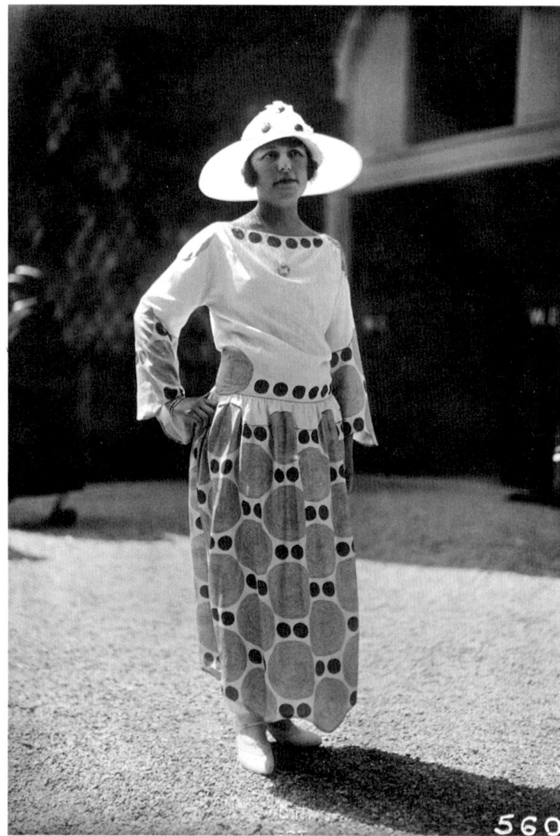

Chantilly, Prix du Jockey-Club, June 11, 1922.

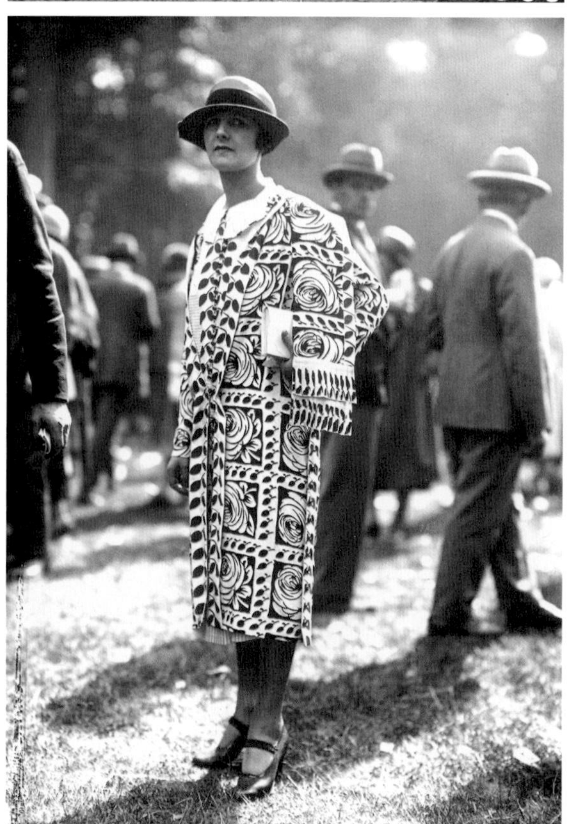

At the races, 1925.

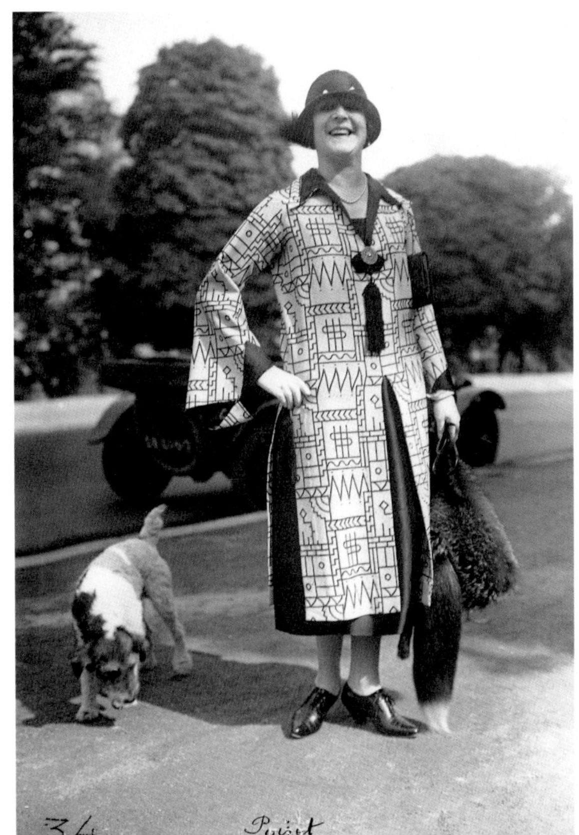

Poiret dress, Longchamp, September 1924.

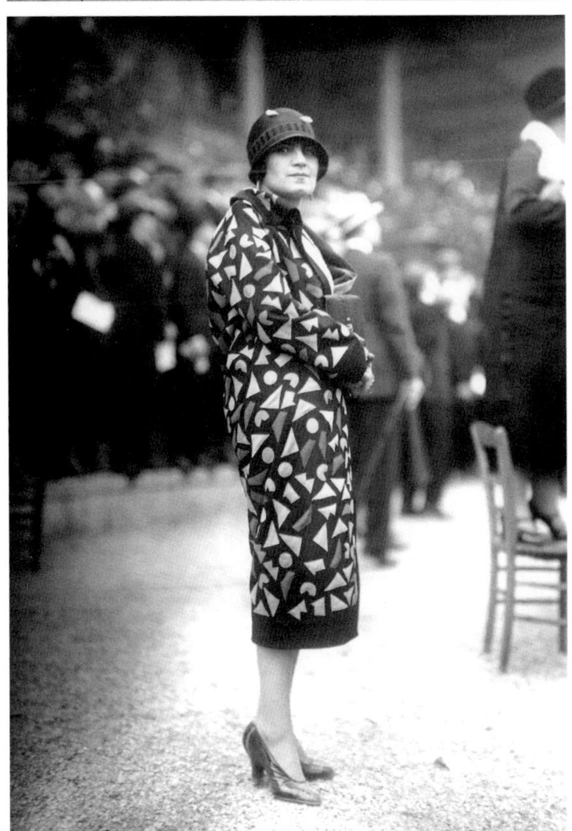

September 1925, at the races.

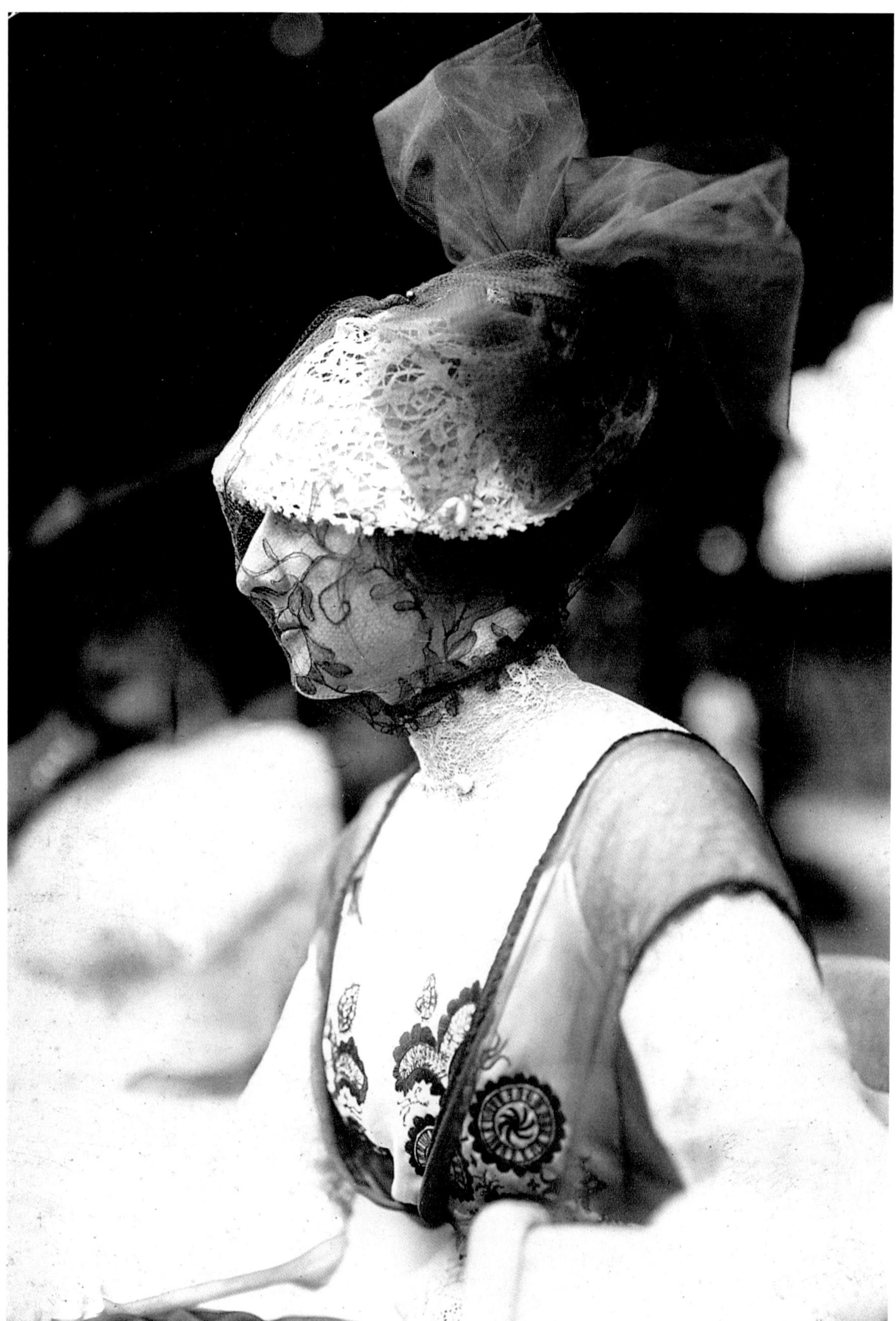

Deauville, 1912.

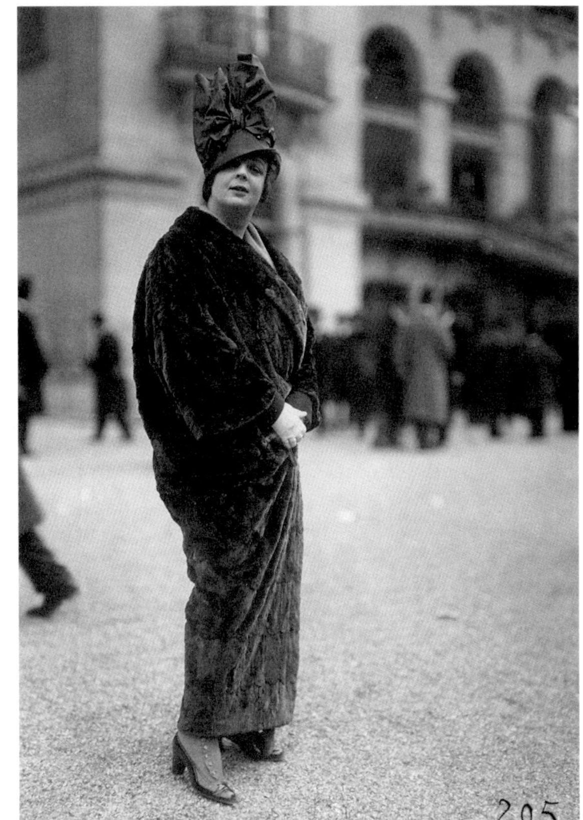

Spring 1913.

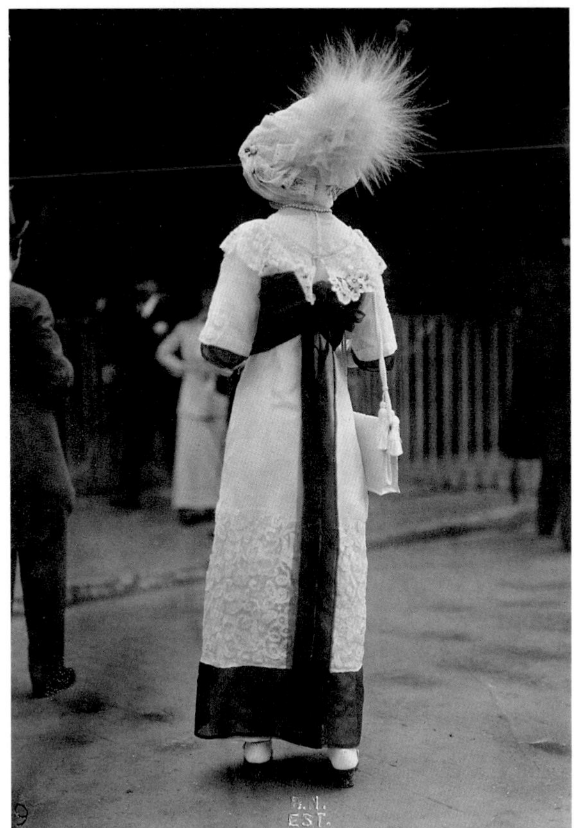

Drags Day, Auteuil, 1911.

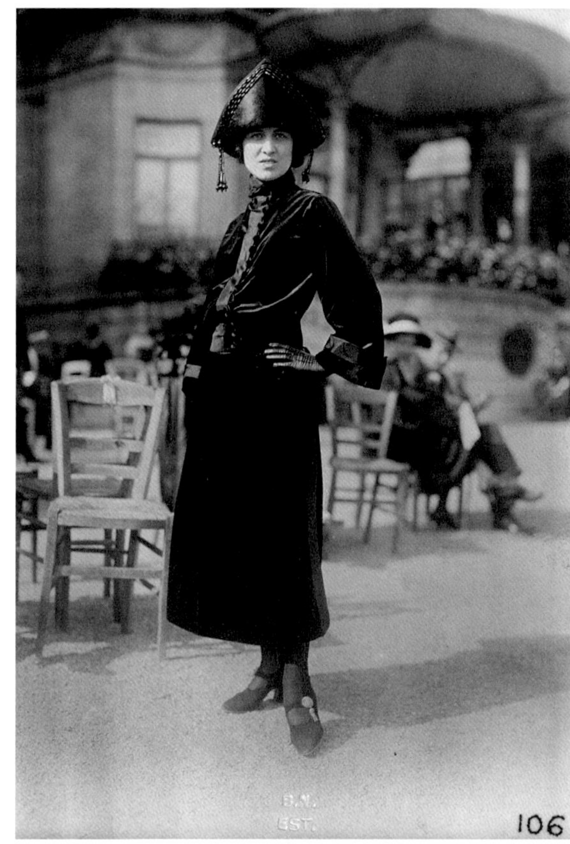

Longchamp, September 25, 1921.

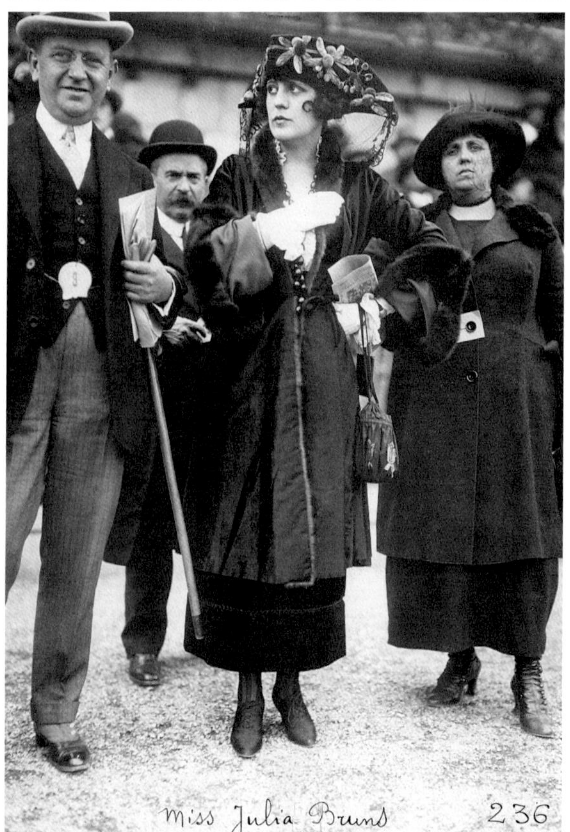

Julia Bruns, Atlantic City beauty queen, at the races in October 1919.

Gaby Mono hat,
Deauville, August 1926.

Jean Patou hat,
Longchamp,
April 21, 1929.

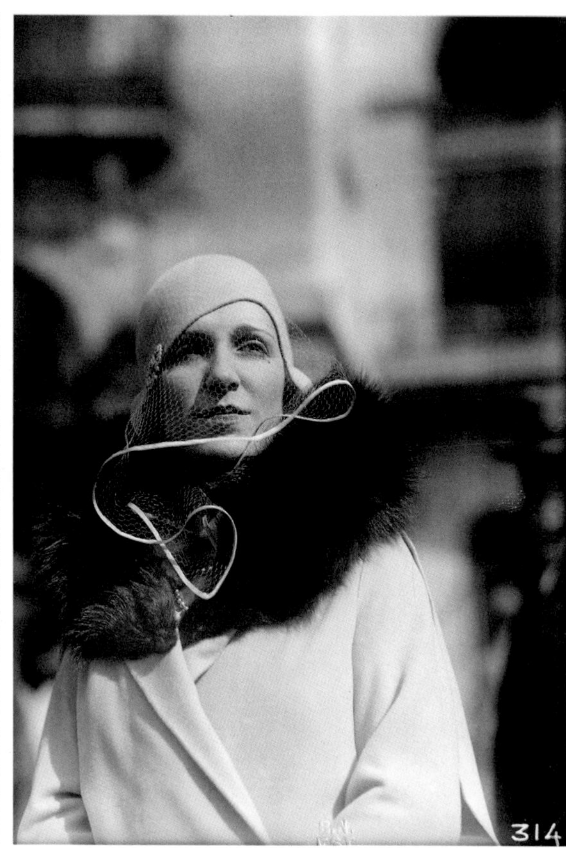

Gaby Mono hat,
Touquet, Grand Prix,
July 31, 1927.

Caroline Reboux hat,
Auteuil, March 4, 1928.

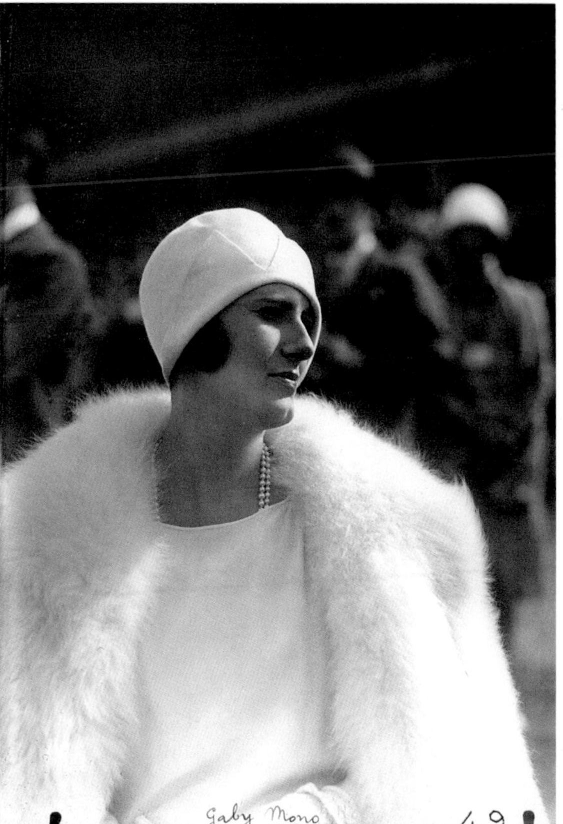

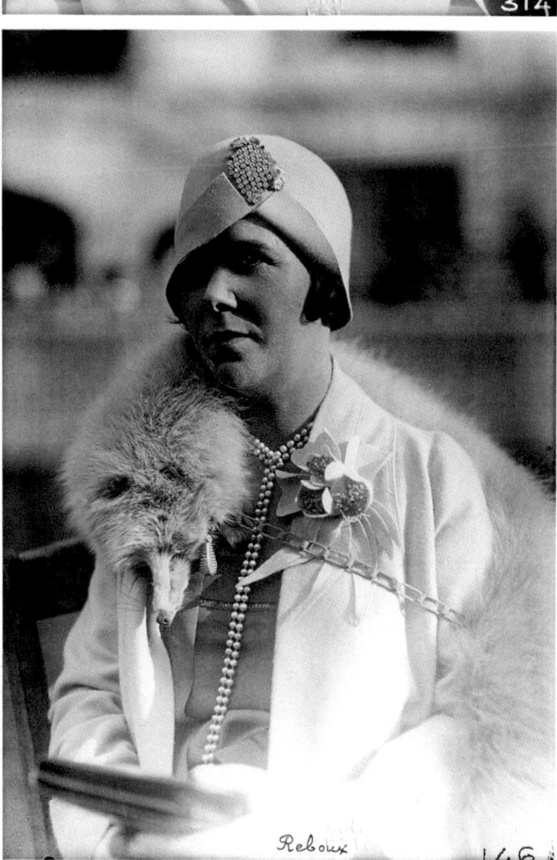

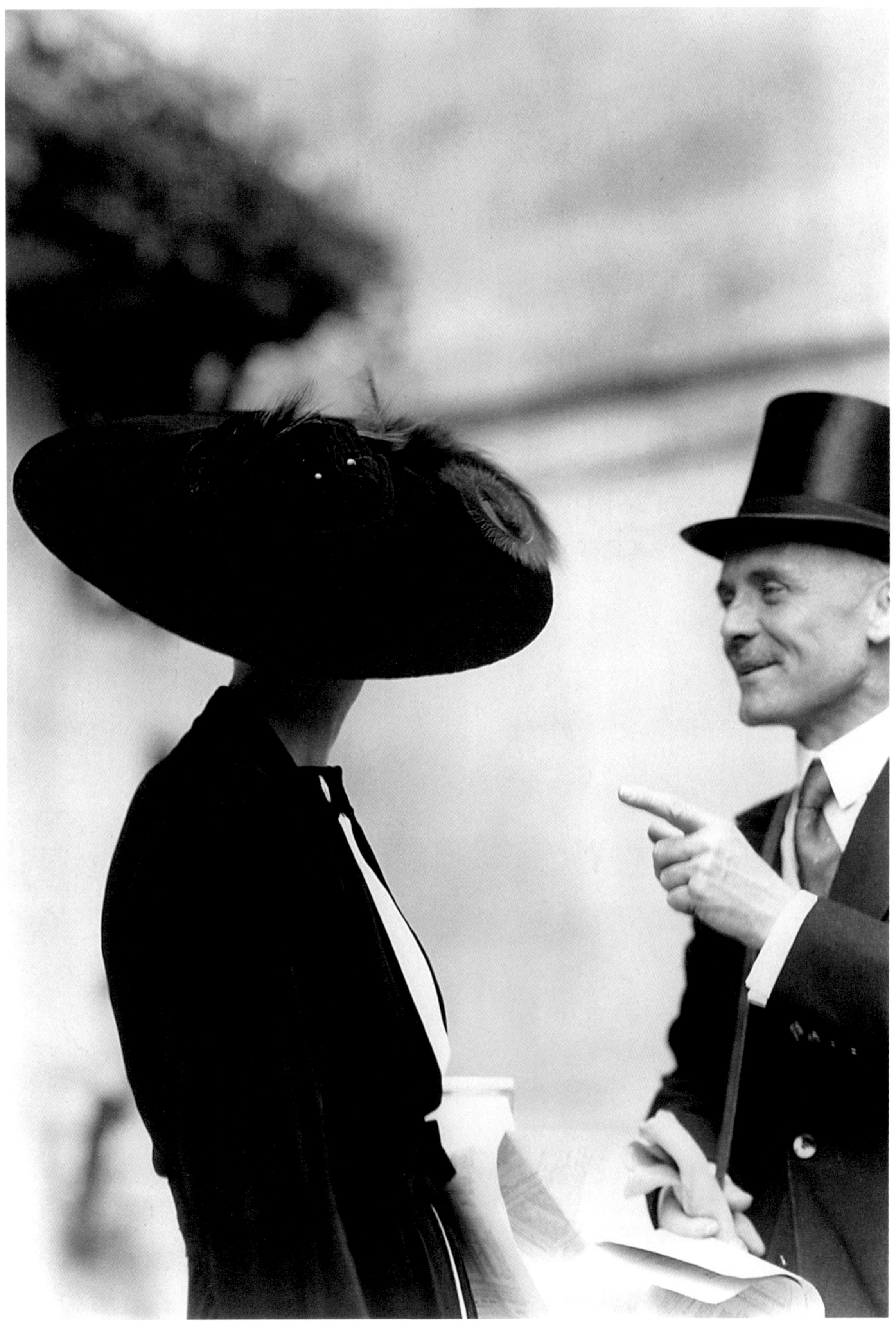

*Countess Élie de Ganay,
née Nadège de Fontenay,
wearing Worth,
Grand Prix de Longchamp,
June 24, 1934.*

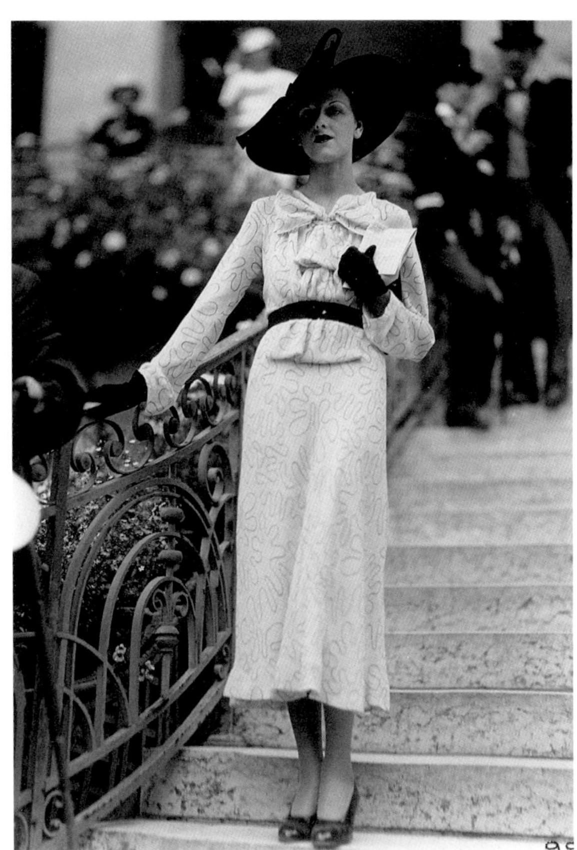

Countess Alain de la Falaise in Schiaparelli, wearing a hat by Suzanne Talbot, Grand Prix de Longchamp, June 24, 1934.

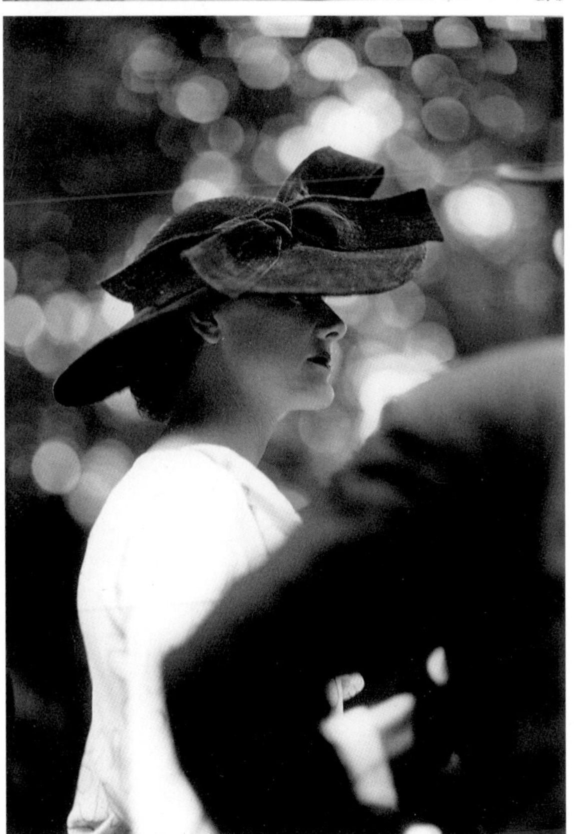

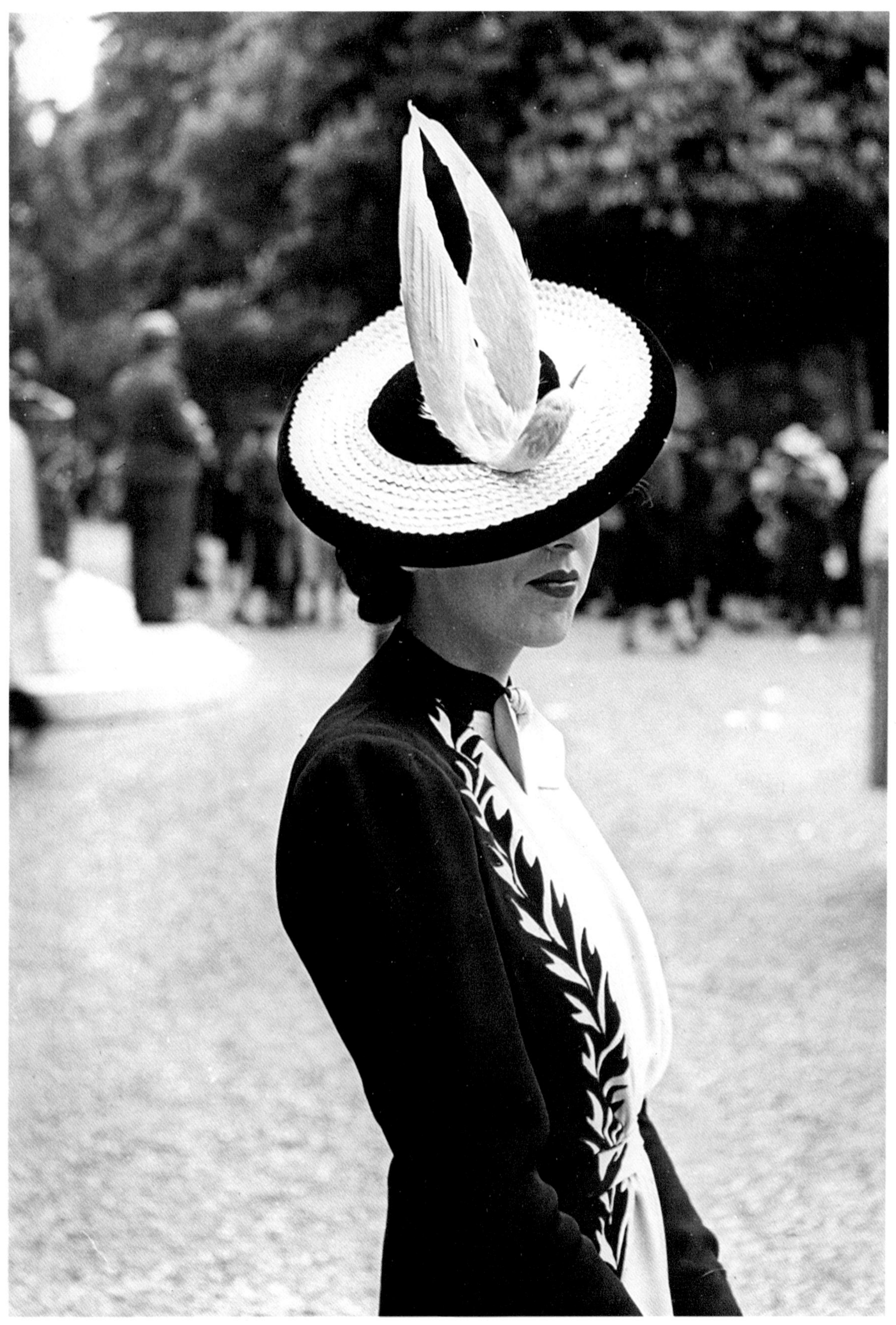

Christina Claudel, née Diplarakos, wearing a dress by Gaston and a hat by Braagaard, Longchamp, May 15, 1938.

Mme Revenga wearing a dress by Marcel Rochas and a hat by Schiaparelli, Longchamp, May 21, 1939.

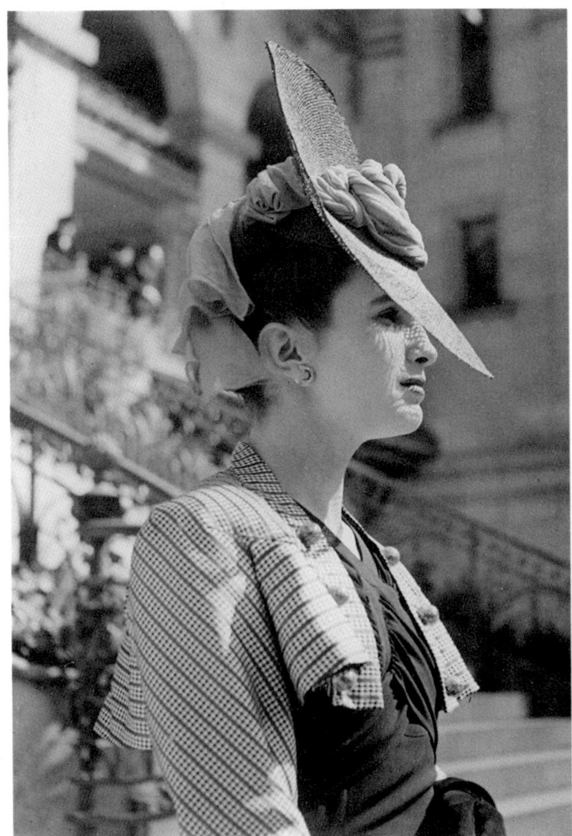

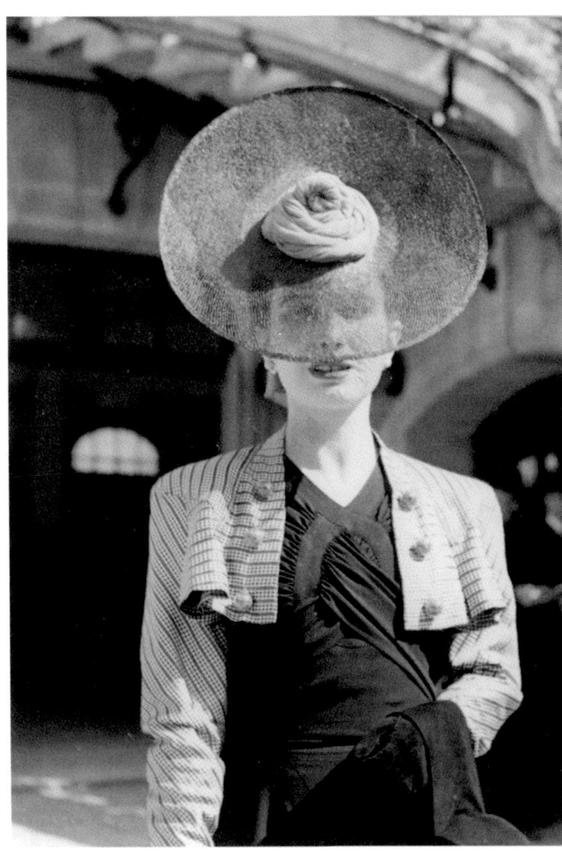

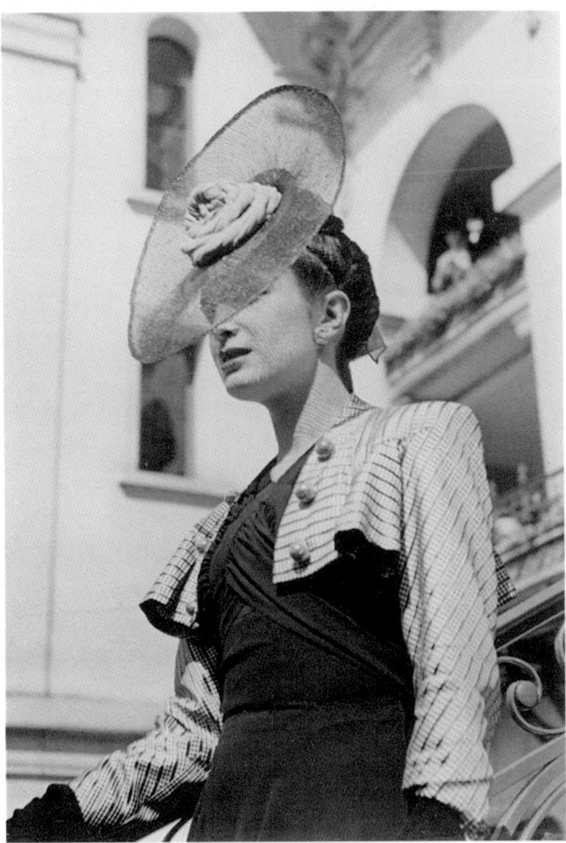

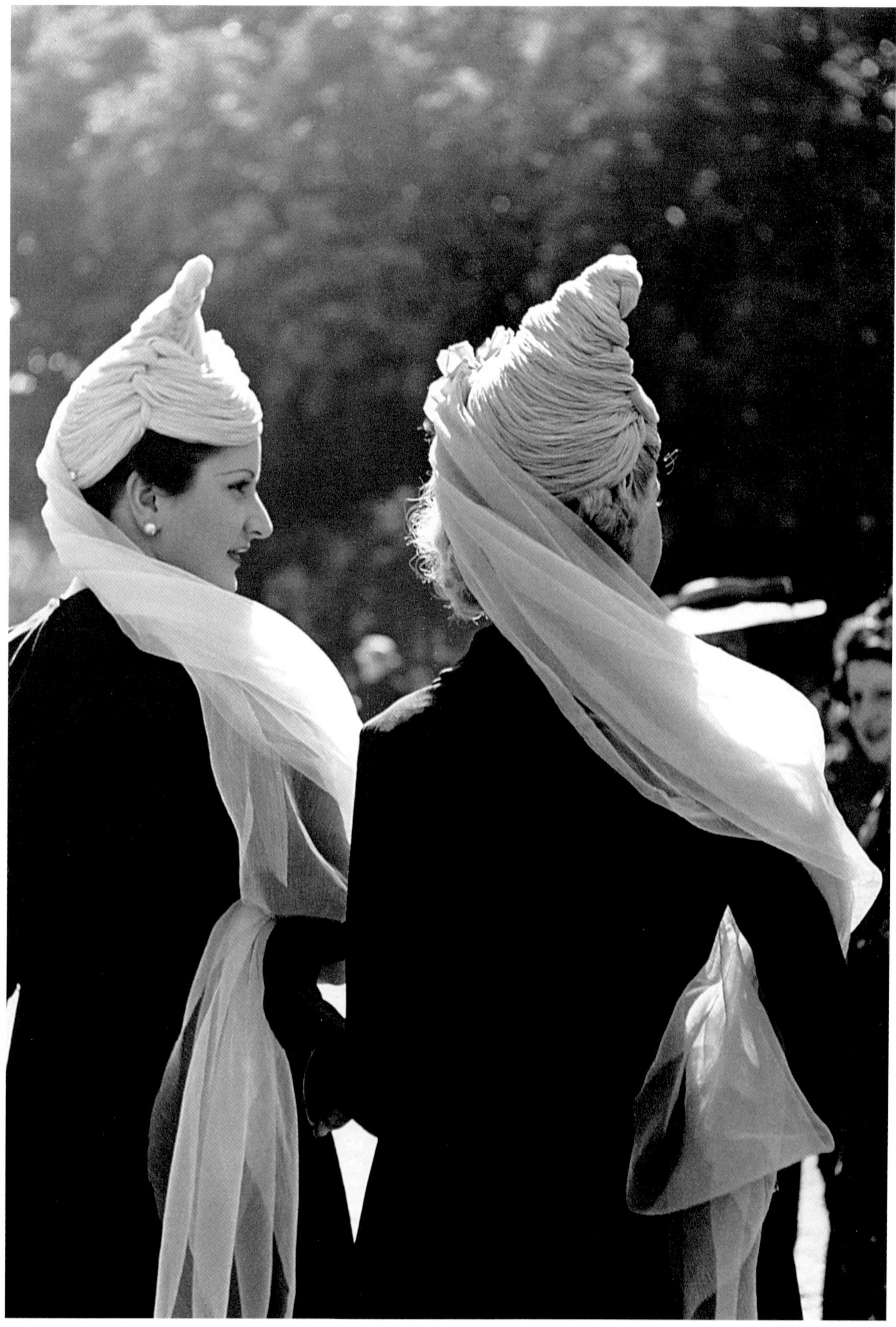

Turban model "Idole" by Agnès, Grande Course des Haies, Auteuil, June 22, 1938.

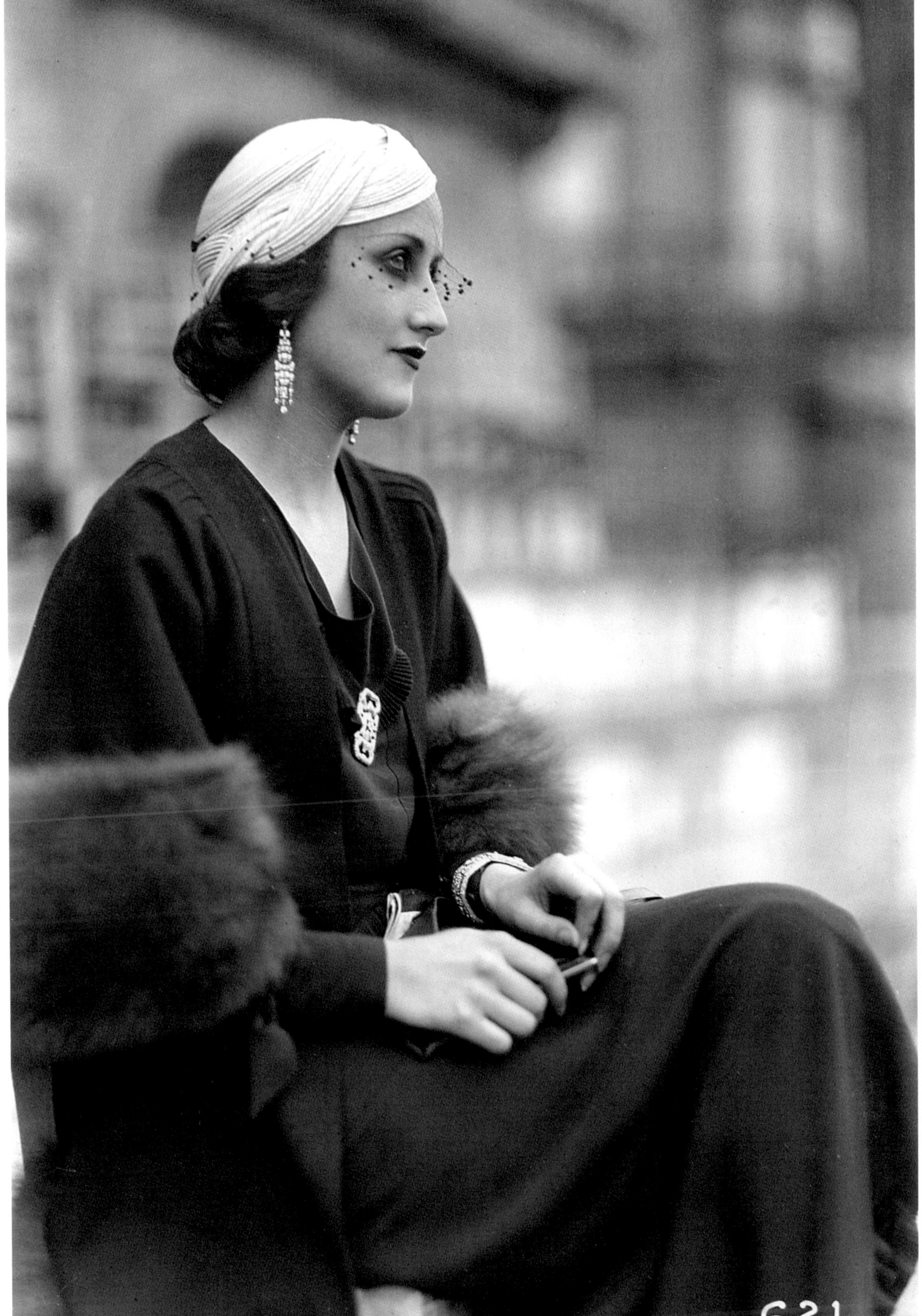

Hat by Gyne, Longchamp,
May 14, 1933.

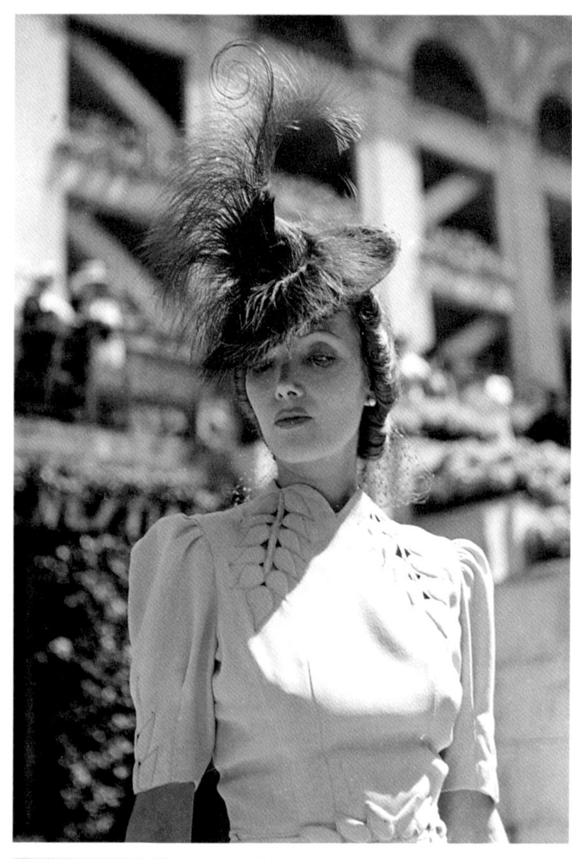

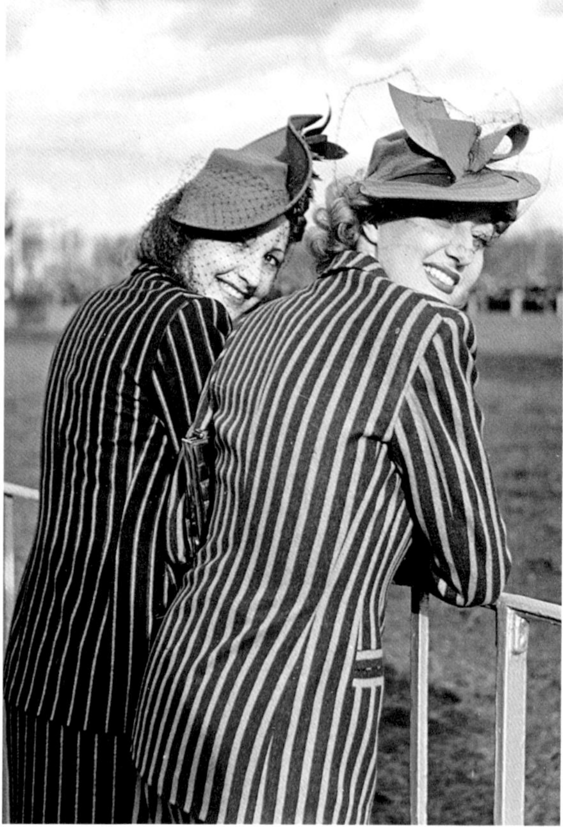

Dress by Émilienne Manassé, hat by Annette Daumont, Auteuil, Drags Day, June 23, 1939.

Striped suits by Freddy, hats by Louise Bourbon, Auteuil, March 5, 1939.

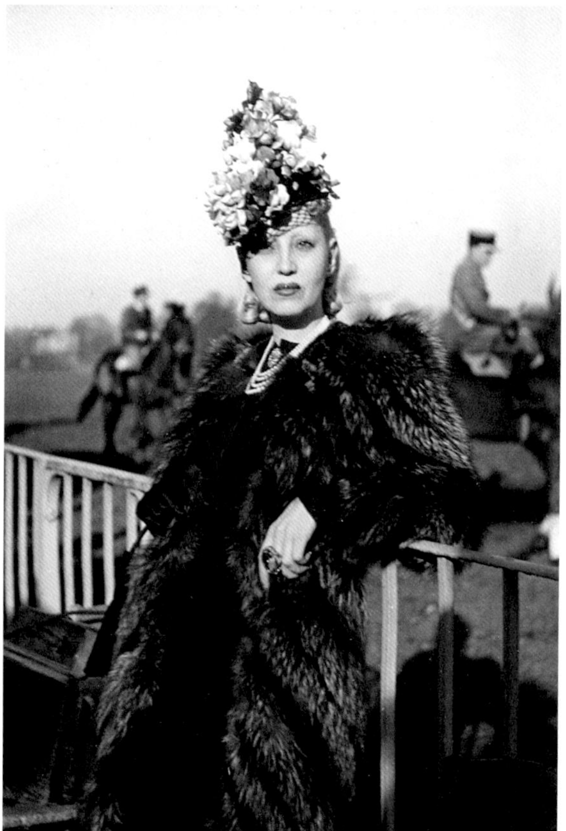

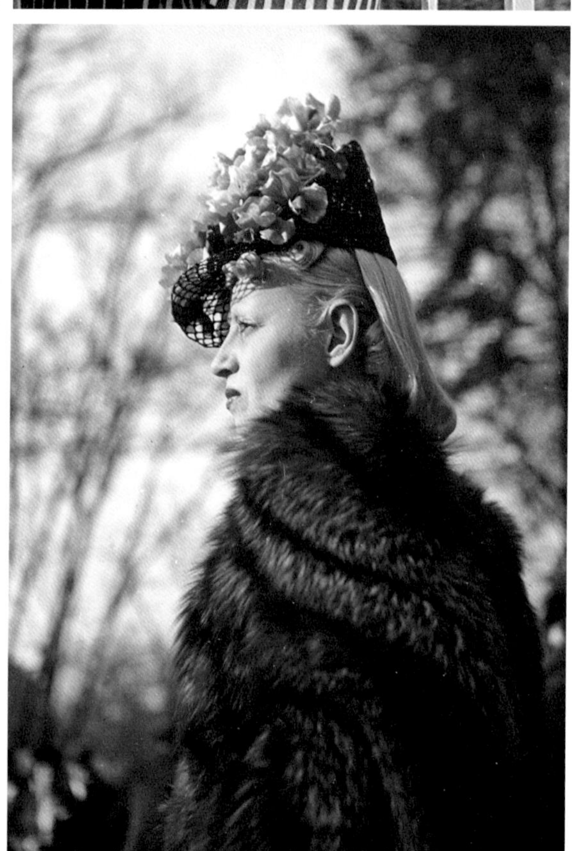

Hat by Dunton, Auteuil, Prix Murat, March 20, 1938.

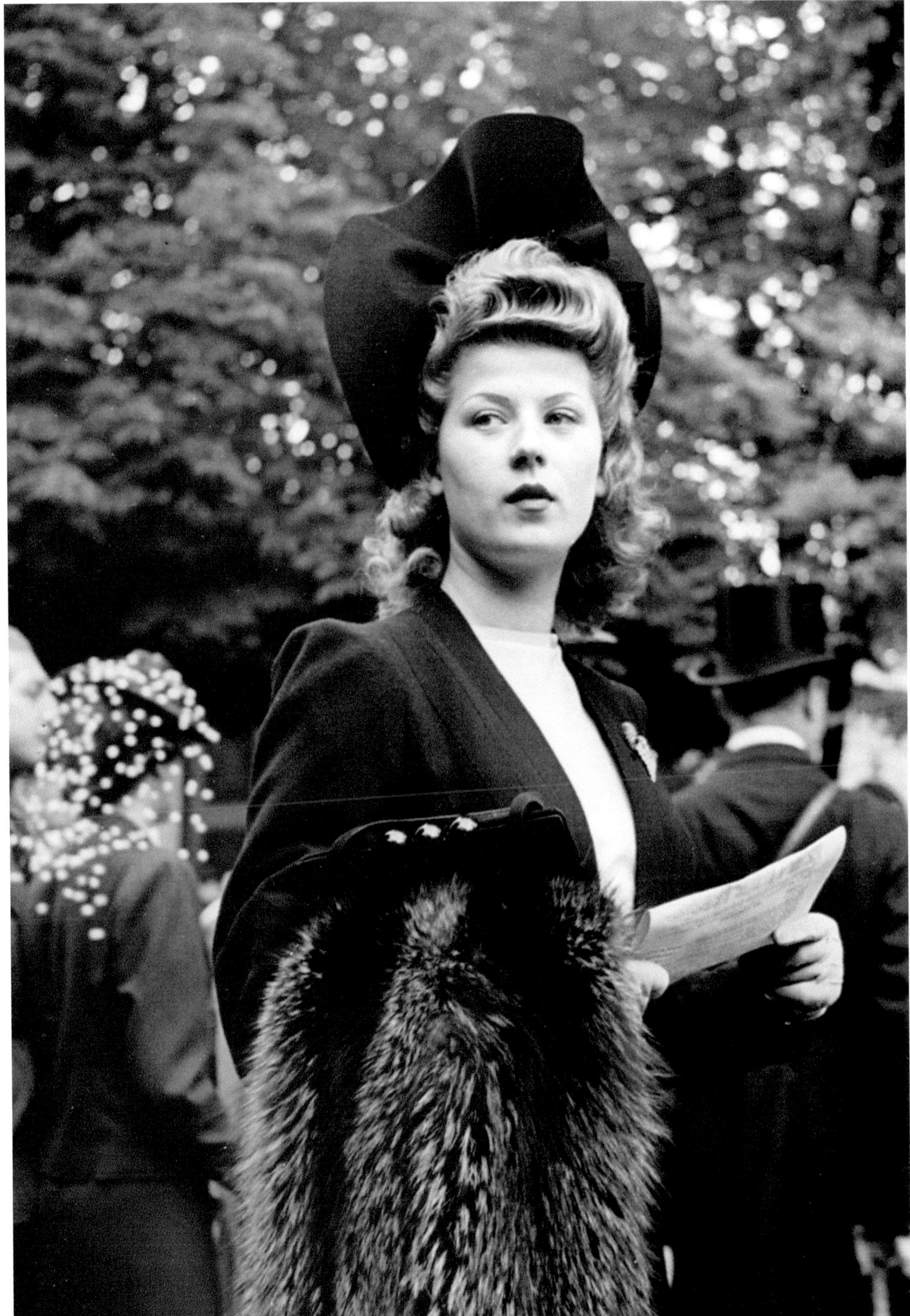

Hat by Rose Valois, Longchamp, Grand Prix, June 25, 1939.

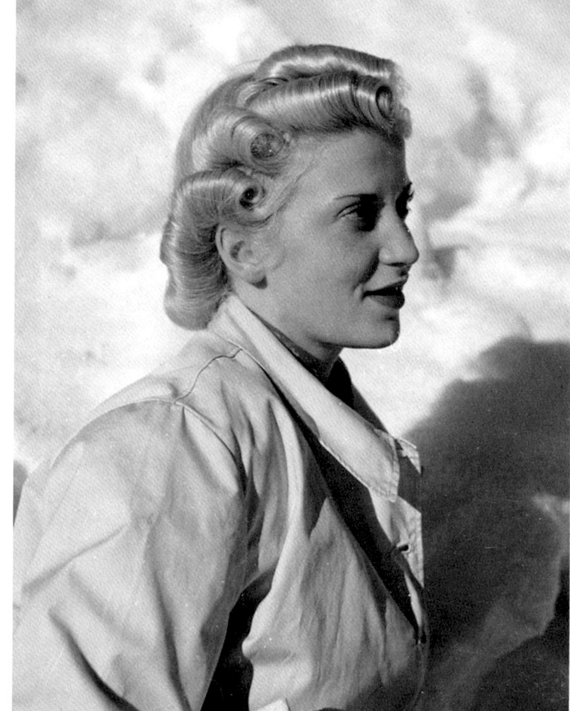

Saint-Moritz, New Year's Eve celebration, 1937/38.

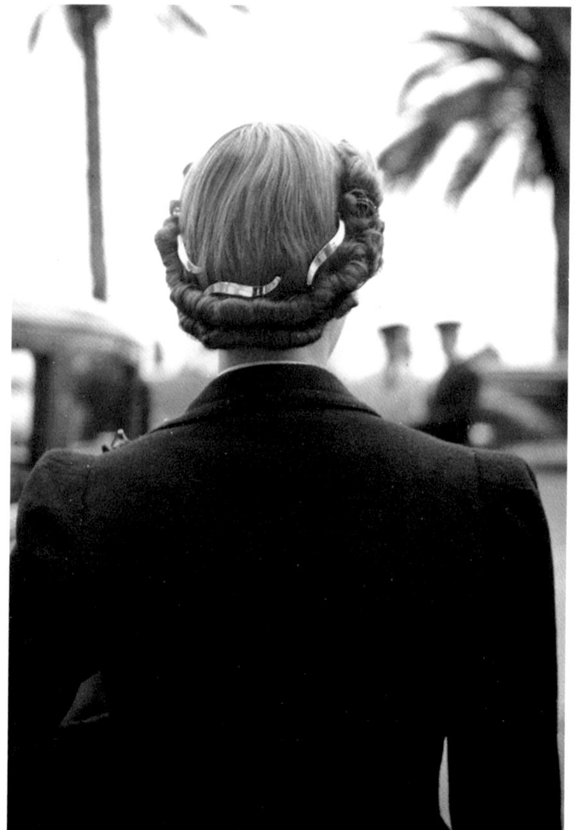

M[me] Arpels seen from behind, with combs by the jeweler Van Cleef & Arpels in her hair, Cannes, Easter, 1937.

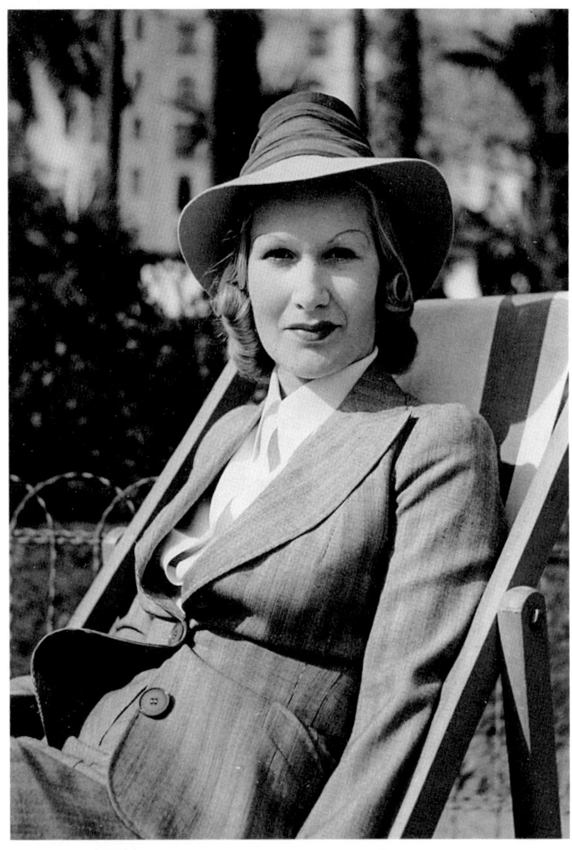

Magda Belmont, film actress, wearing a Jean Patou suit, hat by Maria Guy and hairstyle by Claude, Cannes, April 1938.

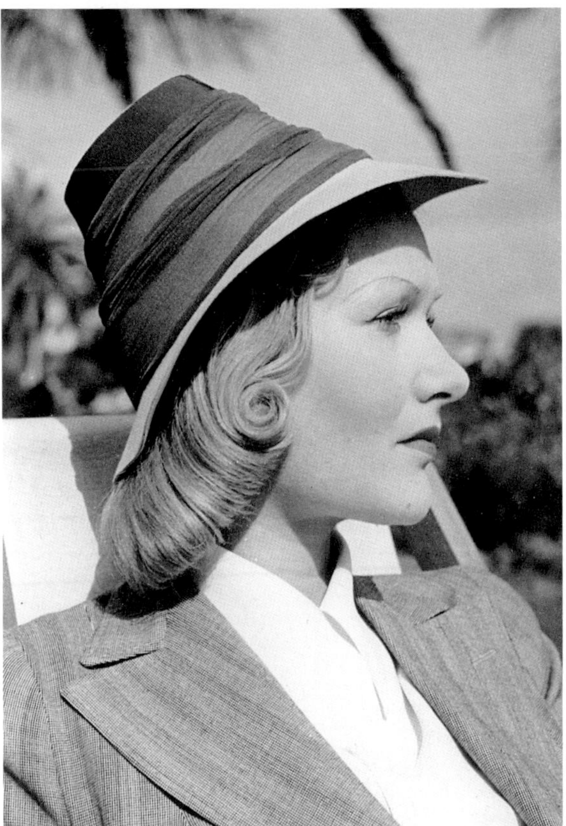

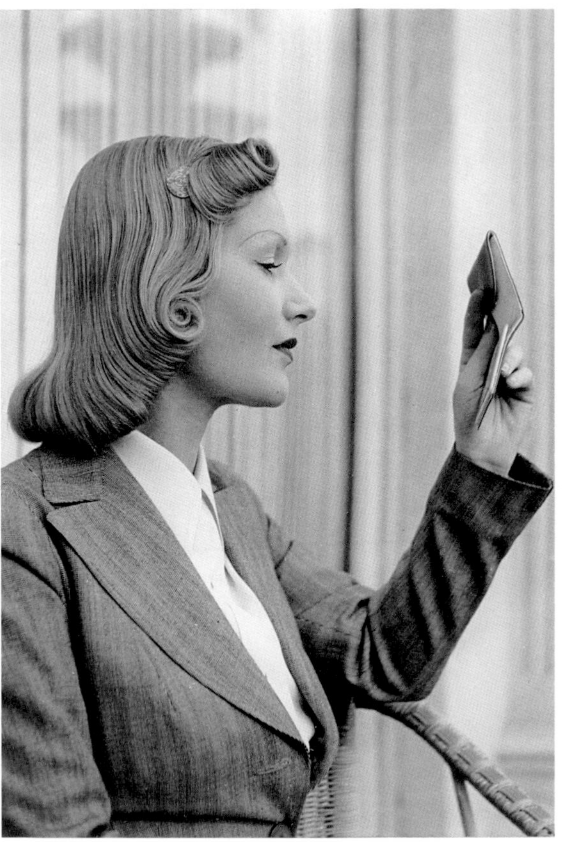

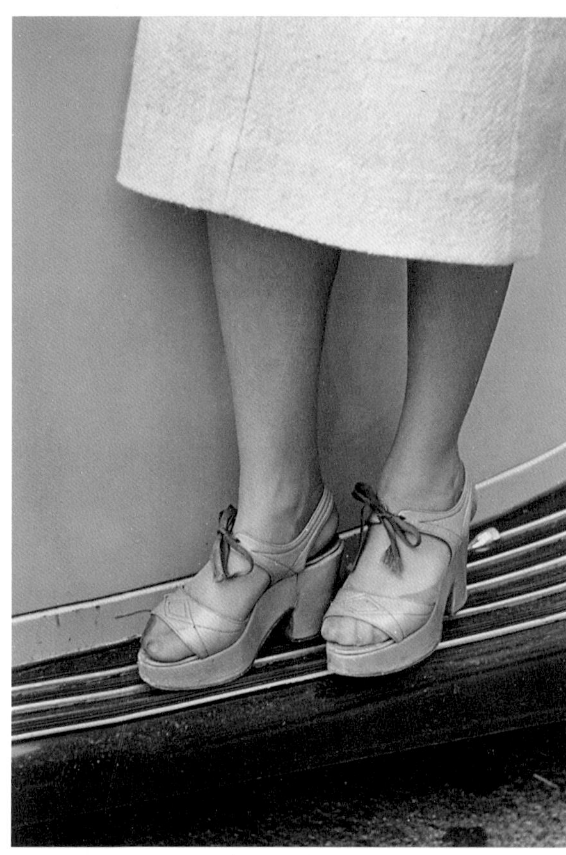

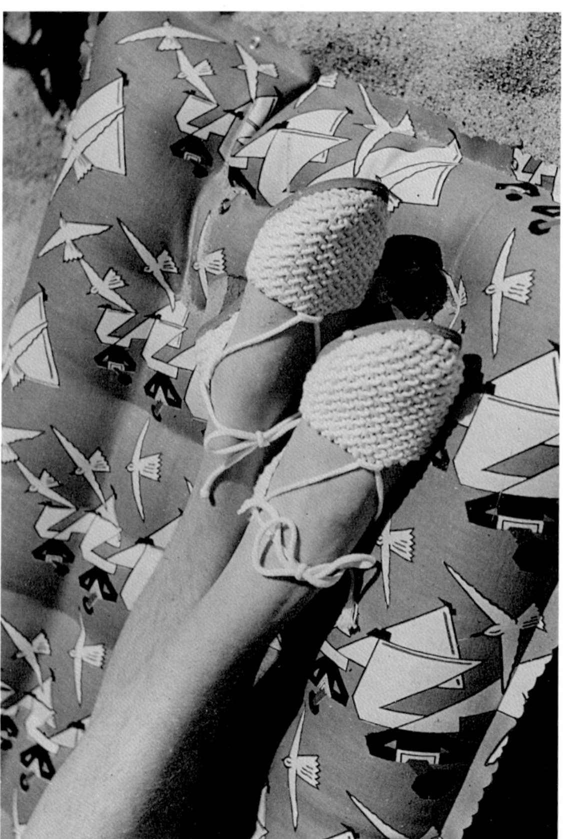

Cédric shoes,
Cannes, April 1939.

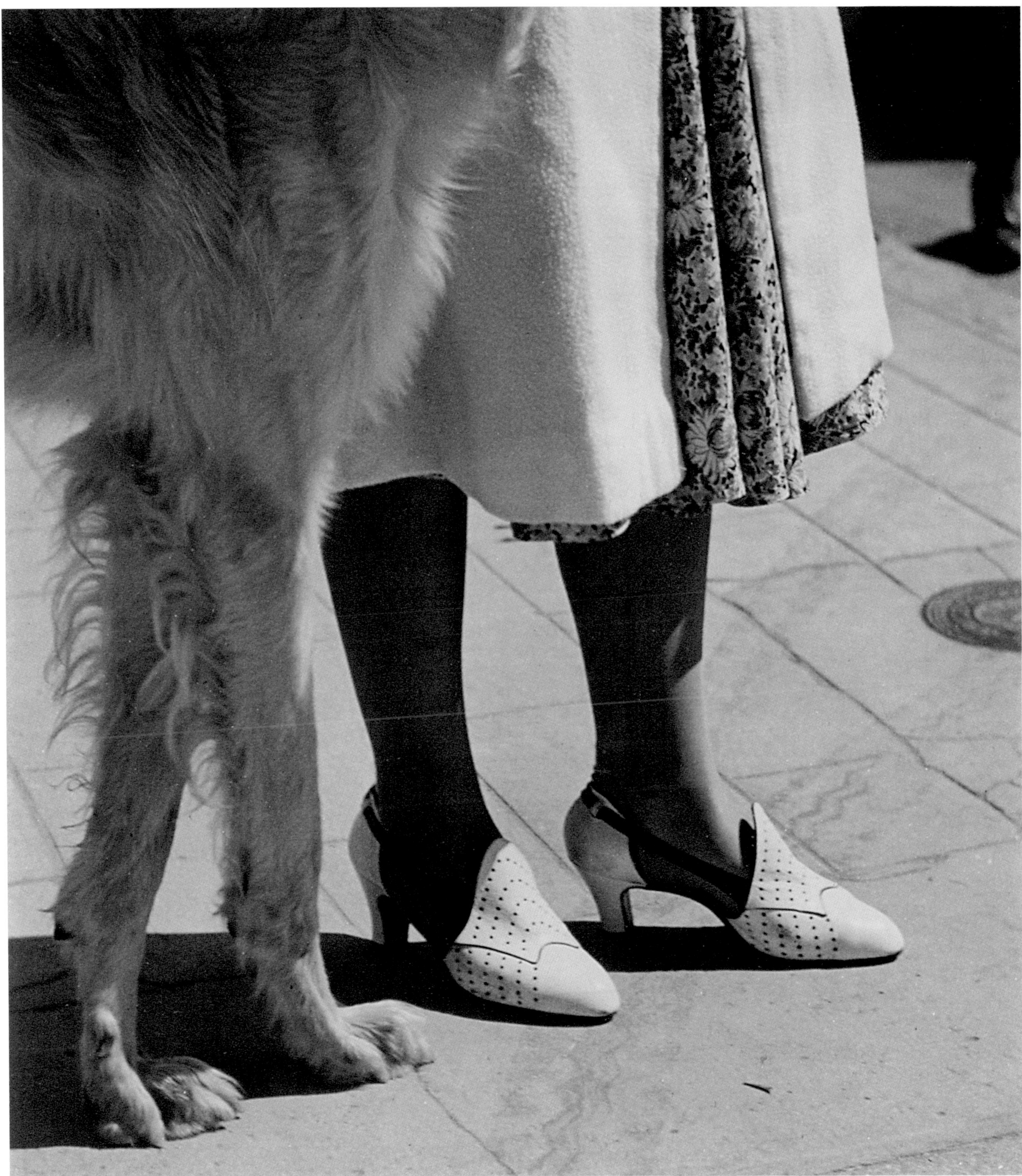

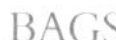

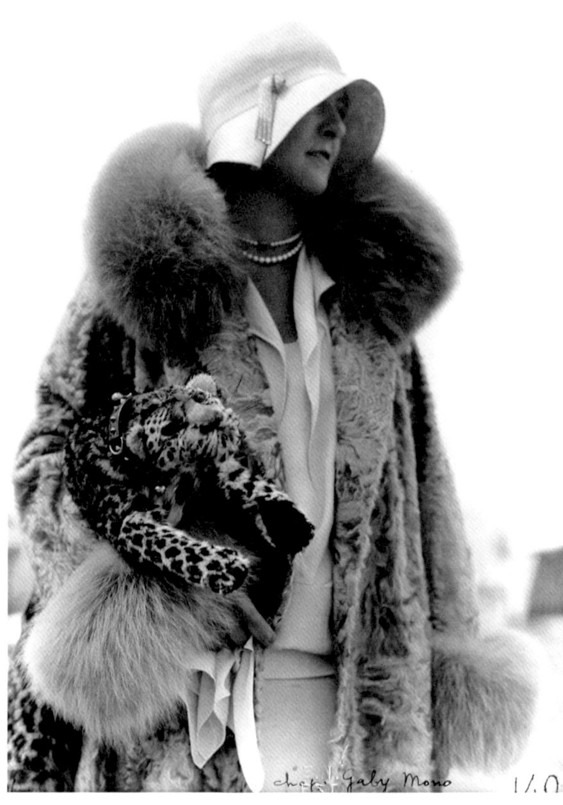

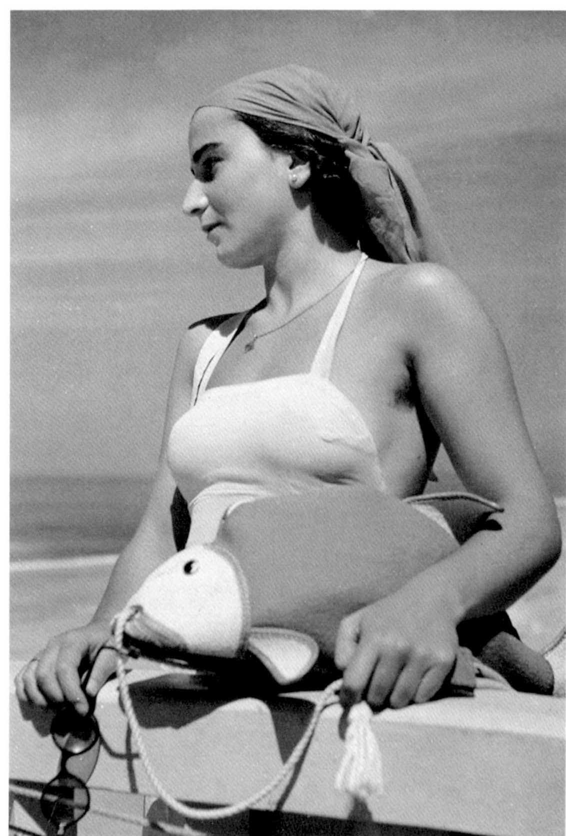

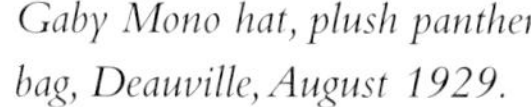

Gaby Mono hat, plush panther bag, Deauville, August 1929.

M[lle] de Szilagyi, Biarritz, September 1935.

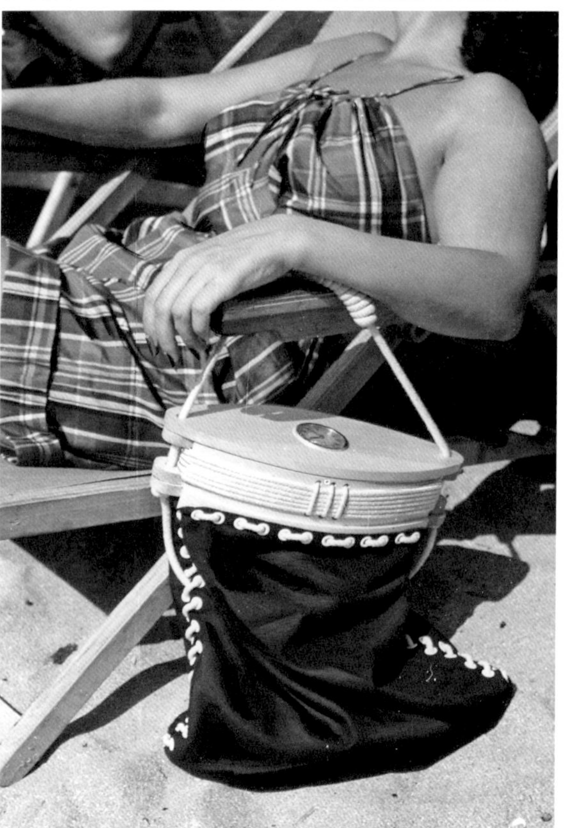

Schiaparelli bag on the beach at Deauville, August 13, 1939.

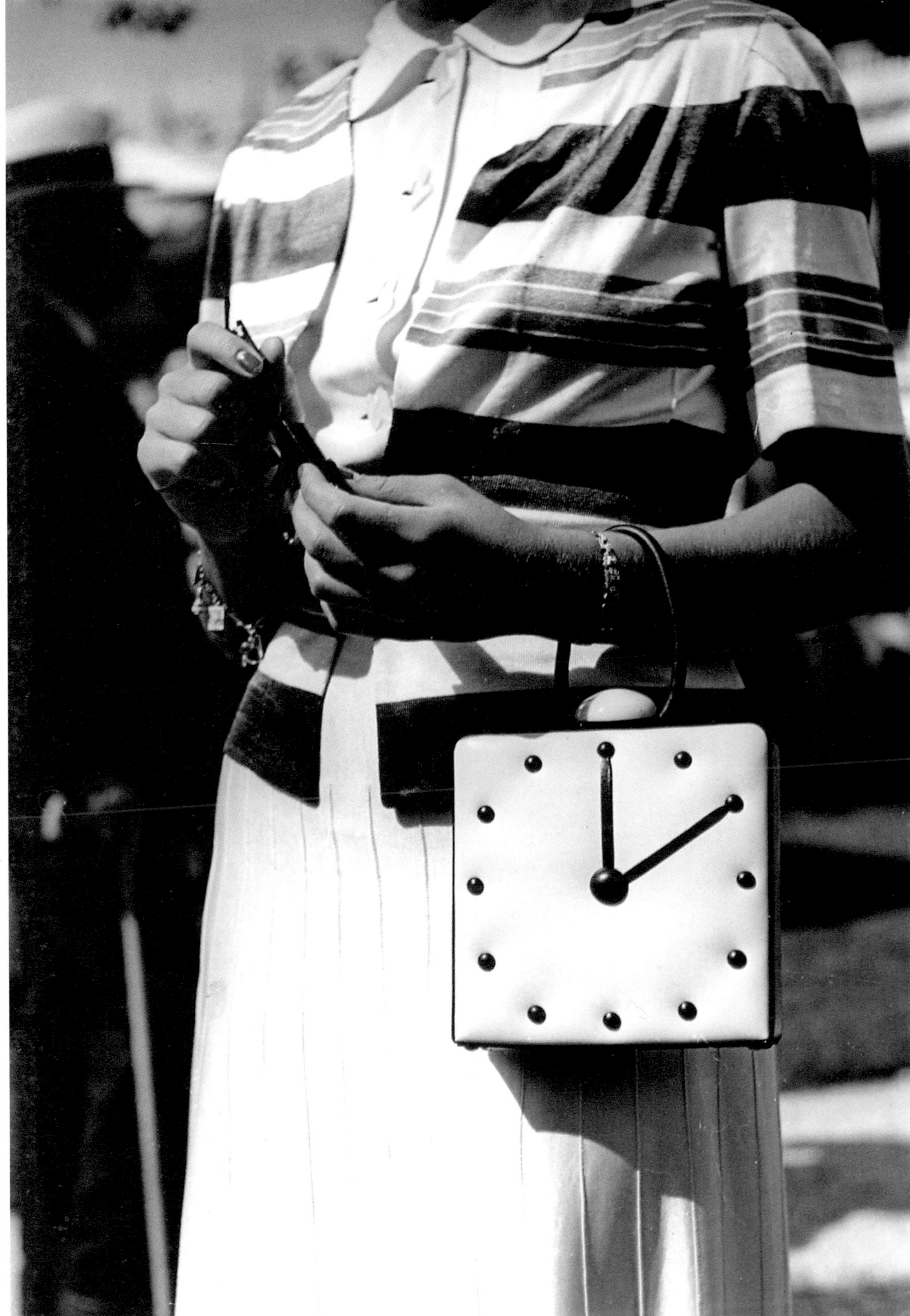

Scarlet Gresham at the races,
Deauville, August 7, 1938.

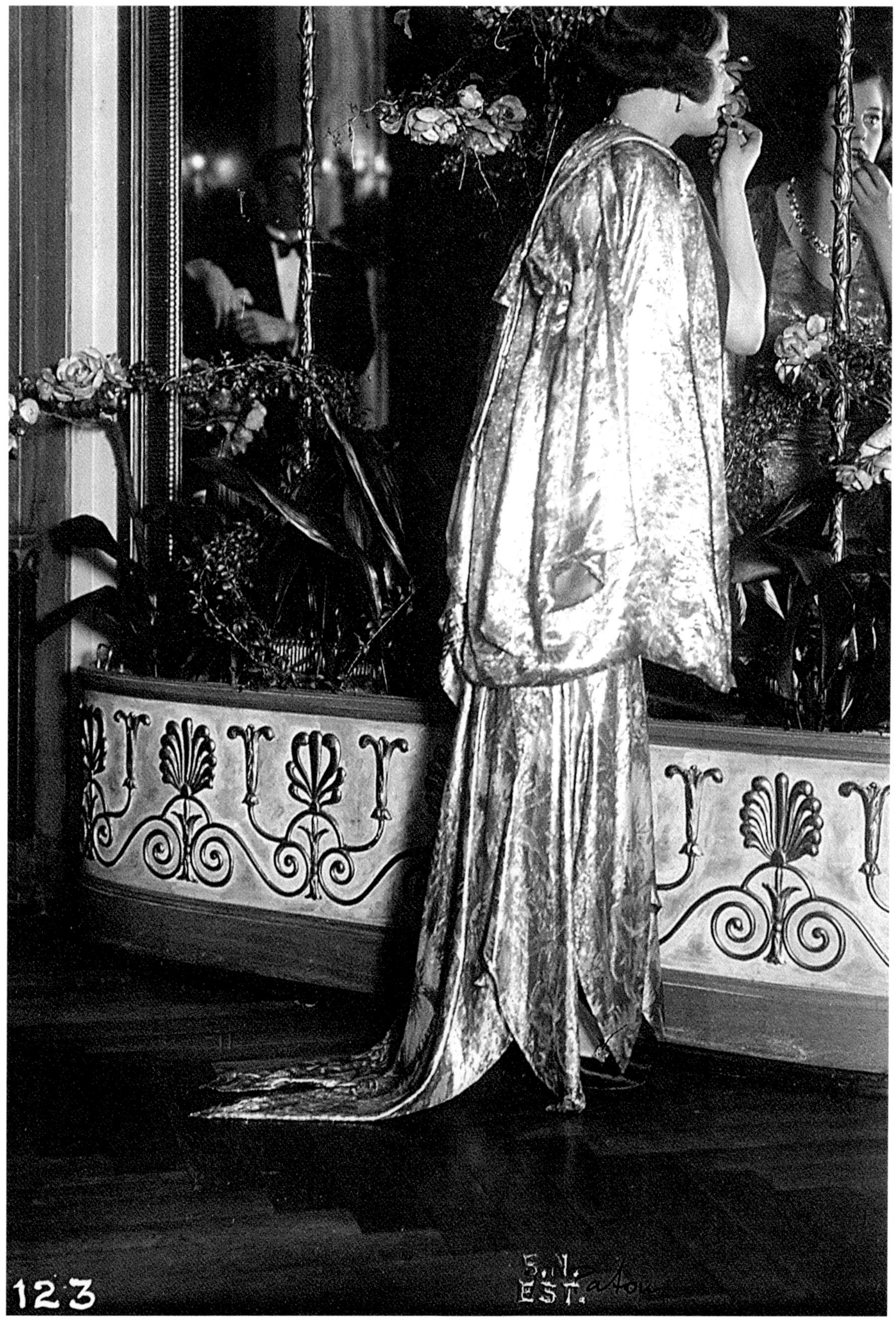

Evening gown by Jean Patou, Saint-Moritz, January 1930.

Rose Valois hat, opening day at Longchamp, September 13, 1936.

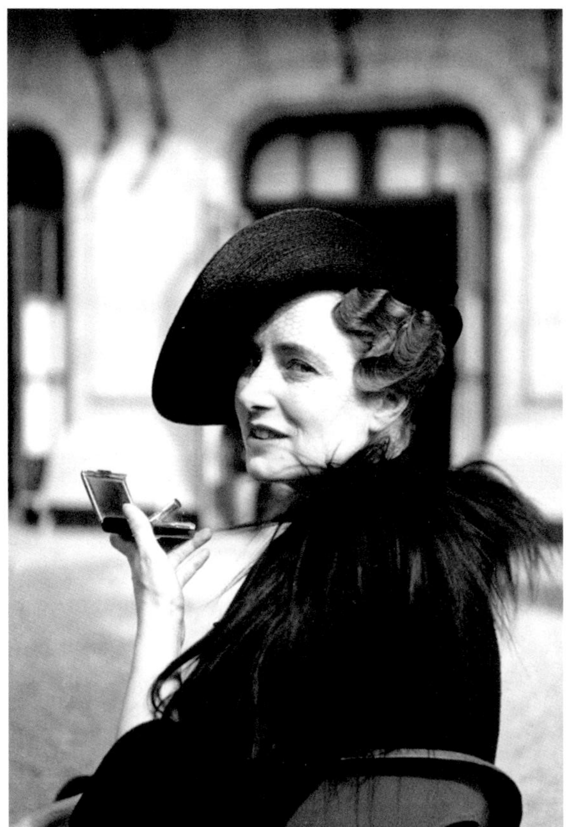

Countess Élie de Ganay, née Nadège de Fontenay, in Worth, Longchamp, May 5, 1935.

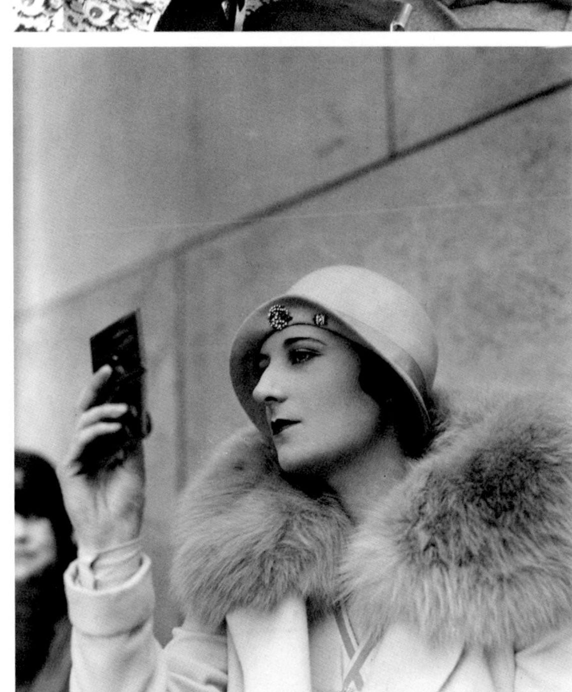

Hat by Rosa Descat, Longchamp, May 6, 1928.

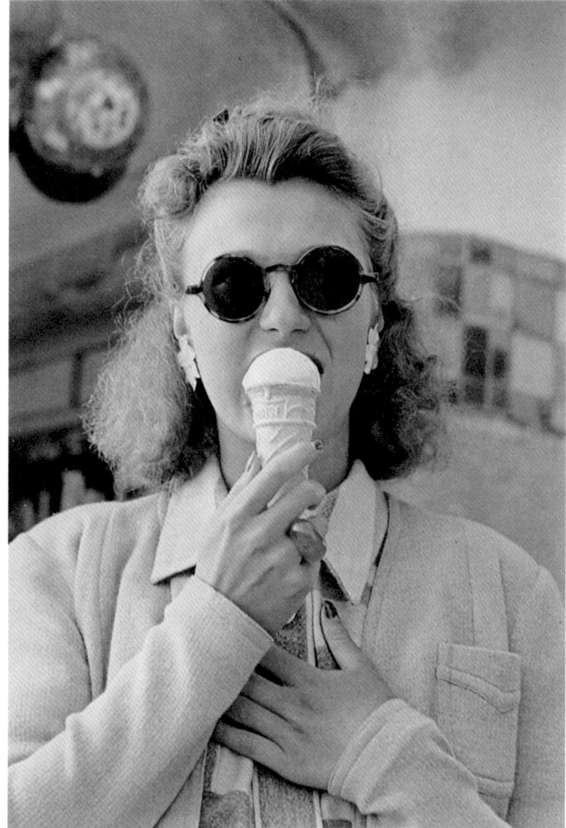

Young woman eating ice cream, Deauville, August 1939.

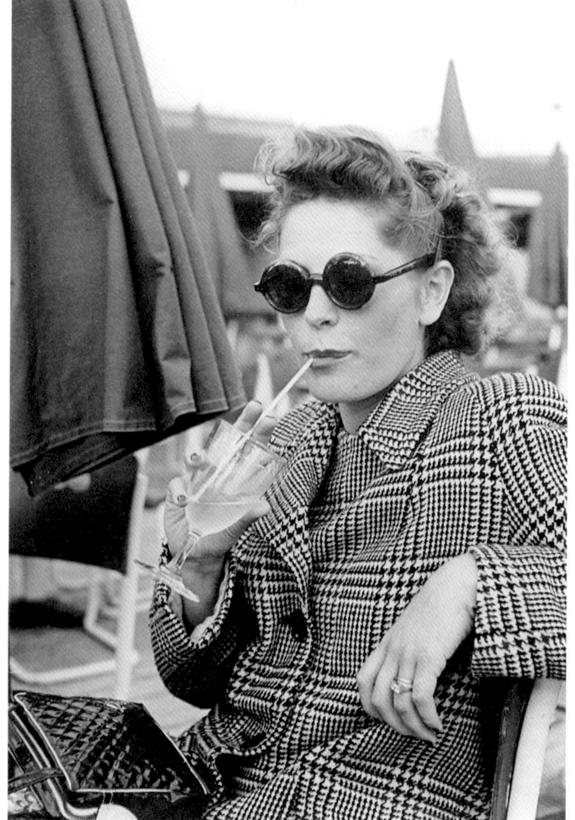

Young woman drinking a lemonade, Deauville, August 1939.

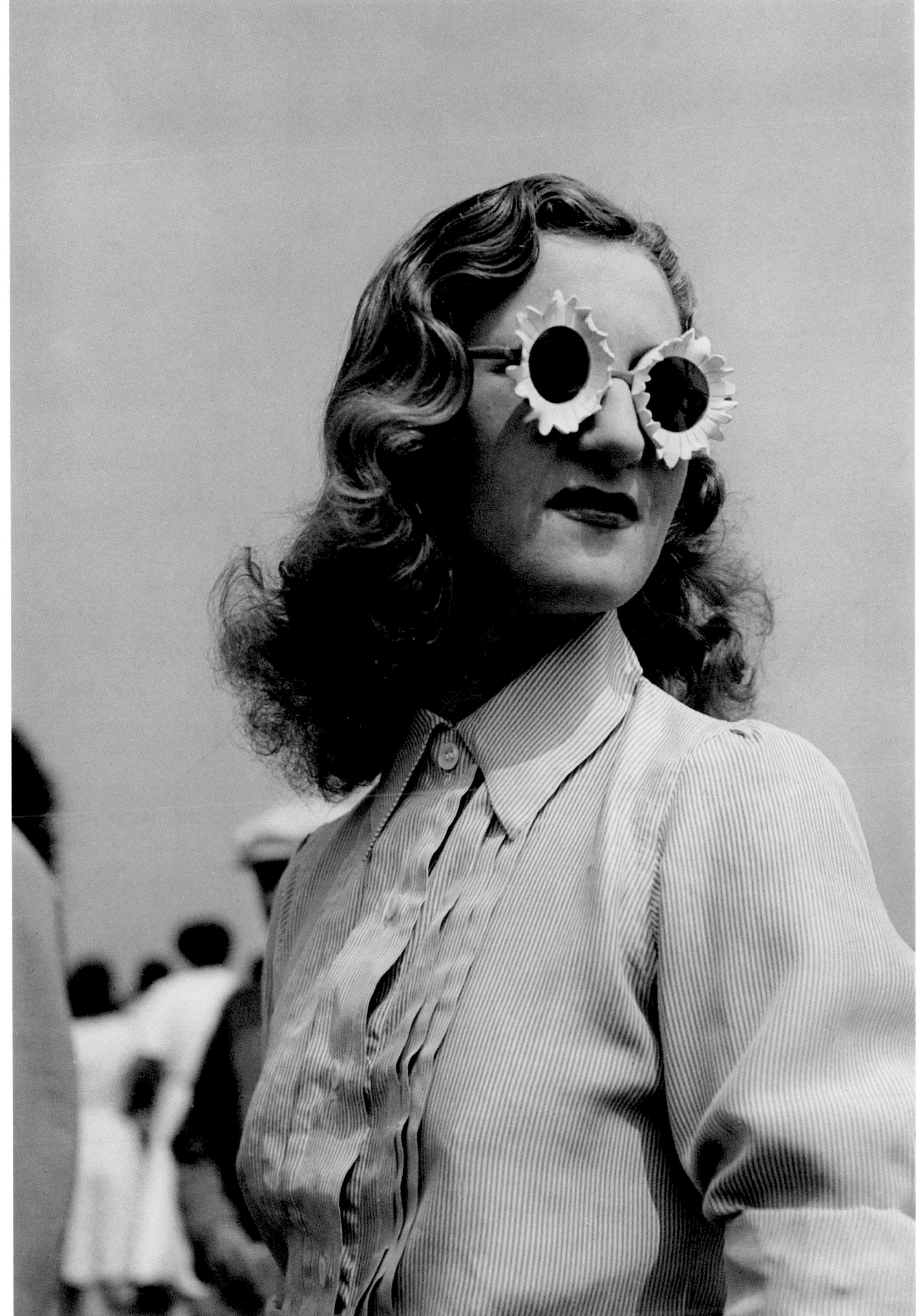

Mme Henri Gouin,
Deauville, August 1939.

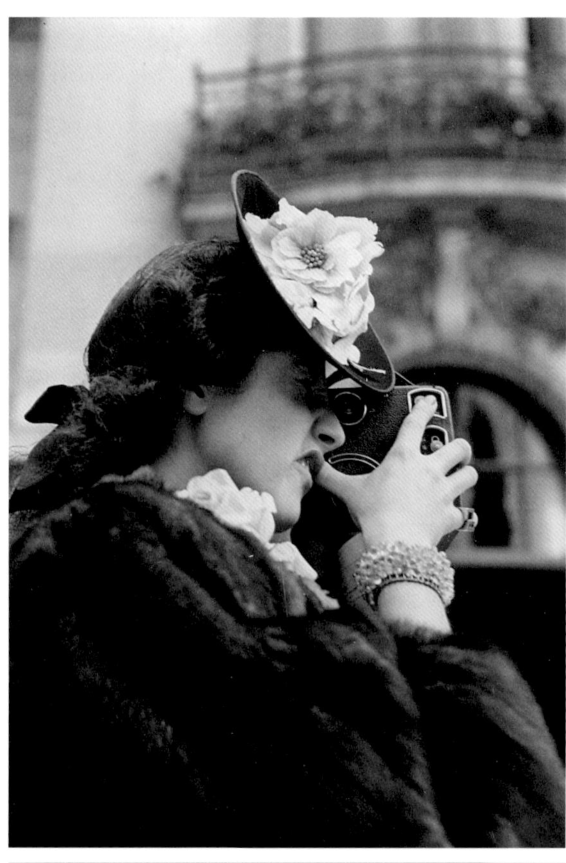

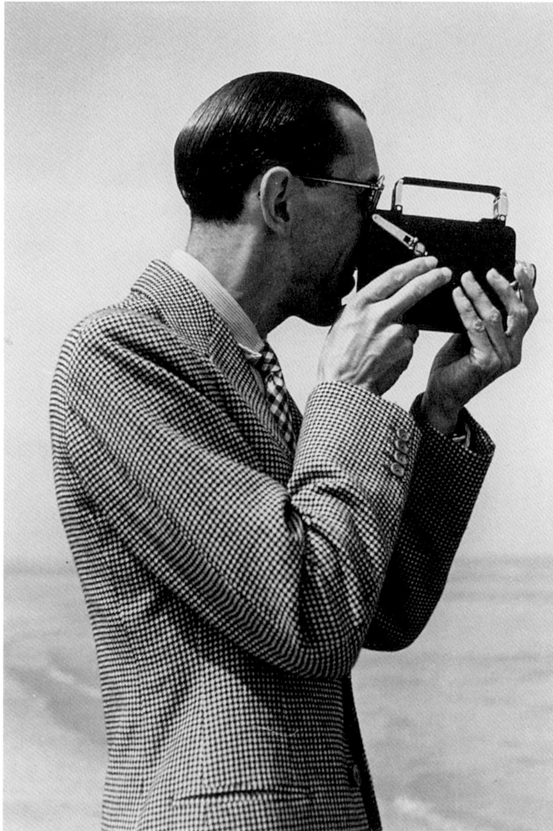

Young woman at Longchamp, September 1938.

Paul Dubonnet at Deauville, August 1938.

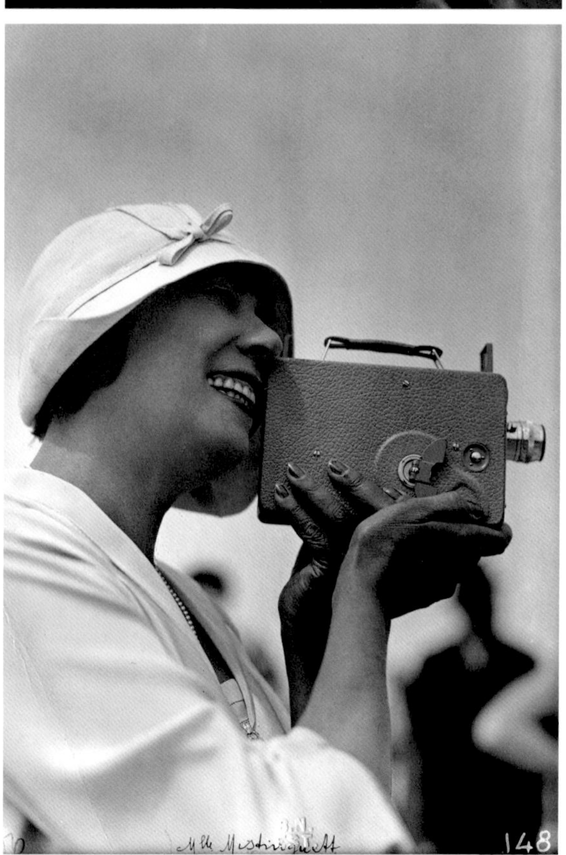

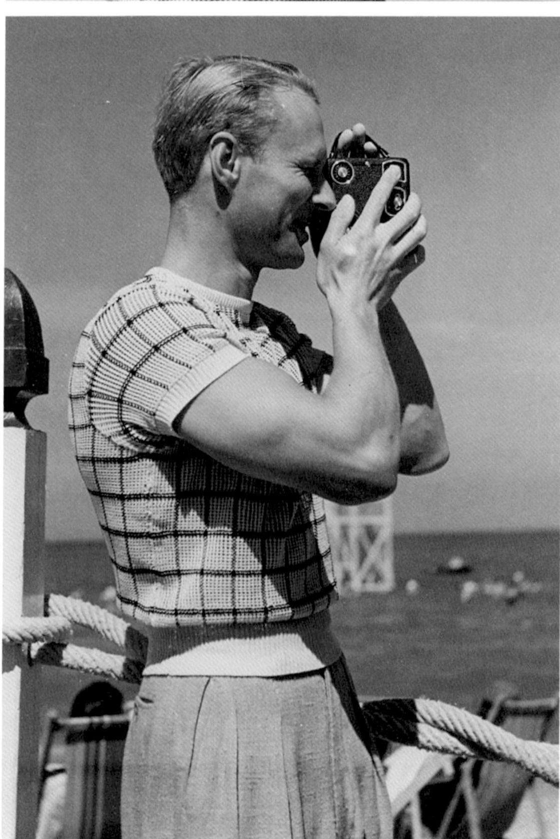

Mistinguett at Deauville, August 1929.

Eric Bagge at Deauville, August 1939.

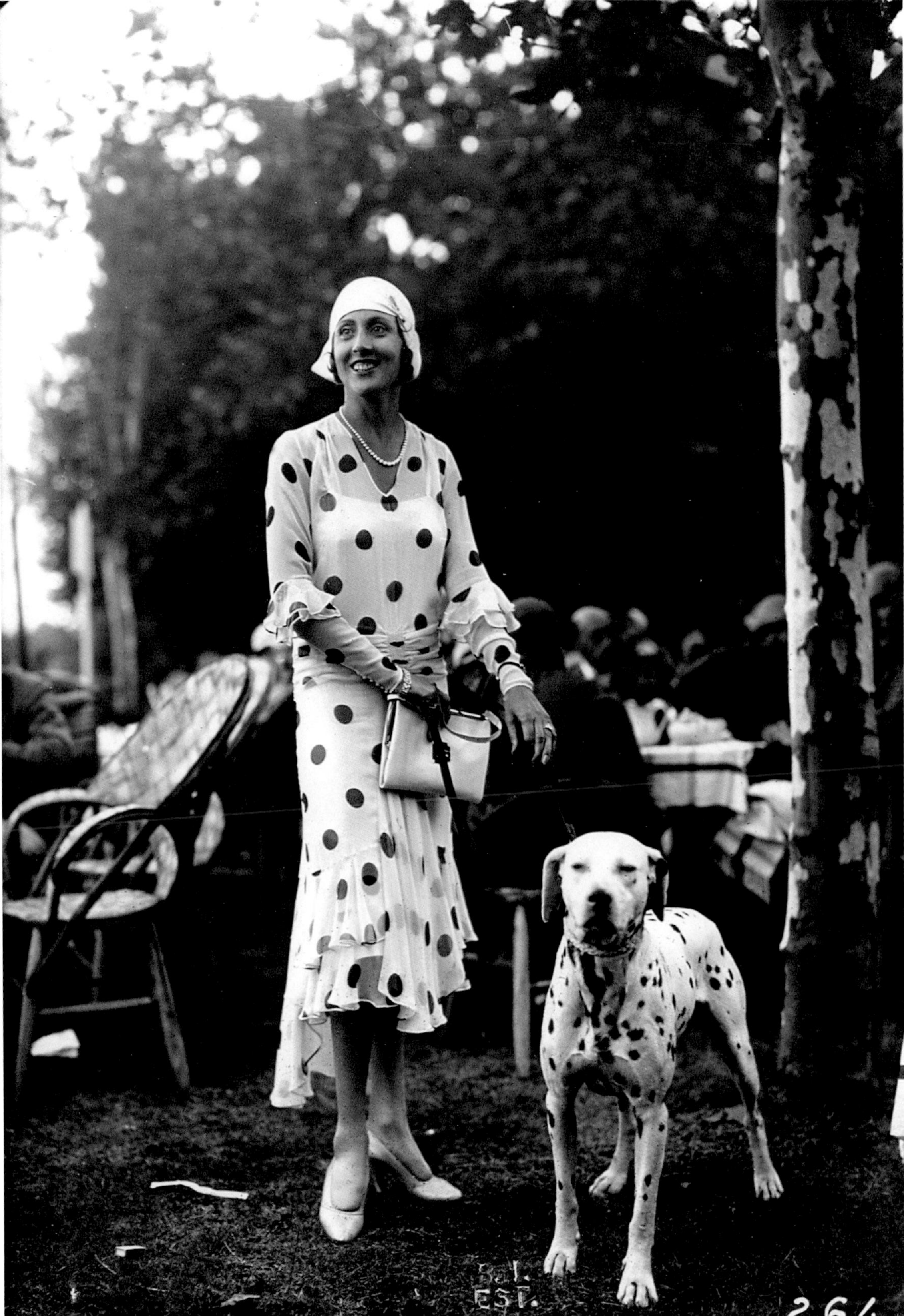

Woman dressed by Jenny,
Biarritz, September 1929.

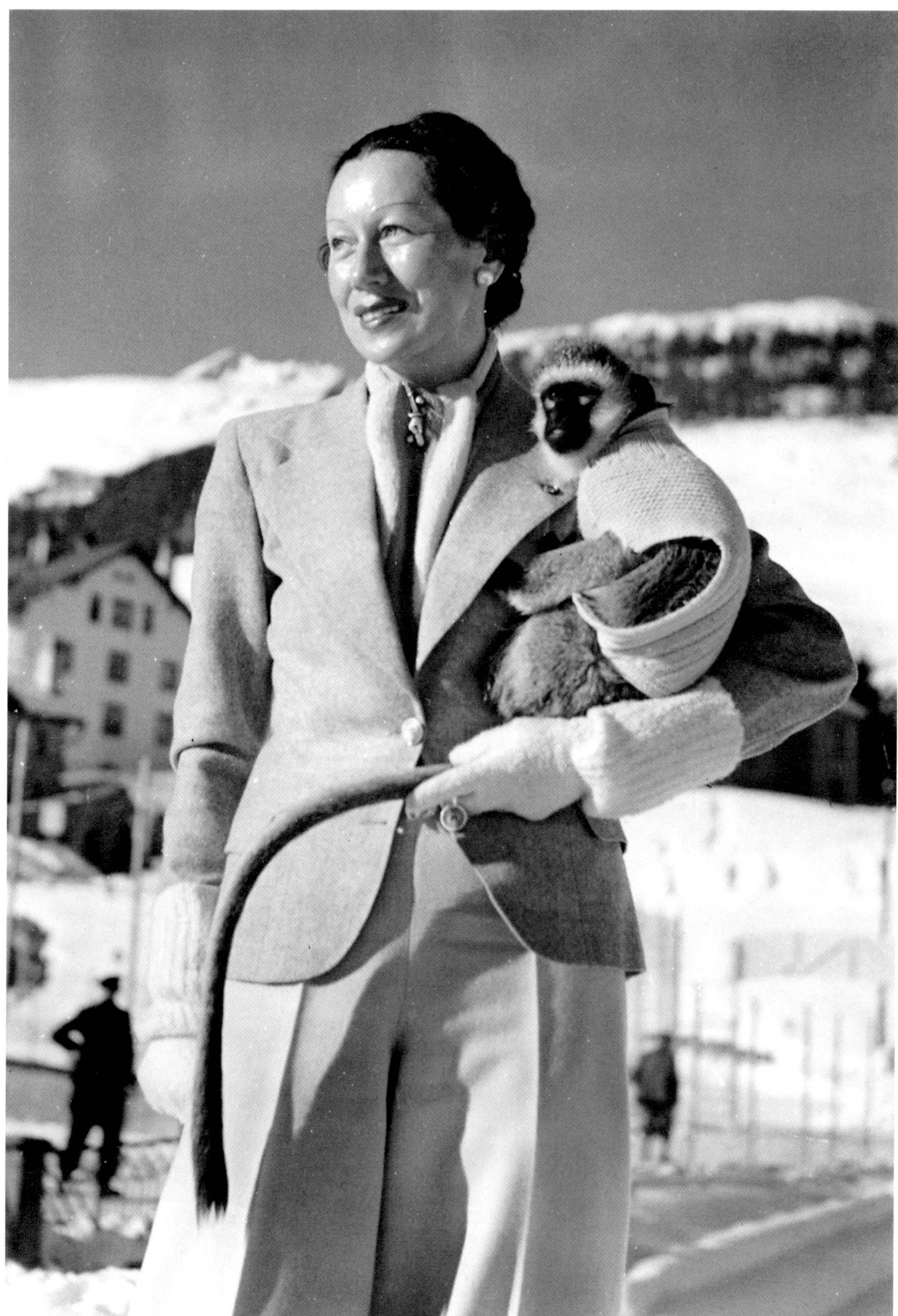

Mme Kade at Saint-Moritz, January 1937.

Mme Gay, Biarritz, September 1935.

Nikitina (1904–1978), ballerina with the Ballet Russes from 1923 to 1929, in Hermès, Biarritz, September 1933.

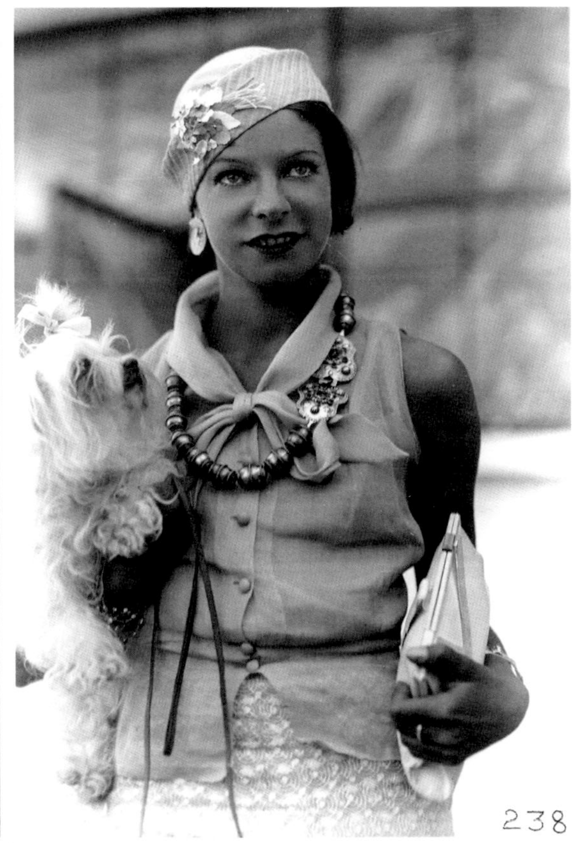

Young woman dressed by Jane Régny, Deauville, August 1931.

Mme Rodocanachi in Hermès, Biarritz, September 1935.

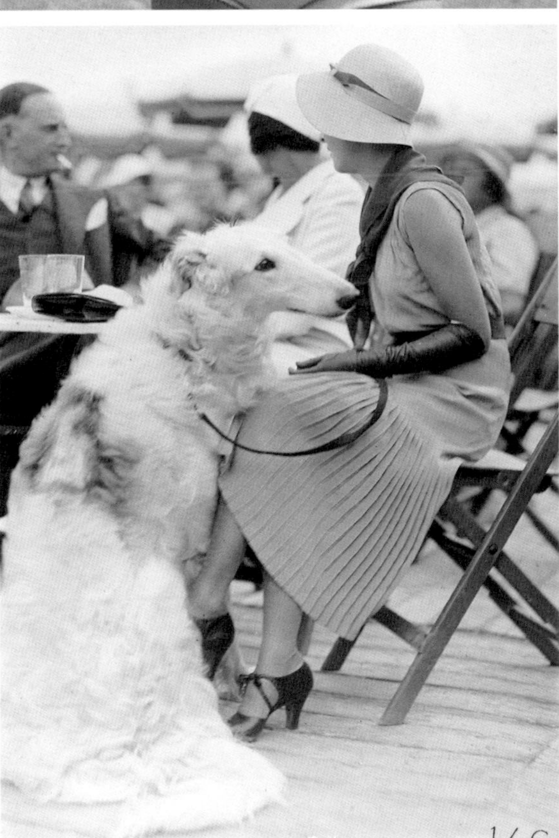

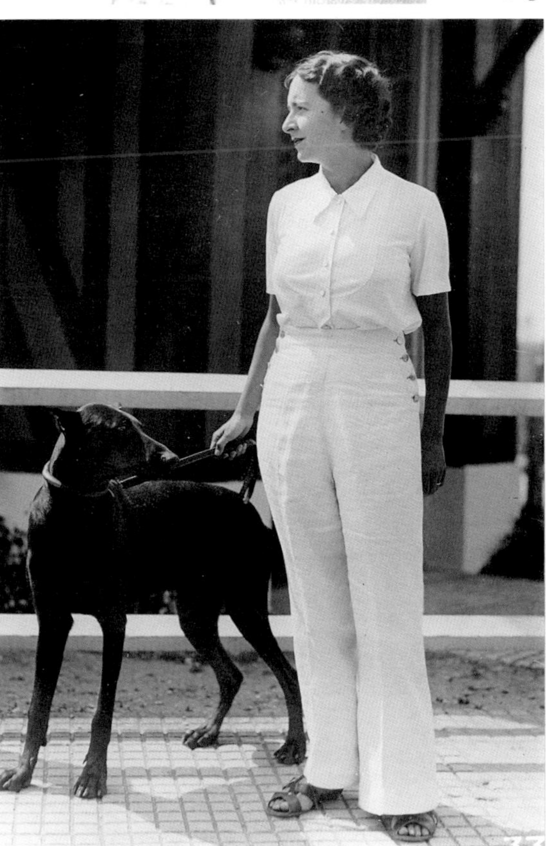

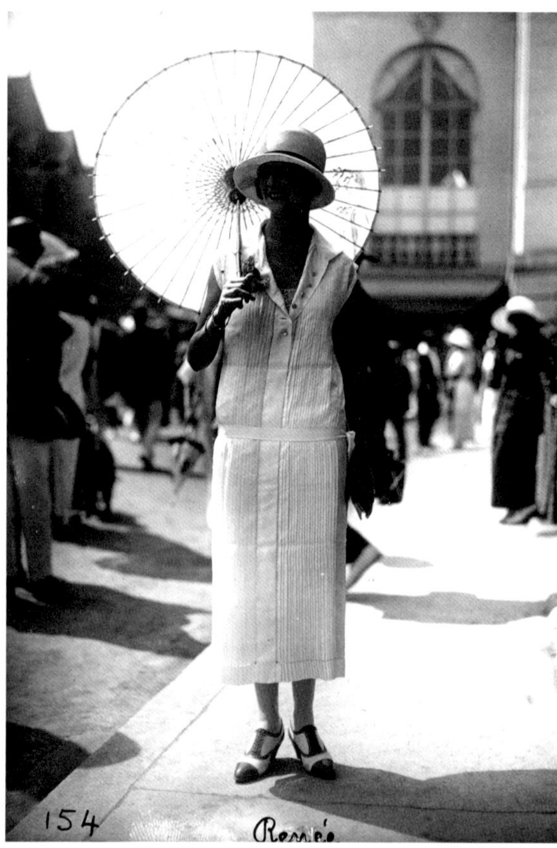

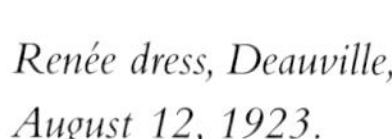

Renée dress, Deauville, August 12, 1923.

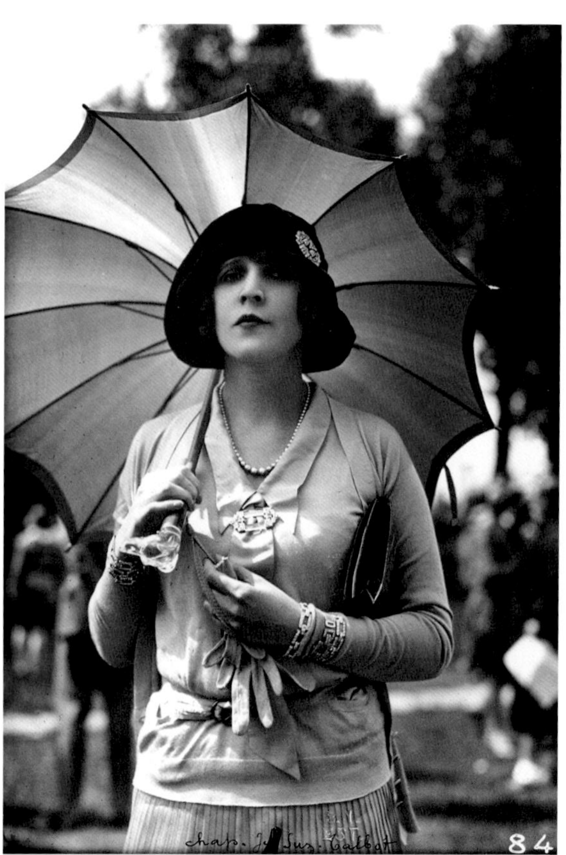

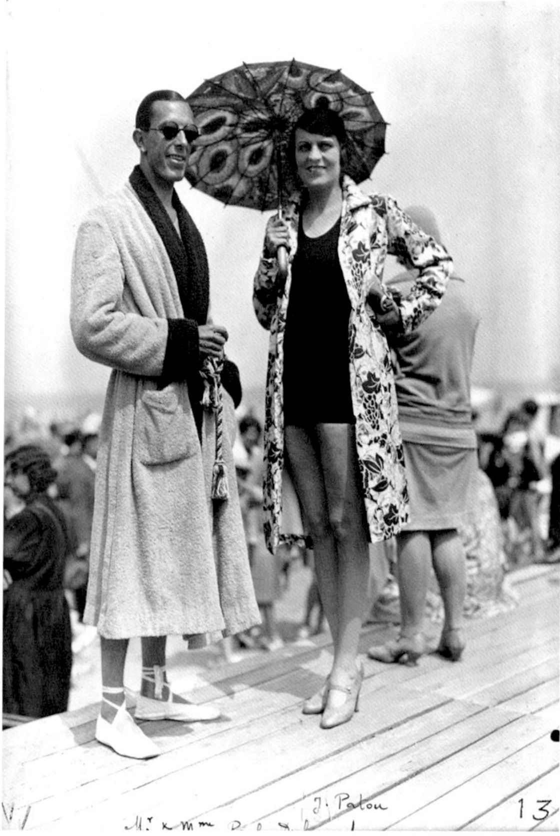

Arlette Ryan wearing a hat by Suzanne Talbot, Deauville, August 3, 1929.

Paul and Jane Dubonnet, Deauville, July 28, 1929. Mme *Dubonnet, née Donaldson, the fifth wife of Mr. Paul Dubonnet (of the aperitifs), is wearing Jean Patou.*

Gown and parasol by Christiane Jo, Auteuil, Drags Day, June 28, 1935.

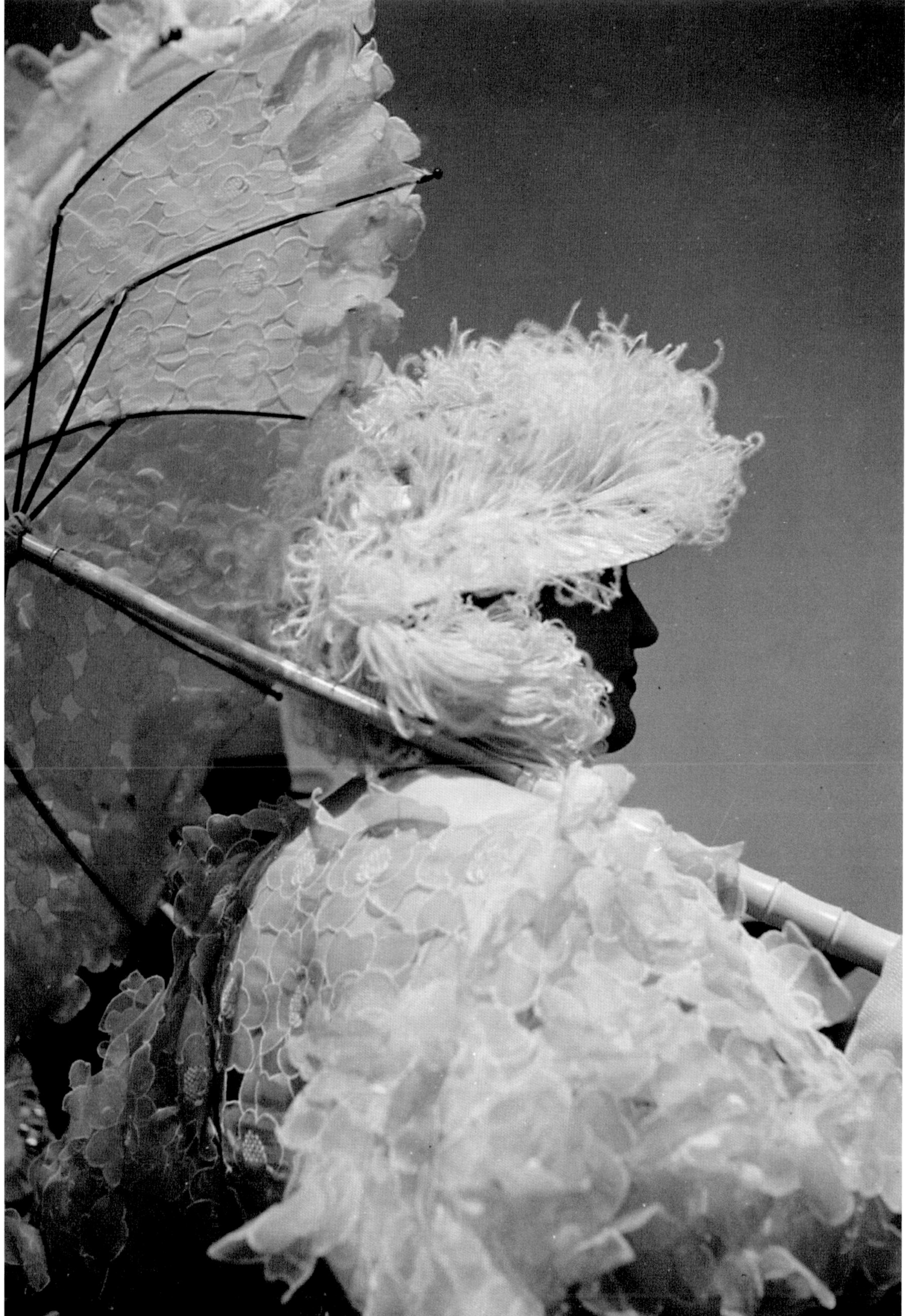

HOLIDAY RESORTS

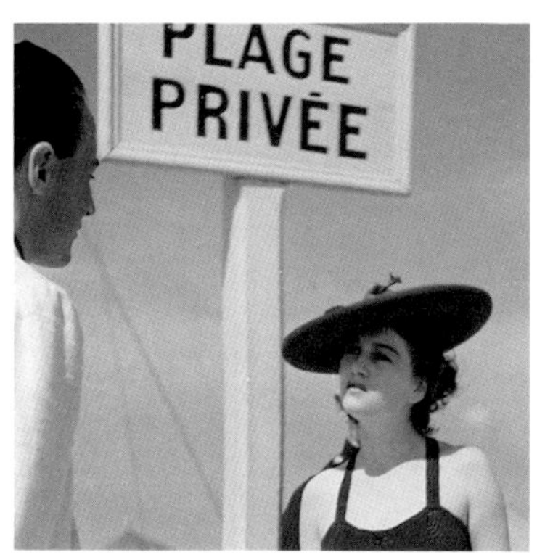

HOLIDAY RESORTS

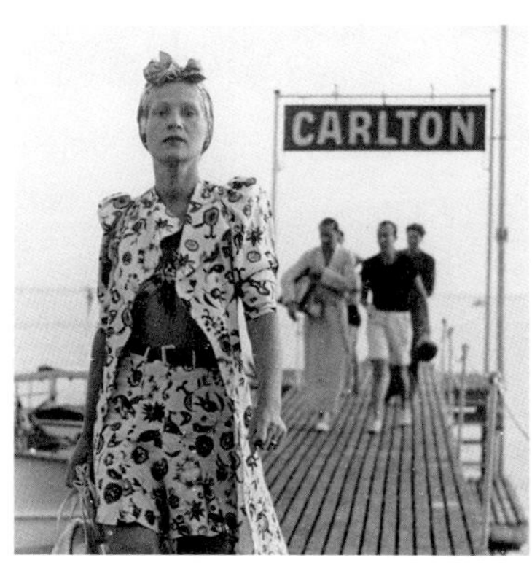

HOLIDAY RESORTS

Sylvie Aubenas

The Séebergers' photographs are journalism drawn from real life, and therefore (and this is not least of their charms) reflect the calendar and peregrinations of high society life. Apart from public or private soirées, which were not really their specialty—although some examples of these are to be found—the Séebergers sought new fashions where they first appeared, i.e. at the racetrack,[49] but also in those spots where it behooved one to be and to be seen. Until the 1920s, they kept to the racecourses, by far the best places to find new styles. As Janine Alaux recalled in her contribution to a biography of Jeanne Lanvin: "this was also why she went into the field with her sister Marie-Louise. The field was Longchamp, the appointed place for all that was to be seen, worn, and done. Incidentally, the horses were less important than those who rode them or watched them arrive."[50] Thus in summer the Séebergers followed the racing season in Deauville, and moved seamlessly from the track to Les Planches and the beach.

During the 1920s, their calendar was relatively fixed: they visited Deauville, *the* place to be in Normandy during the period between the wars, in July and August, Biarritz in September, Cannes at Easter, and Saint-Moritz for the New Year. There were other well-regarded holiday resorts, of course, including Trouville, Dinard, Nice, Monte Carlo, Venice, the Italian Lakes, Gstaad, and so on. But the Séebergers were organized to cover some places and events rather than others, where colleagues and competitors went in their turn. That meant that the magazines, which now regularly planned articles around the society seasons and migrations, knew in advance for which cities they could count on the Séebergers' photographs.

By a process established since the Second Empire, the development of these fashionable locales was in the hands of investors, financiers, politicians, and press barons. The example of Deauville,[51] studied by Paul Smith,[52] is particularly striking, but the same process (with local variations) was at play everywhere. In Deauville there was an alliance between the Letellier family[53] and the architect George Wybo (1880-1943),[54] who between 1910 and 1920 built, among other things, the sea swimming facilities, the casino, a branch of the Parisian department store "Le Printemps," and a showroom for the firm of André Citroën (with whom he had been associated since 1916). André Citroën had himself been a mainstay of the resort since 1912, renting the beautiful villa *Les Abeilles* (The Bees) for his family, and (far more interesting for readers of the local gazettes) winning—or rather losing—staggering sums at the casino in the company of the Aga Khan or Jean Patou. Those who strolled along Les Planches—the Citroën family or the beautiful Mme Letellier—were certainly ambassadors of chic, but they were also promoters with a personal stake in the success of the season.

Launched as early as the Second Empire, Deauville, Biarritz, and Cannes took on different forms as life and habits changed. New hotels and casinos were built. The restaurants, café terraces, and bars—to which beaches, swimming pools, and golf courses were added—became suitable haunts for society women and ever more sought-after by those in the public eye. Fashionable life no longer took place exclusively behind the closed doors of chateaux and villas, but at least some of the time, in public. It was enough for a photographer to take up a strategic location at the right time. Many celebrities, especially at Cannes and Saint-Moritz, were thus captured on film while exiting their hotel or nearby, while at Deauville and Biarritz, the seashore, Les Planches, or the bar *La Chambre d'Amour* were the best places.

It was extremely important for each resort's notoriety—and thus closely monitored by the office of tourism, which was obviously managed by investors such as those mentioned above—that each season should bring its quota of royalty and nobility, exotic beauties, movie stars, industrialists' families, and so on. This was how the reputation of a resort (and the value of the investments made in it) was built and maintained. These arrivals were therefore announced daily in the local press, in the foyers of the hotels where the celebrities arrived, and—better still—in the national and international media.

This was mainly the light in which the Séebergers' work as published in *Vogue* and other magazines was appreciated. They arrived on the scene, equipped with letters of introduction from the publications on whose behalf they had come;[55] the letters certify their mission as special correspondents and express hope for speedy publication of prints. They also obtained passes on location. Hence this letter dated July 3, 1925, on the Deauville casino letterhead: *"I authorize the Séeberger brothers to take photographs in our hotels and casino and request that the Baths, Polo Ground, Golf Course, Clay Pigeon Shoot, Trouville Casino, the Palestra, etc. etc. kindly facilitate Messrs. Séeberger in their task, these photographs being needed for various French and foreign publicity materials. The Chief of Publicity, George Loiseau."*[56]

Fashion in itself remained essential, of course. The latest activities of the socialites on holiday offered plenty of opportunities to wear a variety of outfits, both sporting and those with a studied informality. Patou and Chanel invented haute couture sportswear, which was particularly becoming in these places where the beauty of the site was carefully orchestrated. From now on, tanning[57] put light-colored fabrics and beachwear at a premium.

To retain their customers who deserted the capital for long periods, the great couture houses opened branches at the resorts. The head office in Paris would delegate some of its personnel, saleswomen, models, and seamstresses. In *Journal d'un mannequin* ("Diary of a Model"),[58] the author relates how she was sent successively to the salons at Cannes and Saint-Moritz following the seasons. Obviously, the clothing presented was adapted to place and season.

Gabrielle Chanel inaugurated her first shop in Deauville in 1913, in the rue Gontaut-Biron, the same street where the casino had opened the previous year. The establishment of twenty luxury boutiques was planned under its aegis, one of which was Van Cleef & Arpels, which had been installed there since 1912. Chanel's venture was so successful, even during the war, that she opened another branch in Biarritz in 1915, entrusting its management to her sister Antoinette. There, she gained the Spanish royal family as clients. Patou opened a shop in Deauville in 1924 called *Jean Patou, ses costumes de bains & plage* (Jean Patou, swimsuits and beachwear), and another in Biarritz the same year. In that same city—which he had discovered in 1921 through his brother-in-law, Basque tennis champion Raymond Barbas—he had a sumptuous villa (decorated, like his Paris mansion, by Süe et Mare) built on the hill of Ustarritz. Jeanne Lanvin and Madeleine Vionnet finally settled there as well, in 1925.

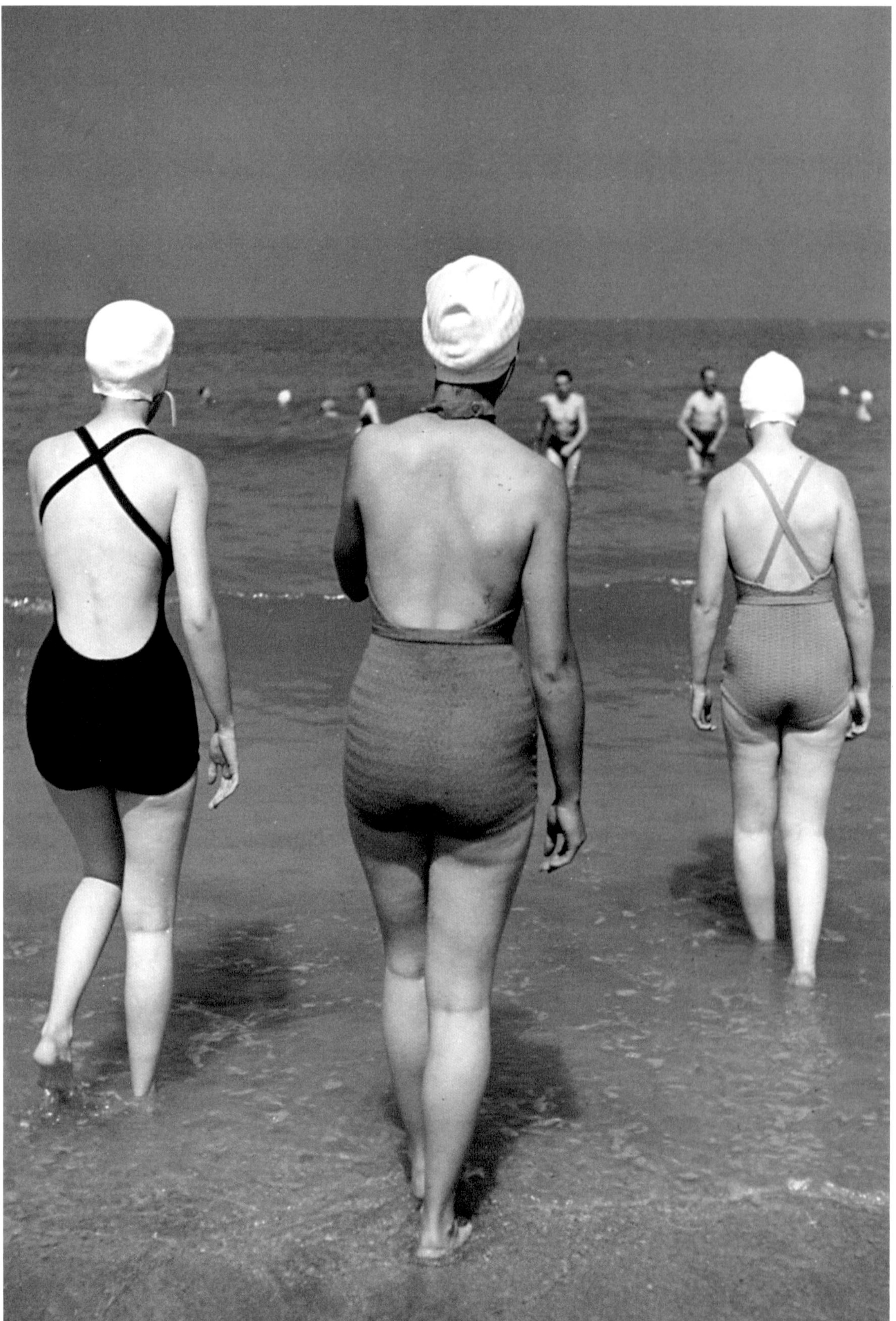

Deauville, August 15, 1936.

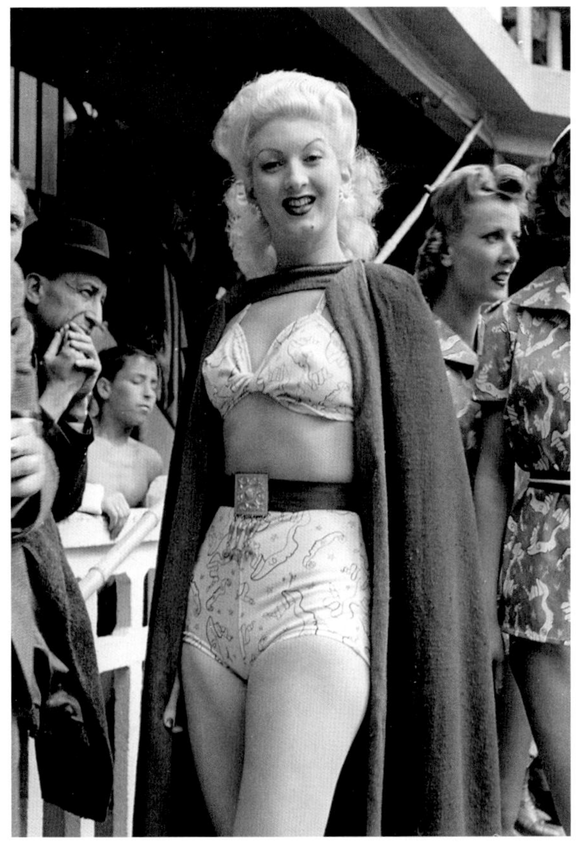

Two-piece swimsuit by Jean Farrel, fabric designed by Jean Cocteau, Water Festival, Molitor swimming pool, June 19, 1939.

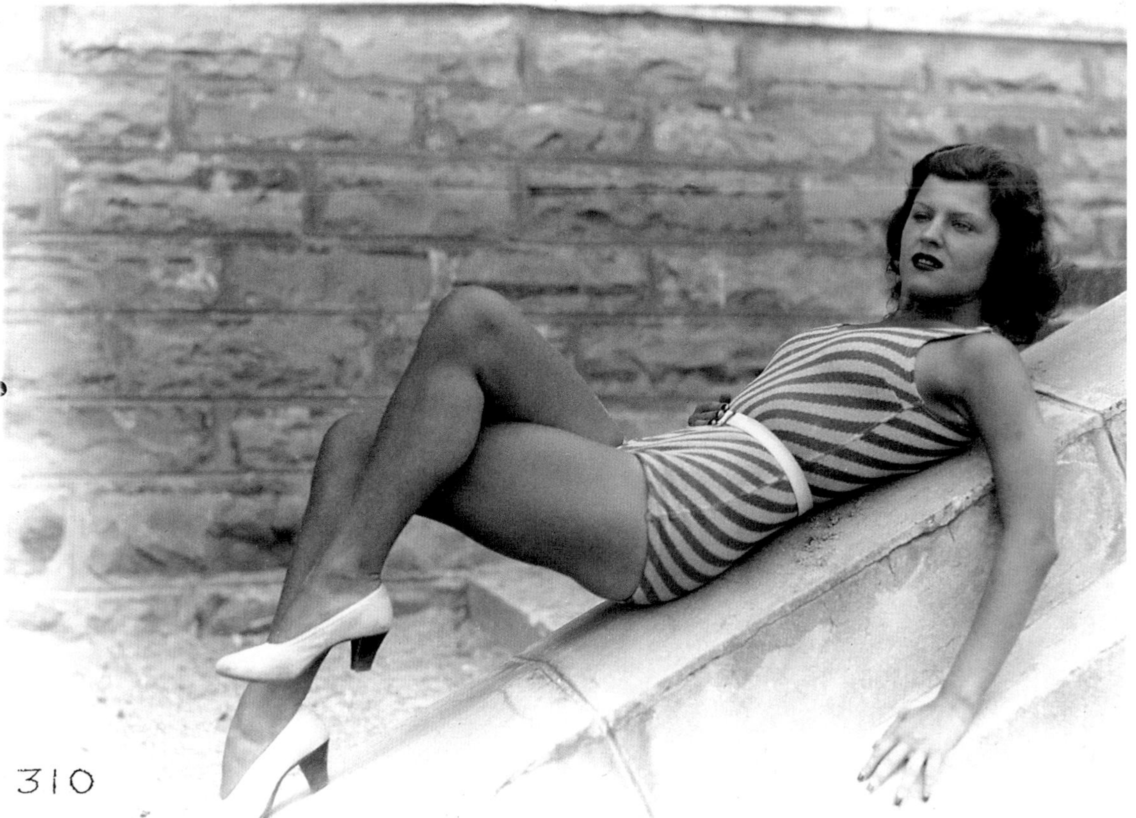

Kate de Nagy (1909–1973), Hungarian actress, bathing suit by Heim, Biarritz, September 1933.

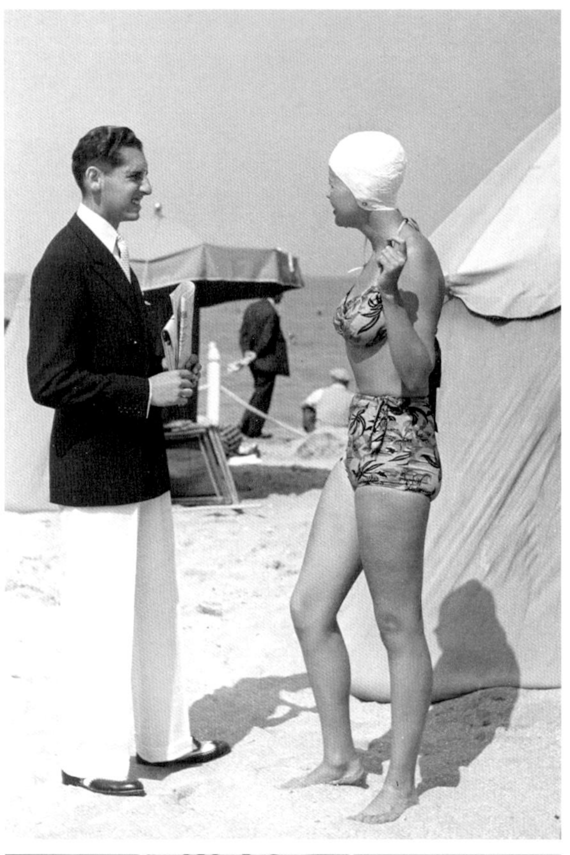

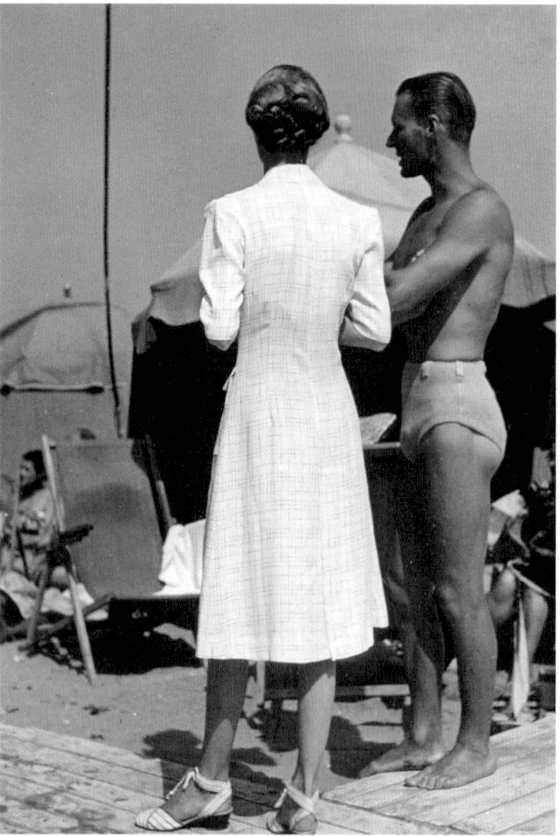

Mr. Fribourg on the beach with a friend, Deauville, August 28, 1938.

Eric Bagge (1890–1978) on the beach with a friend, Deauville, August 28, 1938. Mr. Bagge, an architect, decorated the liner Isle-de-France in 1927.

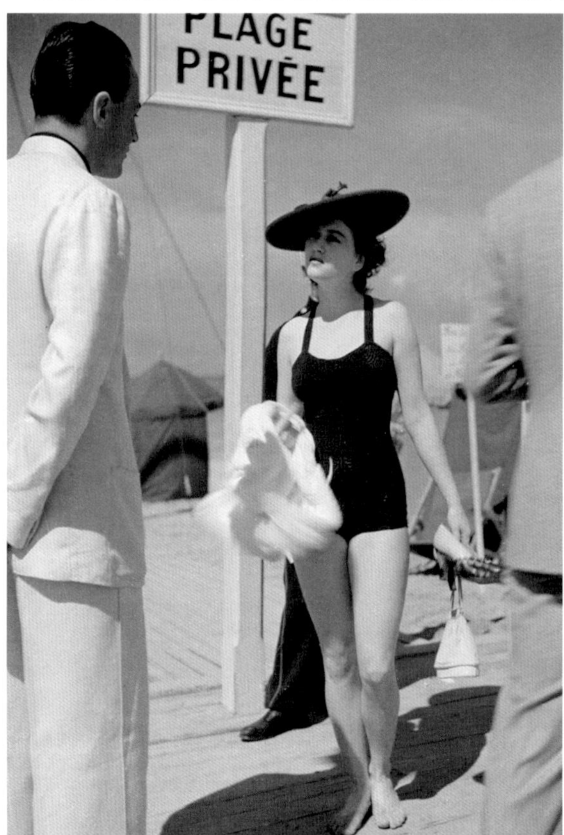

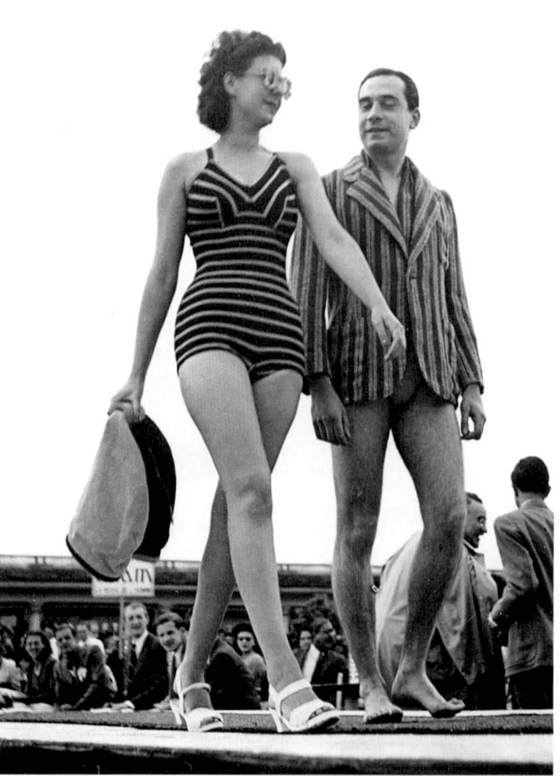

Private beach, Deauville, August 25, 1935.

Presentation of bathing suits and summer wear, Deauville, July 16, 1939.

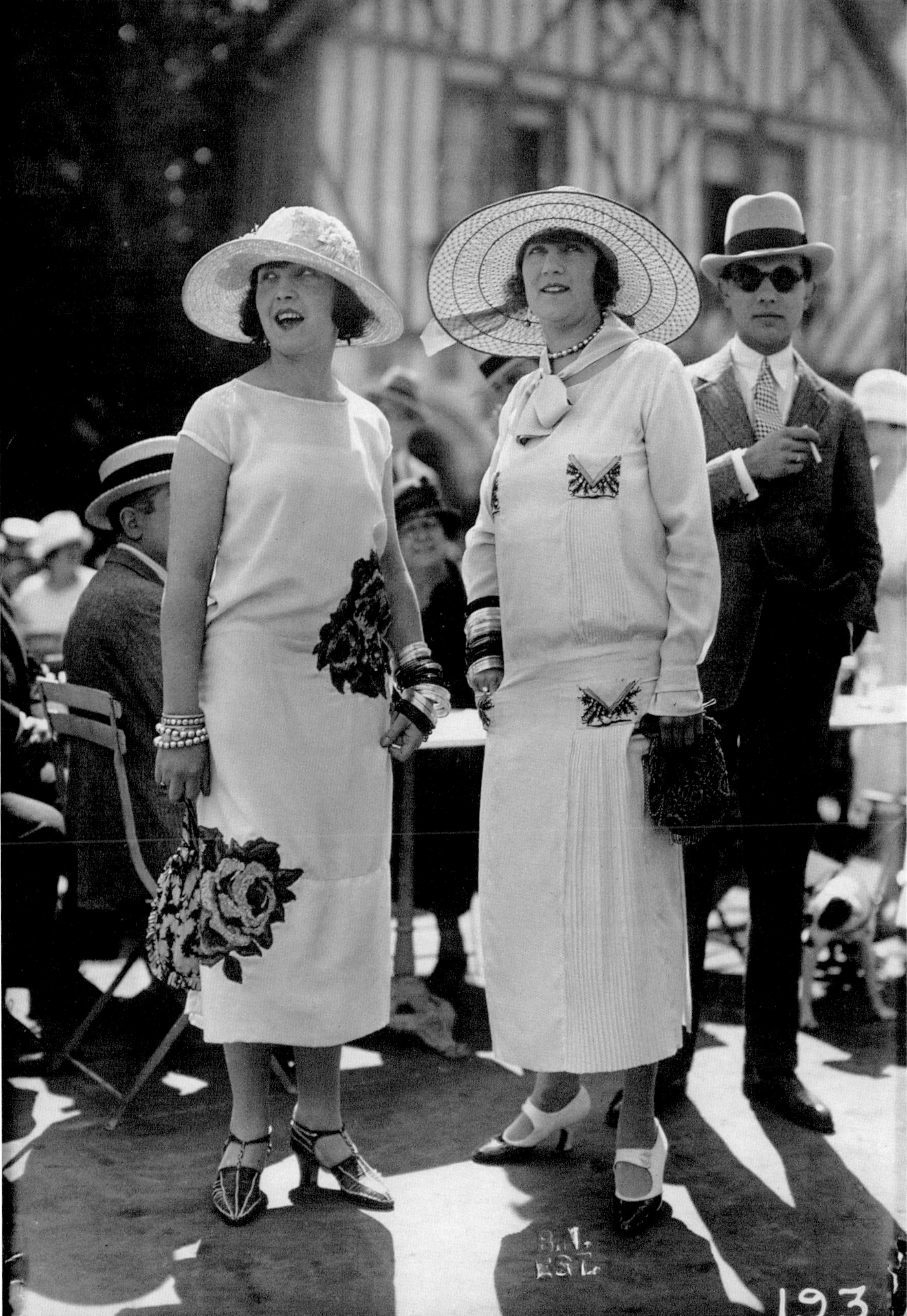

Young women in white,
Deauville, August 10, 1924.

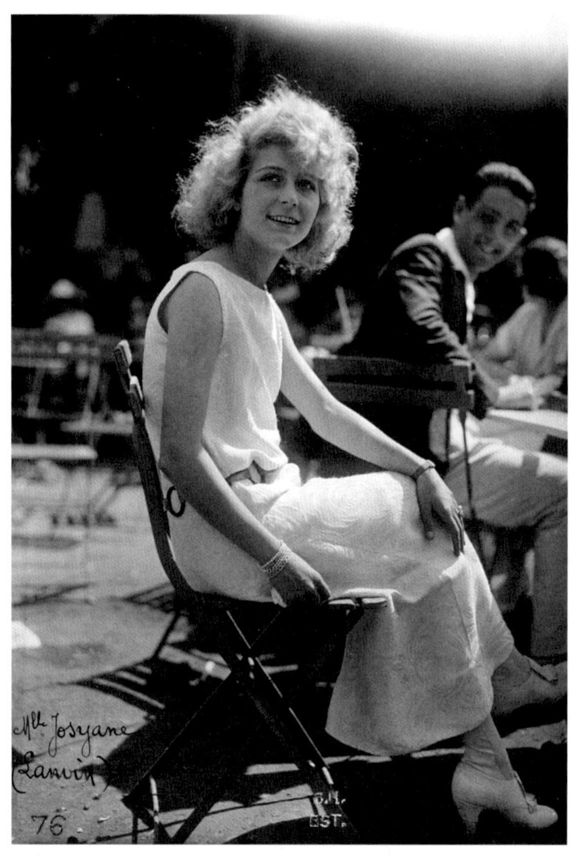

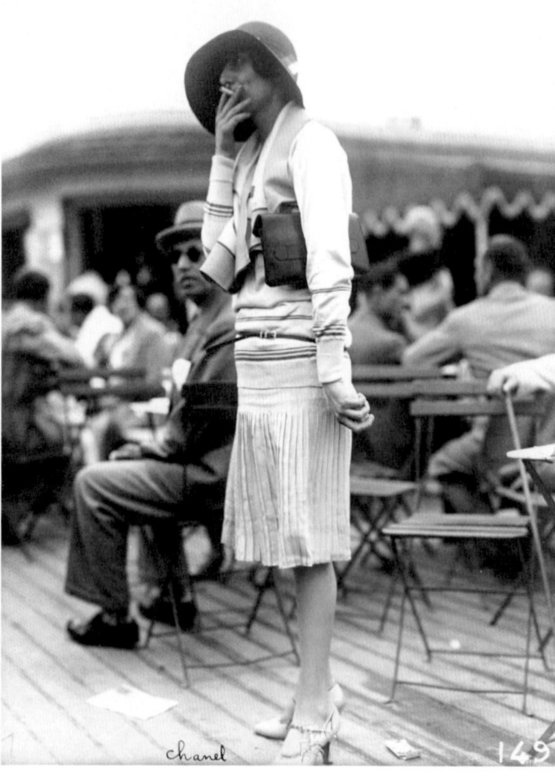

Mlle Josyane in a Lanvin dress, Deauville, summer 1922.

Chanel dress, Deauville, Grand Prix day, August 26, 1928.

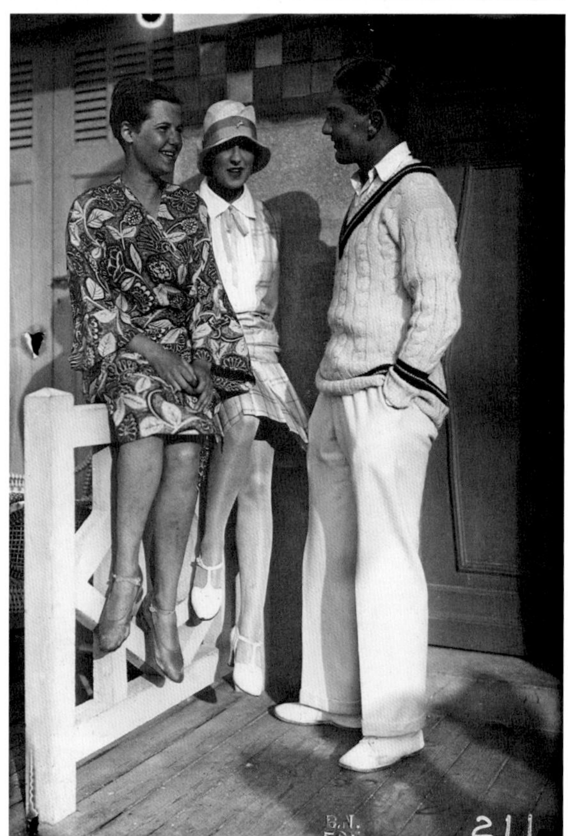

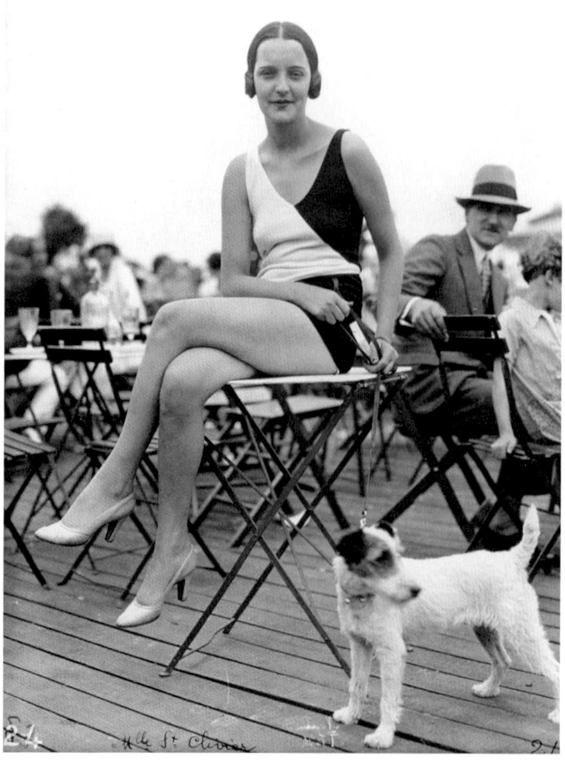

Young woman, center, in a Jenny dress, Deauville, August 1927.

Mlle Saint-Clivier, Deauville, July 28, 1929.

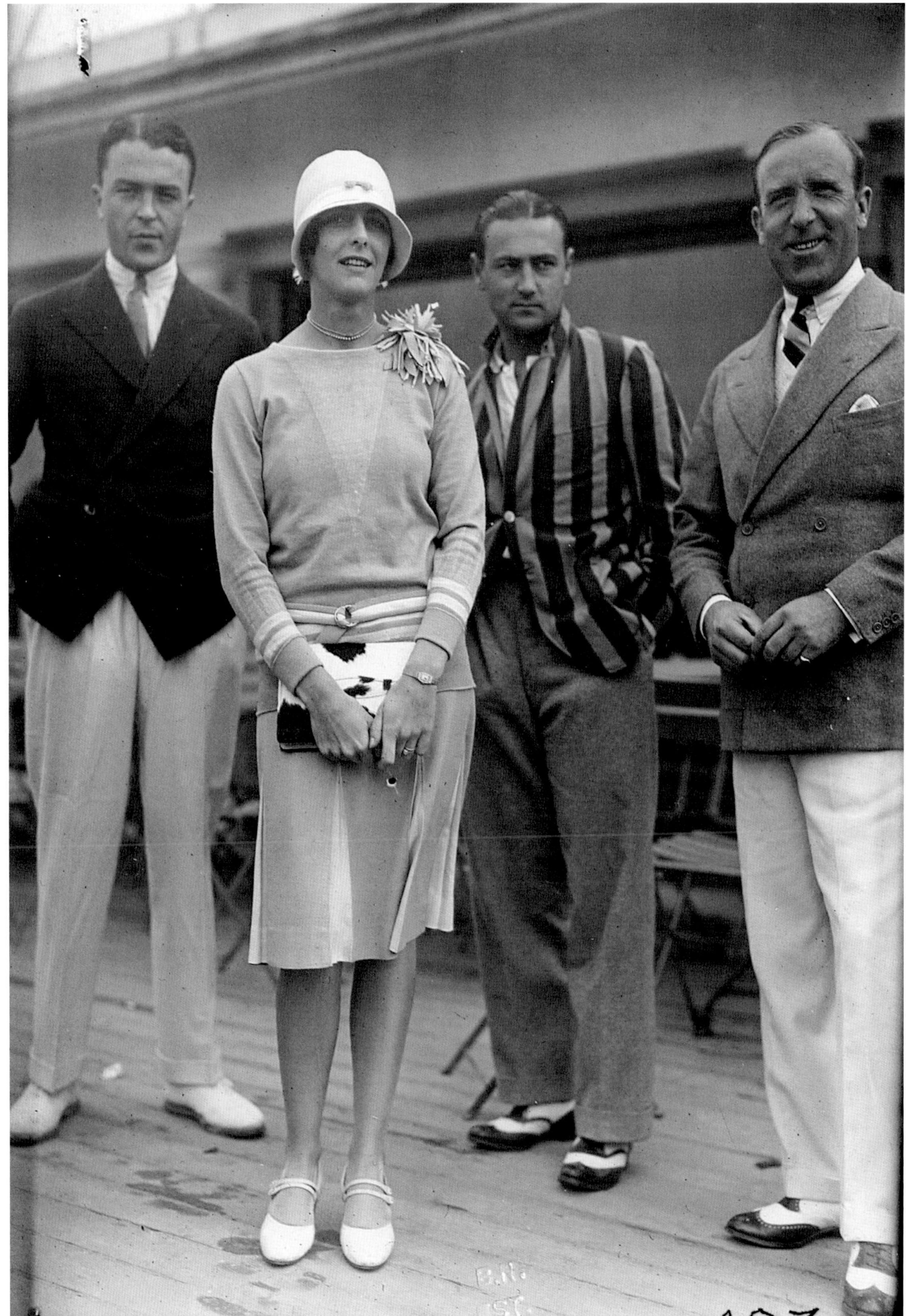

At Les Planches,
Deauville, August 1926.

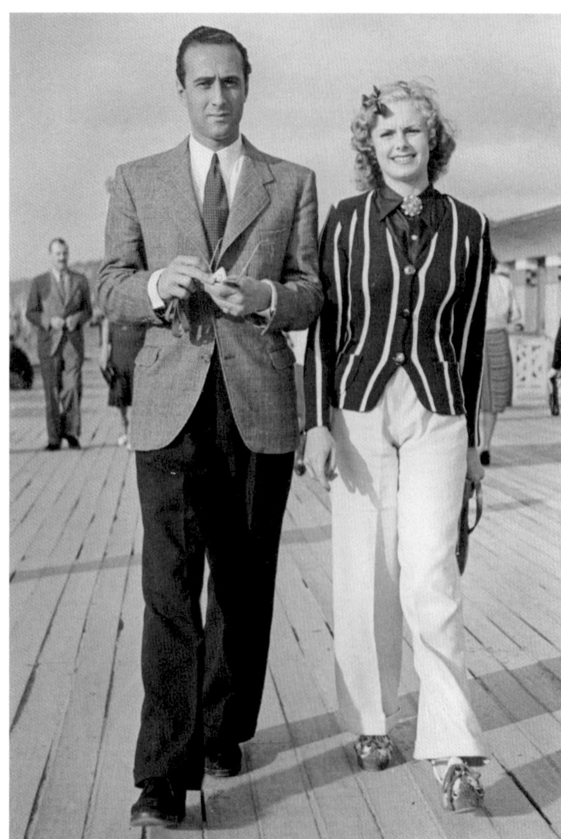

Count and Countess de Gozaloff wearing Jones outfits, Deauville, August 6, 1939.

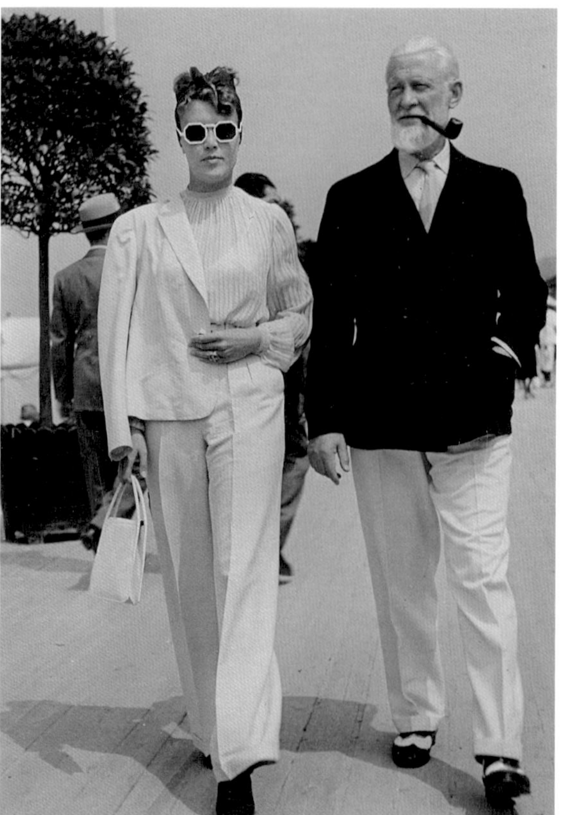

The artist Kees Van Dongen (1877–1968) and a friend, Deauville, August 6, 1939.

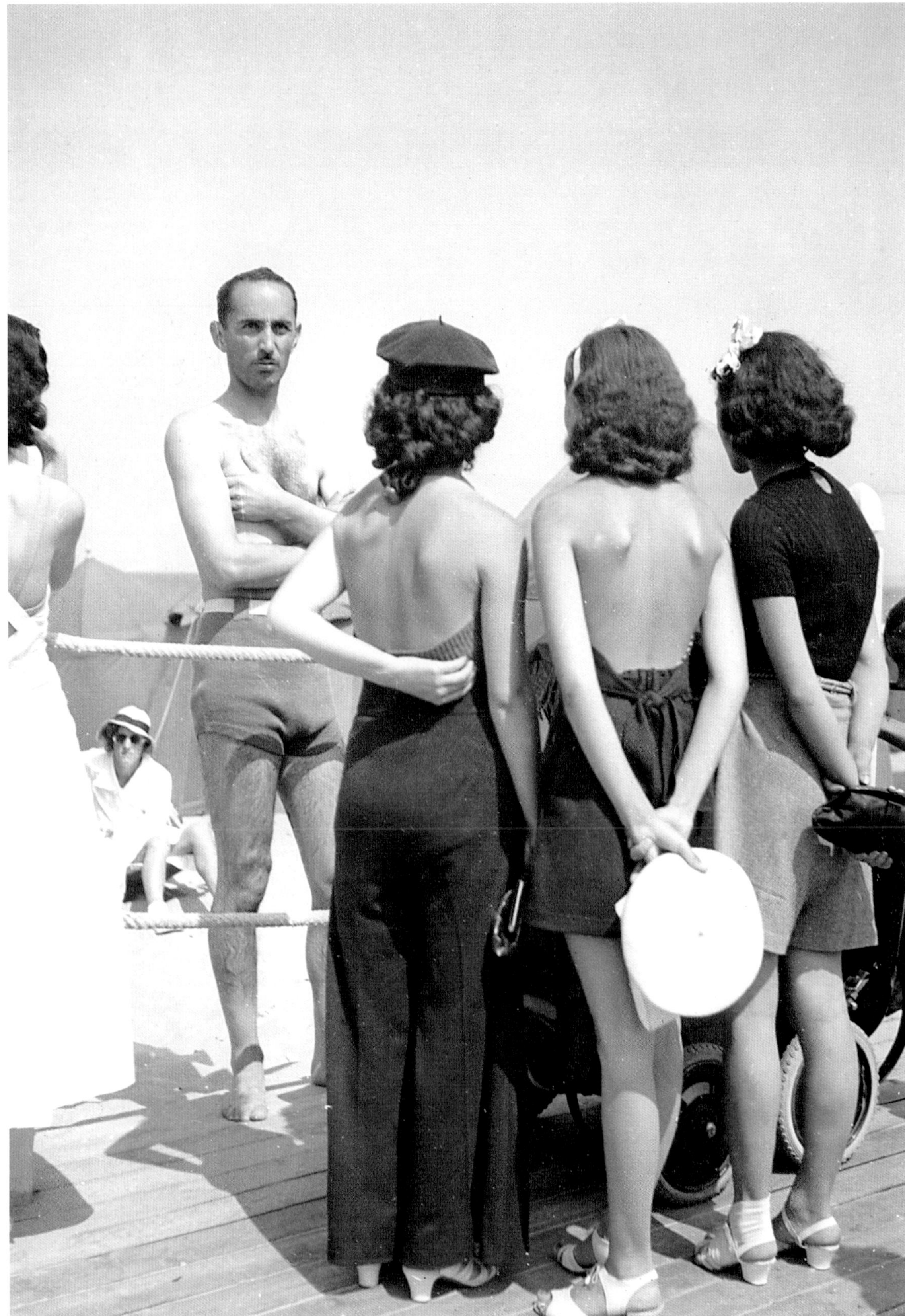

Prince Charles d'Arenberg (1905–1967) on the beach at Deauville, August 1935.

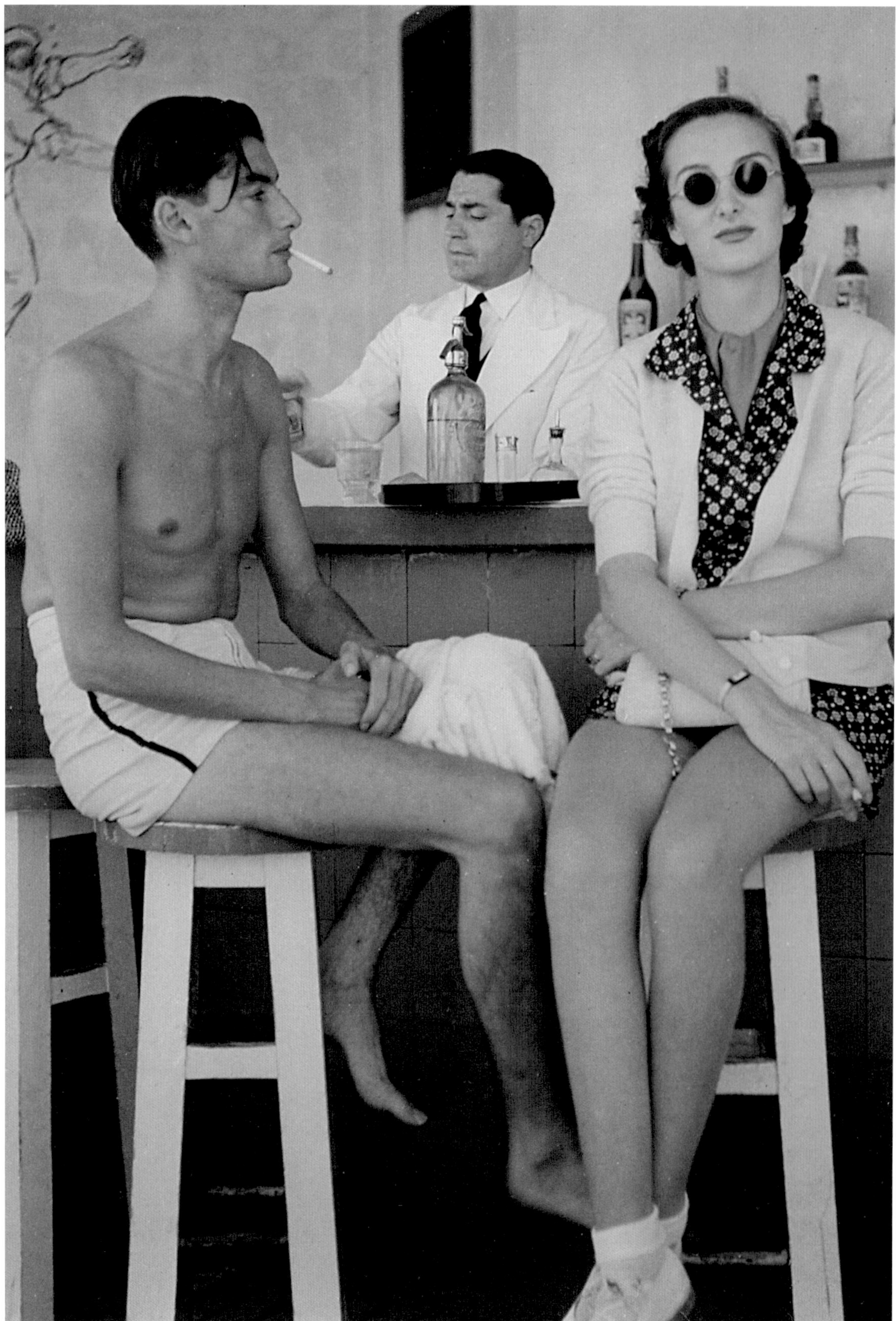

Mme Christian Dufaure seated at the bar of La Chambre d'Amour, *Biarritz, September 1935.*

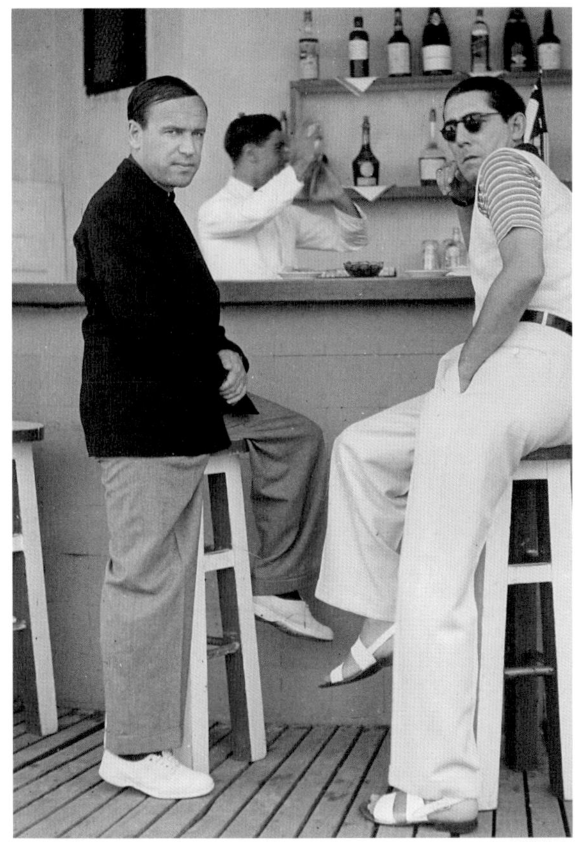

Jim Mollison and Martinez at the bar in La Chambre d'Amour, *Biarritz, September 1938.*

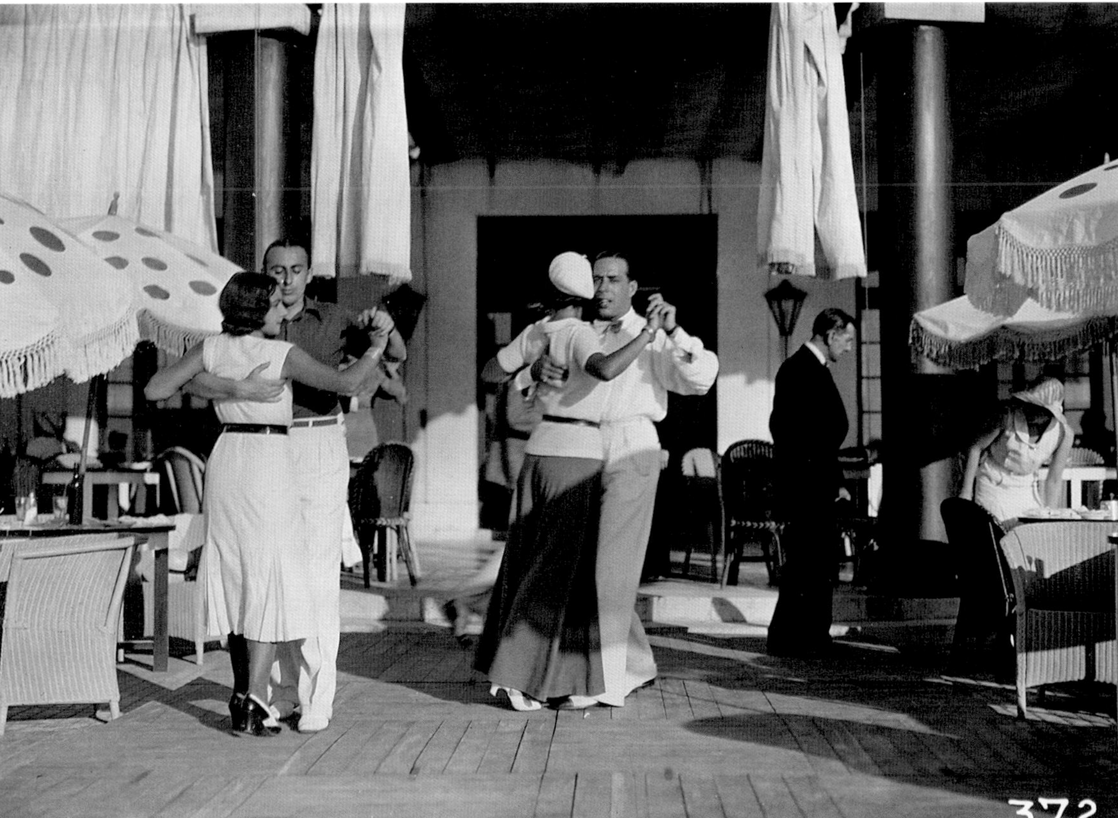

Dancing on the terrasse of La Chambre d'Amour *from five to seven, Biarritz, September 1931.*

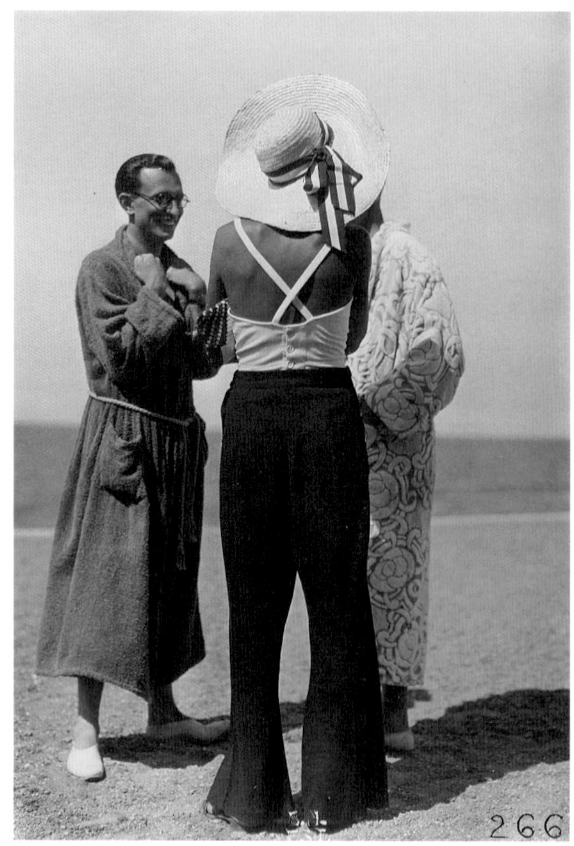

Hilda Sturm, Swiss ski champion, seen from behind, outfitted by Jane Régny, Biarritz, September 1930.

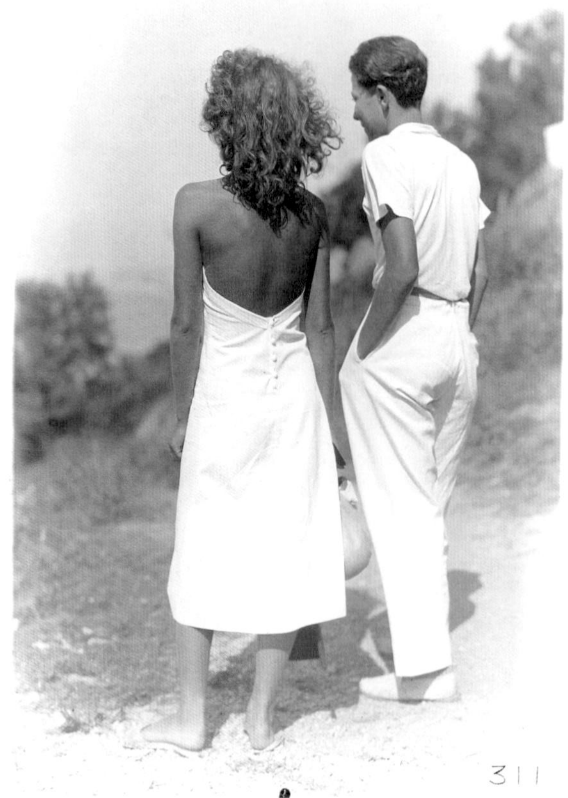

Young couple, Biarritz, September 1933.

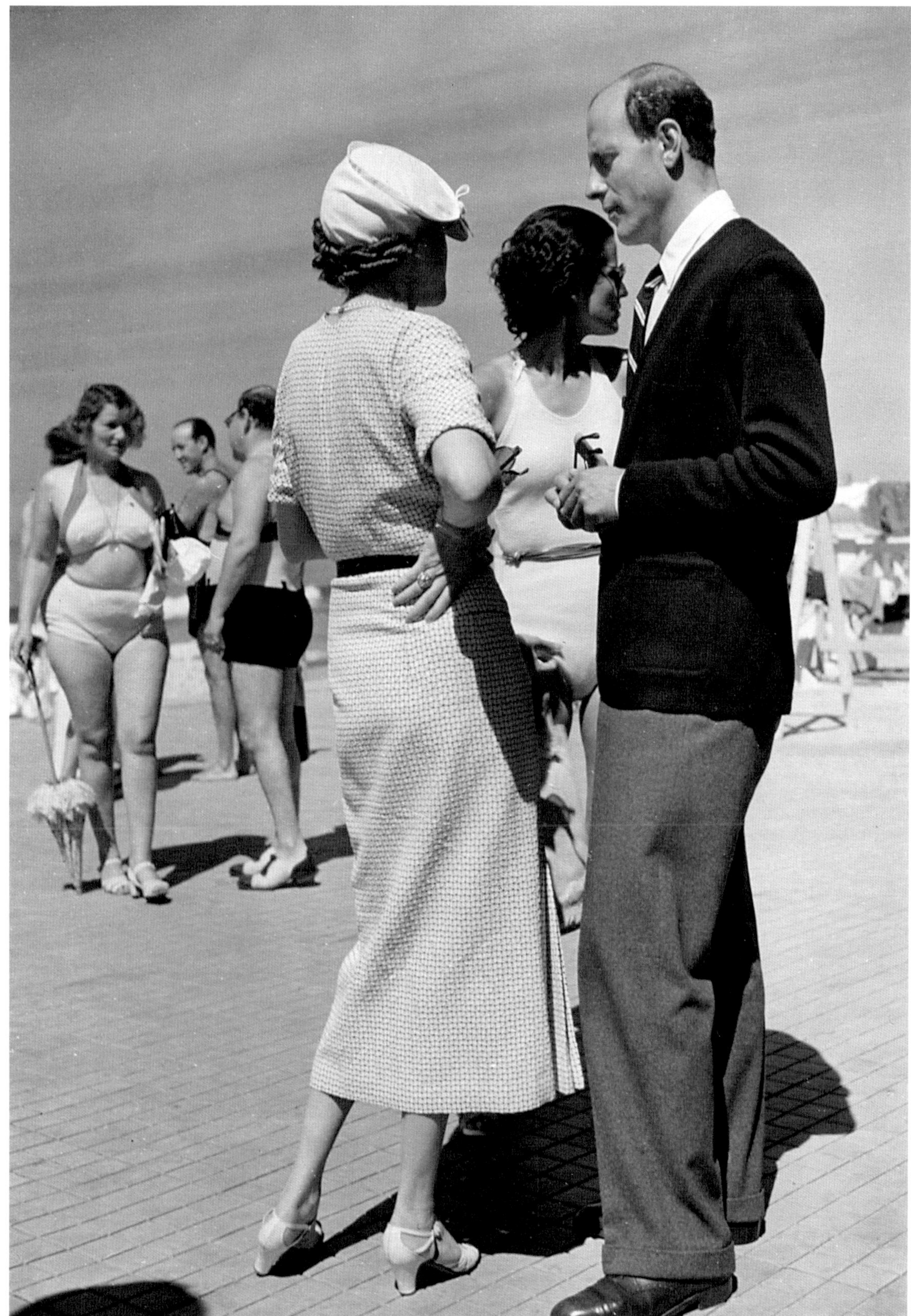

Marquise de La Fressange (in the foreground) and André Cellier, Biarritz, September 1935.

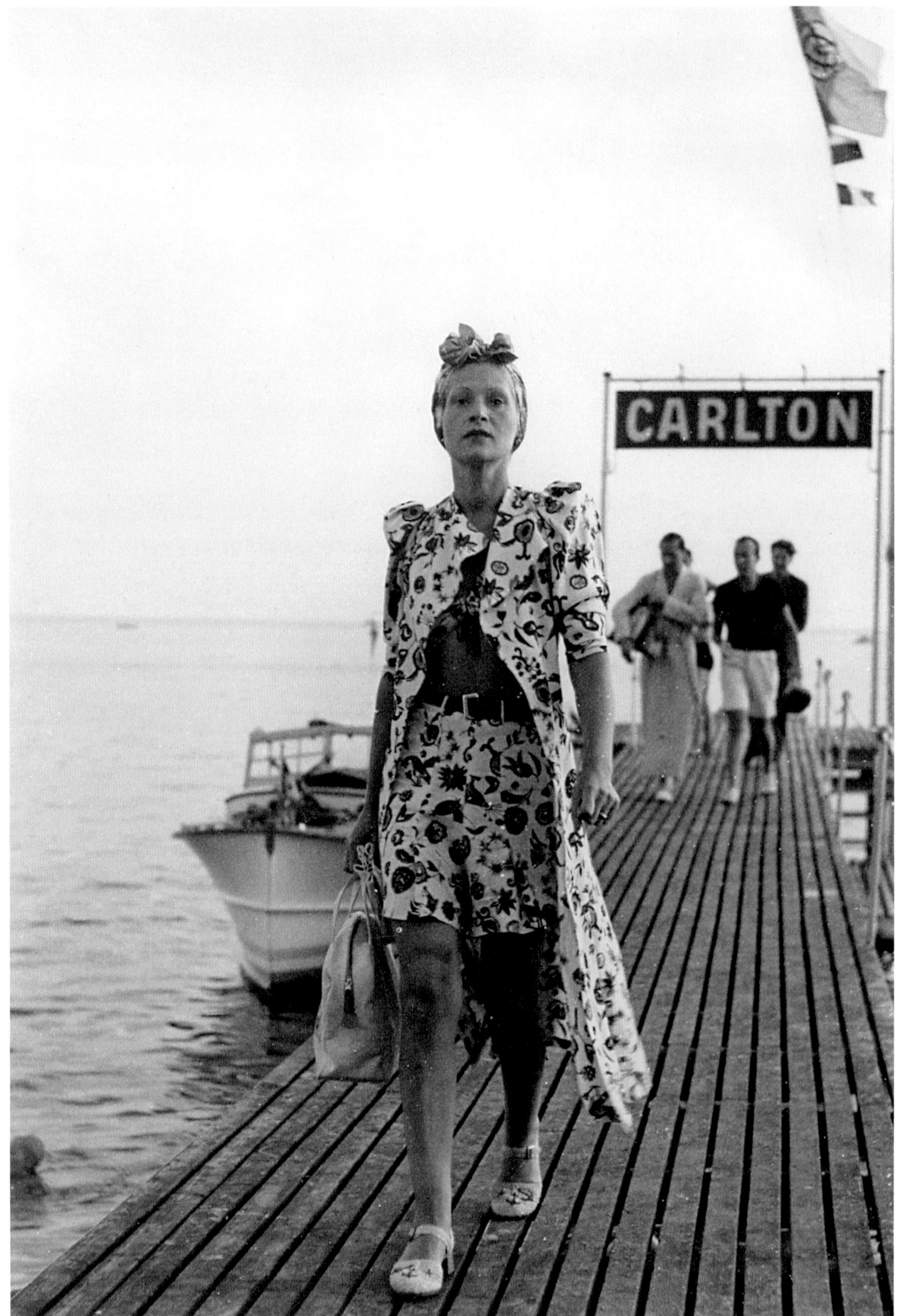

Mme Cuttingham on the pier of the Carlton Hotel, Cannes, September 1936.

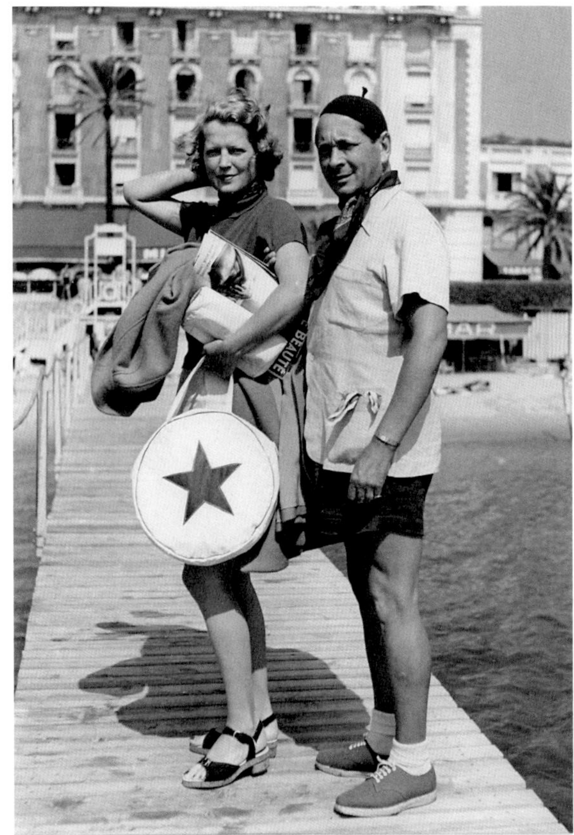

Mr. Ostertag and a friend, Cannes, September 1936.

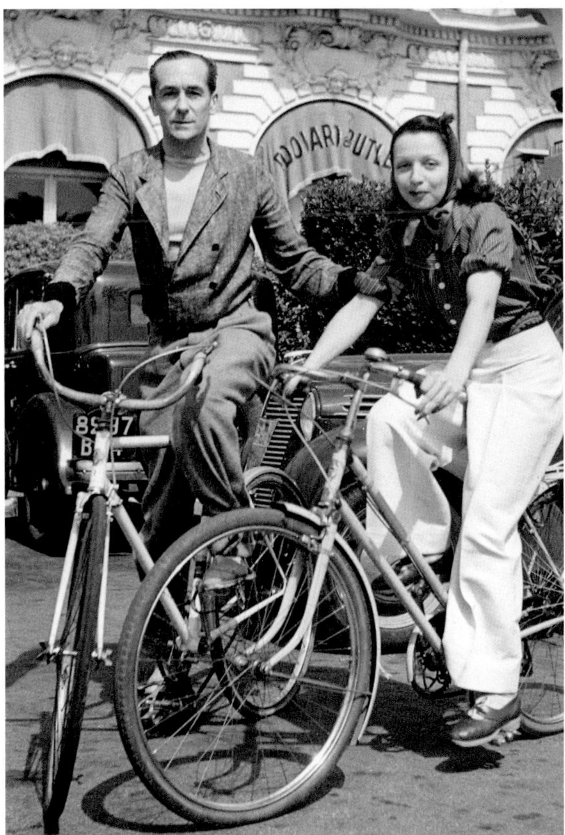

The photographer Jacques Henri Lartigue (1894–1986) and his second wife, Marcelle Paolucci, known as Coco, married in 1934, Cannes, April 1939.

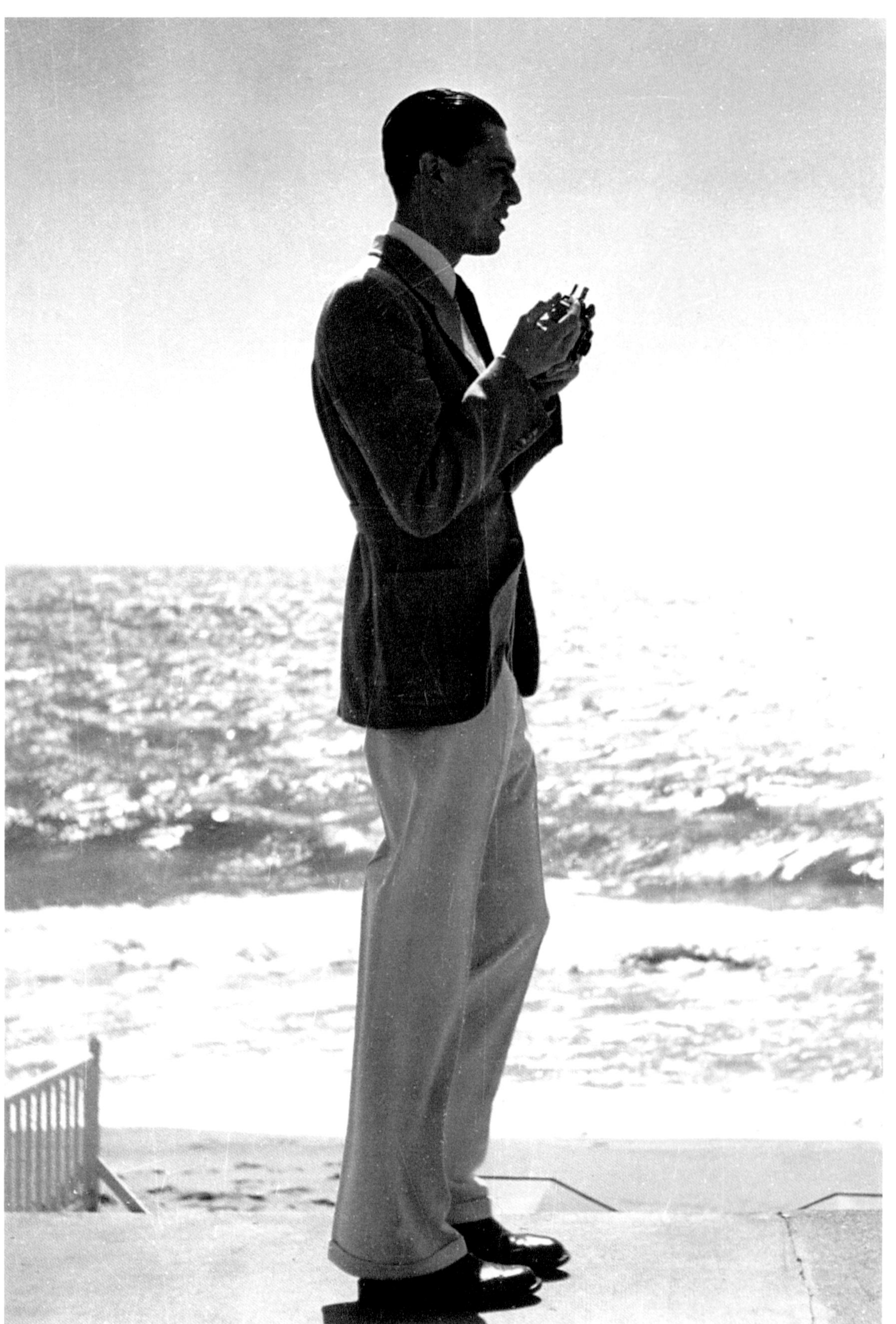

Elegant young photographer on the beach, Cannes, Easter, 1936.

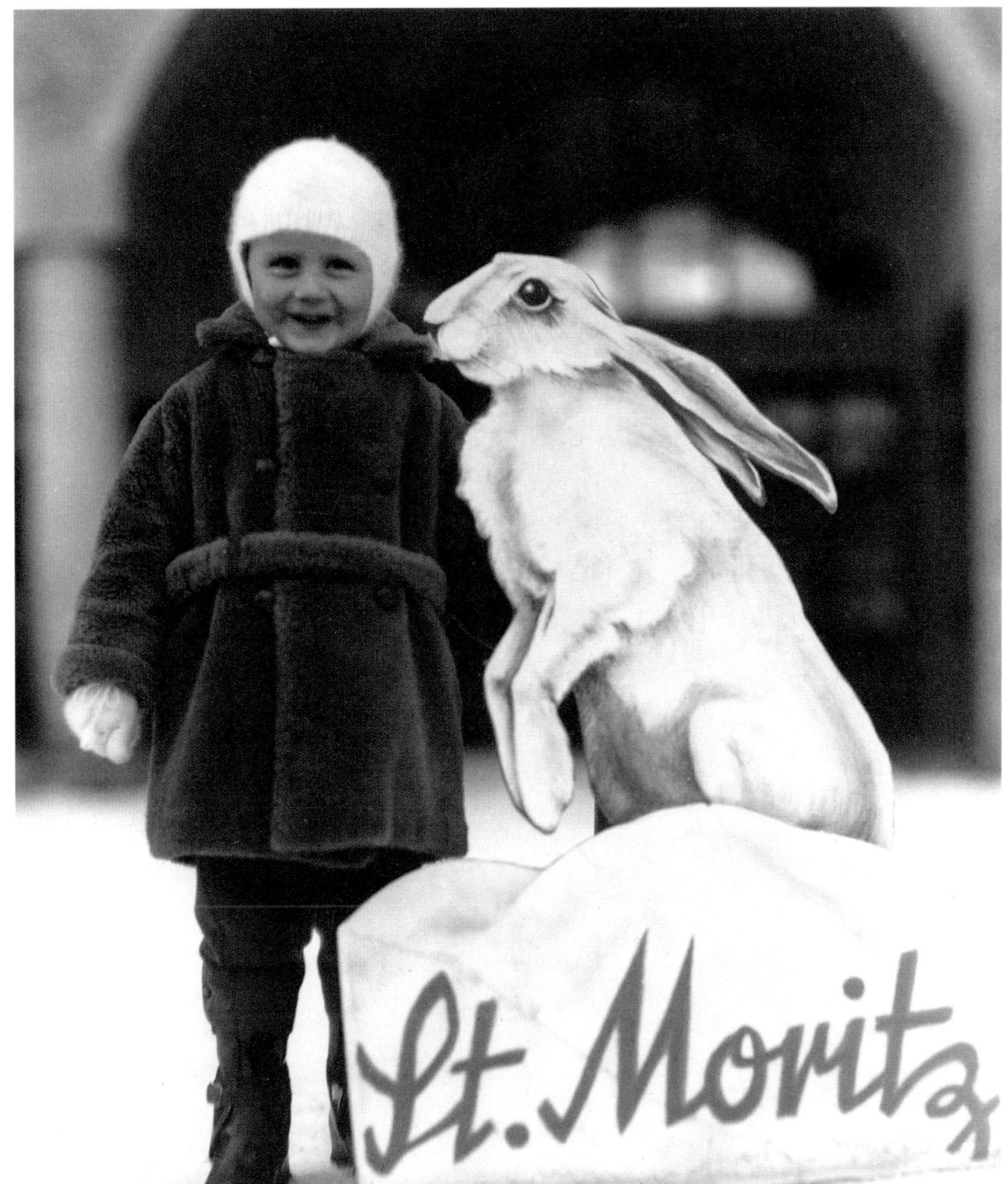

*Saint-Moritz,
New Year's Eve, 1933/34.*

117

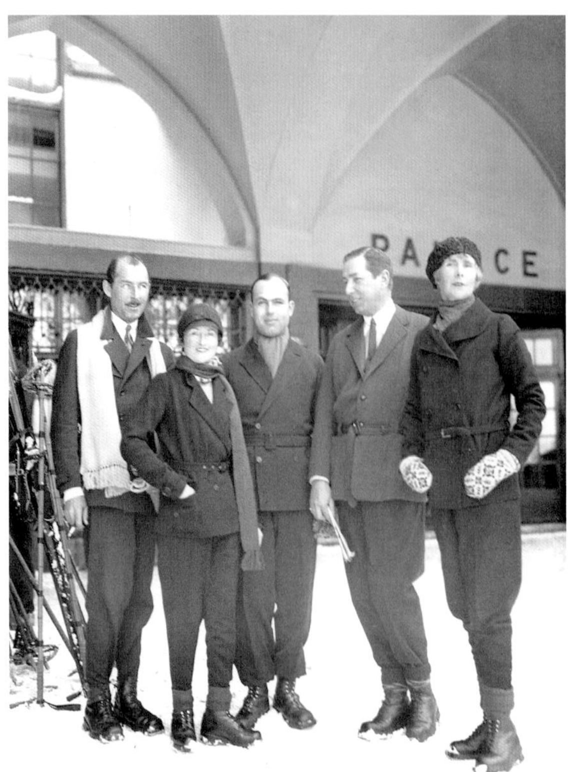

72 Mr x Mrs Richard Parke Baron x Baronne Demeyer

Mr. and Mrs. Richard Parke with (on the right) Baron Adolphe (1868–1946) and Baroness Olga de Meyer, née Caracciolo, Saint-Moritz, January 1930. One of the pioneering fashion photographers of the early twentieth century, Adolphe de Meyer collaborated especially with Vogue *(1914–1922) and then* Harper's Bazaar *(1922–1934); he and his wife—married in 1899—made a fashionable artistic team.*

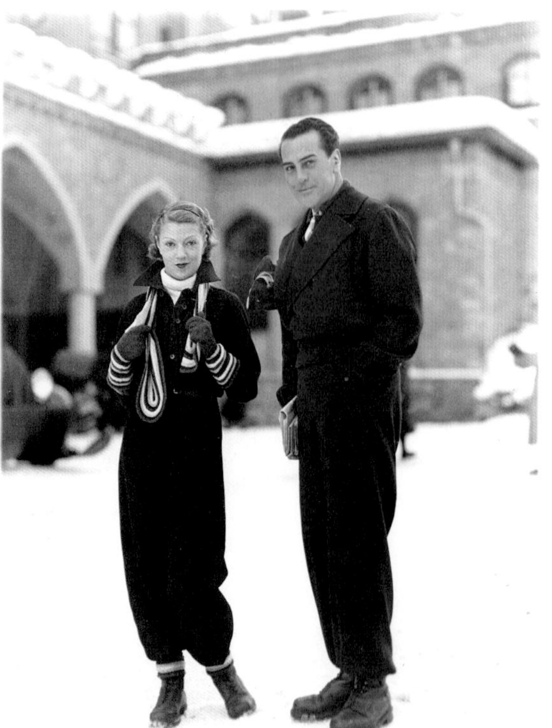

37 Mlle Annabella Mr Jean Murat

Film actor Jean Murat (1888–1968) with his fiancée, Annabella (1907–1996), an actress, Saint-Moritz, New Year's Eve, 1933/34.

Ilse Maria Remarque (1901–1975), née Ilse Jutta Zambona, Saint-Moritz, New Year's Eve, 1936/37. She and German writer Erich Maria Remarque (1898–1970), author of All Quiet on the Western Front, *were married twice, first in 1925, and again in 1938, in Saint-Moritz.*

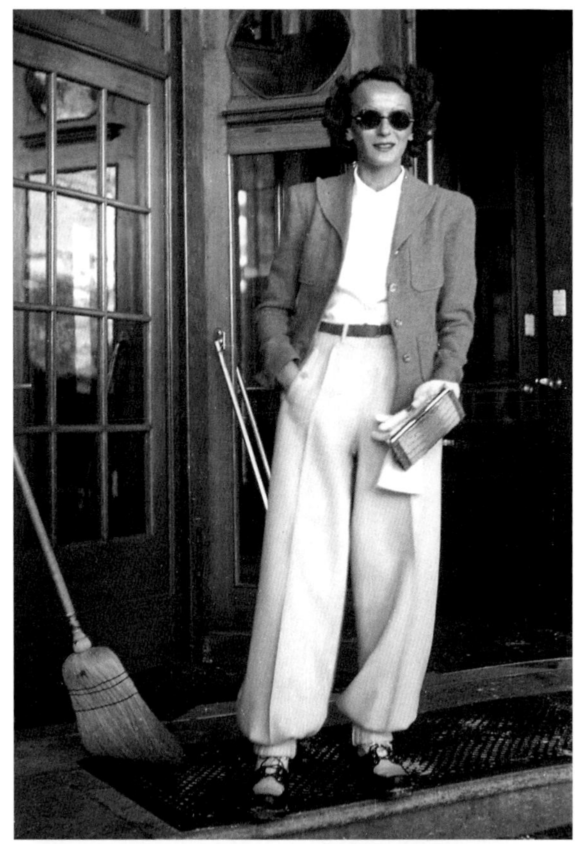

Princess Anna Boncompagni Ludovisi (1923–1946) in Chanel, Saint-Moritz, January 1933.

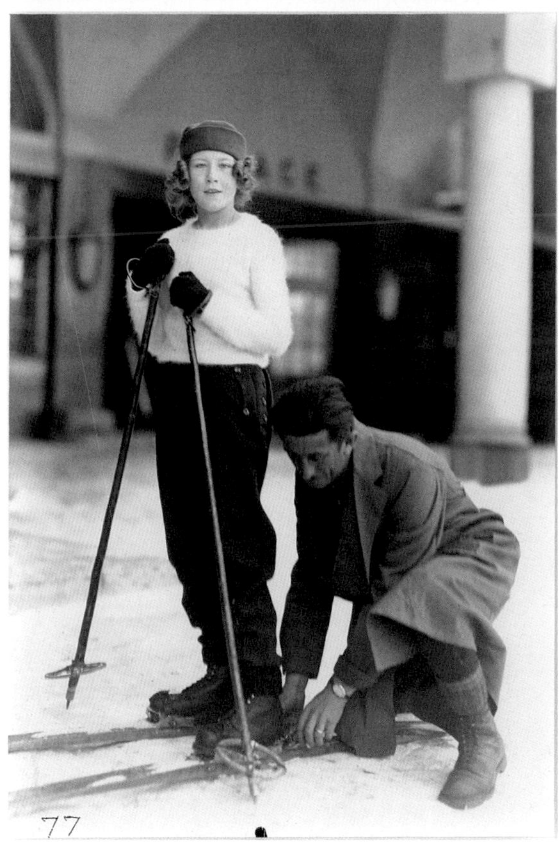

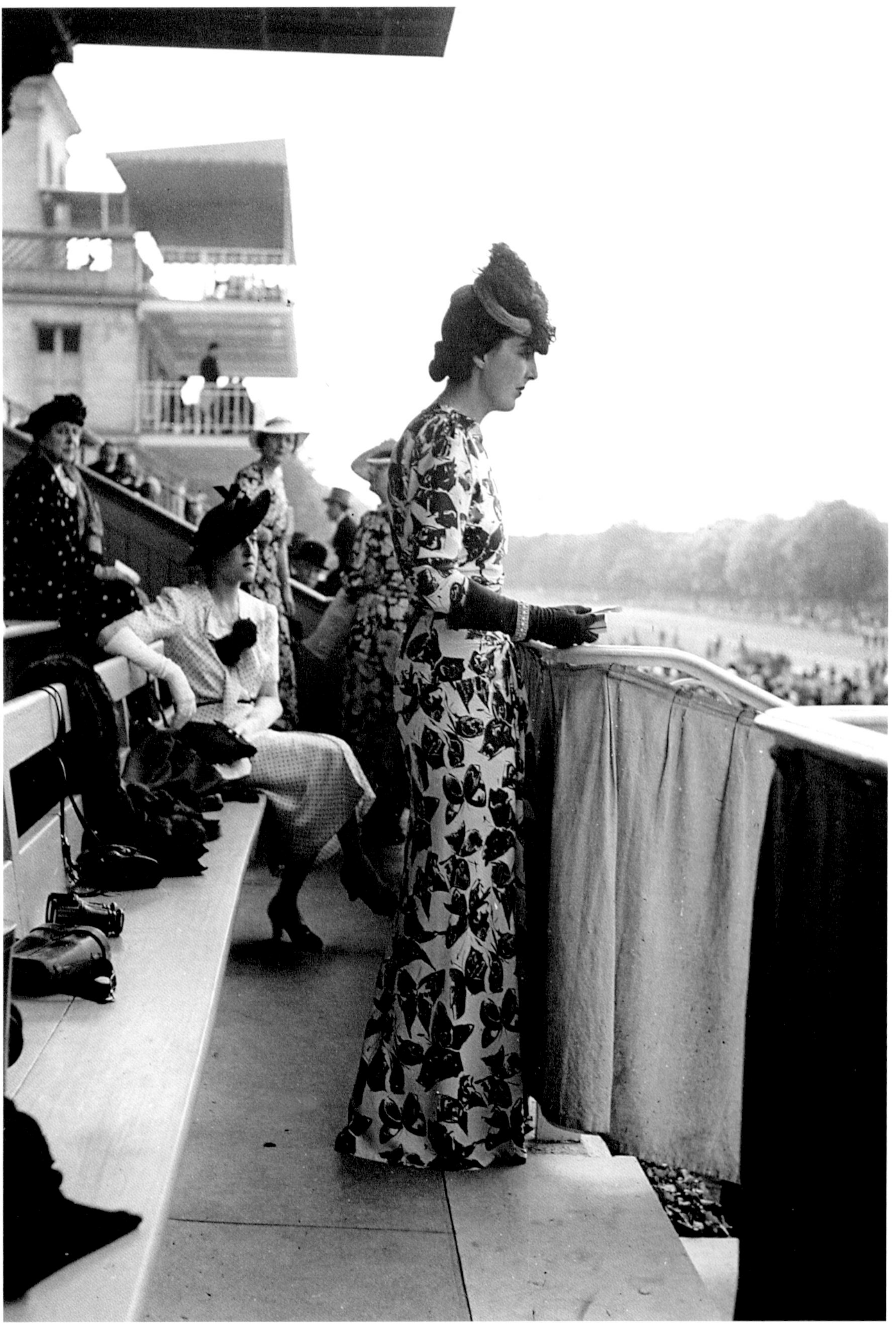

Countess Robert de Montjou, née Alice de La Laurencie, in a gown by Maggy Rouff and a hat by Talbot, in the stands at Chantilly, Prix de Diane, June 6, 1937. Seated behind her is the princess Amédée de Broglie.

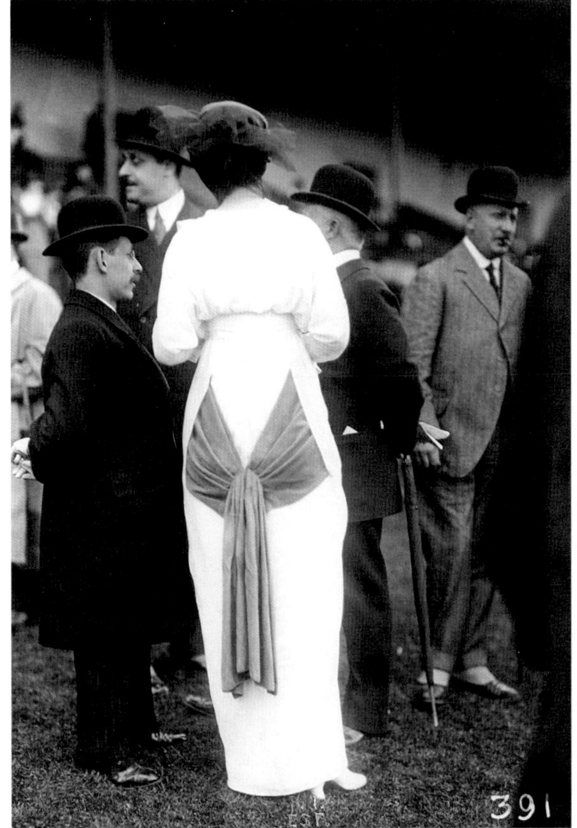

Chantilly, June 1913.

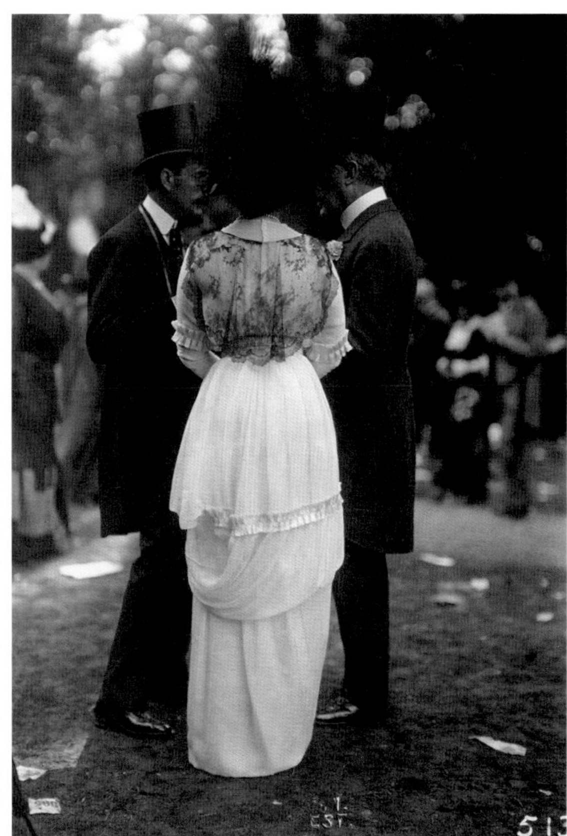

Grande Course des Haies, Auteuil, June 1912.

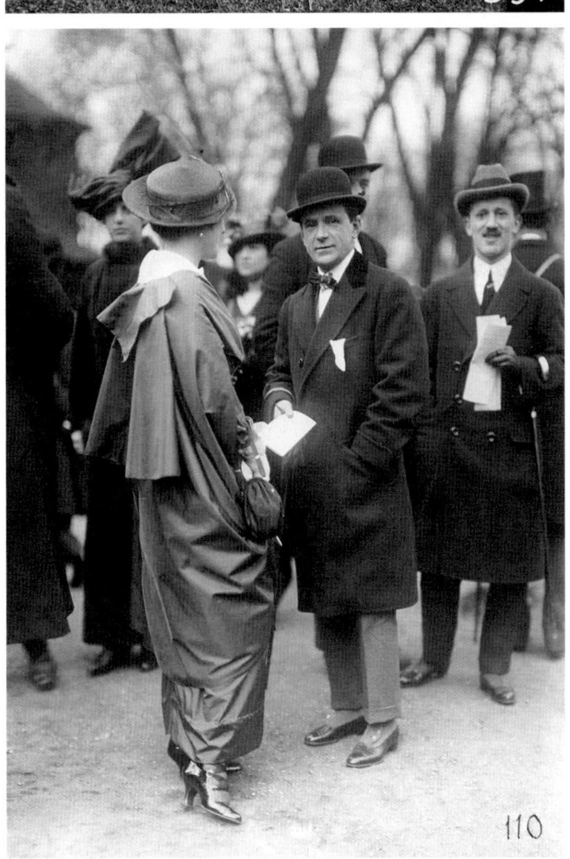

The caricaturist Sem (pseudonym of George Goursat, 1863–1934) at the Auteuil races, March 29, 1914. Sem, one of the most assiduous personalities of the racetracks and high-society resorts, met with astounding success when he published his first album, Turf, *in 1909; he is famous for his portraits of Parisian celebrities, created on the fly.*

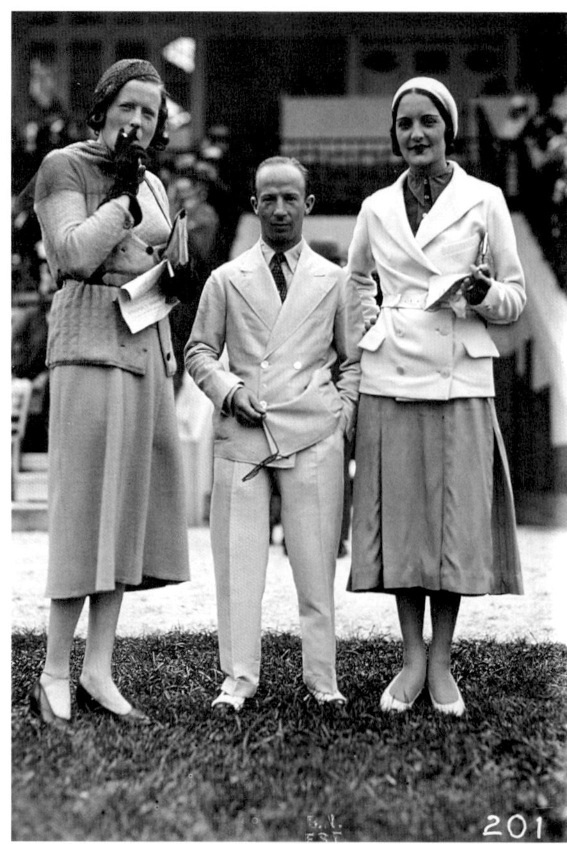

The jockey Gabriel Vatard, who rode in the colors of Princess de Faucigny-Lucinge, between Laure Jarny and Mlle Saint-Clivier, Deauville races, August 9, 1931.

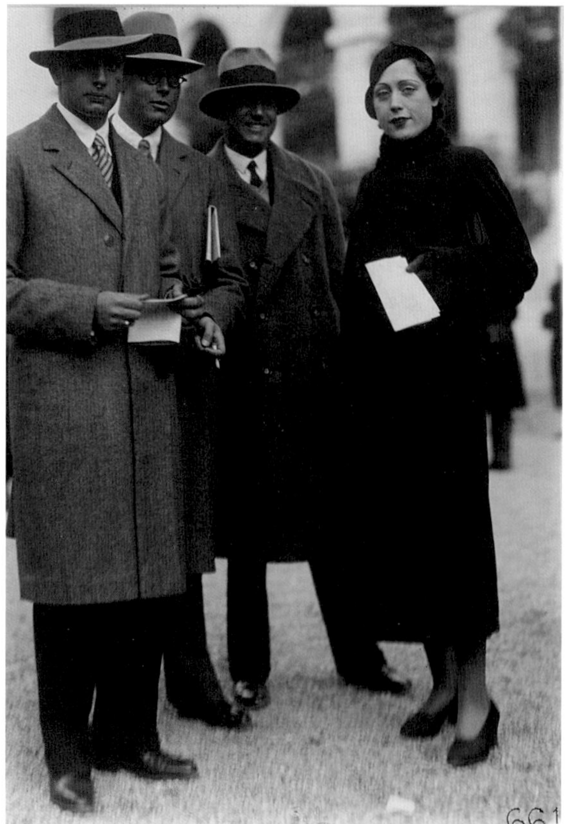

Mme Monari at Longchamp, October 18, 1931.

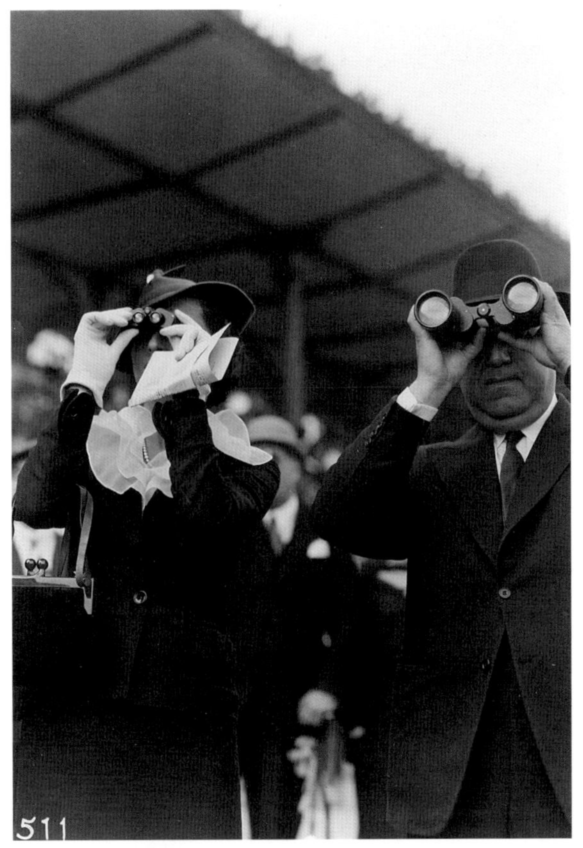

Young woman in Jean Patou, Longchamp, Prix Royal Oak, September 16, 1934.

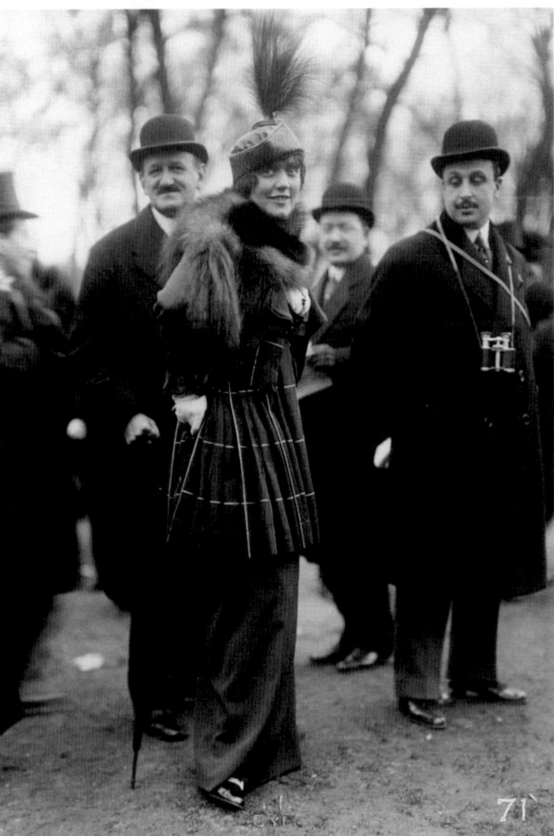

At the races, March 1914.

A Poiret dress at the racetrack, May 1921.

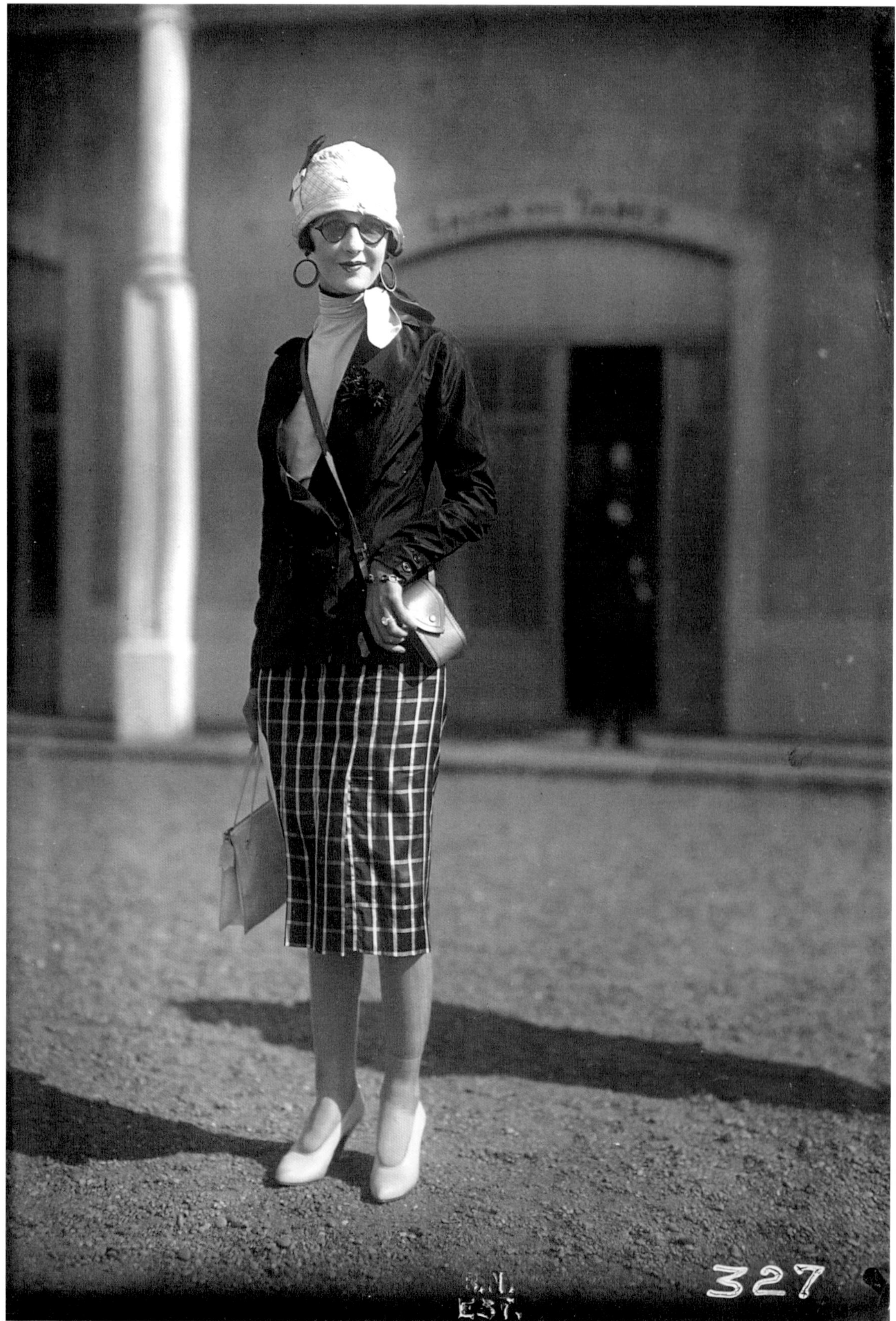

Biarritz, September 1925.

Mlle Magnus, at the reopening of Longchamp, September 9, 1934.

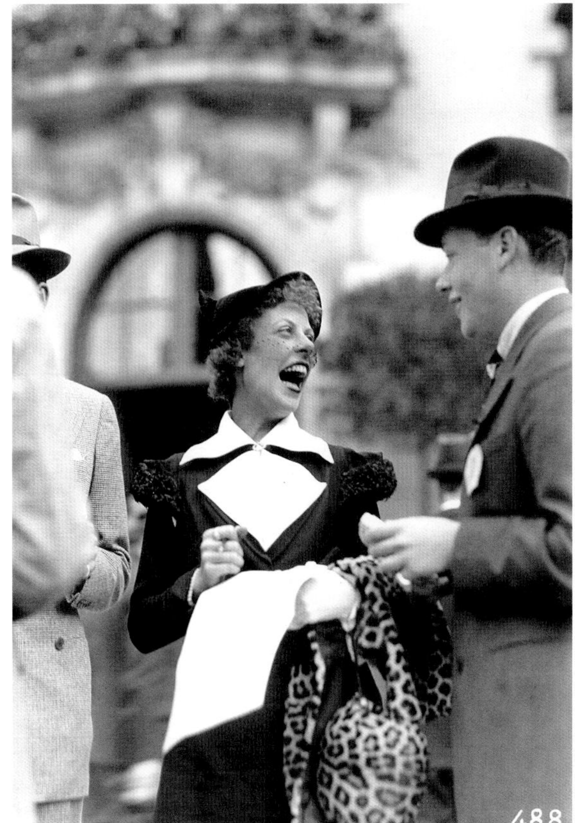

The Boulevard actress Jane Marnac (1892–1976), née Mayer, outfitted by Callot, Deauville, August 19, 1923.

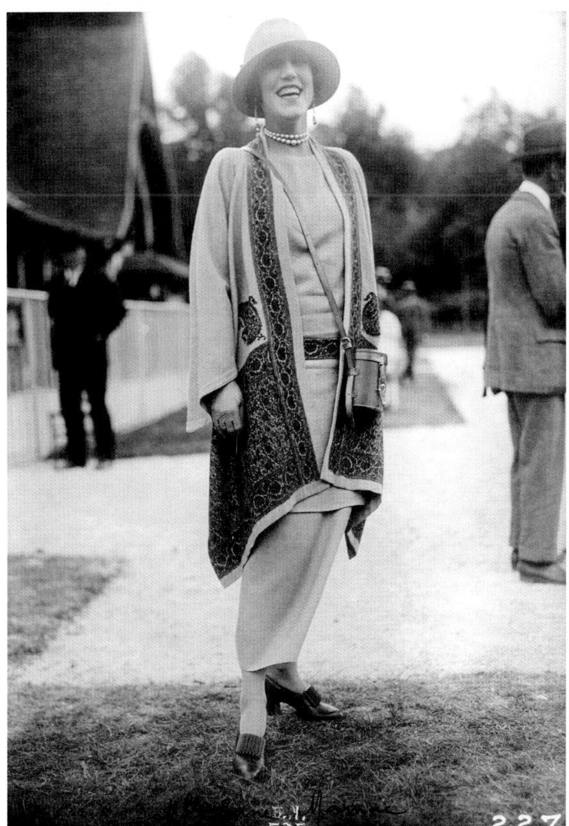

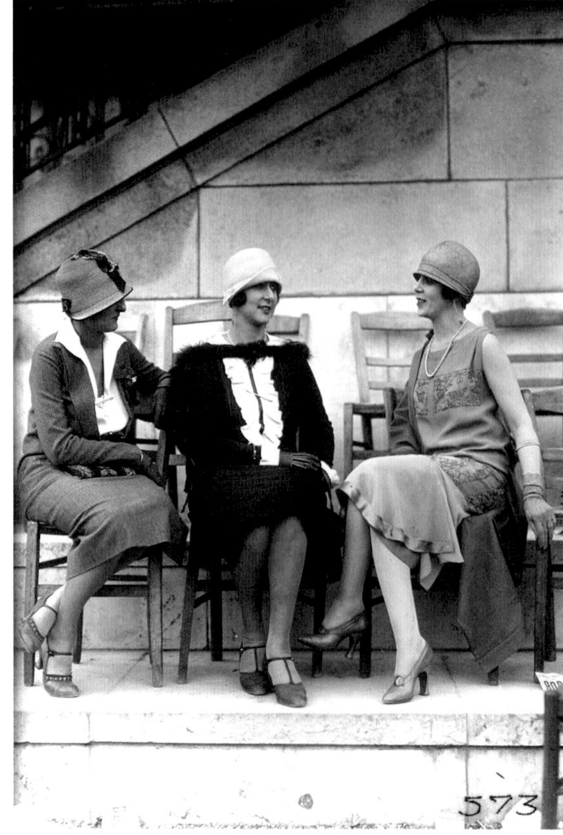

At the races, 1925.

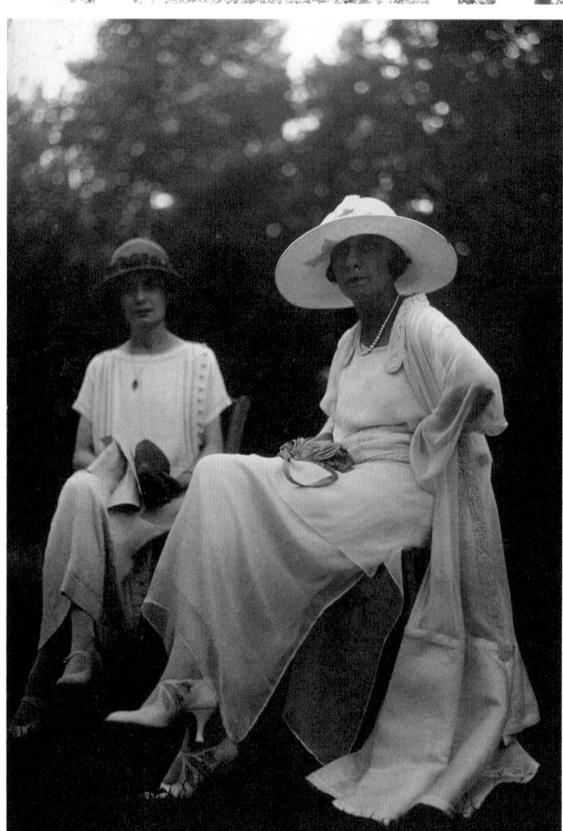

Seated woman in a Chéruit gown, Deauville, August 12, 1923.

The Hobsons, May 1914.

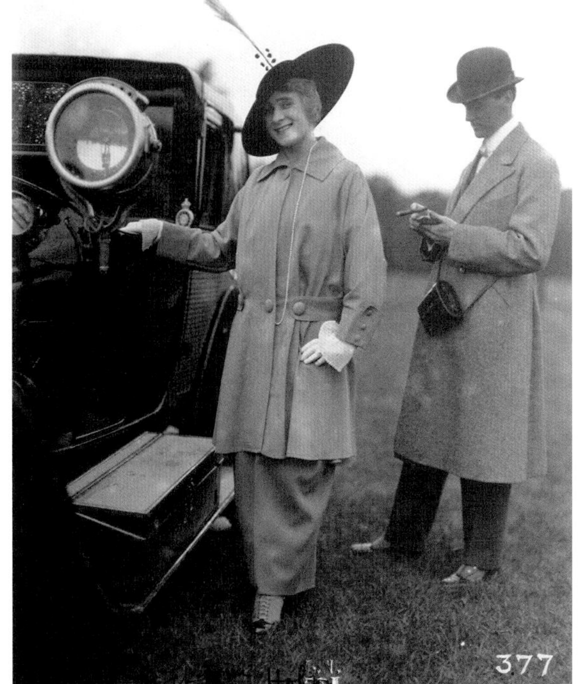

Acacia allée in the Bois de Boulogne, March 22, 1931.

Yvette Laurent in a Drécoll-Beer dress, concours d'elegance car show at the Parc des Princes, 1930.

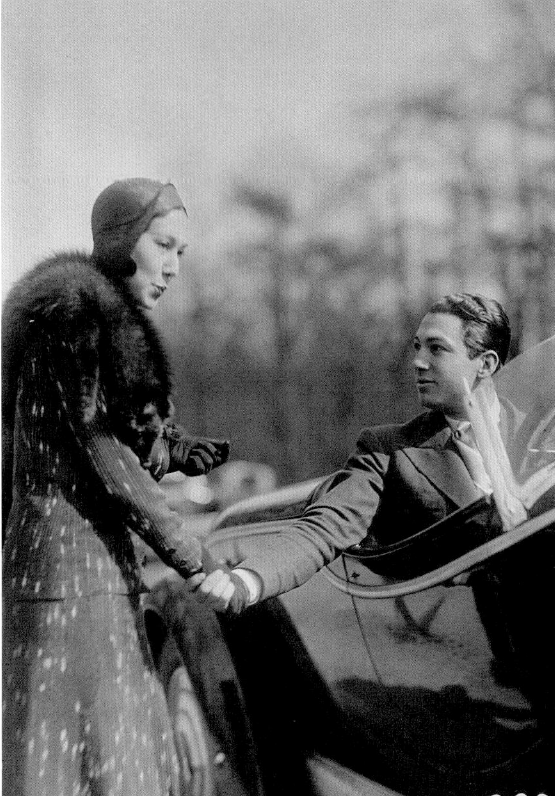

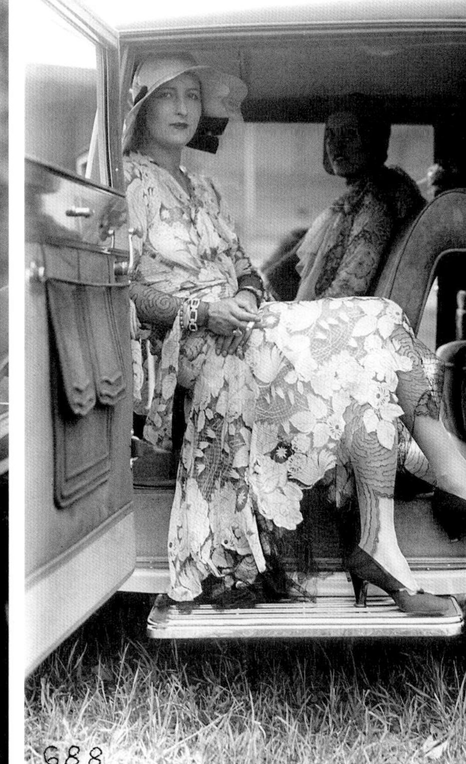

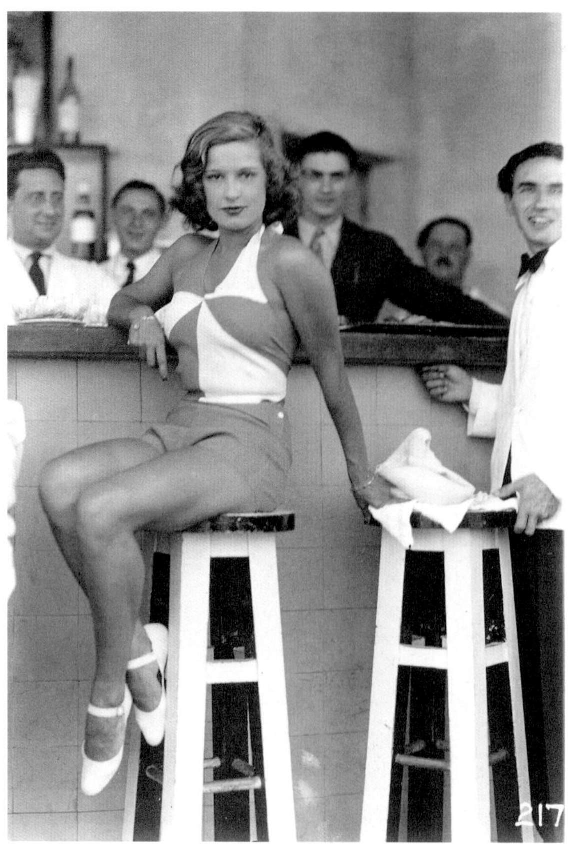

French actress Lily Damita (1904–1994), née Liliane Carré, wife of Errol Flynn from 1935 to 1942, Biarritz, September 1933.

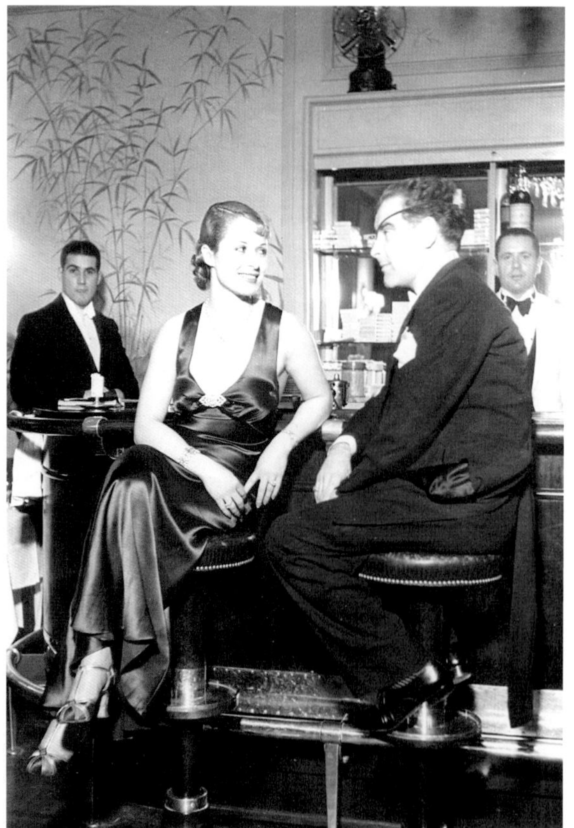

Mona Rico (1906–1994), Mexican actress, wearing Schiaparelli, in the company of Arthur Wiesenberger, at the bar of The Embassy, Saint-Moritz, New Year's Eve, 1935/36.

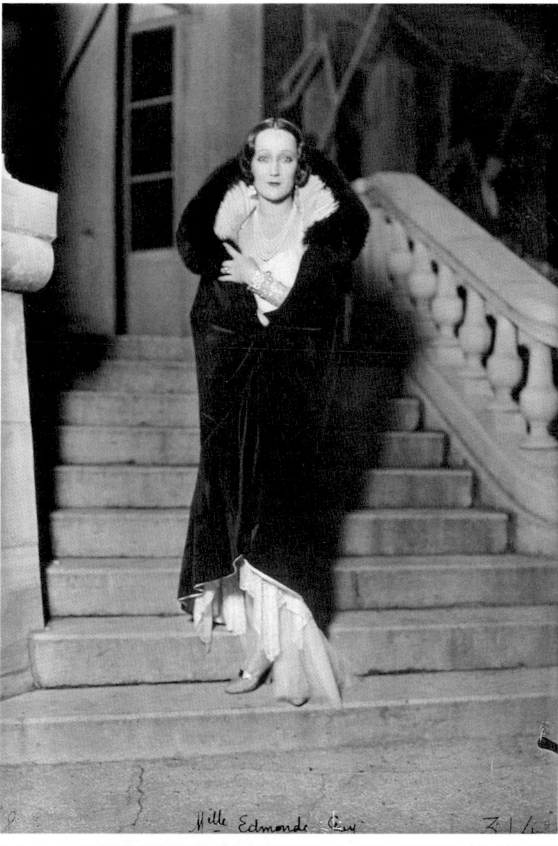

Edmonde Guy, née Eugénie Goubé, top billed music-hall star, sister of the milliner Maria Guy, Biarritz, September 1929.

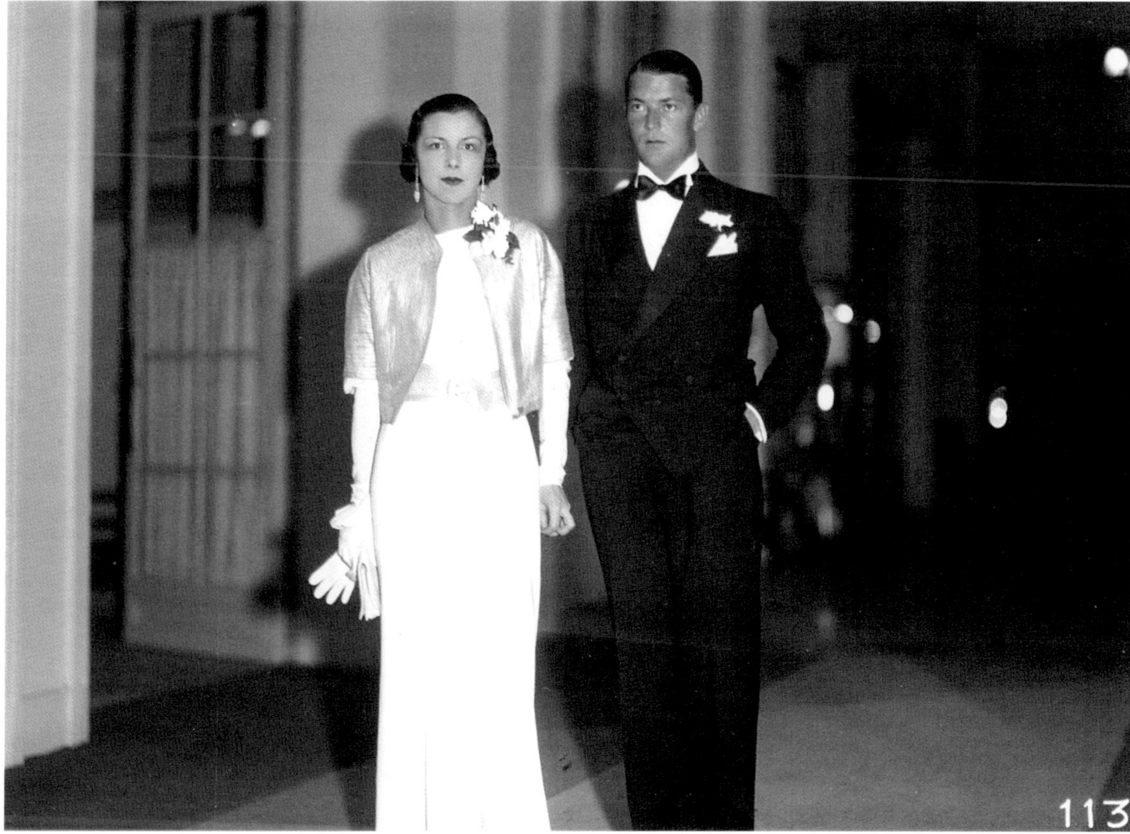

Michael Farmer (1902–1975), Irish actor, at the Golf Hotel gala, Deauville, August 12, 1934. Here shown with a friend, just after his divorce from Gloria Swanson, whom he had married in 1932.

PERSONALITIES

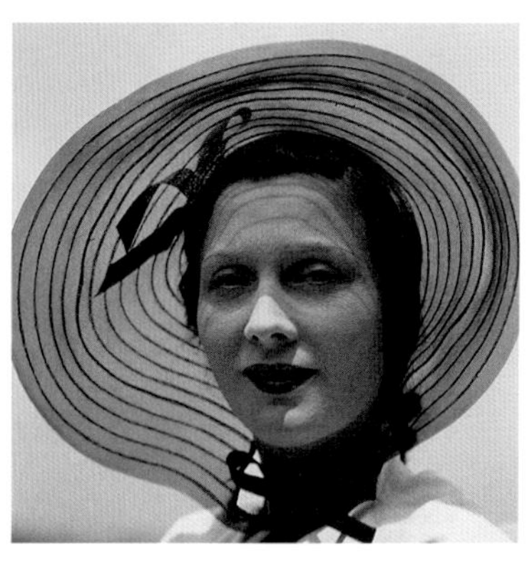

PERSONALITIES

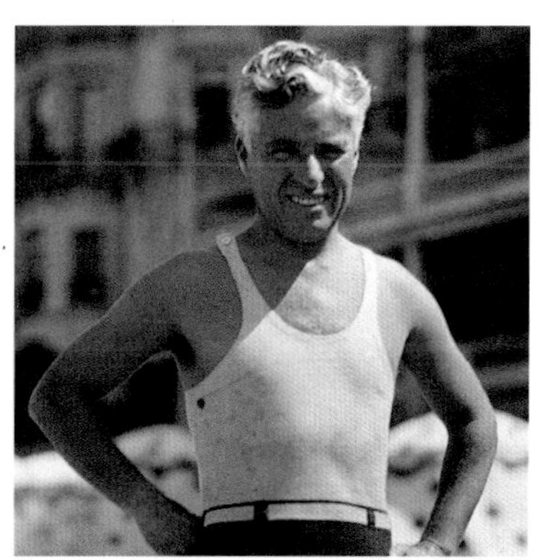

PERSONALITIES

Xavier Demange

The Séebergers not only photographed fashions, they also photographed people. Although many are now unknown to us, a diligent eye and careful attention to the various annotations on the photographs themselves can extract the more familiar features of the personalities of the period from this mass of anonymous faces. Indeed, the Séebergers generally indicated the name of the couturier or milliner at the bottom of each image, and sometimes the models' names, almost certainly for submission to their foreign customers (the practice was rarely observed during the first decade of their business, but much more frequently after 1929).

An entire world, a sampling of the Who's Who of the period between the World Wars processes before us: high society, artists of all kinds, models, athletes, and wealthy foreigner tourists are recorded in places as varied as the racetrack, seaside resorts, winter sporting events, or (more rarely) private receptions. As mentioned above, many well-known women wore haute couture creations for the sole purpose of allowing themselves to be photographed without restraint at the society gatherings they attended. Stars of the stage, music hall, and cinema were quickest to exploit this. The upper crust was represented by a handful of society women whose notoriety was no longer disputed and who could invariably be recognized, season after season, over the years. The social elite and financial elite were each represented by a few select personalities.

STAGE ARTISTS

The Séebergers' most-photographed celebrities belonged to the world of the Parisian music halls. First and foremost was the indefatigable Mistinguett (illus. p. 211), who held the spotlight without fail for nearly fifty years. She was seen at the heart of all the great society gatherings between the two wars. In the eyes of the civilized world, she came to represent the quintessential "Parisian," but she controlled her public appearances particularly carefully. It was whispered that, as a fearsome businesswoman, she insisted on being paid by the couture houses that solicited her to wear their outfits, and simply kept those that pleased her most. An unreliable payer, she was always involved in lawsuits with her suppliers–though this did nothing to dampen the enthusiasm of her adoring public.

Two sisters were close behind her in the ranks of the Séebergers' most-photographed stars of the 1920s: the Dolly Sisters (illus. p. 207). Rosie and Jenny, née Deutsch, naturalized American dancers of Hungarian descent, personified the style of the flapper years with their identical bobbed haircuts and makeup, their extravagant outfits and fabulous jewelry. Their artistic career in France extended from 1922 to 1928.

Another music-hall artist, an American greatly loved by the public, was Joséphine Baker, who was also known as the Black Pearl. She made her entire career in France and attended the races in the 1930s. The Séebergers also photographed her at her home in Vésinet in 1932 for a report that has never been published (illus. p. 203).

A singing star at her debut in the 1920s, Suzy Solidor was much photographed in Deauville by the Séebergers (illus. pp. 204–205). An impossible-to-ignore personality of the garçonne period, she was especially known for her extravagant clothing and various escapades at that time. Becoming a full-scale artist in the 1930s, she drew all Paris to her cabaret in rue Sainte-Anne.

Other variety stars less often represented in the Séebergers' oeuvre were no less popular: Jane Marnac and Spinelly were operetta queens, but also Boulevard actresses. Not to be forgotten are the beautiful Edmonde Guy, the American Jenny Golder, Florelle, Gaby Deslys and her dance partner Harry Pilcer, and Laure Diana, all of whom headlined at the Paris Casino, the Moulin-Rouge, the Folies-Bergère, the Palace, the Cigale, and so on. Among the stage actresses are none who were employed by the state-subsidized theaters, but a great many stars of the Boulevard theaters: Maud Loty, who played leading roles at the *Variétés*; Gisèle and Nadine Picard (two very elegant sisters); Jane Renouardt; Gaby Morlay; Regina Camier; the incandescent Rumanian Elvire Popesco; Geneviève Delubac, who married

Sacha Guitry; Huguette Duflos; Alice Cocéa and Simone Berriau, who headlined at the Ambassadeurs Theater and the Antoine Theater respectively; as well as a bevy of actresses who had the gift of making Parisians laugh for more than thirty years and, for the most part, are quite unjustly forgotten. The Séebergers' images restore to us their smiles, their extravagant garb, and the intangible air of a vanished time when they twirled to the last applause of their admirers.

Most of these artists enjoyed success on both the stage and on the screen. After World War I, a great American silent film star, Pearl White, was often seen at the Paris racetracks. She came to love France so much that she lived there until her death. Gaby Deslys also made a career in Hollywood, but died prematurely in 1922. Jacqueline Forzane began her career as a model before the war and played in many films, but only after the advent of talking films were significant numbers of the great film stars seen at society gatherings: Simone Simon; Brigitte Bardot of the 1930s; Lily Damita, who married Errol Flynn; Jean Murat and his wife at the time, Annabella; Tino Rossi and his friend Mireille Balin; Arletty; Josette Day, whom Cocteau later launched into the public eye; and Corinne Luchaire (illus. p. 217), who was destroyed by political passions after the war. From abroad, prestigious actors including Charlie Chaplin, Buster Keaton, and Douglas Fairbanks, the enigmatic Eric von Stroheim, and sultry Marlene Dietrich would briefly condescend to strike a spontaneous pose before the Séeberger viewfinder (illus. p. 213).

Still other artists mingled in the permanent party that ruled this cosmopolitan society until the outbreak of war, to draw inspiration from it and to transcend it in their personal work. First among these must be the celebrated caricaturist Sem, habitué of the races and Deauville, where for more than thirty years he untiringly launched biting penciled salvos at the idiocies of contemporary society, recorded in his famous albums. The Séeberger brothers made no mistake in photographing him frequently, because their shared status as privileged observers of their time implied some kind of tacit complicity between them. Two great photographers who recorded aspects of this world destined to disappear in the storm, each in his own style, Jacques Henri Lartigue and Baron Adolphe de Meyer, were photographed in quiet moments with their wives by the vigilant Séebergers (illus. pp. 177 and 180).

THE ELITE

Like the fashionables, the upper echelons of society were also among the crowds: aristocrats, major financiers, and racing stable owners. Royalty made furtive appearances, as well: the king of Spain, Alphonse XIII (illus. p. 198), invited to Deauville by resort manager Eugène Cornuché during the 1922 season, was roundly condemned by all the European consulates for lending himself to a shameless advertising campaign. Titled nobility still enjoyed great prestige, and their presence—duly recorded by the Séebergers—gave the horse shows an undeniable cachet, eagerly relayed by the fashion reviews, which commented on the women's most attractive toilettes. Among the most elegant of this group were the French: the countesses d'Audiffret-Pasquier, Élie de Ganay, Robert de Montjou, Le Chartier de Sédouy, Jean de Moustiers, de la Guère, de la Falaise, Gabriel de La Rochefoucauld, and the princesses Amédée de Broglie and May de Faucigny-Lucinge. Among the foreigners were the countesses de Muñoz, Celani, Sanjust di Teulada, Gozaloff, Cartier, Lady Edwina Mountbatten, Ellen von Lee, and others.

One might also run into members of the Rothschild family, such as Baron Édouard, owner of one of the biggest racing stables in France, and his very elegant wife, née Germaine Halphen (illus. p. 200). Baron Maurice, their cousin, who was more eccentric in appearance, also had a stud farm of thirty horses. Another legendary great owner, Aga Khan III, raced his horses for more than forty years on all the courses in France and England. His third wife, Begum Aga Khan, née Andrée Carron (illus. p. 199, top right), combined sound French good taste with an unlimited fortune to promote Parisian haute couture.

Great industrialists like the Berliet brothers or André Citroën (illus. p. 202, top left), the one-man band of the time, famous sportsmen like the boxer Georges Carpentier, or tennis champions like Suzanne Lenglen and Jean Borotra, international playboys like Georgian prince Alexis Mdivani or the Dominican diplomat Porfirio Rubirosa, "Americans in Paris" like Jimmy Walker, mayor of New York City—a brightly colored kaleidoscope parades before us, a somewhat dizzying vanity fair, a world sucked into the vortex of time revived briefly by the magic of photography and fixed permanently in our memories by the historian.

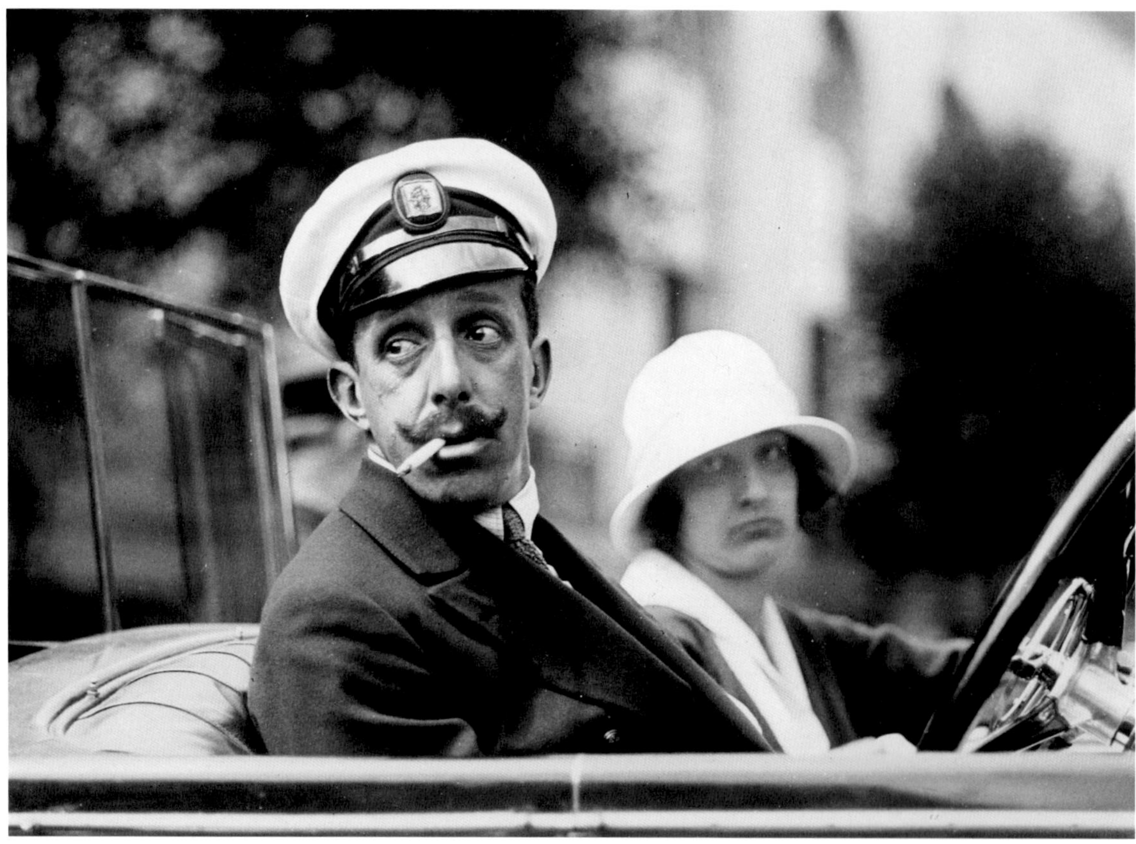

King Alphonse XIII of Spain (1886–1941), Deauville, August 15, 1922. Séeberger family collection, Paris.

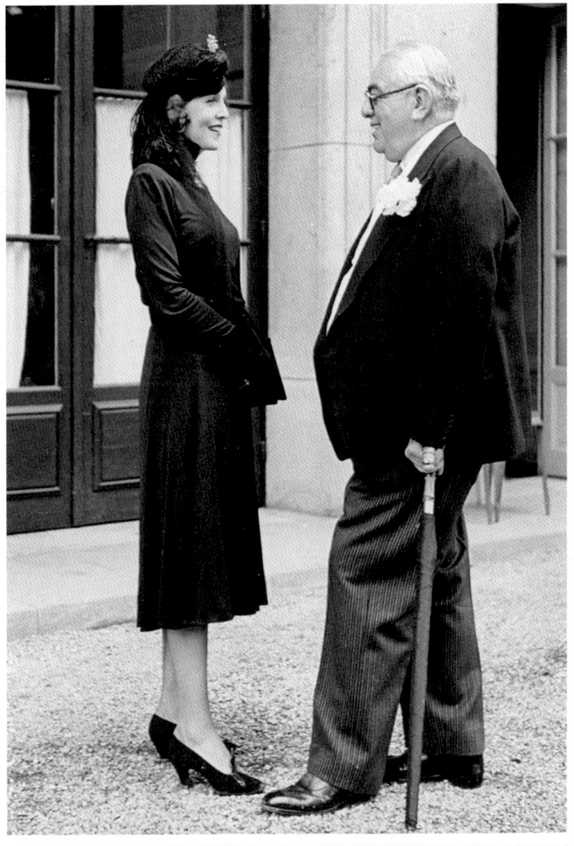

Prince Mohammed Aga Khan III (1877–1957) with Arlette Ryan at the races, La Grande Semaine, summer 1939.

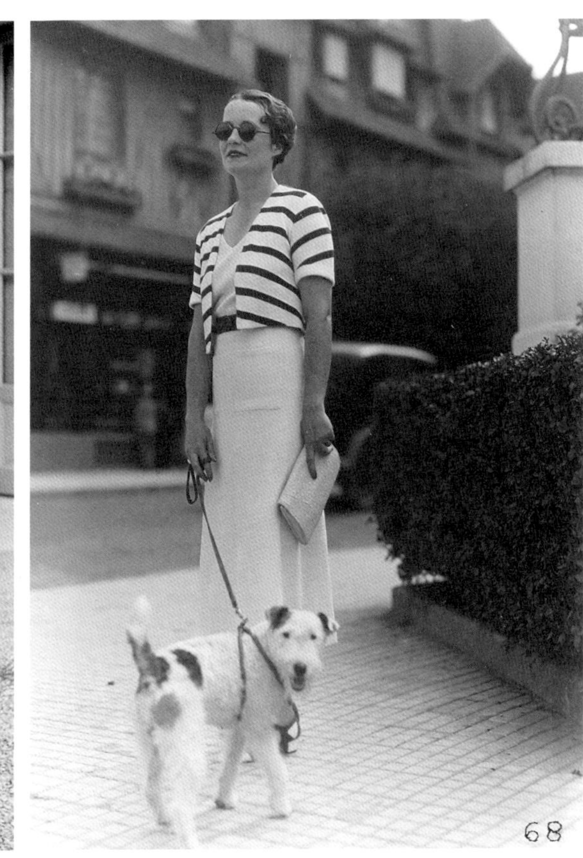

Begum Aga Khan (1898–1976), née Andrée Marcelle Carron, third wife of Mohammed Aga Khan III, Deauville, Feast of the Assumption, August 15, 1933.

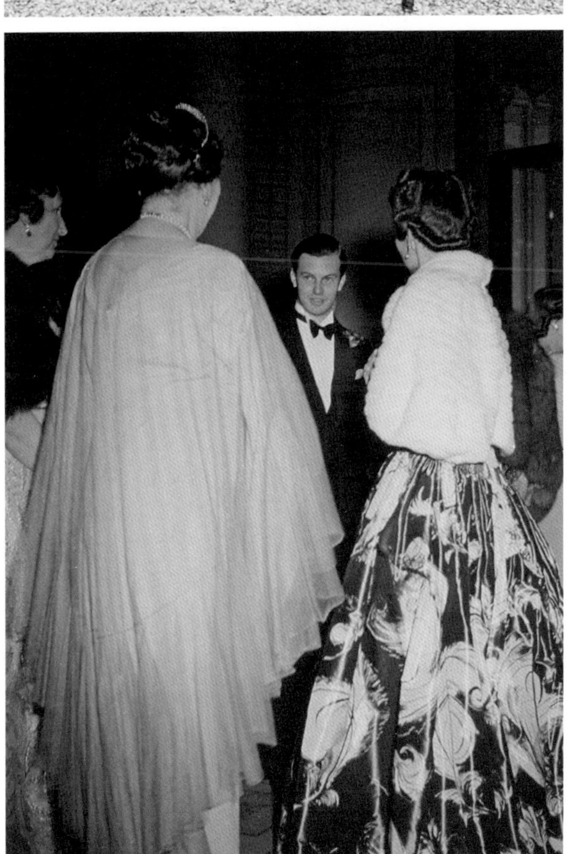

Prince Ali Khan (1911–1960) with the Duchess of Vendôme (1870–1948), née Henriette of Belgium, and Princess Aga Khan (seen from behind) in a gown by Jeanne Lanvin, at a Cannes casino, April 1939. Ali Khan, son of Aga Khan III and his second wife, Teresa Magliano, married the American actress Rita Hayworth as his second wife and died tragically in a car accident in 1960.

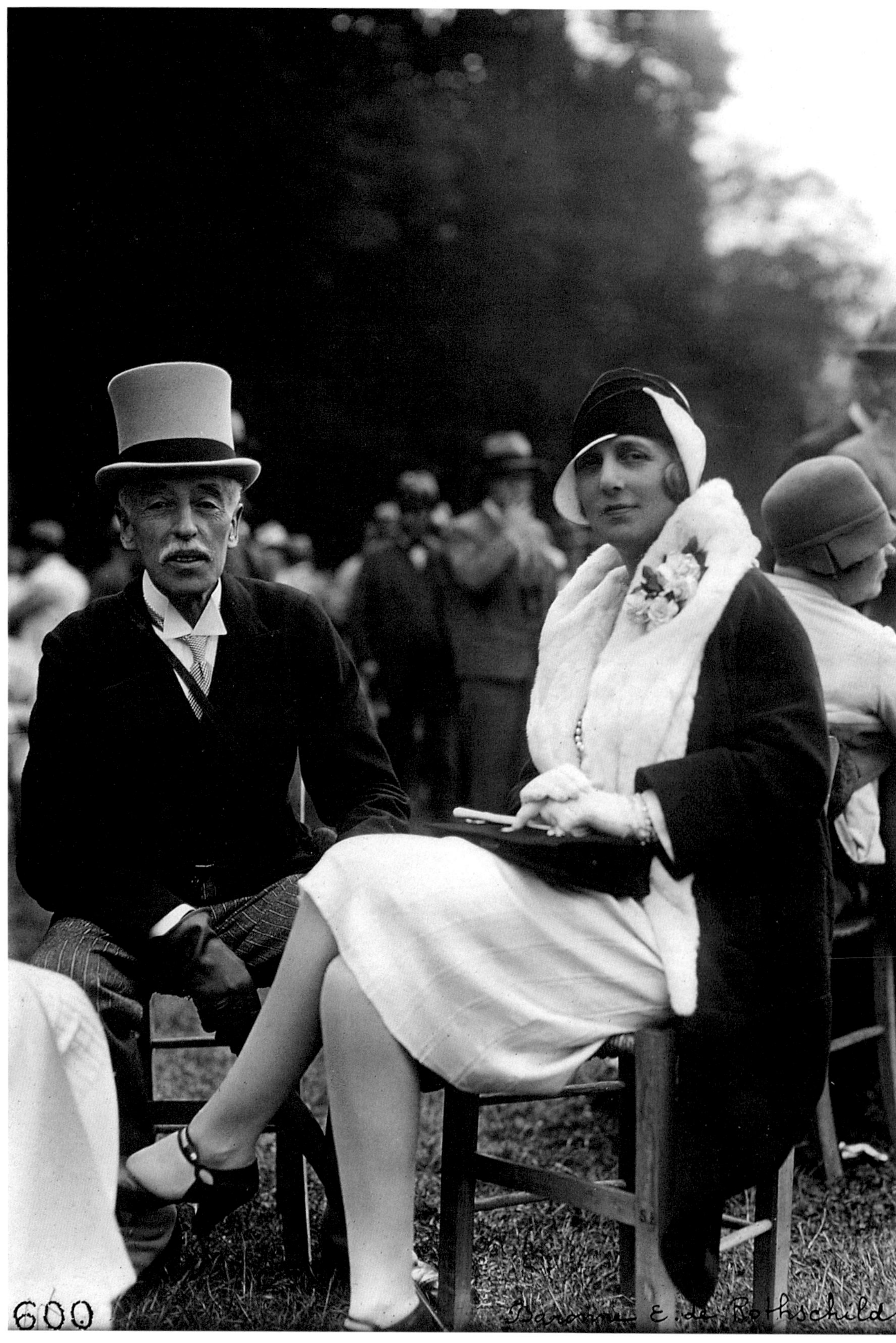

Baron Édouard de Rothschild (1868–1949) and the baroness (1884–1975), née Germaine Halphen, wearing a hat by Caroline Reboux, Chantilly, Prix du Jockey-Club, June 16, 1929.

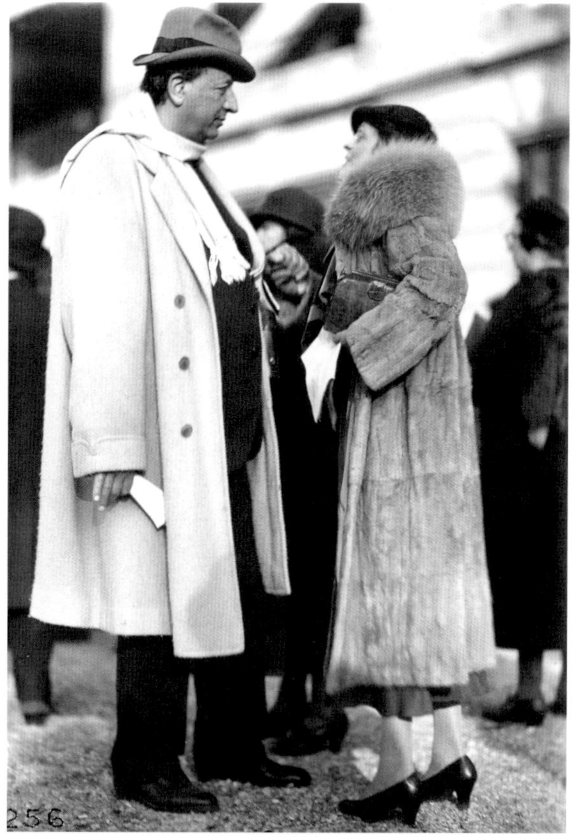

Baron Maurice de Rothschild (1881–1957) and Marie Porgès, née Brodsky, at the Prix d'Auteuil, March 12, 1933.

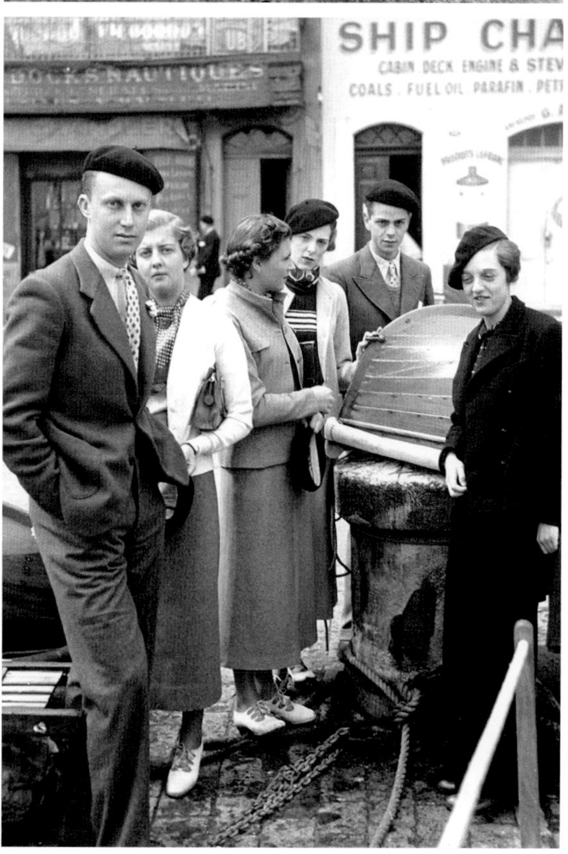

From left to right: Baron Frédéric de Cabrol (1909–1997), Eliane d'Audiffret-Pasquier, Mlle de Saint-Sauveur, Daisy d'Harcourt (born in 1915), her brother Bernard d'Harcourt (1919–1984), and Bethsabée de Rothschild (1914–1999), Cannes, April 1936. Daisy d'Harcourt married Frédéric de Cabrol in 1937, and Bethsabée de Rothschild (1914–1999) was the wife of D. Bloomingdale.

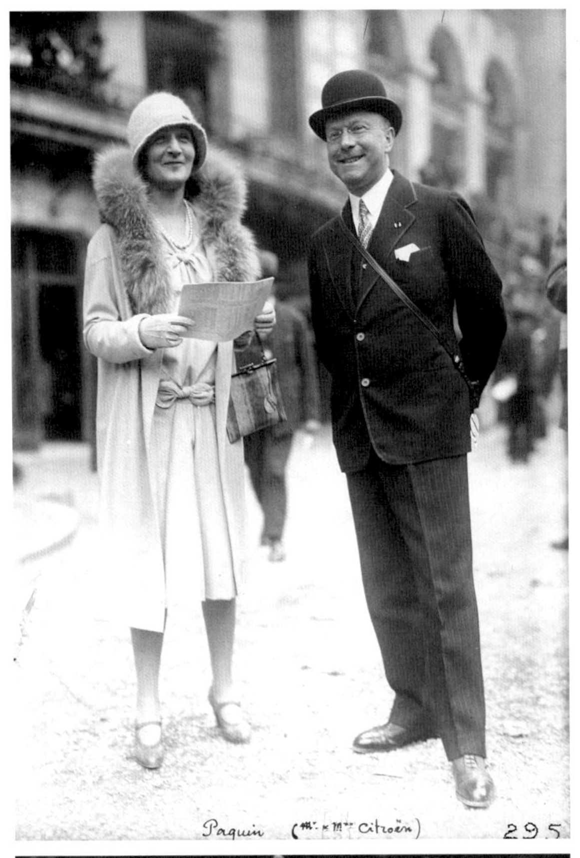

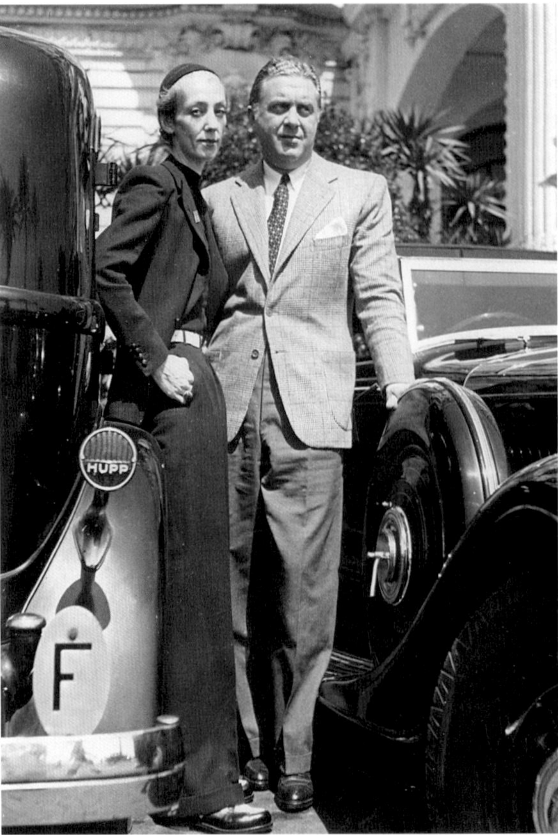

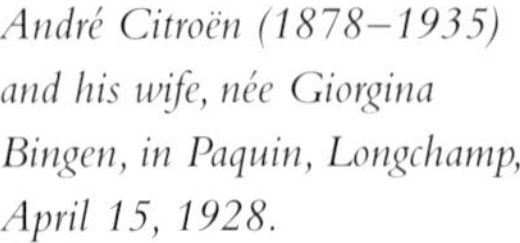
André Citroën (1878–1935) and his wife, née Giorgina Bingen, in Paquin, Longchamp, April 15, 1928.

Roussy, wife of the Spanish artist José Maria Sert, and her brother, Prince David Mdivani, Cannes, April 1938.

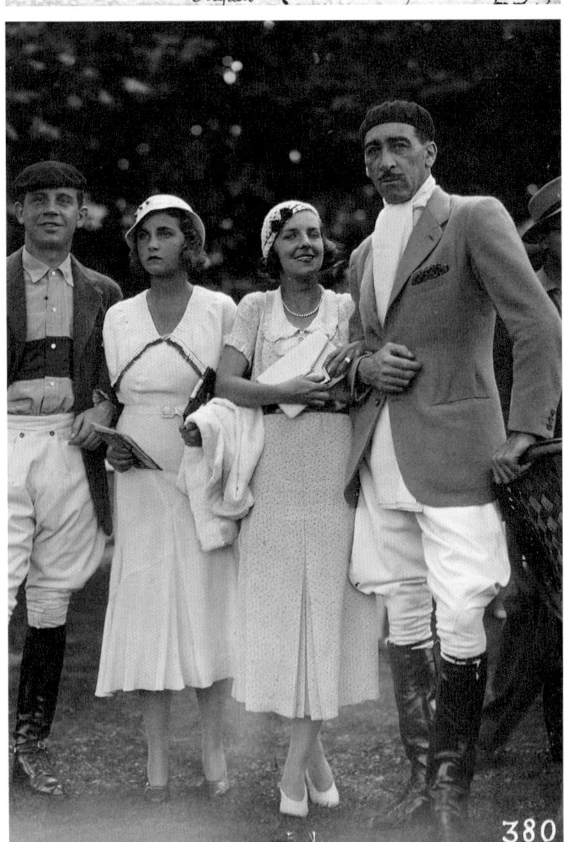

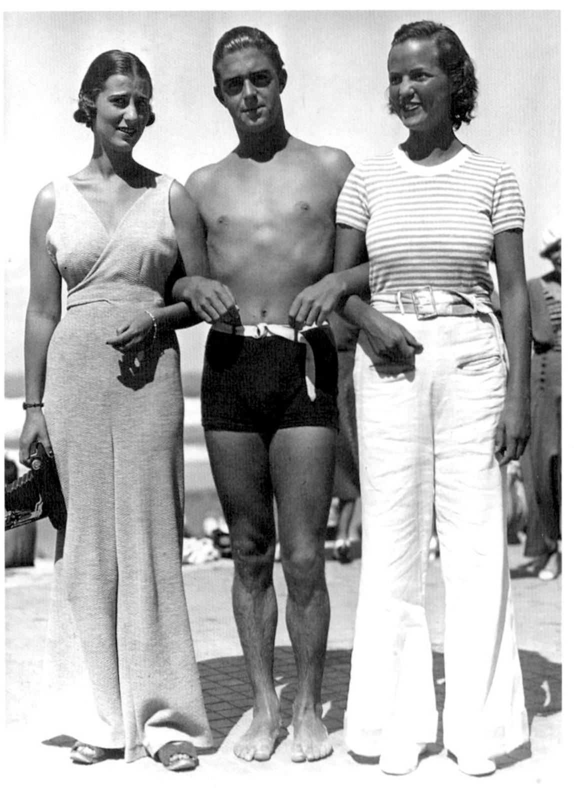

Prince Alexis Mdivani (died in 1935) and the Marquis de Portago, cinema producer, flanking Barbara Hutton (1912–1979), then married to Mdivani, wearing Chanel, and a young woman in Patou, Biarritz, September 1931.

The Marquis de La Puente, with Mlle Rosenberg in Schiaparelli on his left arm, and on his right arm Mary Perine outfitted by Germaine, Biarritz, September 1932.

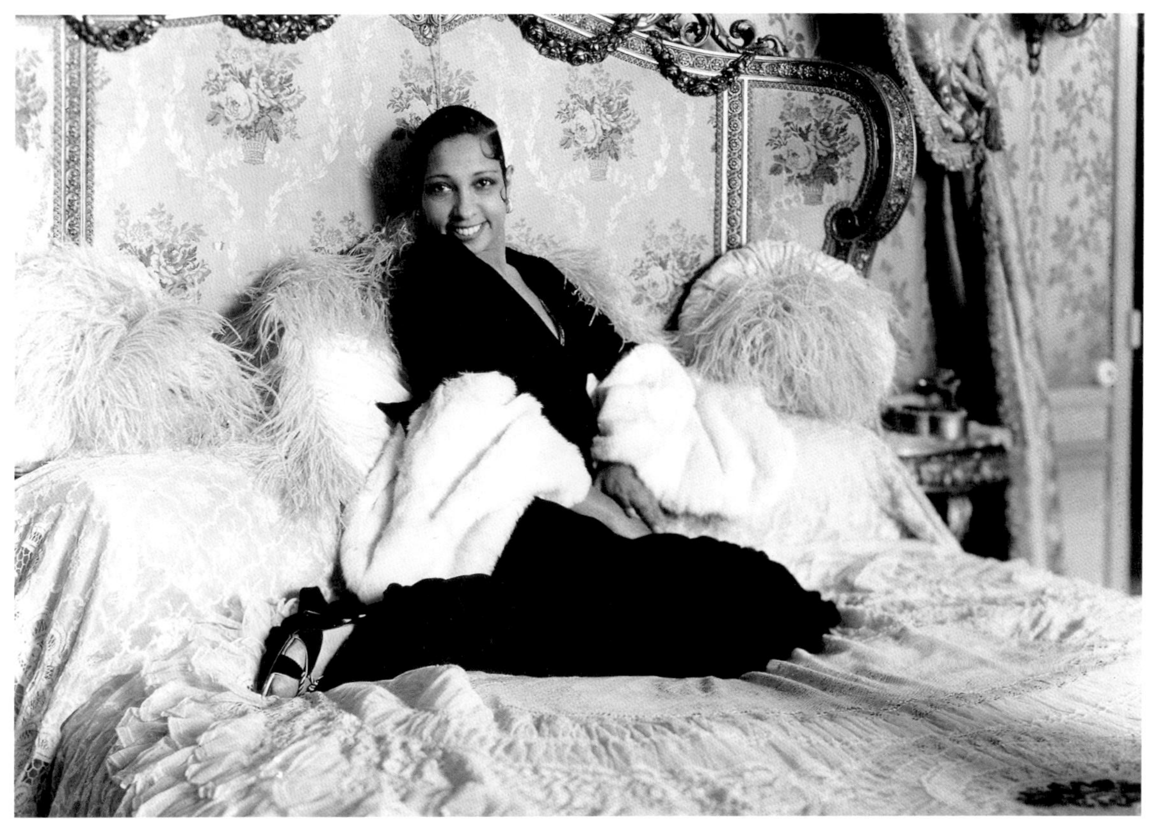

Joséphine Baker (1906–1975) at Vésinet, winter 1931/32. Séeberger family collection, Paris.

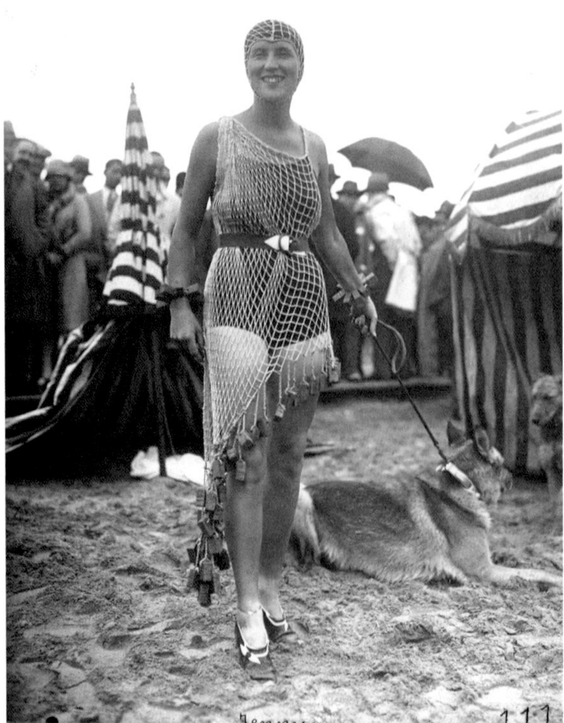

Suzy Solidor (1900–1983), née Suzanne Rocher, in a Jenny swimsuit, Deauville, August 14, 1927.
Before becoming a successful realist singer in 1933, Suzy Solidor began as a model and posed for a great many artists, including Foujita, Lempicka, Domergue, Picabia, Van Dongen, Man Ray, and others. Her androgynous style and her connection with the antique dealer Yvonne de Brémond d'Ars made her an icon of the garçonne, *the French equivalent of the flappers, and a personality in Deauville in the 1920s, even before the start of her cabaret career.*

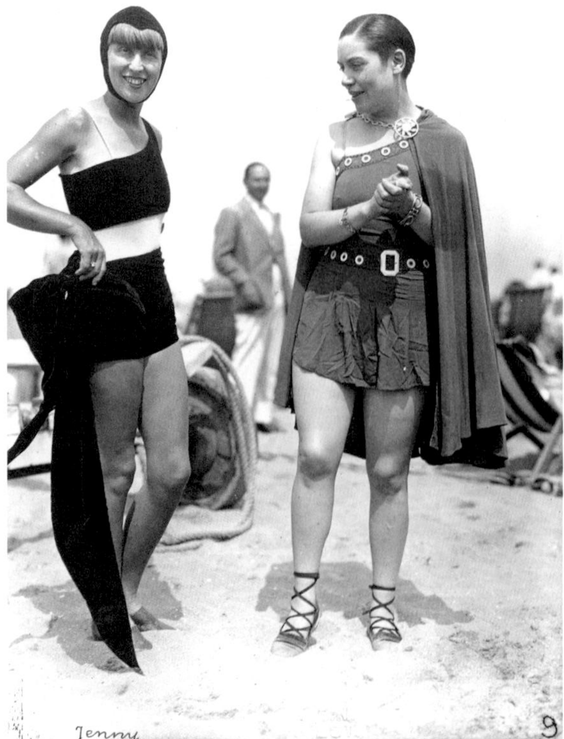

Suzy Solidor in a Jenny swimsuit, Deauville, July 28, 1929.
At right, her friend, Yvonne de Brémond d'Ars.

Suzy Solidor in a
Jenny swimsuit, Deauville,
August 9, 1928.

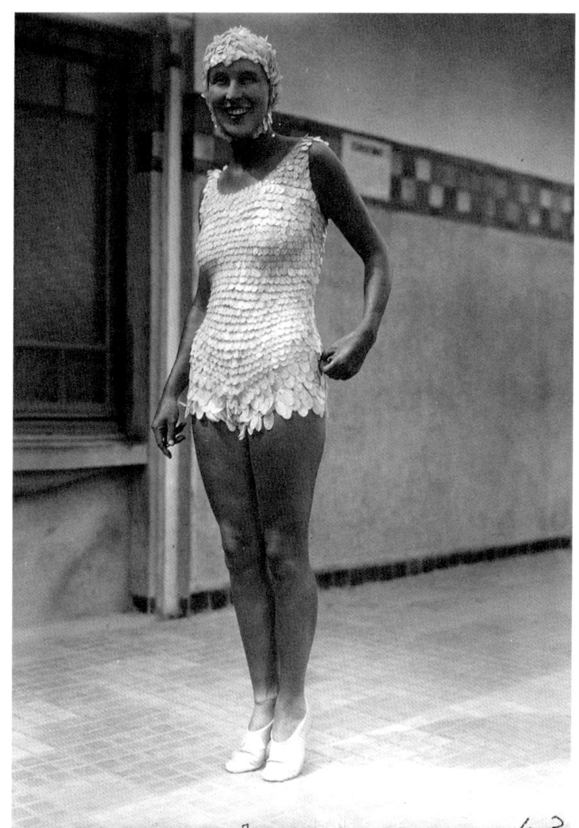

Suzy Solidor at Deauville,
August 15, 1936.

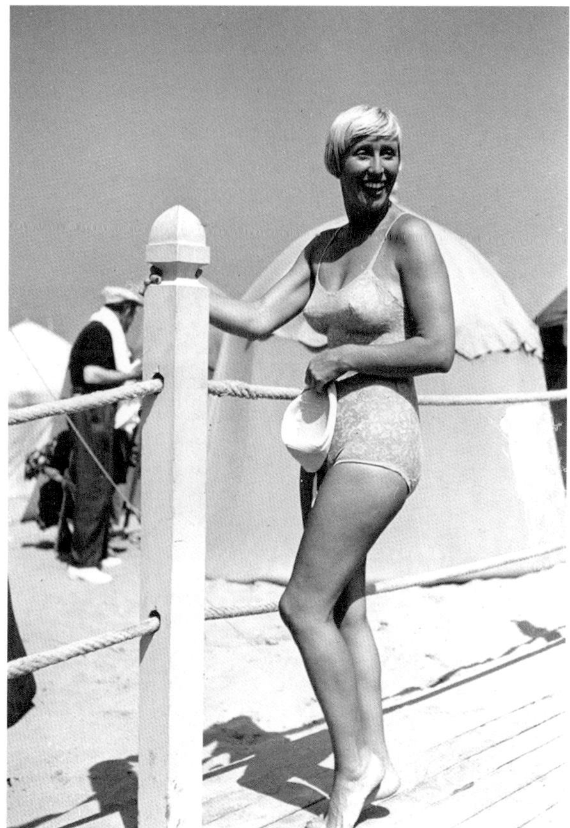

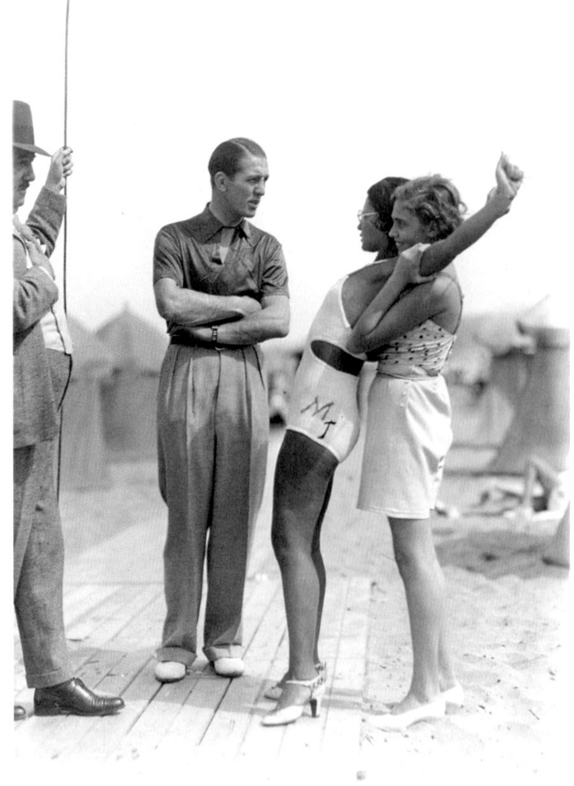

178

The boxer Georges Carpentier (1894–1975) with admirers, Deauville, August 19, 1934.

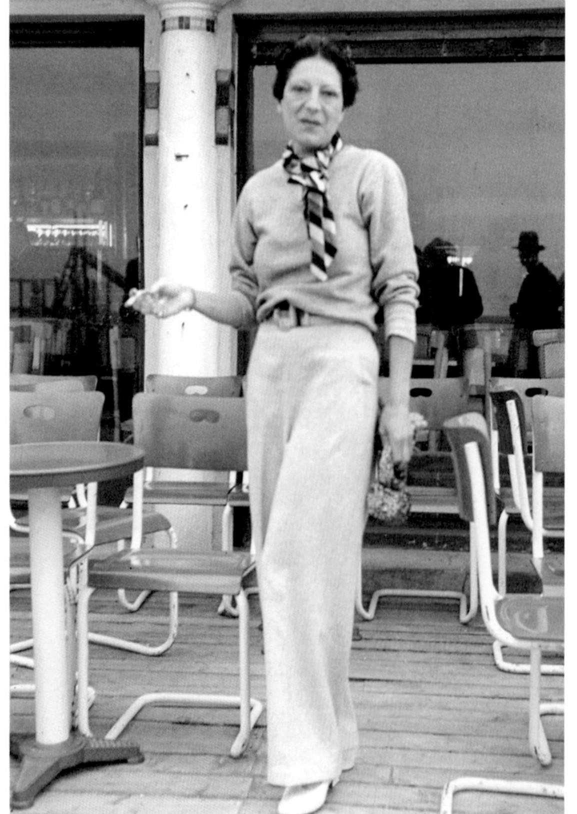

Tennis champion Suzanne Lenglen (1899–1936) in Patou, who was her appointed couturier, Deauville, August 9, 1936. Patou's brother-in-law, tennis champion Raymond Barbas, introduced him to Suzanne Lenglen and many other great sporting figures.

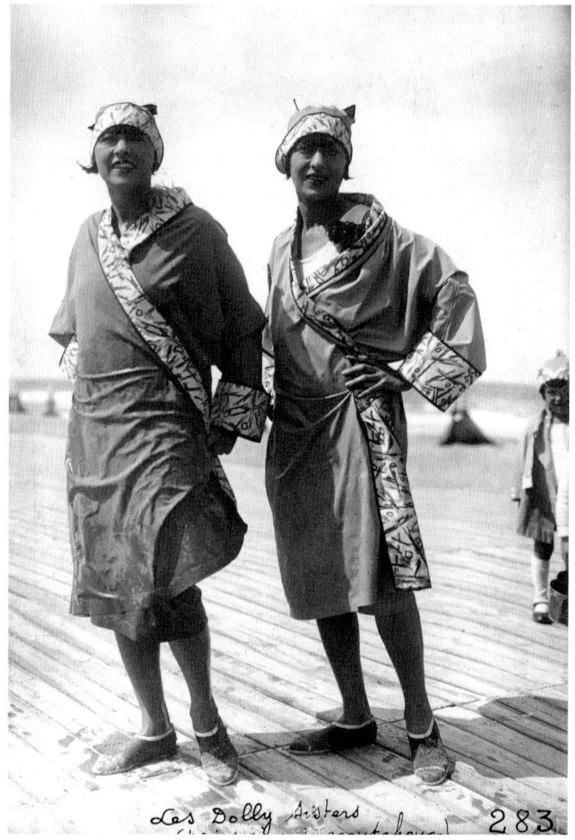

The celebrated twins Rosie (1892–1970) and Jenny (1892–1941) Deutsch, known as the Dolly Sisters, in rubber beach robes, Deauville, August 15, 1926.

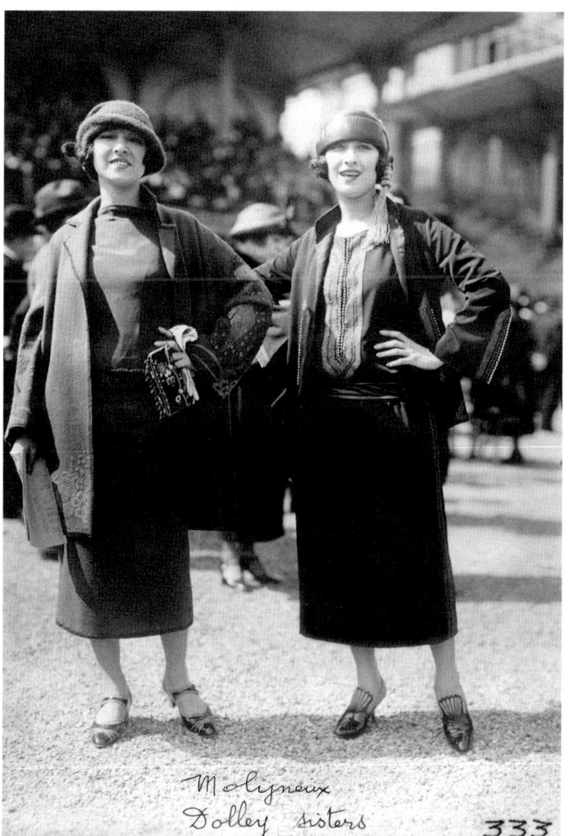

The Dolly Sisters in Molyneux, Longchamp, May 7, 1922.

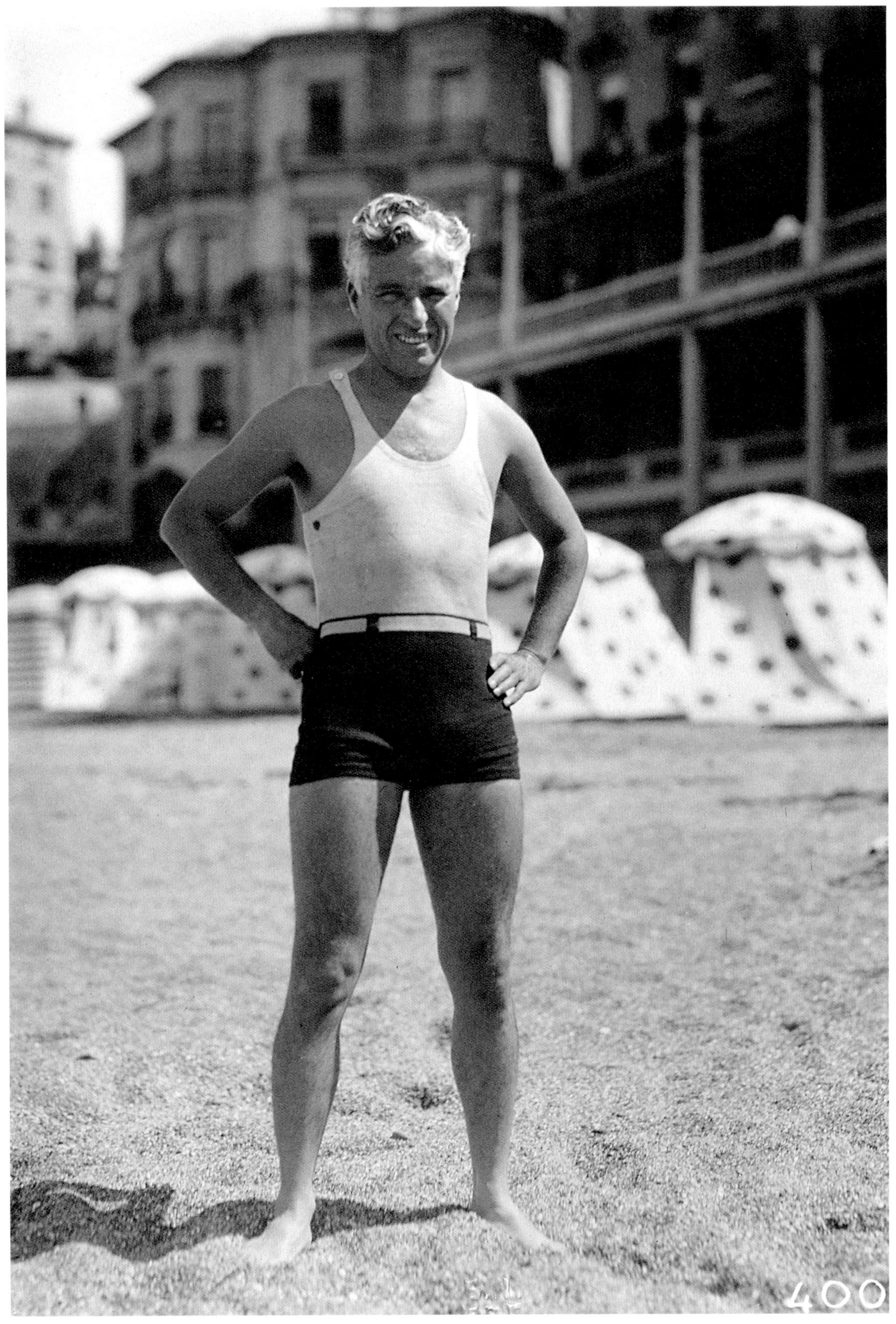

Charlie Chaplin (1889–1977) on the beach at Biarritz, September 1931.

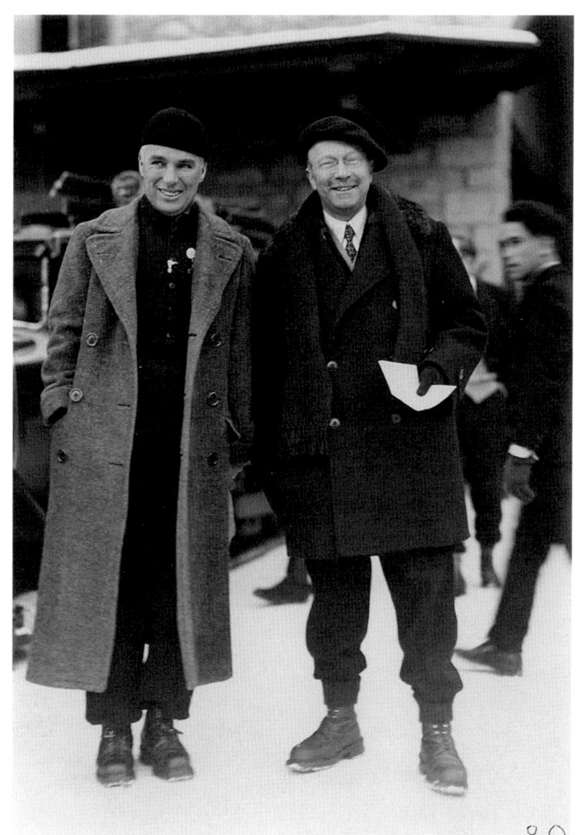

Charlie Chaplin with André Citroën, Saint-Moritz, New Year's Day 1932.

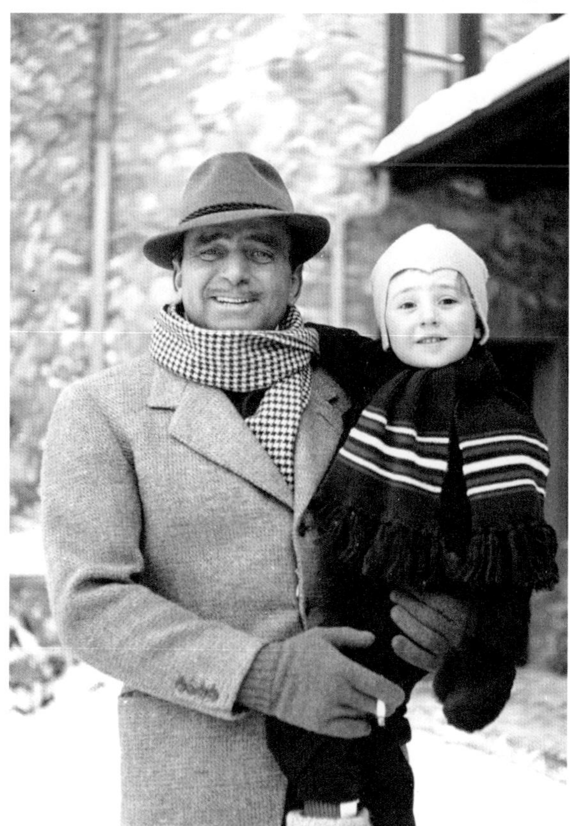

The actor Douglas Fairbanks (1883–1939), Saint-Moritz, New Year's Eve, 1935/36.

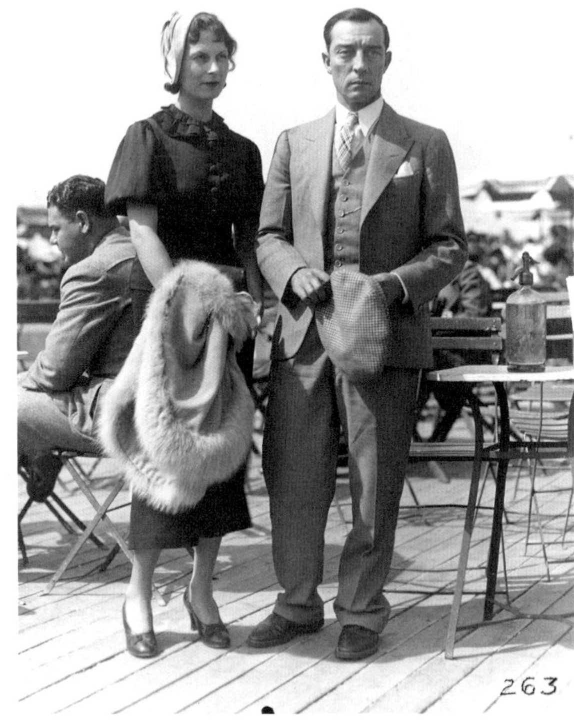

Mr. and Mrs. Buster Keaton (1895–1966), Deauville, Grand Prix Day, August 26, 1934.

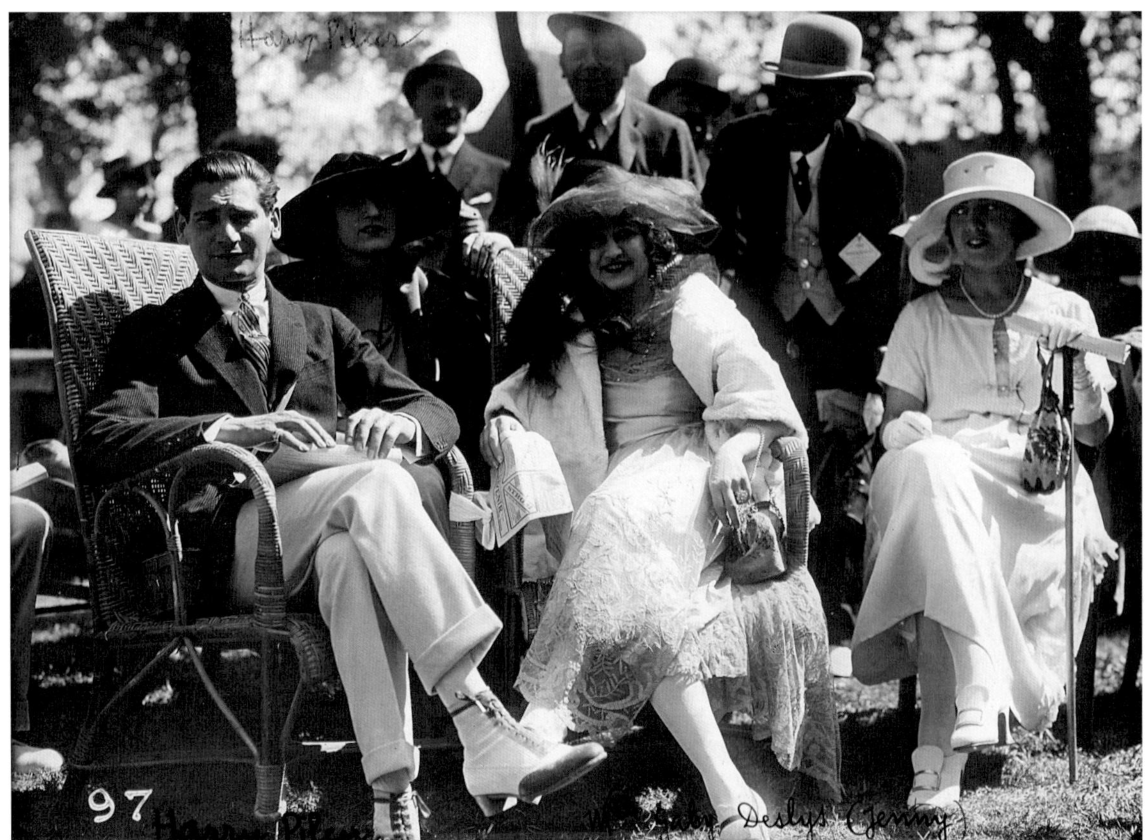

Harry Pilcer (1885–1961) and Gaby Deslys, née Caire (1881–1920), in a dress by Jenny, Deauville, 1919. In 1910, music-hall singer Gaby Deslys brought singer Harry Pilcer from Broadway to France. In 1917, they inaugurated the great staircase of the Casino de Paris with Laisse-les tomber. *She also introduced jazz to the French music hall scene.*

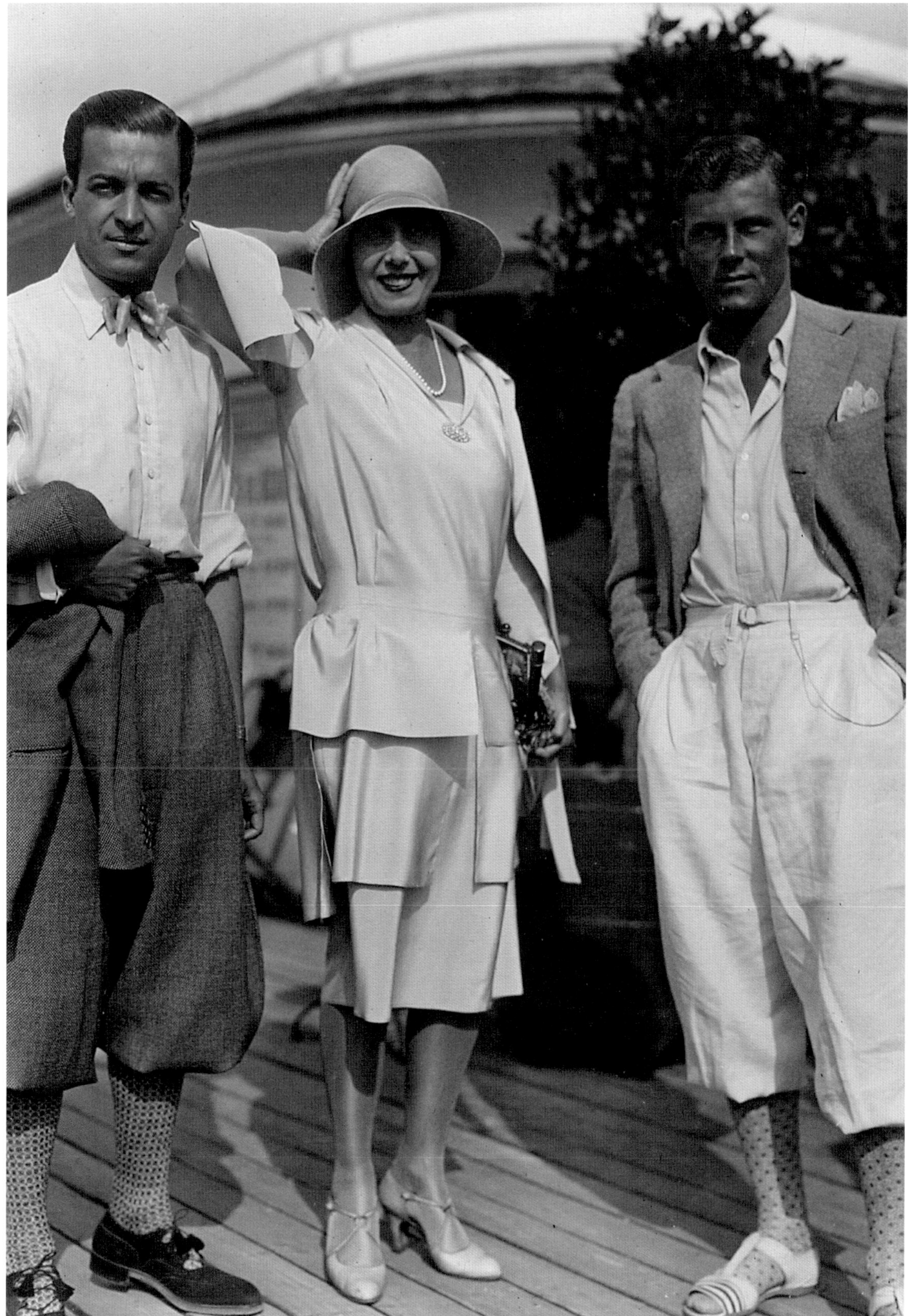

Mistinguett (1872–1956), née Jeanne Bourgeois, wearing a Louise Baker gown and Agnès hat, Deauville, July 28, 1929.

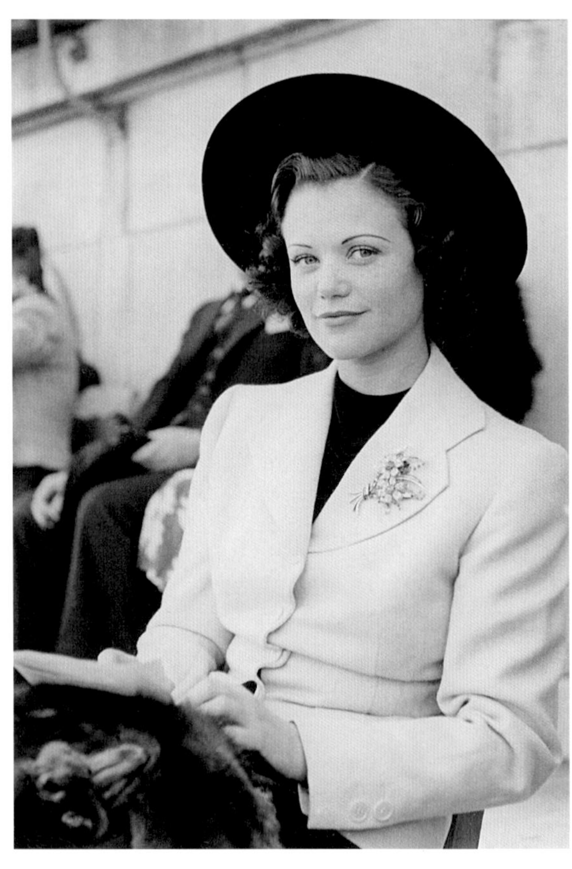

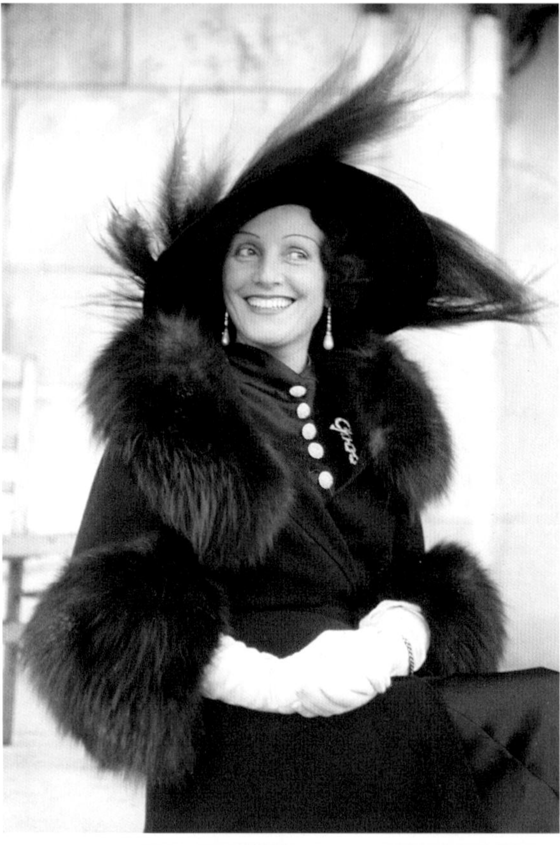

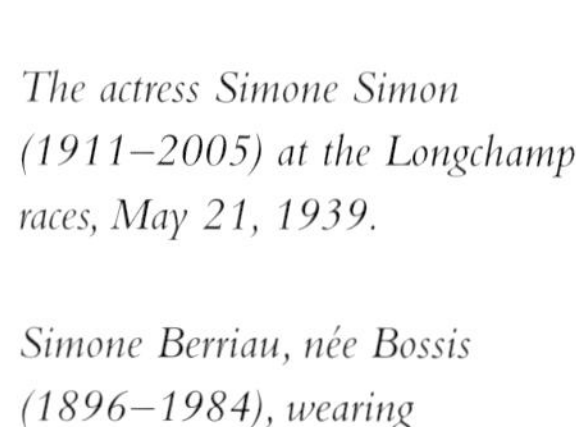

The actress Simone Simon (1911–2005) at the Longchamp races, May 21, 1939.

Simone Berriau, née Bossis (1896–1984), wearing Vionnet with a hat by Agnès, Longchamp, Grand Critérium, October 13, 1935. A film actress during the 1930s, Simone Berriau directed the Théâtre Antoine after the war.

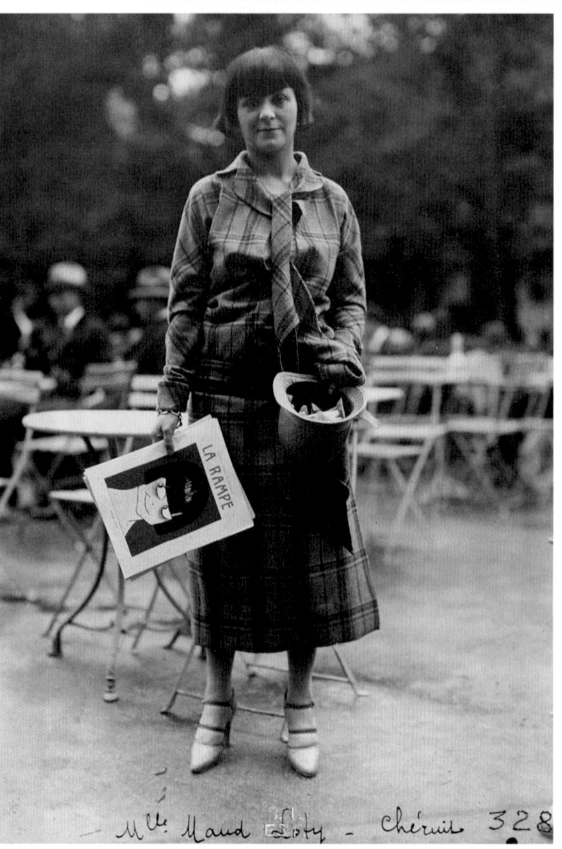

A Théâtre des Variétés actress, Maud Loty is wearing an outfit by Chéruit and holds in her hand an issue of La Rampe *featuring a caricature of her on its cover, Grand Prix de Deauville, August 24, 1924.*

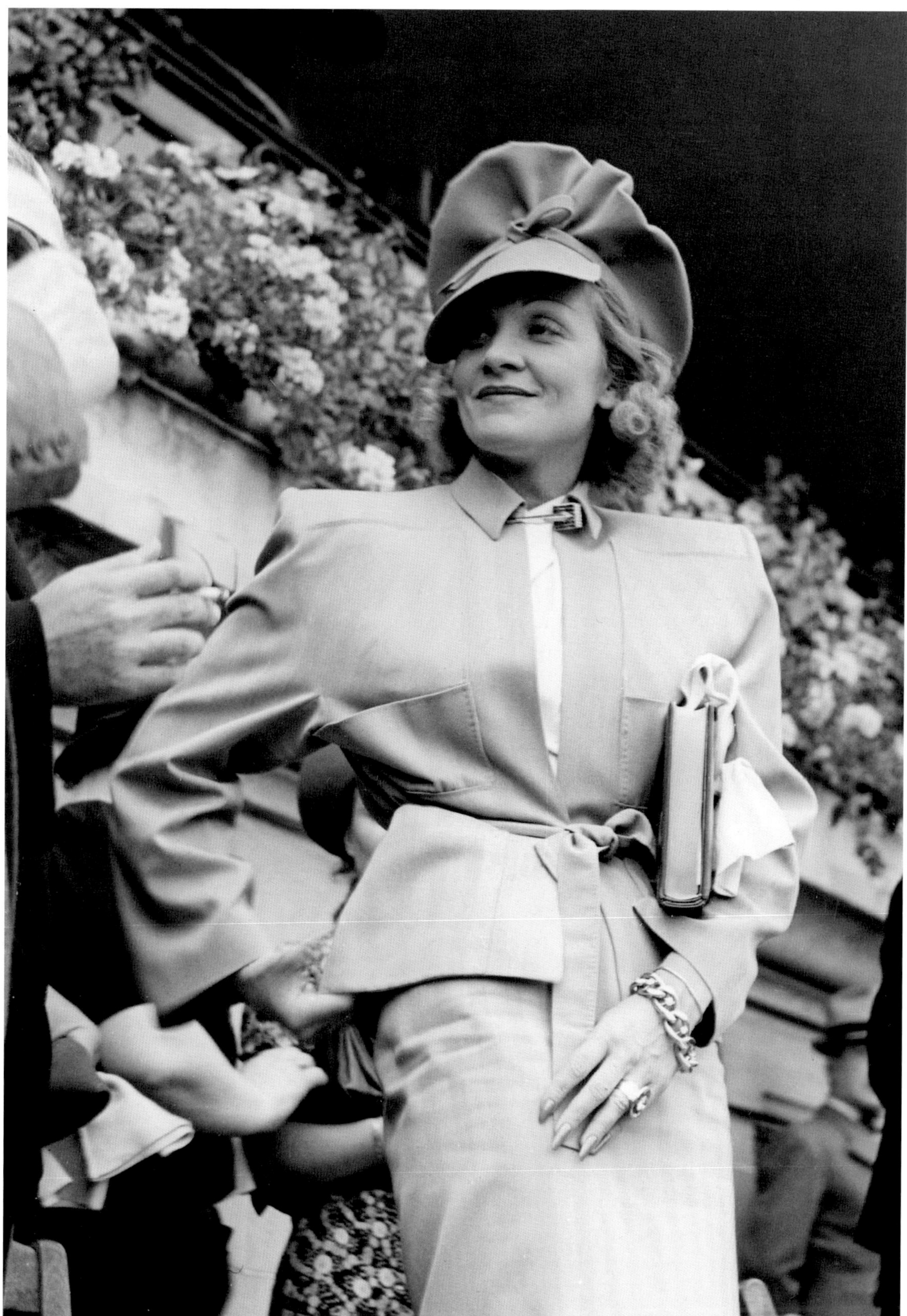

Actress Marlene Dietrich (1901–1992) at the Auteuil races, June 21, 1939.

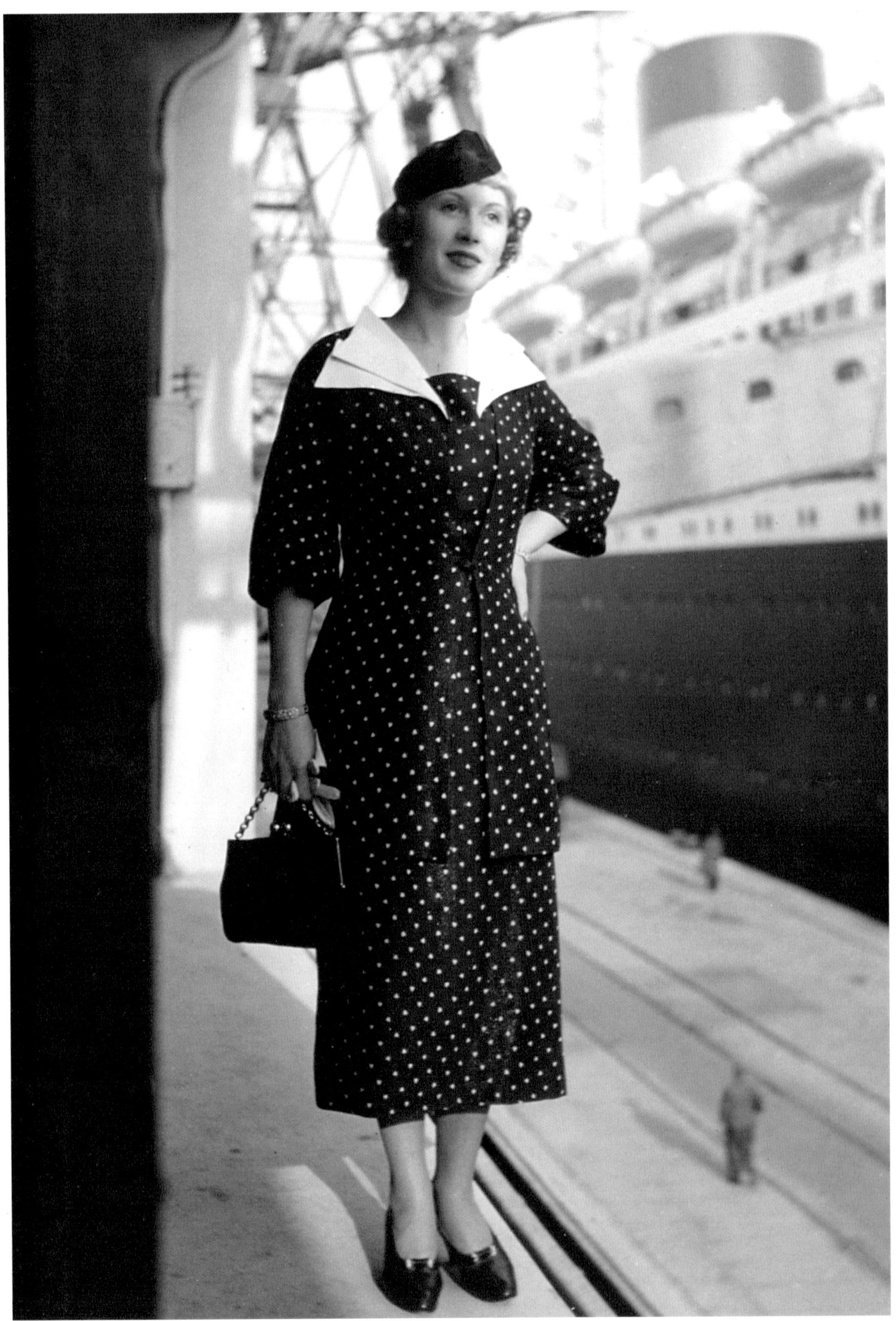

Film actress Josette Day (1914–1978) about to board the Normandie *in a Patou suit on the evening of the steamer's inauguration, May 25, 1935.*

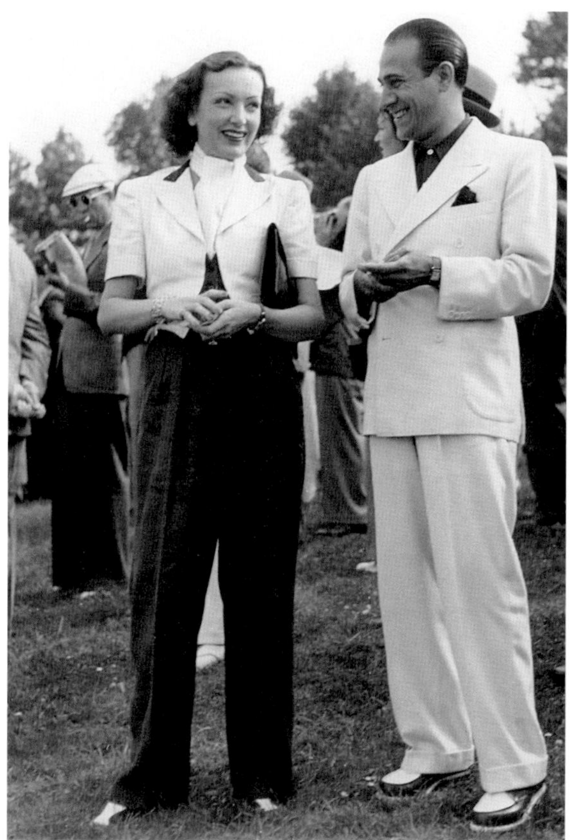

Tino Rossi (1907–1983) and his friend, actress Mireille Balin (1911–1968), outfitted by Marcel Dhorme, Deauville, August 1939.

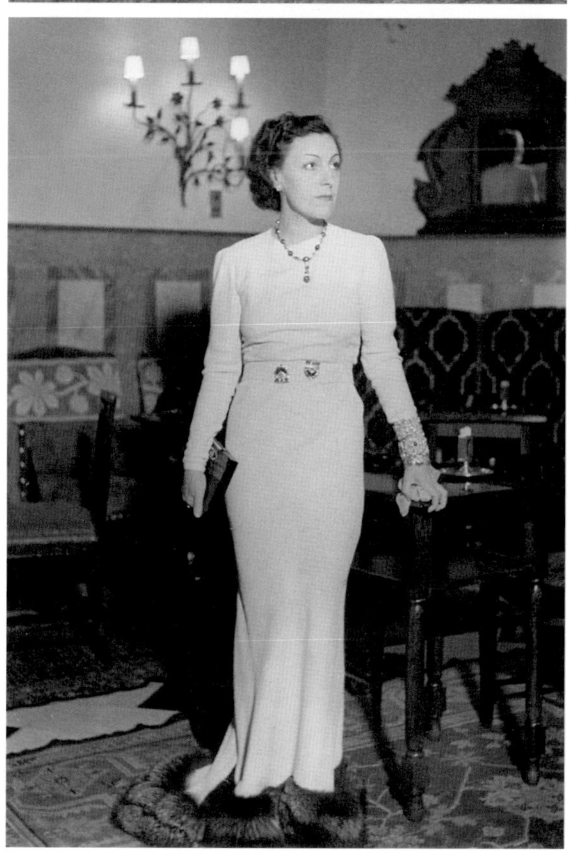

Film actress Gaby Morlay (1893–1964) wearing a Lucile Paray gown, Saint-Moritz, New Year's Day, 1936.

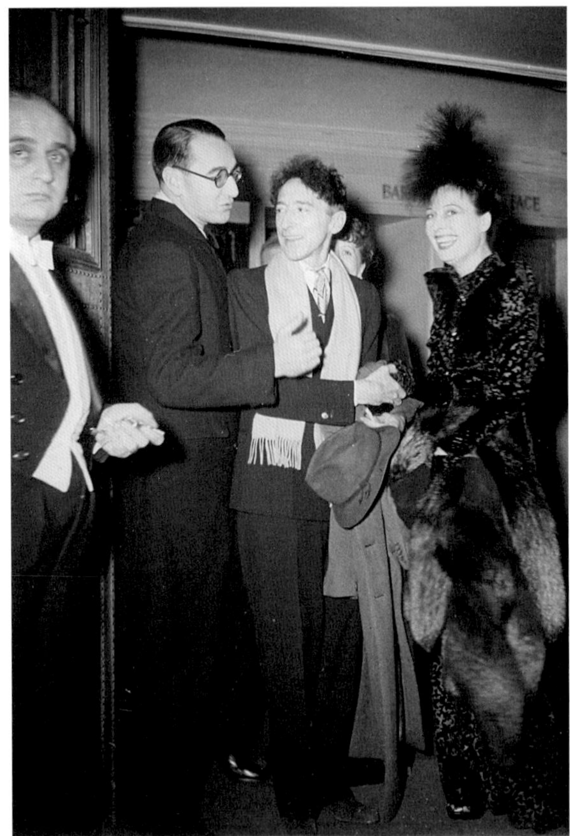

Marcel Achard, Jean Cocteau, and Arletty on the opening night of Marcel Achard's play, Adam, *at the Théâtre du Gymnase, November 1938.*

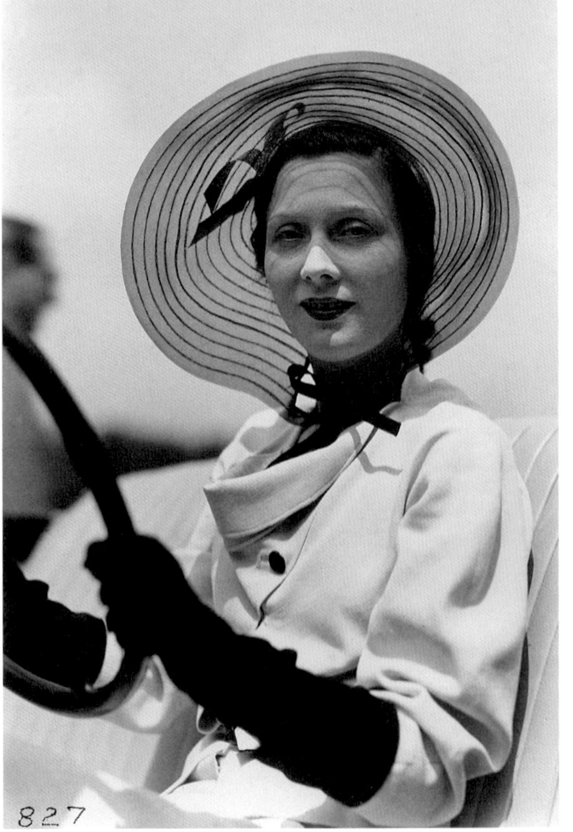

The actress Arletty, née Arlette-Léonie Bathiat (1898–1991), wearing a hat by Suzanne Talbot at the concours d'elegance custom automobile show in Bagatelle, June 15, 1934.

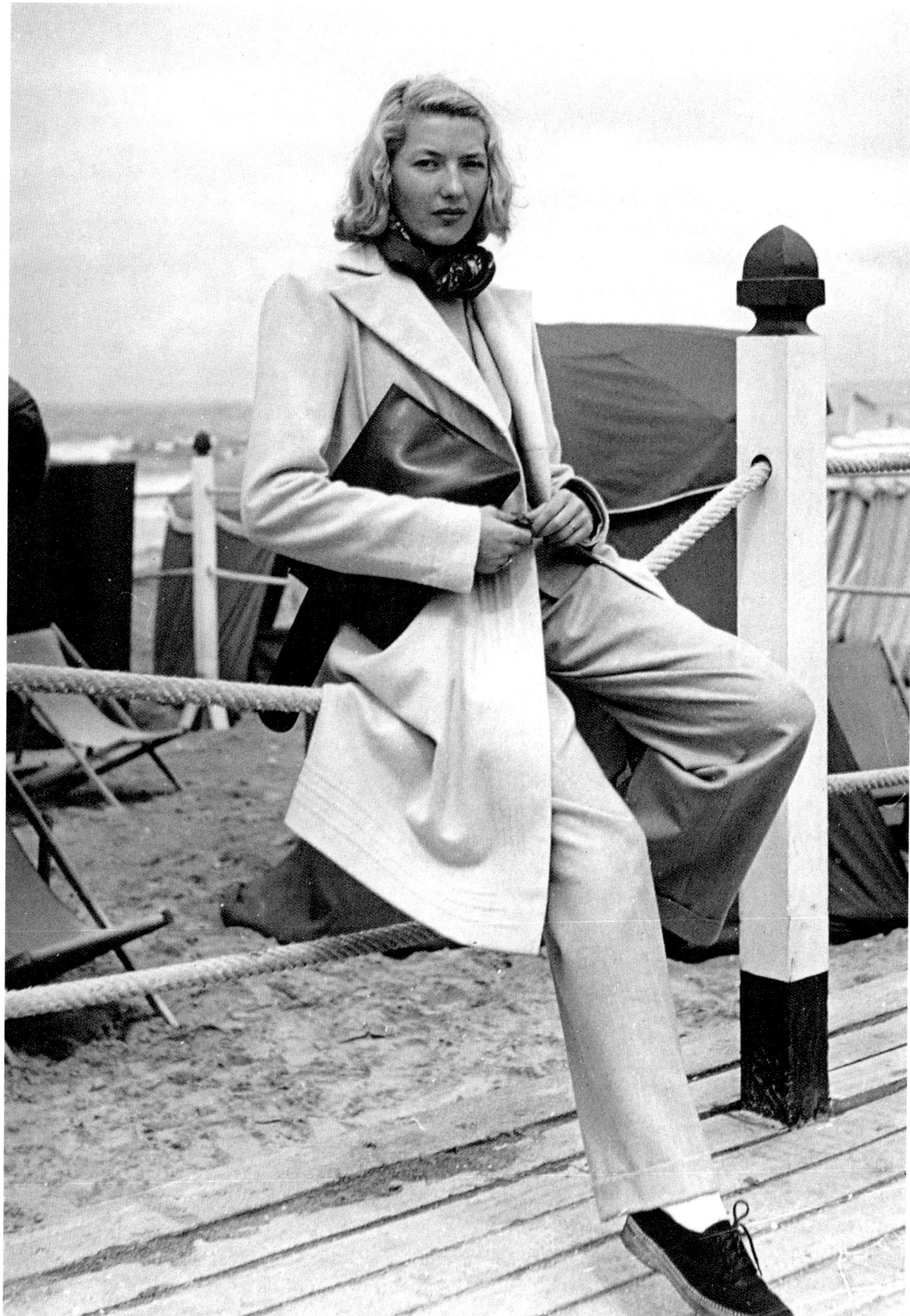

Film actress Corinne Luchaire (1921–1950) in a trouser suit by Freddy and a coat by Heim, Deauville, August 6, 1939.

Notes

1. The 1977 book by Nancy Hall-Duncan and the article published by Françoise Ducros in 1994 will be quoted in particular. All cited works are included in the bibliography.
2. For complete biographical information, see the Chronology, pages 220-222.
3. The initiative for this undertaking came from Michel Melot, who was director of the Department of Prints and Photography at the time.
4. The Bibliothèque nationale de France acquired 35,000 negatives and prints from the period 1909-1939 in 1975, and in 1977 accepted the donation of 25,000 prints from the period 1941-1975.
5. Primarily Paris and the greater Paris area.
6. Séeberger family archives.
7. Jean-Claude Gautrand, *The Séebergers. L'aventure de trois frères photographes au début du siècle (The Séebergers: the adventures of three photographer brothers at the beginning of the century)*, Paris, La Manufacture, 1995, p. 20.
8. It is easy to understand why the use of a tripod is counterproductive for journalism. Moreover, tripods were strictly prohibited in all of the exclusive places that were the Séebergers' hunting grounds.
9. See the list of periodicals with which the Séebergers collaborated, p. 223.
10. Nancy Hall-Duncan, *op. cit.*, p. 26.
11. *Op. cit.*, p. 83.
12. The workshop closed on April 1, 1977, to be precise.
13. See the bibliography at the end of this book.
14. New York Times Agency.
15. Célestine Dars met Jean and Albert Séeberger; Jean Claude Gautrand and Françoise Denoyelle, after the death of Jean in 1979, talked with Albert alone.
16. Françoise Denoyelle, *La Lumière de Paris*, p. 286.
17. Recorded on January 5, 2006. Daniel Séeberger was Jean's son and worked in the family studio from 1959 to 1970.
18. Anecdotes on this subject abound in biographies of the great couturiers, for whom the departure of a talented employee to a rival house was experienced as treason and a minor drama.
19. Marshall Field and Co, John Wanamaker, The Eaton Co, Messrs. Gimbel Brothers, *Dry Goods Economist*, A.M.C., la Société française de commission pour l'étranger, America latina.
20. A small notebook from the early 1920s containing the addresses of these particular customers is a veritable handbook on high society, the demimonde, and the Parisian stage.
21. Letter dated September 9, 1938, Séeberger family archive.
22. Which explains why it could be passed on to us.
23. Among the Séeberger brothers' foreign clients should be noted: Drapers Organizer, Bonwit Teller, The General Art (Agency in London), Strawbridge & Clothier, Harry Angelo Company (Séeberger family archives), and see note 19.
24. Elisabeth de Gramont, *Les Marronniers en fleurs.*
25. The first fashion parades took place in 1901 at Lucile, the couture house of Lady Duff Gordon, rue de Penthièvre. The models were generally designated by a first name (Blanche, Georgette, Gaby, Violette) and their identity was little known until the end of the 1920s, when the first American "top models" made their appearance at Patou. Their profession was glorified in the popular press (Fantasio, La Corbeille des plus jolis mannequins de Paris, 1914). Mention should be made of "Mlle Cass (Cyber mannequin) 23 rue Lauriston" in the Séeberger address book (Séeberger family archives).
26. *Le Cri de Paris*, November 17, 1929.
27. "A type of swaying walk or very slow belly dance, a way of oozing along in waves, a seal's waltz." (*La Vie Parisienne*, March 23, 1918) In the same period, Cocteau described the couturier Chéruit shouting at his models as they filed down the catwalk: "Ladies, stick out the belly! Bend, bend, stick out the belly!" (Cecil Beaton, *Cinquante Ans d'élégance et d'art de vivre [The Glass of Fashion: Fifty Years of Dress and Decor]*, London and Paris, 1954, p. 147.)
28. The Department of Prints and Photography has a collection of photographs taken by the Séeberger brothers at the racetracks in the years 1910-1914 that could be called a collection of rejects (Oa 574 petit folio); this is the humble admission of these craftsmen photographers to their groping beginnings.
29. In connection with the influence of fashion designers on photographers of high society life at the beginning of the twentieth century, see the catalog of the exhibition at the Musée Galliéra, *Le Dessin sous toutes ses coutures. Croquis, illustrations, modèles, 1760-1994*, Paris, Paris Musées, 1995.
30. "Barely a bra and slight girdle are tolerated by the fashionable couturier. The free and flexible body must be inferable under the gown, without artifice." (*Fantasio*, February 15, 1911) The "body" or corset had already been eliminated from female fashion between 1795 and 1825.

31. "At Longchamp, a young beauty splendidly tacked up in a triple-trained gown. Before long, there will be no difference between the racing stand and the ballroom." (*Journal des dames et des modes*, July 10, 1912)
32. "The reign of the straight line is over. There is nothing but panniers, frills, ribbons, tulle, and flowers. Fat ladies accustomed to encasing their opulent forms in sheathes are in despair." (*Fantasio*, June 15, 1912)
33. "What female fashion has taken from menswear: the top hat, dinner jacket, starched shirt, pajamas, sports shorts, cycling socks, and the cane." (*Femina*, July 1924)
34. As proof of this, the return to exaggerated female curves was promoted by American actresses like Mae West. At the same time, German national-socialism valorized the "new German woman," with full chest, broad hips, and narrow shoulders.
35. Schiaparelli promoted the platform shoe for the beach in 1938, a fashion from Italy, where the embargo imposed by the League of Nations in reprisal for the Italo-Ethiopian war had rationed the use of leather. As early as 1936, the Italian shoemaker Ferragamo had responded by creating a shoe design with wooden soles (see the article "Socques, cothurnes et zoris de Perugia" in *Vogue* [French edition], February 1938).
36. See note 33.
37. *L'Irrégulière ou mon itinéraire Chanel*, Paris, Grasset.
38. "For the Prix de Diane, Mme Martinez de Hoz chose a broad-brimmed hat festooned in pale blue velvet, whose brown tulle base allowed her hair to show. At the Derby, she was all in pink, a broad-brimmed hat by Reboux in Italian straw decorated with two roses, and a barrette of foliage in her hair, to the left." (*Femina*, July 1934, two photographs by Schaal, and *Femina*, July 1927)
39. *Vogue* (French edition), July 1934.
40. "Mme Revel, very simple in her black outfit, short and plain, with a tiny hat, teamed with a pearl choker and low heels, reflects exactly what fashion currently requires of a woman: she is of unparalleled elegance – but why?" (*Vogue* [French edition], June 1925.)
41. *Femina*, August 1933 (see also a Mourgues sketch in *Femina*, July 1933).
42. Lud (Ludmilla Feodoseyeva), the photographer Horst's preferred model in the 1930s, and Alla Illchun, star model at Dior in the 1950s, were the most photographed Russian beauties in the fashion magazines from the 1930s through the 1950s (see Alexandre Vassiliev, *Beauty in Exile*, Harry N. Abrams, Inc. Publishers, 1998).
43. Mme Louis Arpels, fleeing racial persecution during the German occupation, took refuge in the United States after the war. She opened a luxury accessory boutique on Park Avenue, New York City. She counted among her customers Mrs. Rose Kennedy, mother of John F. Kennedy.
44. *Femina*, July 1934.
45. That is, baubles treated as seasonal accessories that change along with fashion.
46. *La Philosophie de l'élégance*, Paris, 1942, pp. 141 - 142.
47. "And then we had our fixtures, Mme Citroën, Mme Revel, and Mme Martinez de Hoz, whom one always saw at the races, and who turned up in magazines with the Vionnet-Reboux reference (since our hats were almost always produced by Reboux)." [Mireille, first saleswoman at Vionnet, quoted by Jacqueline Demornex in *Madeleine Vionnet*, Paris, Éditions du Regard, 1990, p. 91].
48. As was the beret, which, before becoming popular headwear, was adapted as a chic, informal hat at the beginning of the 1930s.
49. See Xavier Demange, Trend Setters at the Racetrack, pp. 28 - 37 in this book.
50. In Janine Alaux, François Baudot, Sylvie de Chirée, and Patrick Mauriès, *Jeanne Lanvin*, Milan, Franco Maria Ricci, 1988, pp. 18 - 19.
51. Regarding the development of the seaside resorts, see especially the proceedings of the conference *Les Réseaux de a villégiature, In situ*, No. 4, March 2004. They are accessible online at www.culture.gouv.fr/culture/revue-inv/insitu4/index4.html.
52. *Ibid.*, "La place de l'automobile dans le développement des stations."
53. Eugène Letellier, mayor of Trouville from 1904 to 1910 and silent partner of the news daily *Le Journal*, and his son Henri, mayor of Deauville between 1925 and 1928 and director of the same newspaper.
54. He also erected the Le Journal building in Paris, 100 rue de Richelieu.
55. The family archives preserve letters from *Vogue*, *Harper's Bazaar*, *L'Officiel de la Couture*, and *Fairchild*.
56. *Ibid.*
57. In 1927, Patou launched the first sun lotion, l'Huile de Chaldée.
58. Lucy Clairin, *Fasquelle*, 1934.

Chronology

SÉEBERGER BROTHERS, OR PHOTOGRAPHY IN THE FAMILY
Virginie Chardin
A history established through the Séeberger family archives

1839 (August 1)
Birth of Jean-Baptiste Séeberger, in Wolfertschwenden (Bavaria).

1841 (March 9)
Birth of Louise Vauterin, in Saint-Galmier (the Loire).

1869 (April 28)
Jean-Baptiste Séeberger, a trade worker, marries Louise Vauterin, widow of Peyrachon and already mother of a young girl named Félicie, in Lyon. By marrying Séeberger, Louise loses her French citizenship.

1872
Birth of Jules, in Vienna (Isère).

1874 (February 7)
Birth of Louis, in Lyon.

1876 (November 28)
Birth of Henri, in Lyon.

1878
Birth of Claudius, in Lyon. He died prematurely in 1895.

1883
Louis is awarded a first prize for drawing, in the eighth grade of the lycée, or high school, in Lyon.

1886 (May 17)
Naturalization of Jean-Baptiste Séeberger and reinstatement of Louise Vauterin as French citizens.

Between 1886 and 1889
The family settles in Paris.

1889
The Séebergers live at 17 rue d'Hauteville. Jules and Louis are enrolled in training at J. Souchon to study fabric design there. This reputable atelier, located at 23 rue du Sentier, specialized in the design of "high innovations, gowns, ribbons, damask linens, Jacquard fabrics, and drafting."

1891
Jules takes evening drawing classes at the Ville de Paris and wins a second prize.

1892
The Séebergers live at 39 rue Lafayette. Louis wins the Danton Jeune prize, a scholarship intended for a poor child at the Ville de Paris art school. Jules, prizewinner of the open drawing competition, wins a travel grant from the Ville de Paris to the principal cities of the coast of Normandy and North. Henri takes the first year classes at the municipal school for the application of fine arts to industry, where he will take a first prize the following year.

1894
Death of Jean Baptiste. In the following years, the three brothers work as fabric designers.

1896
The Séeberger family lives at 13 rue Fénelon.

1899
The three brothers, jointly, are awarded second prize in an amateur photography contest organized by the newspaper *Lectures pour tous*.

1903
First documentary photography competition at the Ville de Paris. Jules Séeberger takes part with pictures of the Seine riverbanks taken between 1900 and 1903, and wins a silver medal (exhibition inaugurated January 15, 1904, at the Petit Palais). These photographs are preserved at the Musée Carnavalet.

1904
Second documentary photography competition at the Ville de Paris. Jules submits fifty large-format prints of Montmartre and the Bièvre and wins the medal of honor (exhibition at the Petit Palais from January 15 to February 15, 1905).

1905
Publication of portfolios in *L'Illustration* and *Le Monde illustré*, and publication of fifty postcards of Montmartre and the Bièvre through Kunzli Frères. Henri becomes Jules' partner. They are represented at tenth salon of the Photo-Club of Paris and at the international exhibition of photographic postcards (non-competitors' Medal of Honor). Third documentary photography competition at the Ville de Paris. Jules and Henri take part with large-format photographs of the Marais and the Île Saint-Louis (new medal, and exhibition at the Petit Palais from January 15 to February 15, 1906). The photographs are preserved at the Musée Carnavalet.

1905 (October 17)
Louis marries Anna Durieublanc, a sales person at the lace department at La Samaritaine. They move to 41 rue Monge.

1906
Louis and Anna team up with Jules and Henri, and install a laboratory at 41 rue Monge. Publication of a set of color postcards entitled *Le Marais et l'Ile Saint-Louis* bearing the signature J.H.L.S.

(Jules Henri Louis Séeberger) through Kunzli Frères using the wet plate process. Jules takes part in eleventh salon of the Photo-Club of Paris.
Fourth competition at the Ville de Paris, on the Luxembourg gardens, the botanical garden and the old residences, houses or castles of the Seine Département. The Séebergers send in 300 large-format proofs, under the name Séeberger Brothers (non-competitors' gold medal). The photographs are preserved at the Musée Carnavalet.
Travels in Switzerland and France for the editor Léopold Verger: Pays de la Loire in February, Switzerland in spring, the Normandy coast from Lisieux to Berck in summer, Burgundy and the Rhone valley in winter. Series on the Bois de Vincennes and the Bois de Boulogne. Launch of the series on the fun fair and the Seine riverbanks, published by M. and Co, or M. S. and Co.

1907–1908

Report on the 1907 Festival of Flowers and the 1907 Neuilly Festival. Continuation of travels for Léopold Verger, including the Riviera in winter, Auvergne in February, and Guernsey in summer. Series on the life of the sailor and the infantry. Participation in the 1908 salon of the Photo-Club of Paris, with portraits using the Rawlins process.

1909

Installation of a photography studio at 33 rue de Chabrol, near 13 rue Fénelon, where Jules, Henri, Félicie, and their mother live, and where their offices are established.
Participation in the Photo-Club of Paris salon, with color studies using the oil process.
Beginning of style and fashion reports.

1910 (August 10)

Birth of Jean, first son of Louis.
Report on the flooding of Paris, published as postcards by the Staerck brothers.
Jules takes part in fifteenth salon of the Photo-Club, with portraits and still lifes, and presents a seminar on the oil color process, called the Rawlins process, before the *Cercle des amateurs photographes* (Amateur Photographers Circle).

1913

Publication of the first volume of *Le Monde et la Science* encyclopedia. Jules exhibits nudes and female portraits at the Paris salon, and publishes a series of postcards featuring the monuments of Paris.

1914

Jules exhibits at the Paris salon.
Louis and Henri are mobilized. Jules, unwell, continues to carry out fashion reports, assisted by his mother and his sister, Félicie.

1914 (October 31)

Birth of Albert, second son of Louis.

1917 (December 26)

Death of Louise Vauterin.

1919

Louis and Henri return to the business. Louis is secretary-treasurer of the Union of Fashion Reporters. From now until 1939, the Séeberger Frères studio will be devoted almost exclusively to fashion and style reports from the major society events.

1920

Jules exhibits paintings at the Salon des Indépendants and the Salon de l'école française. He will gradually withdraw from the business during the 1920s to devote himself to painting.

1923

First commission from the International Kinema Research agency for photographs of typically French places and people for Hollywood artistic directors and studio designers. The Séebergers worked for this agency regularly until 1931.

1927

Jean joins the family business.

1930

Albert joins the family business.

1932 (January 8)

Death of Jules at Henri's home in Galluis (Seine-et-Oise).

1935

First advertising studio shoots. The 13 x 18 cm glass plate format was abandoned in favor of 6 x 6 cm format flexible film. Use of Rolleiflex for outdoor shoots.

1936

Jean marries Suzanne Juncker, who will join the studio in 1942. They will have two children, Daniel (1937) and Geneviève (1943).

1939

Jean and Albert are mobilized.
Henri retires to Galluis, and Louis to Guérard (Seine-et-Marne).

1941–1944

Henri marries Kazimiera Napadlek.
Jean and Albert return from the front and launch a new Séeberger

Brothers. Many photos of occupied Paris and steady collaboration with the Théâtre national populaire and the Paris Opéra.
Jean photographs the liberation of Paris, August 19–26, 1944.

1945–1970

Studio increasingly specializes in fashion and publicity, and to a lesser extent, journalism.
Regular collaboration with the magazines *Noir et blanc, La Donna, l'Illustré, France tricots, La Femme chic, l'Officiel de la couture, Chapeaux de Paris, Collections,* and *Mariages*. Hunting reports for the magazine *Adam*. Many publicity pieces, notably for Van Cleef & Arpels, Mauboussin, Meller, Prestinox, Komura, Roche-Bobois, Thermor, Coryse Salomé, Télémécanique La Broderie suisse, Desarbre, Coca-Cola, and Prénatal.

1946

Death of Louis.
Jean Séeberger takes part in the creation of the Group des XV. Albert will join the organization later.

1947

The studio is moved to 112 boulevard Malesherbes.
Albert marries Cécile Dumont, who also touches up photographs. They will have three children, Michèle (1948), Jean-Louis (1949), and Emmanuel (1962).

1949

Death of Félicie.

1956 (March 7)

Death of Henri.

1963

Death of Anna Durieublanc.
Adaptation and use of the Transflex process (invented by Alekan and Gérard) to project background images in the studio, giving the illusion of natural backgrounds. First publications with Simone d'Aillencourt in the magazine *Collections*.

1973

Beginning of collaboration with the Bibliothèque historique de la Ville de Paris. Prints of old photographs of Paris, made from original glass plates by the Séebergers and Charles Marville.

1975

Article on the Séebergers and portfolio of their work in the *Sunday Times Magazine* of April 6.
Transfer of 35,000 fashion plates (negatives and 13 x 18 contact prints), covering the period 1909–1939, to the Bibliothèque nationale de France.

1976

Donation of negatives and prints to the Musée de l'Air and the Établissement cinématographique et photographique des armées (Fort d'Ivry).
Gift of an additional 25,000 plates (negatives and contact prints) from the period 1941–1975 and 1,800 large-format modern prints to the Bibliothèque nationale.
Transfer of 3,042 negatives on glass plates by the first generation of Séebergers, and a collection of flexible negatives from the period 1935–1975, to the Architectural division of the Ministry of Culture.

1977 (April 1)

Final closure of the boulevard Malesherbes studio.
Remittance of equipment, printing materials, magazines, and fashion prints to the Musée de Bièvre.
Livre de Paris 1900 is published by Belfond éditions.

1978

Donation of hunting photographs to the International Hunting Museum, in Gien.

1979 (June 20)

Death of Jean.
Publication of *A Fashion Parade: The Séeberger Collection* by Blond & Briggs, and *La France 1900 vue par les frères Séeberger*, by Belfond éditions. Two exhibitions: "Les Parisiens au fil des jours (1900–1960), Séeberger Frères" at the Bibliothèque historique de la Ville de Paris, and "La mode 1900–1975" at the Zabriskie Gallery, Paris.

1992

Pontault-Combault mounts an exhibition at the Centre Photographique d'Île-de-France, and the study *The Séebergers. L'aventure de trois frères photographes au début du siècle*, is published by éditions La Manufacture.

1994

Thirty-five glass plates of Montmartre are transferred to the Architectural division of the Ministry of Culture.

1999

Exhibition "Les frères Séeberger. Une lignée de photographes" at the Château des Bouillants, Dammarie-les-Lys.

1999 (June 3)

Death of Albert.

2005 (July 15)

Death of Suzanne.

Journals in which the Séebergers' photographs were published

Agence Express: 1917
Adam: 1937-1939
L'Art et la Mode: 1931
L'Art vivant: 1939
Associated Press: 1937-1939
Les Champs
Chiffons: 1916-1917
Comoedia
Diane: 1937-1939
Les Élégances parisiennes: 1916-1929
L'Époque littéraire et artistique: 1939
Excelsior: 1914-1917
Fairchild Publications: 1930-1939
Femina: 1916-1935
Le Figaro illustré: 1939
La Femme chic, Les Chapeaux de la femme chic (and other Louchel publications): 1916-1939
La Femme chez elle
The General Art and Photography Agency: 1919
Good Housekeeping: 1929-1935
Harper's Bazaar: 1918-1939
L'Illustration
L'Intransigeant
J'ai vu: 1916-1918
Le Jardin des modes: 1929-1939
Le Jour: 1937
Le Journal: 1916-1917
The Ladies' Home Journal (Philadelphia): 1924
Lectures pour tous: 1921-1922
Le Monde illustré
Marianne
Marie-Claire: 1937-1939
Minerva
Le Miroir des modes: 1918-1919
La Mode pratique: 1909-1939
Les Modes: 1917-1925
La Nacion (Buenos Aires)
New York Herald Tribune (Paris)
L'Officiel de la couture et de la mode de Paris: 1931-1939
Paris artistique: 1918
Paris Soir: 1938-1939
Plaisir de France: 1937
Le Petit Écho de la mode: 1916-1919
Pantagruel
Pour vous: 1938-1939
Rester jeune: 1937-1939
La Revue de la femme: 1927
The Times: 1920
La Vie féminine: 1919
La Vie parisienne
Voilà: 1938
Votre beauté
Vu: 1928-1939
Vogue (all editions combined): 1916-1939

Periodicals Consulted

Aux Écoutes
Candide
Le Cri de Paris
Fantasio
Journal des dames et des modes

About the Séebergers

BRIGHELLI, Jean-Claude, and Claude MALÉCOT, *Les Jardins parisiens à la Belle Époque. Photographies Séeberger frères*, Paris, Éditions du Patrimoine/Monum, 2005.

CABAUD, Michel, and Guy FEINSTEIN, *La France 1900 vue par les frères Séeberger*, preface by Hubert Juin, Paris, Belfond, 1979.

CHARDIN, Virginie, *Séeberger frères*, Arles, Actes Sud, coll. "Photo poche," nr. 105, 2006.

DARS, Célestine, *A Fashion Parade: The Séeberger Collection*, London, Blonc & Briggs, 1979.

DHEURLE, Michel, "La dynastie Séeberger," in *Les Cahiers des 30 x 40*, nr. 6, 3/79, pp. 1-3.

GAUTRAND, Jean-Claude, *The Séebergers. L'aventure de trois frères photographes au début du siècle*, Paris, éditions La Manufacture, 1992.

Les Parisiens au fil des jours, 1900-1960, exhibition catalog, Paris, Bibliothèque historique de la Ville de Paris, 1980.

Le Montmartre des frères Séeberger, exhibition catalog, Paris, Galerie Roussard, 13, rue du Mont-Cenis, 75018 Paris.

About Fashion Photography

DEVLIN, Polly, *Vogue Book of Fashion Photography*, NY, Simon & Schuster, 1979.

DENOYELLE, Françoise, *La Lumière de Paris. Le marché de la photographie, 1919-1939*, Paris, L'Harmattan, 1997.

DUCROS, Françoise, "L'imaginaire de la beauté," in *Nouvelle Histoire de la photographie*, Paris, Bordas/Adam Biro, 1993, pp. 535-553.

GERNSHEIM, Alison, *Fashion and Reality: 1840-1914*, London, Farber and Farber, 1963.

HALL-DUNCAN, Nancy, *The History of Fashion Photography*, New York, Abrams, 1978.

LAWFORD, V., *The Work and the World of a Great Photographer of Fashion and Society*, Hardmondsworth, Penguin/New York, Knopf, 1985.

MOORE, Doris Langley, *Fashion through Fashion Plates: 1771-1970*, New York, Clarkson N. Potter, 1971.

PENN, Irving, *Inventive Paris Clothes 1909-1939*, NY, The Viking Press, 1978.

Vanités. Photographies de mode des XIXe et XXe siècles, Paris, Centre national de la photographie, 1993.

About Fashion Photographers

BRANDAU, Robert, ed., *De Meyer*, preface and biography by Philippe Jullian, New York, Knopf, 1976.

EWING, William E., *The Photographic Art of Hoyningen-Huene*. NY, Rizzoli, 1986.

FRENZEL, H. K., *Hoyningen-Huene. Meisterbildnisse*, Berlin, Verlag Dietrich Reiner, 1932.

ESTEN, John, *Man Ray: Bazaar Years*, NY, Rizzoli, 1988.

FABER, Monika, *Madame D'Ora, Wien-Paris. Portraits aus Kunst und Gesellschaft, 1907–1957*, Vienna, Christian Branstätter, 1983.

LAWFORD, Valentine, *Horst, his Work and his World*, New York, Viking, 1984.

LONGWELL, Dennis, *Steichen: The Master Prints 1895–1914. The Symbolist Period*, NY, Museum of Modern Art, 1978.

Horst: Sixty Years of Photography, London, Thames and Hudson, 1991.

Martin Munkacsi, Bielefeld/Düsseldorf, Marzona, 1980.

STEICHEN, Edward, *A Life in Photography*, Garden City, Doubleday & Co, 1963.

About the History of Fashion and the Great Couturiers

BARD, Christine, *Les Garçonnes, modes et fantasmes des années folles*, Paris, Flammarion, 1998.

BARTHES, Roland, *The Fashion System*, 1967, transl. Matthew Ward and Richard Howard, NY, Hill, 1983.

BATTERSBY, Martin, *Art Deco Fashion: French Designers 1908–1925*, NY, St. Martin's Press, 1976.

BEATON, Cecil, *The Glass of Fashion*, preface by Christian Dior, London, Weidenfeld & Nicholson, 1954.

BERTIN, Célia, *Haute Couture, terre inconnue*, Hachette, Paris, 1956.

BESANÇON DE WAGNER, Maggy, *Ce que j'ai vu en chiffonnant la clientèle*, Paris, Librairie des Champs-Élysées, 1938.

BESANÇON DE WAGNER, Maggy, *La Philosophie de l'élégance*, Paris, Éditions littéraires de France, 1942

BONY, Anne, *Les Années trente d'Anne Bony*, Paris, Éditions du Regard, 1987.

CHASE, Edna Woolman and Ika Chase, *Always in Vogue*, NY, Double Day and Co., 1954.

CLAIRIN, Lucy, *Journal d'un mannequin. Feuillets d'une année*, Paris, Fasquelle, 1937.

DUMAS, Françoise, *Actualité artistique et créateurs de mode de 1909 à 1939*, Université de Provence, Aix-Marseille I, 1988.

ETHERINGTON-SMITH, Meredith, *Patou*, NY, St Martin Marek, 1983.

HALL, Caroline, *The Thirties in Vogue*, NY, Harmony Books, 1985.

HOWELL, Georgina, *Six Decades of Fashion in Vogue*, London, Penguin Book Ltd, 1976.

LEHNERT, Gertrud, *Histoire de la mode au XX*[e] *siècle*, Könemann, 1999.

MCDOWELL, Colin, *Fashion Today*, NY/Paris, Phaidon Press, 2003.

MORAND, Paul, ed., *L'Allure de Chanel*, Paris, Hermann, 1976.

MULVAGH, Jane, *The Vogue History of 20th Century Fashion*, NY/London, Viking, 1988.

POIRET, Paul, *En habillant l'époque*, Paris, Grasset, 1930.

RILEY, Robert, *The House of Worth*, NY, Brooklyn Museum, 1962.

SCHIAPARELLI, Elsa, *Schocking*, Paris, Denoël, 1954.

SEEBOHM, Caroline, *The Man Who Was Vogue: The Life and Times of Condé Nast*, Lonon, Weidenfeld and Nicolson, 1982.

TRAHEY, Jane, *Harper's Bazaar: 100 Years of the American Female*, NY, Random House, 1967.

About the Historical Context

Annuaire du monde artistique. Guide national des artistes, Paris, J.P. Lenormand, volumes 1921 and 1922.

Bottin mondain, Paris, Annual report of Didot-Bottin for the years 1926, 1933, and 1938.

COSTON, Henri, ed., *Dictionnaire des dynasties bourgeoises et du monde des affaires*, Paris, Éditions A. Moreau, 1975.

CUNY, Hubert, *Le Gotha français. État présent des familles ducales et princières*, Paris, Librairie académique Perrin diff., 1989.

GEORGES-MICHEL, Michel, *La Vie à Deauville. Trois époques, 1913–1923*, Paris, Flammarion, 1924.

GRAMONT, Élisabeth de, *Les Marronniers en fleurs*, Paris, Grasset, 1929.

PASSEK, Jean Loup, ed., *Dictionnaire du cinéma*, Paris, Larousse, 1986.

Le Tout-Paris. Annuaire de la Société parisienne, La Fare, 1939.

TRARIEUX, Jean, *Le Pesage*, Paris, Nouvelle Société d'éditions, 1928.

TRARIEUX, Jean, *Journal d'un homme de courses, 1900–1945*, Paris, Fayard, 1945.

VALYNSEELE, Joseph, *Le Sang des Rothschild*, Paris, 2005.

VIGARELLO, Georges, *Histoire de la beauté. Le corps et l'art d'embellir de la Renaissance à nos jours*, Paris, Le Seuil, 2004.